For Bernard,

With my very best wishes –

Melvin

John Dos Passos' Correspondence with Arthur K. McComb

John Dos Passos'
Correspondence with
Arthur K. McComb
or
"Learn to sing
the Carmagnole"

Narrative and editing by

Melvin Landsberg

UNIVERSITY PRESS OF COLORADO
Niwot, Colorado

Publication of this book was made possible, in part, by
a grant from the Eugene M. Kayden Memorial Fund.

Library of Congress Cataloging-in-Publication Data

Dos Passos, John, 1896–1970.
    John Dos Passos' correspondence with Arthur K. McComb, or,
"Learn to sing the Carmagnole" / narrative and editing by Melvin
Landsberg.
        p.   cm.
    Includes bibliographical references.
    ISBN 0-87081-137-1
    1. Dos Passos, John, 1896–1970—Correspondence.
2. McComb, Arthur K. (Arthur Kilgore), 1895–1968—
Correspondence. 3. Novelists, American—20th century—
Correspondence. 4. Art historians—United States—Correspondence.
I. McComb, Arthur K. (Arthur Kilgore), 1895–1968.
II. Landsberg, Melvin. III. Title. IV. Title: Learn to sing the
Carmagnole.
PS3507.0743Z487   1990
813'.52—dc20   89-24775
[B]   CIP

To my mother

Anna Landsberg

Contents

List of Illustrations

"... ein jeder, nur zehn Jahre früher oder später geboren, dürfte, was seine eigene Bildung und die Wirkung nach aussen betrifft, ein ganz anderer geworden sein." "... anyone born only ten years earlier or later might have become, as regards his education and his effect on others, a totally different person."

Goethe, Preface to *Dichtung und Wahrheit*

Preface and Acknowledgments

*T*HIS EDITION OF John Dos Passos' letters to Arthur K. McComb grew out of my interest in Dos Passos' biography. When I added to his letters to McComb a selection of McComb's letters to him, I found myself listening to two voices, each with its distinct timbre, and attending to an interplay of two very different personalities. Reading and rereading the Dos Passos–McComb dialogue, I sometimes fancied that I was involved in an epistolary novel. However, reflection upon my fancy evoked only the adage that fiction imitates life. Quite matter-of-factly, then, this volume is offered as a scholarly edition, one which benefited from the memories and specialized skills of many people.

I could not have prepared this edition without the aid of Elizabeth Dos Passos (Mrs. John Dos Passos) and a number of Dos Passos' and McComb's friends, as well as of scholars at the University of Virginia, the University of Kansas, and elsewhere. Dudley Poore, a mutual friend of Dos Passos and McComb, helped me interpret many matters in both their histories. My regret that Poore—who died on January 9, 1982— did not see this volume is considerable, but it is as nothing compared to my regret at the death of this generous and cultivated man.

For information on Dos Passos I am especially indebted not only to Poore and Elizabeth Dos Passos, but also to Lucy Dos Passos Coggin, Dos Passos' daughter. For information on McComb I am especially indebted to Robert Lynch, Professor Kelly Lynch, of Babson College, Poore, Professor Sydney J. Freedberg, of Harvard University, Constance R. Worcester, and the late David M. K. McKibbin, of the Boston Athenaeum.

Others who gave me information for this study include Professor Pamela Askew, of Vassar College, Richard Beatty, Professor Charles W. Bernardin, of Villanova University, Slater Brown, the late Brodnax Cameron, Mrs. Paul Fenimore Cooper, Professor Alexander Dallin, of Stanford University, Dr. Sydney Fairbanks, the late Dr. Horsley H. Gantt, Ray Lord, of the New York Public Library, Doreen A. Lostanlen,

Enid McLeod, Laurette Murdock, Professor Jean Peytard, of the University of Besançon, in France, Mrs. P. Russell (Information Officer, Lloyd's Register of Shipping), Professor Ernest Samuels, of Northwestern University, Dorothy de Santillana, Professor Francis Sweeney (S.J.), of Boston College, Alice, Arthur, and Nora Sweeney (all three of Andover, Massachusetts), Hood van den Arend, the late Dr. Walter Muir Whitehill, of the Boston Athenaeum, the late Gurdon Saltonstall Worcester, and Professor Peter Wülfing, of the University of Cologne, in West Germany. At the University of Virginia, Professors Frederick Hartt, Peter L. Heath, Thomas H. Hunter, Jacob C. Levenson, David A. Sensabaugh, and Floyd Stovall provided information, and at the University of Kansas, Professors Richard T. deGeorge, Rose L. Greaves, Roy E. Gridley, Wallace S. Johnson, Elizabeth A. Kuznesof, Chu-tsing Li, Arnold H. Weiss, and the late Professor Carl Leban did the same. Professors Joel J. Gold, Edward F. Grier, and Charles Masinton, all three of the University of Kansas, made editorial suggestions.

Without the contributions of several generous scholars, I could not have provided adequate translations of the portions of the Dos Passos–McComb correspondence which are in foreign languages. At the University of Kansas, Professor Vernon Chamberlin spent many hours translating Spanish passages, and Professor Michael H. Shaw translated material from the Latin and Greek. At the University of Virginia, Professor Lionel R. Duisit gave me many hours of help with the French, Professor David T. Haberly gave me much help with the Portuguese, Catalan, and Spanish, and Mrs. Francesca Langbaum translated most of the Italian.

For additional aid with the translations I am indebted to Professor Arthur F. Stocker, of the University of Virginia, Professor John C. McGalliard, of the University of Iowa, Professor Francis M. Rogers, of Harvard University, Professors Robert E. Anderson, Frank Baron, Jean-Pierre Boon, David A. Dinneen, Rose L. Greaves, Helmut E. Huelsbergen, Ted Johnson, Janice M. Kozma-Southall, Elizabeth A. Kuznesof, Norris J. Lacy, Oliver C. Phillips, Jr., Raymond Souza, Alfonso Verdu, Jon S. Vincent, Arnold H. Weiss, and Gerhard H. Zuther, all of the University of Kansas, and to Ray Lord, Dr. Terence Boring, Professor Jean Peytard, and Professor Peter Wülfing.

After this edition was in galley proofs I received still further help with language and translation problems from Professors John T. Alexander, Michael M. T. Henderson, Gerald E. Mikkelson, and Dr. Marie-Luce Parker, all of the University of Kansas, and from Professor Stephen L. Baehr, of Virginia Polytechnic Institute and State University.

A number of scholars read all or most of the manuscript and made suggestions which improved the edition. For this help I am deeply grateful to Professor William W. Abbot, of the University of Virginia, Dr. Mary Davidson and Professors David M. Katzman and Edward L. Ruhe, all three of the University of Kansas, Professor Bernard Semmel, of the State University of New York at Stony Brook, and Professor Ronald M. Hartwell, of Nuffield College, Oxford. I am also deeply grateful to Professor Paul Barolsky, of the University of Virginia, who looked over most of my notes in art history and made corrections and suggestions.

For access to the bulk of Dos Passos' letters to McComb, I am indebted to Miss Margaret Mills, Executive Secretary of the American Academy and Institute of Arts and Letters, and to her predecessor Miss Felicia Geffen. For access to still others of Dos Passos' letters to McComb, I am indebted to Robert Lynch. I am indebted to him also for information regarding McComb's estate, and grateful to Professor Pamela Askew for generously facilitating my publication of McComb's letters to Dos Passos. For access to the bulk of those letters and to McComb's diaries, I am indebted to Elizabeth Dos Passos, and to Edmund Berkeley, Jr., Curator of Manuscripts of Alderman Library, at the University of Virginia, as well as to Michael F. Plunkett, Gregory Johnson, and others in the Manuscripts Department.

My debt to Alderman Library is an especially strong one, not limited to members of the Manuscripts Department. I am grateful to Dr. Ray W. Frantz, Jr., the University Librarian, to the entire staff of the Reference Department, who helped me with much of the annotation, and to numerous other members of the library staff. My debt to the Reference Department of Watson Library, at the University of Kansas, is considerable also, and I wish to thank Mrs. Marilyn S. Clark, the former head, and the Reference staff. At the Boston Athenaeum I received help from the late Walter Muir Whitehill, the director and librarian, and more recently from Rodney Armstrong, the present director and librarian. At Harvard University I made extensive use of the university archives for my narrative and notes, and I wish to thank Kimball C. Elkins, Senior Assistant in the archives, for his help there. At Harvard I also used the resources of the Fogg Art Museum, and I wish to thank Mrs. Phoebe Peebles, the archivist there, for her help.

Dr. Mary Davidson, while a graduate student in English, typed most of the Dos Passos letters and proofread them with me, Phyllis White typed the McComb letters and proofread most of them with me, and Pam Loewenstein typed the notes. The edition owes much to the encouragement and patience of John T. Schwartz, Director of the Colorado Associated University Press. Working with him and Frederick R. Rinehart, my editor there, was a pleasant experience.

M.L.

Abbreviated Forms

Almost all the abbreviations in the notes in this edition are common scholarly ones or are readily interpretable.

Harvard, A.B., 1918 (21) would mean that a student received his Harvard A.B. degree in 1921 as a member of the Class of 1918.

ML stands for Melvin Landsberg.

OED designates *The Oxford English Dictionary.*

Guide to People Mentioned by First Name or Nickname

A number of people in our letters are usually mentioned only by first name or nickname. To identify each of them continually would cause readers many unwelcome interruptions. We have tried to identify these people as often as necessary, and as a safeguard we offer the following guide:

Bob, Bobby, or Bobs	Robert Hillyer
Cuthbert	Cuthbert Wright
Dudley	Dudley Poore
Gazelle	George Locke Howe
Great Auk or Auk	Stewart Mitchell
Hardinge	Hardinge Scholle
Van	Frederik Francis van den Arend

Editing Dos Passos' Letters

WHEN JOHN DOS PASSOS gave me permission to edit his letters to Arthur K. McComb, in August 1969, he did so with the provision that they be published "with their original punctuation, including misplaced and garbled or misspelled words."

"May I," I had written, "make a few editorial changes in the interest of readability? Ampersands might become 'and's' and dashes at the ends of sentences might become periods, etc." His answer, explaining the provision, was: "I'd much rather have you transcribe them exactly as written—they did that in a recent volume of E E Cummings' letter[s] and I thought it worked very well."*

In imposing his conditions Dos Passos possibly knew that he was differing from his friend Edmund Wilson, who in his controversy with the Modern Language Association shortly before had declared a certain kind of faithfulness impedimental to readability. Wilson wrote in a letter to the editors of the *New York Review of Books* (June 5, 1969, p. 36):

> I have had some respect for Mr. [Gordon N.] Ray on account of his edition of Thackeray's letters—though I was slightly annoyed by his following Thackeray's epistolary shorthand so pedantically as to print all his *and*'s as ampersands and his contractions of such common words as *should* and *which*, when a note of explanation or the facsimile of the page of a letter would have been enough to indicate this practice and leave the editor free to present a more readable text.

Scarcely three years after Dos Passos' death a large edition of selections from Dos Passos' letters and diaries appeared, its title *The Four-*

---

*Dos Passos' provision was in a "To Whom It May Concern" letter of August 9, and the explanation accompanying it was on a letter that I had written him on August 7.

teenth Chronicle and preface implying that it was a direct continuation of the corpus of Dos Passos' work. The editor, describing his book as a reading edition, wrote that he had corrected Dos Passos' spelling and sometimes his use of foreign languages, and had also inserted needed words. I think that Dos Passos felt that what would be lost in a "reading edition" of this sort, even a careful one, would be an immediate sense of his writing habits, which reflected the cataract-like rush of his thoughts and words, and thus significant aspects of his personality.

In *"Learn to sing the Carmagnole"* I have sought to transcribe all of Dos Passos' correspondence as he wished. The edition consists of all his letters, cards, telegrams, and notes to Arthur K. McComb that I have discovered, and a selection of McComb's similar writings to him. Altogether there are about 93 pieces by Dos Passos, including one or two fragments and possible fragments. None of his pieces has been published in its entirety before, although some scattered excerpts have appeared. I have used all of Dos Passos' writings in their entireties. Of McComb's letters, etc., to Dos Passos, there are about 174, including several fragments. Of these I have used 108, most of them only in part.

My major reason for omitting much of McComb's material is that I have intended his letters to be a gloss on those of Dos Passos. Another reason is that I have tried to produce a viable book which would retain McComb's especially interesting comments, dramatize the friendship between Dos Passos and him, and give a sense of the balanced correspondence which existed. Although McComb's writings appear only in part, they make up over half of the published text of the letters.

DETAILS OF TEXTUAL PROCEDURES

In editing Dos Passos' letters, I have reproduced original spellings and punctuation. When words seemed miswritten, I have dealt with them according to individual circumstances, keeping in mind Dos Passos' desire for fidelity. When crossed-out words seemed of significance or interest, I have recorded them. To interpolate material, I have used square brackets, and to indicate and explain conjectural readings, footnotes. I have avoided the use of *sic,* as misspellings and miswritings in Dos Passos' letters are so numerous that its employment would be more of a nuisance than a help to the reader. Sometimes I have used a footnote or brackets to indicate the correct spelling of a word or a proper name, but I have often passed over an error.

I should have liked to position the different parts of Dos Passos' letters, e.g., headings and complimentary closes, faithfully relative to one another, but as almost all his letters are handwritten, this was impossible.* Although Dos Passos showed himself a master of simultaneity in sections of *U.S.A.*, his letters here are by no means "concrete poems." Consequently I finally resigned myself to regularizing their parts, except when something of the original positioning seemed reproducible and perhaps worth reproducing. I have placed in conventional positions wraparound lines and postscripts gathered from corners, and I have usually regularized the positions and indentations of headings. I have often done the same with complimentary closes, and I have sometimes regularized salutation and paragraph indentations. Similarly, I have eliminated flourishes, as having no typographical equivalents, and I have eliminated a number of originally expedient lines (such as lines setting headings off from bodies of letters) because their functions would not be clear on the printed page.

In presenting the letters, I have transcribed as closely spaced all of Dos Passos' series of three periods. I have also left a space before and after each such series, except where Dos Passos' passage is in French. (With French passages I have followed French practice for points of suspension—using closely spaced periods and a space after, but not before, a series.) My purpose in using closely spaced periods has been to prevent Dos Passos' periods from being taken for editor's ellipsis points. Of course, since Dos Passos' letters to McComb, where they are preceded by identifying numbers, appear in their entireties, no ellipsis points of my own occur in them. However, such points do occur in the numbered McComb letters.

Every dash in the texts of Dos Passos' letters is his own, unless it is otherwise described in a footnote. Editor's dashes occasionally occur in the footnotes to indicate illegibility in the text. In such instances their use is made evident by the commentary.

Except as noted here, I have edited McComb's letters in the same manner as those of Dos Passos. A few features in McComb's letters required special handling. Among them were his sometimes omitting commas, periods, etc., at the ends of lines, and his using linear spaces within conventional paragraphs to indicate additional paragraphs. Wherever McComb's omissions of end-of-line punctuation appeared confusing or awkward, I have inserted punctuation marks in brackets.

*Of Dos Passos' letters, postcards, etc., to McComb, all but Letters 69 (a telegram), 192, and 194 are handwritten. Letters 192 and 194 are typewritten; both have handwritten corrections, and Letter 192 has a handwritten postscript. All but one of McComb's messages in this edition are handwritten. His Letter 54 is typewritten.

McComb's internal paragraphs seemed in keeping with his style, and perhaps his anti-contemporary outlook, and I have retained them whenever possible.

Another problem arose from McComb's sometimes writing random comments on the picture sides of his art postcards. Where these comments were not related to the primary messages on the cards and drew their meanings from the art reproductions, I have not treated them as parts of the messages, and have not noted their omissions with ellipsis points.

I have described McComb's picture postcards only insofar as they are of interest for the correspondence, but I have described all of Dos Passos' picture postcards. Where McComb used letterhead paper without clearly intending it to provide his address, I have sometimes omitted the letterhead. For Dos Passos' letters I have indicated all letterheads. Dos Passos in writing Spanish made his inverted question marks face the wrong way. As the symbol he used has no typographical equivalent, I have used the ordinary mark. McComb occasionally used minute lines for periods, sometimes in series which included unmistakable periods, and I have rendered such lines as periods. McComb also occasionally substituted a line for the dot forming the lower part of an exclamation point or question mark. There being no typographical equivalent for either resultant character, I have used the ordinary exclamation point or question mark.

NARRATIVE, NOTES, AND TRANSLATIONS

My narrative is biographical, but I have not sought to write rounded sketches of Dos Passos' and McComb's lives. Rather, I have stressed material that helps explain the contents of the letters and have omitted most material that does not serve this purpose. The notes following each letter complement the narrative in explaining the letter's contents. They have still another major purpose, and that is to throw light on Dos Passos' intellectual history and the operations of his mind. Usually they do this merely by identifying sources for Dos Passos' statements, but sometimes they also discuss his uses of the sources. I know that some readers would prefer a brisk exchange of letters with little or no freight, and I have therefore taken pains to make the letters readily distinguishable from the notes. The reader who wishes only to read through the letters may do so with ease. Afterwards he can look at the notes as curiosity moves him.

Four additional details on the narrative and notes. First, for dating the publications of Dos Passos' books precisely, I have often relied on

Jack Potter, *A Bibliography of John Dos Passos* (Chicago: Normandie House, 1950). Second, in citing the Bible, I have used the Authorized (King James) Version. Third, all interviews cited in notes to the narrative and to the letters were conducted by me unless they are otherwise credited. Fourth, in quoting Baedeker's travel guidebooks and the Blue Guides, I have omitted features attributable to format and coding when these features would be meaningless and confusing outside of the books; thus I have generally omitted asterisks, without using ellipsis points, and I have changed italic and boldface type into regular type, and small capital letters into regular ones. I have likewise altered boldface type for several words in quoting Sir Banister Fletcher's *A History of Architecture.*

Finally, a few comments on my handling of Dos Passos' and McComb's writings in foreign languages. Though I believed that readers of *"Learn to sing the Carmagnole"* would know a host of foreign languages, I was not sure whether a large majority of the readers would know any given one of them. After querying prospective readers and considering my own difficulties, I concluded that I ought to provide translations for most of the material.* Where a word or brief passage in a foreign language contains an error, I have often noted the fact, usually by repeating the material correctly; however, I have left many errors unnoted.

It is important to add that Dos Passos wrote with varying degrees of familiarity in a number of languages, and often mingled words of the Romance tongues. I have offered occasional notes on his usages. In doing so, as in offering translations, I have relied heavily on the aid of professors or native speakers of the languages. Ultimate responsibility for translating and elucidating the foreign-language material is of course my own.

M.L.

*I also decided to substitute translations for the original legends on some picture postcards.

Introduction

JOHN DOS PASSOS' friendship with Arthur K. McComb, the art historian, was one of many for him. He found much of his happiness in friends, sought them and, being a thoughtful friend, usually kept them. One reason for his valuing friends greatly was that for a long time he didn't have much of a family. During his boyhood he didn't even bear his father's name, but instead went by the name Madison, his mother's. Suffering from the consequences of illegitimate birth, shunted off to Europe for a time, seeing much less of his father than was normal, finding little in common with his two older half brothers, he knew a great deal of loneliness as a child.

He was lonely even at school. It would be surprising if his difficult family situation didn't affect his relationships with his schoolmates, if the need to be guarded in speaking of his parents didn't make him a more reserved person than he would otherwise have been. There were other troublesome situations. One sprang from his having learned to speak French fluently as a little boy on the European continent. At an English preparatory school he attended he regarded himself as an American, but going on to Choate, in Connecticut, he found himself nicknamed Frenchy. At Choate Dos Passos was noticeably young for his class—he graduated and was ready for Harvard at fifteen and a half. Besides his youth there was his poor eyesight; perhaps it was because of his eyes that, for all his efforts, sports were an embarrassment.[1]

His loneliness may also have been the loneliness of genius lacking stimulating, responsive companionship. Among his papers there is a diary he kept at Choate in 1911. An entry of April 9, written after listening to a sermon by the headmaster, reads:

I have no friends—There is no one who cares a rap about me. No one ever seems to speak to me unless it is necessary; no one ever comes into my room to talk to me. . . . Is it because I am younger that most of the fellows I am with that they neither respect me, like me, dislike me, hate me? I should rather be hated by every one in the school than looked upon as a nonenity— . . . I do not care what misery I go through now if I can only in the future be great—Be the greatest man the [that] ever lived—Be such a man that they will all treasure the remembrance of me and say with pride—"I went to school with John R. Dos Passos" (if I ever do assume that name)—[2]

When he graduated from Choate in 1911, his father decided to have him wait a year before entering college. A corporation lawyer with a large income, he was able to send Dos Passos on a tour of Europe and the Mediterranean. Traveling with a hired companion, the boy went to England, France, Egypt, Greece, Turkey, and Italy.[3]

He entered Harvard in September 1912 as John R. Dos Passos, Jr., and during his four years there made a fair number of friends, among them Arthur McComb. A British youth who entered college in 1914, McComb was even more cosmopolitan than Dos Passos. He was born in Paris in 1895. His father, Samuel McComb, was a clergyman from northern Ireland, educated there, at Oxford, and in Berlin, and his mother was from Scotland. Arthur first attended school in Hanover, Germany. He studied Latin with a Jesuit teacher in Paris, attended Rugby between 1910 and 1912, and prepared for Harvard at two private schools in Massachusetts, Noble and Greenough School and Milton Academy. From 1906 to 1916 his father worked at Emmanuel Church in Boston, assisting Dr. Elwood Worcester in an Episcopalian movement rivaling Christian Science. The Emmanuel movement combined religion with medical science in treating psychosomatic disorders.[4] Outside Emmanuel Church somebody once placed a huge placard reading: "Dr. McComb says there is hope." Arthur had no idea what the sign meant and was embarrassed by it. The incident helps to illustrate the difference in outlook between him and his parents. The father, a red-faced, outgoing, humorous man, and the mother, a large, charming woman, were disturbed because they didn't think that Arthur had a realistic attitude towards life. When Arthur was about ten his mother placed above his bed a plaque with the blazoned motto: "I ought, I can, I will." A delicate child who had no sympathy with the rugged spirit, he hated the plaque. He did not fight his parents, but was introverted, sad, and lonely. After he entered Harvard, he appears to have come to enjoy life more, for there he found brilliant people who accepted him and were fond of him.[5] In this respect his experience at Harvard was similar to that of Dos Passos.

Both young men found the *Harvard Monthly,* an undergraduate literary journal, important in their social and intellectual lives. Though

It is thawing rapidly, how-
-ever and I think that it
will all be gone by the
morning. Did not go down
to church this morning but
had a service in the
Red Parlor. Mr. St John
gave a very inspiring talk
on being better than those
about you and on being a
sort of fellow that changes the
condition of affairs. I do wish
that I could be a fellow like
that — It is terrible to be in
a school to be anywhere
where no one respects you!
I do not know why it is
but no one ever treats me
as if I were one of them.
Every one is very nice to
me but — that is all
I have no friends — there
is no one who cares a
rap about me. No one

"I have no friends." Page from Dos Passos' diary at Choate, 1911.

Arthur Kilgore McComb, a British subject for most of his life.
Courtesy of Robert Lynch

carrying a normal course load and reading heavily on his own,[6] Dos Passos gave much time to it, and most of his closest friends at college were staff members or contributors. Among these friends were Dudley Poore, a poet who later taught English at Harvard and then worked for the State Department; E. E. Cummings; Robert Hillyer; Stewart Mitchell, later director of the Massachusetts Historical Society; and McComb.*

During his freshman and sophomore years Dos Passos published two short stories in the *Harvard Monthly*. Thereafter his writings appeared more frequently, and among them, in July 1915, were two pieces of non-fiction which require mention here: an essay on Conrad's *Lord Jim* and an editorial supporting the army's summer military camps as a democratic influence but calling compulsory military training barbaric. Most of his publications came in his senior year, when he was a member of the editorial staff: more stories, reviews, a half dozen lyric poems, an essay, and some editorials. His editorial "The Evangelist and the Volcano," in November 1915, declared that the war in Europe was a catastrophe beyond all praise and blame, for the nineteenth century had collapsed, "the good old materialistic nineteenth century, with its self-confidence and its comfortable cosmopolitanism"; the ideals of civilization were tottering, and Americans could not isolate themselves from events.[7] Part of the significance of the editorial is that it shows Dos Passos already viewing social and political issues historically, although most of his courses were in languages, literature, and writing, and he took little history as such.

McComb took a variety of courses during his first year at Harvard, but in his second (which was Dos Passos' last) he took most of his courses in history. He began to publish in the *Harvard Monthly* in July 1915, at first book reviews and then essays, and in both he proceeded to address himself to the overriding issues in the Harvard community — military preparedness and the possibility of entering the European war — and to show his dislike of the rugged spirit. His writings were pacifistic and opposed to militarism, conscription, and the penalizing of unorthodox opinion. His essay "The Meaning of Pacifism," published in March 1916, defined it as the "recognition of the futility of force and the desire to substitute for it in international disputes the use of the human reason." Taking issue with a comment by Theodore

---

*Another close friend on the *Harvard Monthly* was Wright McCormick ('15), who served on the board of editors of the journal and later worked as a reporter for the *New York Times*. He was killed while mountain climbing in Mexico in 1922.

Roosevelt about pacifists' "Chinafying" the United States, McComb said:

> It would be perhaps unfair to expect a man of Mr. Roosevelt's temperament, trained in the tenets of a fighting Christianity, to appreciate the noble and exalted spirit of China. . . . It has upheld the fine doctrine that right does not need the support of might.

The next month he published an essay, "Of Individuality," saying that the European war had stimulated the herd instinct throughout the world. McComb quoted John Stuart Mill's statement: "In this age the mere example of non-conformity, the mere refusal to bend the knee to custom, is in itself a service," and declared that it was even truer now than when Mill made it.[8]

Twice Dos Passos and McComb took opposite views in the pages of the *Harvard Monthly*. First Dos Passos disagreed with one of McComb's book reviews, and next McComb took issue with one of Dos Passos' essays. The first clash came in March 1916 with McComb's review of *The World Decision*. This book, by the American novelist Robert Herrick, contended that the European war was a mortal combat between Latin civilization and Teutonic militarism and materialism. Herrick praised the national instinct which had brought Italy into the war, and he disparaged the pacifism for profit which had opposed it.

McComb disagreed, offering an analysis of Herrick's argument based partly on his own experience in Italy; defending trade as an international bond; and going on to oppose internationalism to chauvinism. "I would point out to Mr. Herrick," he wrote, "that some of us are proud to call ourselves, with Goethe and with Lessing, 'citizens of the world'; proud to own an allegiance not bound by artificial frontiers."[9]

Dos Passos' reply to McComb, in the same issue, was pragmatic. Agreeing with Herrick that the conflict was between the Latin and Teutonic views of civilization, Dos Passos said that the United States had to join one side or the other, for to be neutral, except as a technicality, meant to be indifferent to a fundamental problem. Pacifists were ignoring today's problem while trying to build a war-proof world for tomorrow. Of course almost everyone deplored war and was in a sense a pacifist, he said, adding that "every man whose opinion is worth anything, has decided that, somehow, such a war as the present one must be made impossible in the future."[10]

Three months after his reply Dos Passos published "A Humble Protest," a long essay attacking "the rule of science and its attendant spirits, Industrialism, and Mechanical Civilization." Thought and art had not, he wrote, prospered under their rule. Science was a new superstition, and men were so preoccupied with tabulating facts that they neglected the human spirit. The industrial revolution enslaved men in a human pyramid—three quarters of the world suffering economic slavery so that the other quarter could be enslaved, this time by the "tentactular inessentials of civilization."[11]

McComb rejected Dos Passos' argument and in his reply cited the history of the bourgeois Dutch republic. The ideas in "A Humble Protest," he said, were like those of Ruskin and Morris. Dos Passos disparaged production and wanted a more or less equal distribution of what products there were. But industry and commerce created wealth, which was the foundation of all economic and social excellence. And industry helped bring about art. Private property and the multiplication of wants were a force toward peace, as they led to trade, communication among peoples, and toleration. The best hope for the poor lay in their limiting their numbers and protecting capital, not in emotional solutions.[12]

These and other arguments were not confined to the pages of the *Harvard Monthly*. Whether dining in restaurants or walking by the banks of the Charles River, the two young men argued incessantly. Dos Passos was always sensitive, scrupulous, and tactful, Dudley Poore recalled, but had his emotions less under control than McComb, who combined with enormous charm the restrained manners common among Englishmen.[13]

In the midst of these arguments, in June 1916, Dos Passos graduated from Harvard. Though he may have corresponded with McComb before that time, the mail we have begins soon afterwards, and in it Dos Passos continues the political debate. His letters show his political development vividly from the summer of 1916 till the United States entered World War I. About the time of America's entry he became converted to revolutionary socialism. In the very large number of letters he wrote McComb between 1917 and 1923 he continually voiced enthusiasm for political revolution, and he reaffirmed his views in the scant number we have from later in the twenties. Dos Passos held to these views well into the 1930s. Unfortunately his side of the correspondence with McComb during the 1930s and 1940s is missing, though we know that a few letters and more cards passed between the two friends.* A new round of correspondence, reminiscent and politi-

---

*What we have of McComb's consists of six postcards and two letters written between 1930 and 1937 and one postcard written April 22, 1944. From these we know that Dos

cally conservative on both sides, began in 1951 and continued almost until McComb's death.

Let us speak briefly of the significance of the letters, though it means anticipating their texts somewhat. When the United States entered World War I in 1917 Dos Passos held capitalism responsible and wanted to help tear it down everywhere. For a time McComb was also sympathetic with though not enthusiastic about revolution and saw hope in a new Russia. Both youths left the country in manners revealing different temperaments: Dos Passos rushed off to see the war as an ambulance driver, and McComb took leave from Harvard the next year and moved to Spain, a neutral country. At the end of the war McComb lost whatever sympathy he ever had with revolution. True, the war had shattered his inherited world, but watching the Bolsheviks he found a restored capitalist society preferable by far to the one they seemed likely to substitute for it. In his letters from Spain, McComb argued against Dos Passos' sympathy with the revolutionary left.

After Dos Passos' wartime service, which included over nine months in the United States Army, he went to Spain in August 1919, intending to work on *Three Soldiers*. Dudley Poore came too, and they and McComb saw each other for the better part of a year, most of the time almost continually. During this period Dos Passos and McComb had many opportunities to thrash matters out. But neither could convince or even strongly influence the other, for they differed in basic outlook and temperament. Dos Passos had faith in the viewpoint and instincts of the common man, he enjoyed the drama in social turbulence, and he did not shrink from personal danger. McComb found polite, moneyed society reassuring and was prudent politically and timid personally. As they argued it is unlikely that Dos Passos and McComb foresaw that their differences would be a strand, however slender, in the ideological history of the next two decades.

We should view these two decades against a background of the prewar era. Both Dos Passos and McComb grew up when Europe was

---

Passos wrote McComb at least one letter and one postcard during the 1930s. As Dos Passos was a considerate correspondent, it would be surprising if he did not send more cards, and there is good evidence that he did. Professor Charles Bernardin wrote that McComb, helping him with Dos Passos' biography in December 1962–January 1963, sent him data from seven other cards written in the 1930s and one written about May 1, 1944. Bernardin was trying to establish some of Dos Passos' itineraries. Letter from Bernardin to ML, July 11, 1974.

the center of world power and western civilization. Although McComb spent more of his early years in Europe than did Dos Passos, they both lived, traveled, and received some of their schooling there; moreover, they both found much of their intellectual sustenance in English and continental history and literature. Both young men were shocked by a precipitate decline in European civilization, and their different interpretations of and reactions to it are implicit in their letters.

To appreciate their shock, we must look at certain features of Europe before World War I, namely its economy and its social and moral psychology. John Maynard Keynes in *The Economic Consequences of the Peace* (1919) described pre-war Europe as enjoying a "happy age." (His point of view may have been middle class; but Dos Passos and McComb had some experience of middle class European life in their youths.) Before the war, monetary and trade policies fostered international investment and economic growth, Keynes wrote; in addition, food was relatively cheap when compared to what it had been before 1870. Most Europeans worked hard and had a low standard of comfort but seemed contented. The laboring classes "accepted from ignorance or powerlessness, or were compelled, persuaded, or cajoled by custom, convention, authority, and the well-established order of Society into accepting," a situation in which they appeared to get very little of the product they helped create. The rich meanwhile were well rewarded, but their society stressed the duty of saving. Much of what they earned they invested abroad, where it furthered economic progress, such as building the world's railroads.[14]

When an assassin killed Archduke Francis Ferdinand at Sarajevo on June 28, 1914, Europe had not experienced a general war for almost a hundred years. No war that it had ever known prepared it for the one that developed, a total war involving the human, productive, and moral resources of large industrial nations. As regards casualties, World War I was the most calamitous in Europe's history. Over ten million soldiers and still more civilians died, most of them Europeans.[15] But the deaths were only part of the story. World War I intensified national hatreds and begot new ones. It led to major economic dislocations and monetary troubles in Europe. And it created economic and political conditions for the Bolsheviks' seizure of power in Russia (1917), Mussolini's ascendancy in Italy (1922), and Hitler's appointment as chancellor of Germany (1933). The Bolsheviks' extremist ideas of class warfare and the Nazis' extremist ideas of nationalism and race had origins in treatises of the nineteenth century and thereabout. Now these ideas became government philosophies and devastating forces in twentieth-century Europe.*

Less than seven years after Hitler gained power, Leonard Woolf (who was a friend of Keynes) published the book *Barbarians Within and Without*. There Woolf described the decline of European civilization between what Keynes had called the "happy age" and early 1939. Before World War I Europe had a class civilization, Woolf wrote, but it had standards of civilization. Legislators and judges might display atavistic savagery, and most countries had loosely drawn laws enabling the governing classes to suppress persons and opinions they disliked. But virtually throughout the continent except in Russia (which was nevertheless humane compared to Russia in 1939) a rule of law seemed firmly established. The Dreyfus affair (1894–1906) involved the frameup of a single officer in the French army. But millions of Europeans regarded it as a test case for their civilization and its outcome as a matter of intimate concern.

Besides having a class civilization, Woolf wrote, Europe had an imperialist one. European imperialism was beneficial in many instances, though in some others it involved exploitation which violated civilized standards. When great barbarity and savagery became known, as with the Congo atrocities, European public opinion was outraged. Perhaps the effect of this opinion was often exaggerated. However, public opinion in the decade prior to World War I compelled Belgium to reorganize the Congolese government and its administrative methods.

When a Londoner opened his *Times* in the morning in say 1907, Woolf wrote, he did not expect to find its pages filled with "horror piled upon horror"—mass persecution, imprisonment, torture, expropriation. Nor did he read of tens or hundreds of thousands of people labelled for destruction and liquidated as kulaks or Jews or social democrats or communists or capitalists.

---

*Julien Benda in *La trahison des clercs* (1927) gives important clues as to why these ideas became devastating forces. He accused most of the clerks (i.e., intellectuals) of his time of betraying civilization in favor of state, class, or race. "Our age," he wrote, "is indeed the age of the *intellectual organization of political hatreds*." Benda added: "The extent to which the modern 'clerks' have made innovations may be judged by the fact that up till our own times men had only received two sorts of teaching in what concerns the relations between politics and morality. One was Plato's, and it said: 'Morality decides politics'; the other was Machiavelli's, and it said: 'Politics have nothing to do with morality.' To-day they receive a third. . . . 'Politics decide morality.' " Julien Benda, *The Treason of the Intellectuals,* trans. Richard Aldington (New York: William Morrow and Co., 1928). The quotations are on pp. 27 and 109–10 respectively.

There were, no doubt, in those days innocent men in European prisons and judicial murders pompously perpetrated in European courts, but even the most virile realists did not regard the slaughter of innocents as a normal method of government and a masterpiece of political sagacity. You might have travelled from one end of Europe to the other (without a passport) and you would nowhere have found prisons and concentration camps filled with hundreds and thousands of persons, who had committed no offence or crime known to any law, against whom no legal charge had ever been made. . . .[16]

Events in or involving Russia, Italy, Germany, and Spain gave Woolf reason to write of barbarism as he did in 1939. In Russia vast numbers of kulaks had died in the forced collectivization of agriculture Stalin began in 1929 and in the famine of 1932–33 that followed. At least three or four million in the famine, William Henry Chamberlin wrote in his 1934 edition of *Russia's Iron Age*. Many other Russians were killed or imprisoned in the series of political purges that Stalin initiated late in 1934.[17]

Italy in 1935 and 1936 disregarded its obligations to the League of Nations and invaded and conquered Ethiopia, using aerial bombs and poison gas against its ill-equipped people. Germany in 1933 excluded Jews from many phases of national life, and in 1935 it promulgated the Nuremberg Laws, depriving them of their citizenship. In the Kristallnacht pogrom of November 9, 1938, the Nazis destroyed over seven thousand Jewish-owned shops and attacked and tormented thousands of Jews, killing nearly a hundred. Following the pogrom, the Nazis barred Jews from German schools, prohibited them from visiting public places such as theaters and beaches, forced Jews out of their businesses, and sent some thirty thousand of them to concentration camps.[18]

The Spanish Civil War began in 1936 and continued for almost three years. Primarily a class and ideological war, it led to foreign intervention along ideological lines, with Hitler and Mussolini providing troops and arms to aid Francisco Franco's insurgent government, German and Italian planes bombing Spanish cities, Stalin sending supplies and a military mission to the Loyalists, the Communist International organizing brigades, and many non-Communists going to Spain to fight fascism. By the end of the war the toll was perhaps 130,000 murders and executions, 10,000 civilian deaths in air raids (most of them in Loyalist areas), and about 200,000 deaths in battle.[19]

We need an addendum to our recital of barbarisms, as the Dos Passos–McComb letters continue to 1967. Like the recital, our addendum is brief and incomplete and includes a few relevant events outside of Europe.

The Spanish Civil War was a prelude to World War II, which began with Nazi aggression in Europe. Without doubt World War II was the most destructive in human history. Figures for total dead are uncertain and range from forty to fifty million. We are too close to the war to speak of its full effects, but immediately after Hiroshima there was no doubt that in the atomic bomb twentieth-century technology had created a dismaying danger to civilization. Or rather to its remnants. For in World War II German civilization reached its nadir as the Nazis, using death factories, murdered almost six million Jews and hundreds of thousands of Gypsies and created need for a new word—genocide.[20] The war brought Hitler's Reich to an end, but it left Stalin's empire larger than before.

From the 1940s to the 1960s the world got new divulgences of the extent of Stalin's barbarism. Examining this evidence, Robert Conquest estimated in his book *The Great Terror* (1968) that there were eight million victims of political purges in Soviet labor camps in 1938. (Woolf in 1939 had written of tens of thousands of such victims killed or imprisoned.) Conquest estimated that twelve million people died in Soviet labor camps between 1936 and 1950 and that a million prisoners were executed throughout the U.S.S.R. in these years. And he called his figures conservative.[21]

We offered the recital of barbaric events since 1914 as context for our remark that the ideological differences between Dos Passos and McComb in 1919 continued for many years and constitute a bit of the history of the next two decades. During these decades the two friends agreed that the civilization they had known was badly diseased. But they disagreed strongly in their diagnoses, and sometimes even on the symptoms and specific locations of the disease. For most of the period Dos Passos saw the capitalist system as the breeder of war, depression, and fascism, and consequently the underlying cause of the decline in civilized behavior in Europe and America; thus he believed Sacco and Vanzetti to be victims of post-World War I capitalist society in America and tried to save them by invoking the same standards of civilization that Dreyfus' defenders had upheld.* McComb, on the other hand,

*He wrote that the conviction of Sacco and Vanzetti had "shocked a large part of humanity as has no legal decision since Dreyfus was sent to Devil's Island." Dos Passos, *Facing the Chair* (Boston: Sacco-Vanzetti Defense Committee, 1927), p. 116.

identified much of the horror of the post-World War I era with the emergence of Bolshevism, with Bolsheviks' behavior in Russia, and with their revolutionary activities elsewhere in Europe.

Dos Passos in "A Humble Protest" had in 1916 already objected to a pyramidal structure for society. In 1919 he saw Bolshevism as a revolutionary movement against two oppressive systems, feudalism and industrial capitalism, and as a source of hope for people at the bottom in either system. Although he wrote a friend in October 1919 of his intense suspicion of Marxian socialism and in 1921 said in an article that he looked forward to Bolshevism's being replaced by newer and broader creeds, he long continued to view the Bolshevik Revolution favorably. Until he formed a sufficient idea of Stalin, as he did by late 1934, he continued to hope that the revolutionary brutality and violence in Russia might end.[22]

McComb in early 1919 considered himself a liberal in the traditional English sense. Three years later he said that although he didn't "go in much for labels in these latter days," he thought that conservative-pacifist would be a fair designation for him. But a specific and historical description of his orientation and path is necessary. After World War I he looked back nostalgically to pre-war Europe, and continued doing so for the rest of his life. As between radical leftism and fascism in Europe, he preferred the latter when the question arose. And in the years when people spoke of "choosing sides," he was with fascism. McComb's letters to Dos Passos from 1935 on are those of a royalist and a person of non-religious temperament who nevertheless believed in a strong role for the church in society.[23] For people with conservative views resembling McComb's to identify themselves with fascism was not unusual in the 1920s and 1930s.

Confusion about the meaning of fascism has resulted. Citing it, H. R. Trevor-Roper uses the term "dynamic fascism" for what he considers fascism proper and distinguishes it from ideological conservatism. He defines dynamic fascism as "the cult of force, contemptuous of religious and traditional ideas, the self-assertion of an inflamed lower middle class" in an industrial society weakened by economic crisis. Dynamic fascists, like Mussolini and Hitler, and ideological conservatives (i.e., authoritarian conservatives believing in traditional hierarchy) came together, he says, in a fear of Marxian socialism, and distinctions were confused.

"Fascism, as an effective movement," Trevor-Roper says, was born of the European middle class' fears.

It might have independent intellectual roots; it might owe its form, here and there, to independent national or personal freaks; but its force, its dynamism, sprang from the fear of a . . . 'proletarian' revolution.[24]

McComb was certainly not a "dynamic fascist." But his timidity led him to value the security provided by repressive police and to sympathize with Mussolini and Franco, although they seemed close to making common cause with Hitler in the late 1930s. A paradoxical position for one who despised militarism and the herd instinct—especially for one who in the 1920s and 1930s pointed out to Dos Passos the paradoxes in his own leftist position.

In view of McComb's sympathies with Mussolini and Franco, readers may wonder how Dos Passos could have continued the friendship in the 1920s and 1930s. Probably one reason was that ideological differences are less important in the United States than in countries where they have been resolved, or have threatened to be resolved, by gun battles and executions. And surely another reason was that Dos Passos knew McComb to be a moderate (as, for example, in McComb's disapproval of an Italian court's brazen reasoning in releasing Giacomo Matteotti's murderers in 1925).[25] But the chief reason was probably that Dos Passos valued friends highly. He refused to let political opinions determine his personal relations. We see this refusal in his demeanor at one time or another with a majority of his friends: for example, John Howard Lawson, who one-sidedly ended relations when Dos Passos would not cease denouncing the Communists in the late 1930s; and Edmund Wilson, who engaged with Dos Passos in a mutually exasperating debate about the cold war in the 1950s and 1960s.[26]

It would be dealing in hyperbole to say that for Dos Passos a person's politics were part of his sacred being. But Dos Passos would have subscribed to the sentiments in McComb's college essay "Of Individuality." In commenting on the work of Geoffrey Chaucer and E. E. Cummings, writers over five centuries apart, Dos Passos expressed appreciation of this same trait of individuality.[27] He enjoyed the great variety he found in human beings and abhorred societies that sought to discourage or penalize it—and he himself was a remarkable performer in the drama of his generation, a figure long on individuality, strength, and balance. McComb was long on individuality too. But he became so given to singularities that many of his friends in his later years were more apt to talk about these than about his cultivation and scholarly achievements. McComb's lack of adaptability, which had upset his parents, was as evident to Dos Passos as was his friend's high intelligence, and

Dos Passos must have been disappointed by his shrinking from many of the ordinary challenges of life; he counselled McComb gently against futilitarianism and sought to tutor him on social issues. But McComb's independence made him difficult to counsel, and on social issues he was sure that the situation called for his saving Dos Passos. There was mutual teasing in the correspondence as a result, and certain subjects were touched on lightly.

But the two friends understood a good deal about one another. We have seen that they both had English and continental backgrounds, attended polite New England schools and Harvard, and had a circle of college friends and acquaintances in common. The very individualism they treasured was considered a Harvard trademark by many students there.[28] Both Dos Passos and McComb found World War I traumatic, and both realized how great a change it had wrought, for both saw western civilization historically. (Dos Passos later wrote in his memoirs: "I thought of Arthur as a living exemplar of the nineteenth-century civilization I saw bleeding to death in the nomanslands of France and Flanders.")[29] Besides similar backgrounds, they shared studies and interests. Both knew several modern European languages, as well as one or both of the classical ones, and could view politics, society, literature, and art in relation to the past.[30] Both were devoted to art and literature, and both were perceptive and critical readers. They would recommend books to one another and argue their merits, and McComb was one of the friends to whom Dos Passos sent his early manuscripts for commentary. Writing to him Dos Passos felt an affinity that would allow him to express himself on many subjects and in many moods.

Letters

*A*FTER GRADUATING from Harvard, Dos Passos spent the summer of 1916 on his father's farm in Westmoreland County, Virginia. It was a large farm on the Potomac River and Chesapeake Bay, and and was in those days most accessible by boat. Approaching its landing a visitor would note that it bore the name "Cintra," and if he knew Portugal would connect the name with a town there celebrated for its beauty. A bucolic setting, in the midst of which Dos Passos' thoughts were often on the devastating course of the European war. His mother, an invalid to whom he was very close emotionally, had died in 1915, and her death probably ended any inner constraints he felt about undertaking distant adventures. Now in the summer of 1916 he wanted exceedingly to see the war and had already applied to go overseas with the Norton-Harjes ambulance service.* But his father, seeking to delay him, in hopes that the war would end soon, reminded him that he would not be twenty-one till January and that until then it was a father's business to keep him alive. Though the elder Dos Passos would not let him go off for ambulance service, he offered to send him to Spain, where he could study and prepare to take a course in architecture. On the farm during these months Dos Passos attempted a novel, "Seven Times round the Walls of Jericho," wrote articles, gardened, swam, rode horseback, shot about in an "impromptu sailing canoe,"[1] followed news of the war and America's reaction to it, and corresponded with friends. In September he went to New York, where Dos Passos, Sr., had his law firm and a city residence, and there waited to hear whether Belgian

---

*Early in the war Richard Norton (1872–1918), archaeologist, and son of Professor Charles Eliot Norton of Harvard, had organized an American volunteer ambulance corps to serve in France. This corps, which Norton commanded, was subsequently combined with a unit formed by the Parisian banker H. H. Harjes.

Relief could accept him. Soon the answer came from Europe—he was too young—and Dos Passos resigned himself to Spain. He visited Boston and Cambridge, and on October 14 left New York on the French liner *Espagne,* heading for Bordeaux and intending to proceed to Madrid from there.

McComb did not see Dos Passos before he sailed. He spent part of the summer of 1916 in Cuba, where the father of his college friend Hardinge Scholle had a diplomatic post.[2] Returning to New York from Cuba on October 3, he looked forward to seeing Dos Passos in Cambridge, but on arriving there discovered that Dos Passos had left six days before. From Cambridge McComb wrote Dos Passos regretting that they hadn't met and telling what courses he was taking. McComb's letter contained a drawing of a man in an upholstered chair reading "Against American Literature" in the *New Republic*—a reference to Dos Passos' first publication after college and his first before a national audience.[3]

Settling in Madrid, Dos Passos enrolled at the Centro de Estudios Históricos, where he studied the language and literature of Spain. He also took lessons at a studio in preparation for work in architecture. But much of his education he got less formally, reading on his own, listening to Spanish friends, looking at paintings at the Prado and in churches, taking walks in and beyond Madrid, and at the end of the year taking a longer journey southeast. Late in January 1917 he learned by cable that his father had died. After some indecision he left Spain, and about February 20 he sailed from Bordeaux to the United States.

1

[Cintra
Westmoreland County
Virginia]
July 22$\underline{nd}$ [1916]

[To McComb]

No I won't write you a post card—But to heap coals of fire, here is a letter. Am placidly, bovinely, rusticating here, gradually pining away for want of conversation—Reading Anatole France, Benvenuto Cellini, 'Jean Christophe',[1] French poets and G. Meredith—Writing dully but with fair regularity. Riding and bathing and eating fills up the rest of the time.

Received a letter—a nice long one—from Hardinge[2] this week which I duly answered.

Glad you are reading Conrad—You know, lots of his books are about the Dutch and <u>all</u> about cosmopolites—so there; sit down at once and read him through from "The Nigger of the Narcissus" to "Between Sea and Land"[3]—then will you be ready to approach the throne of the heavenly grace.

Ecrivez une belle lettre je vous prie, mon cher ami, je dévore les lettres comme vous dévorez les salades au Cock Horse![4]

Viva l'España[5]

Dos

1. *Jean-Christophe:* novel in ten volumes (1904–12) by Romain Rolland.

2. Hardinge Scholle (1896–1969). Harvard, A.B., 1918 (21). Contributor to the *Monthly.* Director of the Museum of the City of New York, 1926–51.

3. *'Twixt Land and Sea* (1912). *The Nigger of the "Narcissus"* was published in 1897.

4. [Fr.] "Write me a good letter please, my dear friend. I devour your letters as you devour the salads at the Cock Horse!" The Cock Horse Inn, at 54-56 Brattle Street, Cambridge, was a restaurant McComb loved, but Dos Passos couldn't bear; there was too much decorum there for Dos Passos' liking (telephone interview with Dudley Poore, August 15, 1976). Cf. Letter 111 below. The restaurant was located in the historic Dexter Pratt House, once the home of the village blacksmith celebrated by Longfellow.

5. "Long live Spain." *Viva España* is the proper Spanish form.

2

[Cintra
August 2, 1916]

Ar
thur

—

Ecrivez.
Où êtes-vous?
Que faites-vous?
Que lisez-vous?[1]

I have a new joy. I have an impromptu sail-boat made out of a canoe, in which I skim the bay more or less ungracefully—Today a boom came undone and I came to grief, receiving the mast in the nose and being cast, like Jonah, upon the waters. The affair ended by the whole equipage being trundled ashore and swamped in the surf. You should have seen me dragging mast, canoe, paddles etc out of the breakers. I might add that the wind was high.

Apart from that I read, write, garden, ride and, <u>mostly</u>, pine for

The Cock Horse Inn, on Brattle Street, near Harvard. Dos Passos found it too genteel. (See Letter 1.)

Courtesy of the Cambridge Center for Adult Education

jocund companionship. No plans yet decided. Insanities brewing—
Ecrivez—

Dos

Aug 2nd.

1. [Fr.] "Write. Where are you? What are you doing? What are you reading?"

3

Cintra Westmoreland Co   August 7 [1916]
Va

Dear Arthur,

Let me rest from my labors for a moment to transcrible for you the
following from "Beauchamp's Career" of the Beloved Meredith—

"No one had any desire for war, only we really had (and this was
perfectly true) been talking gigantic nonsense of peace, and of the ever-
lastingness of the exchange of fruits for money, with angels weaving
raw-groceries of Eden in joy of the commercial picture."[1] Voilà—êtes-
vous écrasé?[2] More later— — —

I am beyond compare sleepy having motored all the afternoon over
road incomparably dusty under a hot unblinking sun.

At present I read Francis Thompson,[3] poems of G. Meredith, 'La
Femme de Trente Ans'—Balzac, and a translation by Lady Gregory of
Cuchulain of Muirthemne.[4] I suppose you'll call that an olla podrida.[5]

I agree with you in foaming over Bertrand Russell;[6]—but you pacifists
have,—may I suggest?—a set of cubby-holes into which you arrange
all the actions of the forces of unreason—"official brutality", "fanaticism", "imperialist reaction"—In the battle of phrases you have won:
your catchwords have routed those of the enemy—except in the deeps
of Philistia—but does that mean anything? Your catchwords, mon cher,
must take upon themselves arms and legs and brawny muscles and
poison gas shells before they can rout actuality. I am in terror lest they
are constitutionally unable to stand the weight.

Can you be brutal for righteousness' sake? Can you give up prosperity that you may win peace? Don't you tug too hard at that most
important organ the purse? And at the same time you deify it.

From the depths of ignorance I plead—what is the Malthusian
League? Birth control? If so I approve.

Send me the last Atlantic if you are through with it. No bookstore
nearer than Washington.

I am trying, among other cakes baking, to get out an article on
"Shelley and the Modern Age" deploring the strange sanity of American
young men, their lack of idealism, and their 'redbloodedness'—also a

philippic against "Jean Christophe" as an institution. But the Great Boyg[7] of laziness is hard to hew through.

Do write me soon—I devour mail as I am conversationless—

Au Revoir—you Mancastrian, you Cobdenite,[8]   Dos.

1. From George Meredith's novel *Beauchamp's Career* (1874–76), chap. 3. Meredith has "and it," not "and this," and "waving," not "weaving." The underlining is by Dos Passos.

2. [Fr.] "That's it—are you crushed?"

3. English poet (1859–1907), whose best-known work is "The Hound of Heaven."

4. Published in 1902, with an introduction by W. B. Yeats. Lady Augusta Gregory, selecting and combining versions and elements, translated the story of Cuchulain, a hero in Irish mythology, into the language of contemporary Coole peasants. Yeats called her book "the best that has come out of Ireland in my time."

5. [Sp.] "Spanish stew." Literally, "rotten stew."

6. Soon after Russell's conviction in June 1916 for writing a leaflet defending a conscientious objector, the British government refused him a passport to go to the United States, where he had arranged to give courses at Harvard; moreover, Trinity College, Cambridge, removed him from his lectureship. Dos Passos in his memoir *The Best Times* (New York: New American Library, 1966, p. 25) recalled that McComb "had set me to reading Lowes Dickinson [see Letter 7, n. 6 below] and the pacifist declarations of Bertrand Russell. . . ." Undoubtedly this reading began at Harvard.

7. From Henrik Ibsen's play *Peer Gynt* (1867).

8. Manchestrian: a reference to the Manchester school of English economists, who advocated free trade and laissez-faire. *Mancastrian* might be a play on *Lancastrian*. Richard Cobden (1804–65) was a major leader of the Manchester school and an advocate of a peaceful foreign policy.

4

[Picture postcard: "Sydnor's Residence, Warsaw, Va." Dos Passos' writing to and including his direction "(over)" is on the message side. The remainder is on the reverse side, helter-skelter on the face of the photograph.]

[Cintra

postmarked August 26, 1916]

[To McComb]

Parlant de l'architecture... Et de la belle influence du home American, la douceur de cette atmosphère de foyer. Ecrivez-moi mon cher je vous pris avant de partir pour Cuba—Peut-être avant votre retour je serai partir—Je vous écrirai là[1]   Dos.

(over)

Am reading 'Wilhelm Meister'—in preparation for the first part of my Faust—Qui sera Méphistophèle?[2]

Got nice letter from Hardinge.[3]

"Sydnor's Residence, Warsaw, Va." Picture side of Dos Passos' postcard. (See Letter 4.)

I live on letters & the N.R.[4] Have written an essay for it—"Against American Literature"

Beau Idéal of the Manchester School
  Beauty & utility!
  A sight for Cobden!
  Temple of the Virtues

Really A.
I am dying to go back to Cambridge. Mais jamais de la vie.[5]

Give my love to C.G.[6] when you write

The house depicted on the postcard was built in 1904 by William Sydnor, a Warsaw, Virginia, pharmacist. It was torn down in 1976.

1. [Fr.] "Speaking of architecture ... And the lovely influence of the American home, the sweetness of this home atmosphere. Write me before leaving for Cuba my dear fellow, I beg you. Perhaps I will have left before your return. I will write to you over there."

2. [Fr.] Who will be Mephistopheles?

3. Hardinge Scholle.

4. The *New Republic*.

5. [Fr.] "But I'll never go there." The non-literal translation "But, by my life, never" would keep Dos Passos' antithesis.

6. Probably Charles Gouverneur Paulding. See Letter 5, n. 5 below.

5

[Cintra]
Aug 26th [1916]

Dear Arthur—

Thanks for you letter   Conrad's growing on you—I Knew he would —principally on account of Holland & Cosmopolis but ... I suppose literary merit does count a little—

I wish I had you here to read verses to.

What W.K.[1] means I cannot imagine

Apropos of the war, I have again relapsed into choas—I have no ideas Except a vague and very teasing desire to hack and hew, to agitate against the bogies which are being battened by warfume and are gradually obscuring the fair sky of democracy (the last phrase I shall recommend to Mr. Wilson)   The New Republic is losing verve— Heavens the need to agitate! for sanely enthusiastic to put shoulders to the wheel—

I am dying to get to Belgium & exhaust surplus energy by "going to and fro in the earth and walking up and down in it."[2]

Really Arthur, I am darned serious—"the forces of reason" must get together, must make a fuss—We want a new Enlightenment—new Byrons new Shelleys new Voltaires before whom 19th Century stoginess on the one hand and 20$\underline{th}$ Century reaction on the other shall vanish and be utterly routed "like souls from and enchanter fleeing."[3]

G.B.S.[4] has already formed a nucleus — where are his successors? We want people of personality who can catch the popular imagination and wring tears and blow ardors up like a very bellows —

Tell Governeur[5] that he can publish — if the MS. still exists — that vers libre poem the cher Thacher[6] so tactfully removed from the July number — This is mere spite, but never mind. You must send me copies of all the Monthly's next winter — shall subscribe, but that means nothing. I want to see your articles and Gov.'s —

You can't imagine what I minor prophet's attitude I am getting towards the world and America — it is ridiculous — I hope to eventually explode into the New Republic — I am mad to fulminate. Still, it will be many a day, I fear — as I write more inanely all the time — I think I'm getting softening of the literary lobe.

Écrivez

Dos

Did you see that Liebknecht[7] got 4 years? It makes one feel like an early 'Xtian!

1. Unidentified.

2. Job 1:7. "And the Lord said unto Satan, Whence comest thou? Then Satan answered the Lord, and said, From going to and fro in the earth, and from walking up and down in it."

3. "Like ghosts from an enchanter fleeing." Percy Bysshe Shelley, "Ode to the West Wind," line 3.

4. George Bernard Shaw.

5. Charles Gouverneur Paulding (1896–1965). Harvard, 1914–17. On board of editors of the Monthly from June 1915; editor-in-chief beginning July 1916. Later editor for Commonweal and the Reporter.

6. Thacher Nelson. Harvard, A.B., 1918 (19). On board of editors of the Monthly from June 1915, and at different times advertising manager and treasurer.

7. Karl Liebknecht (1871–1919), German left-wing socialist. A court martial on June 28, 1916, sentenced him to thirty months' imprisonment and dismissal from the army for arranging and participating in a May Day peace demonstration. Liebknecht appealed — and late in August 1916 a supreme court martial gave him a severer sentence.

6

[18 East 56 Street[1]
New York
September or October 1916]

Dear Arthur:

Excuse my long silence — I'm in despair — For the present my age is too tender for the Belgian Relief — they say the Spanish Line is jammed and the next French Line boat doesn't sail till Oct. 14$\underline{th}$ The upshot is—I am sailing on the Espagne to Bordeaux—thence shall to Madrid to Universidad where I have letters to three poets and other amusing people—I shall live in the Resedencia des Estudientes (however one spells it)[2] and study architecture and the Bible like mad—also Cervantes, Calderon, Homer & Vergil's Georgics.—then in the spring I shall go to Paris & make every endeavor to get to the front by hook or by crook—let's hope it'll be the Rhine—(Plans liable to change without notice, as the timetables say)

I have passports on the brain, as I spent the morning being looked at suspiciously by an official who looked like a jail-bird, and swearing allegiance to the United States and that I should support the Constitution (of all baroque absurdities!); also in filling out numberless blanks and signing photos of myself for the benefit of Mr Wilson.[3] Then as if that weren't enough I had to get some one to swear to the truthfullness of my swearing!

Have you read "The Dark Forest", a war novel by Hugh Walpole?[4] It seems to me confoundedly good, and if your pacifism has not made you forget the war entirely, it will interest you if you find it about. I must read "Fraternity"[5] From the description you give, it sounds too much like Arthur K. McComb to be healthy reading for Arthur K. McComb. Pardon, mais je suis 'in a pulpit mood' aujourd'hui.[6]

Have you read "Mr. Britling Sees It Through', one of Well's[7] new score of books? (They are produced in litters—like kittens—I firmly believe)

I have a vivid picture of a poor baffled Arthur on the empty pier— Why is everyone in Cuba so terrified by Infantile Paralysis?—No one in New York is—[8]

There is a faint possibility that I may appear in Boston before long— for a day or so

Au Revoir

Dos

1. New York residence of Dos Passos' father.
2. Residencia de Estudiantes.
3. Woodrow Wilson.
4. Sir Hugh Seymour Walpole (1884–1941), English novelist, knighted in 1937. *The Dark Forest* was published in 1916.
5. Novel (1909) by John Galsworthy.
6. [Fr.] "Beg your pardon, but I'm 'in a pulpit mood' today."
7. H. G. Wells (1866–1946). The novel appeared in 1916.

8. This letter was addressed to Cuba. McComb, in notes accompanying Dos Passos' letters to him at the American Academy of Arts and Letters, says that he missed a United Fruit liner by about twenty minutes; presumably it was sailing for Cuba. New York experienced an infantile paralysis epidemic in the summer of 1916.

7

> Dunster[1] 19.
> Cambridge.
> October 8. [1916]

My dear Dos:

I found your letter waiting for me here on my return from Cuba. For some time I was under the impression you were in Cambridge (Graham Aldis[2] told me so) and only later found out that you had left Monday. That was really too sad. Now I shan't see you at all!

We had a quite pleasant but rather rough trip on the "Pastores" [,] left Havana Fri. Sept 29 arrived New York Tues. Oct. 3. We got regally treated, had special menu every evening etc. Monday night the ship was anchored in the lower harbour because a fog came up and the pilot was afraid to take us up to the docks. We also had a death on board just as the ship was getting into quarantine — it was a passenger, consumption. These are all the incidents of the trip. In Cambridge everything as usual. We have been going through a lot of red tape getting courses fixed and so on.

I am taking 2 of Louis Allards[3] courses. Last year I also took 2. These come at the same time, in the same rooms and I sit at the same seats and he says the same sort of thing. So I feel as if I had been away only a week.

I am also taking International Law and dipping into Fine Arts, taking 2 courses with Edgell[4] who is very charming, one on Flemish painting one on the Central Italian Renaissance painters.

You will be surprised — I have actually pinned up a Raphael Madonna in my bedroom. (Perhaps on second thoughts you won't be so surprised — after all, Raphael— —!)

I am glad you are going on the Espagne, very comfortable boat. Now please don't go into ambulance work when you get over there. It means one is lost to one's friends for six months. You know I expect to come over a year from February and you ought to be in Paris at the Beaux-Arts.[5]

I have not the slightest intention of reading Hugh Walpole's book. He has just been having a discussion in the columns of the London Nation with G. Lowes![6] Besides I hate heroics and heroism too (in the usual sense of that word) and all the silly romance and hypocritical cant which this war is producing. Give me true realism—and by the way let me this minute recommend you a superb and splendid creation. It is a novel 650 pages long by Maugham of the English realist school called "Of Human Bondage"[7] I have just finished it and consider it one of the great books of the era. I commend to you particularly the long passage on El Greco. Do get it and read it on the steamer. It is only fair because I have just read two of your favorites "Small Souls" and "The Later Life". I enjoyed them both immensely but of course the treatment and method are very different from the English novel. And I love the English novel with its philosophizings and remarks on art and literature and politics all interspersed. Still I must say I couldn't leave Couperus[8] for long at a time and am waiting for "The Twilight of the Souls" eagerly. Yes, I read "Mr. Britling sees it through"—it comes serially in the Nation,[9] also "What is Coming" but not "Bealby" or "Boon" or "The Research Magnificent." All these seem to have appeared within about six months! H. G. is a horrid man.

This is all the news at present. Do write me about your journey about Madrid, about your impressions of the Prado, about what you read—everything. You don't know how welcome your letters will be—you, my only serious, only trivial correspondent—

Adios, señor, buen viaje![10]

Arthur.

[Accompanying the letter is McComb's sketch upon Dos Passos' first appearance in the New Republic. See the illustration just below and the narrative, p. 18 above.]

1. A private dormitory.

2. Graham Aldis (1895–1966). Harvard, A.B., 1917 (16); A.M., 1917. Contributor to the *Monthly*. He later headed a Chicago real estate firm founded by his grandfather.

3. Louis Victor Allard. Assistant professor of French, 1911–20. Later professor of French at Harvard.

4. George Harold Edgell (1887–1954). Assistant professor of fine arts, 1914–22. Later professor of fine arts and dean of the Faculty of Architecture at Harvard. Director of the Boston Museum of Fine Arts, 1935–54. Author of *A History of Sienese Painting* (1932).

5. The École des Beaux-Arts.

6. Goldsworthy Lowes Dickinson (1862–1932), English historian, philosophical writer, and essayist. A pacifist during World War I, he was extremely important in the conception of the League of Nations and did much to promote the idea. In the London *Nation* both Dickinson and Walpole dealt with aspects of conscientious objection, but they did not direct their comments at one another.

7. William Somerset Maugham (1874–1965). The novel was published in 1915.

8. Louis Couperus (1863–1923), Dutch novelist. *De boeken der kleine zielen* (1901–03), trans. *The Book of the Small Souls* (1914–18), is a series of four novels. The English titles of the individual novels are: *Small Souls, The Later Life, The Twilight of the Souls, Dr. Adriaan*. Dos Passos had reviewed the translated first novel in the *Monthly* (February 1915).

9. The London journal.

10. [Sp.] "Good-bye, sir, have a good voyage!"

8

My address is
ᶜ/₀ Banco Hispaño Americano
Madrid
España

[18 East 56 Street
New York
October 1916]

Arthur, I was tremendously sorry to miss you in Cambridge—You were one of the reasons for my appearance there—However—your letter was very welcome.

Here's something to enrage over:

Tyranny At Home

A certain journalist writes an article criticizing unfavorably Mr. Wilson's policies.

Said journalist asks for a passport to visit England.

Said journalist is calmly refused one by the State Department.—C'est joli, cette histoire n'est-ce pas?[1]

"The Dark Forest" isn't heroics, and I might suggest Mr. Pacifist that the intolerance of broadminded people …. War is a human phenomenon which you can't argue out of existence. You people are like Christian Scientists with the yellow fever. All Your praying and all your ought not's wont change the present fact. They may change the future, but only through the frank and sympathetic understanding of reality — which is not got by closing doors —

Behold the fast volley of platitudes you've driven me into.

Look!

The most dangerous features of an evil are its virtues.

Discover those; face them by bigger virtues — and the evil will fade like a ghost at cockcrow. And the wost evils are those the thickest clothed with virtues, with "Fine sides" — spoken hath the oracle and Pythia[2] can go home to her soup of leeks and her vin ordinaire.

'Of Human Bondage' interests me — I'll try to get hold of it.

Don't you think Britling — except for the discovery of God — a rather fine work? — It seems to me remarkably sane and sympathetic and honestly and broadly searching for the will-o' the wisp

Look, Arthur — You must write me accounts of Art letters and politics in America, sort of like the eighteenth century newsletter; please do, as I don't want to lose threads. I'll write you lots Madrillense.[3]

Then — send me each copy of the Monthly — please and personal notes, gabble and scandal from Harvard.

Give my love to the Gazelle.[4]

Tell Hardinge[5] I'll write him from the boat.

Oh — I forgot to tell you my news: I have become a money grubber — a barterer of my soul, an intellectual courtisan .... I have been paid thirty dollars for an essay! (I admit that to me at present, tho' I've already spent it in riotous living, it seems a titanic sum) The New Republic — this week I think — is publishing a thing of mind called "Against American Literature" And my head is swelled as the throat of a carrolling canary.

Tell me your criticism of the article —

Au Revoir

Dos

1. [Fr.] "Some story, isn't it?"

2. Priestess said to commune with Apollo and receive his oracles at the Delphi temple.

3. Probably an invented word. The Spanish adjective for *Madrid* is *madrileño* (masc. sing.). It adds *s* in the plural.

4. Dos Passos' name for George Locke Howe, a lively youth who was a college roommate of McComb's and a contributor to the *Monthly*. Howe took an A.B. (1918) and an M.Arch. (1924) from Harvard and became an architect and writer. This identification of the Gazelle as Howe is based on Dudley Poore's recollection (during ML's telephone interview with him, October 20, 1974) and on a comparison of comments in Letters 58 and 60 below.

5. Hardinge Scholle.

9

[Madrid]

Nov 16th [1916]

Arthur!

'Scuse pencil, but I am writing you between sips of café con leche[1]—in my little room in the "Pension Boston" above the Puerta del Sol,[2] Madrid's amusingest and noisyest—The actual[3] sol is trying hard to lift himself over the house roof opposite & take a look at me ... He succeeds as I write & a faint warthm permeates the Midrileño chilliness ... Gulps of café con leche ... delicious dark honey—a pancillo[4] & coffee!—one doesn't even need a lightly clothed "Thou" beside one singing—particularly when all Madrid shouts & jingles & plays a concertina below your window—Oh the raucousness of the morning papers. Honestly, since landing in Madrid I have thought of nought else but food—The Spaniards do nothing but eat—those of them that aren't starving to death—and the deliciousest pastries and "breadillos"[5] about in an infinite variety.

Another cup of coffee ...

Received your letter yesterday—There, speaking of Amy[6] the beloved you crossed out 'food' in the enumeration of the things she could do— why man, she becomes positively lyric over food—You can see that she has a proper poetic appreciation of butter & hotrolls and fruits! She is par excellence, the poet of food & crockery

Alas, the last bit of roll has been crunched, the last sip of café con leche sipped, the last smudge of honey licked from the inside of the spoon (how apt and neat the tongue is for licking the inside of spoons held upside down!) and we will turn to more spiritual matters.

Unluckily I landed—without knowing it—in an American pension, where English is the rule at meals—At present a vague Spanish family, two Andalusian students, an unclassified old gentleman, an American authoress with husband & small daughter,[7] and a recently arrived social worker who has come to learn Spanish and qui m'agace,[8] eat the numberless courses at 'almuerzo & comida,[9] Also two delightful Anglophile Spaniards, one a Ph.D. & the other something I've forgotten, come & give intellectual tone to the excellent cookery—Ah, I forgot, there is, to boot, the American vice-consul—a stupid young man who thinks he's a gay dog & who irritates me by speaking better Spanish than I do ...

Am eagerly awaiting "thoughts on the election & the state of the Enlightenment" by A. K. McC. Esq.—I think of nothing but food &

Spanish, also dibujo, drawing, which I'm taking a course in until I can find enough Spanish for architecture.

In the Prado are two rooms full of Teniers & Brueghel, which would I am sure delight your soul—brrr—[10]

Madrid is very chilly and my fingers become numb as I pen articles which I destroy and stories which bore me. My muse may need a warmer climate, you know.

but my chief joy is the Sierra Guadarrama, the long range of brown mountains to the north & west. Behind them the sun sets with numbing glory—I've never seen such sunsets—They stir up your soul the way a cook stirs a pot of broth, but with what a golden spoon! Then, every Sunday, in company with a charming Spanish gentleman[11] & all Madrid, dressed in alpine costume—knapsacks & the rest—I betake myself to them and there climb. The most wonderful views are everywhere—From the summits you can see the two plains of New & Old Castilla—one to the north a ruddy yellow, the other straw yellow to the south until it is lost in the mists at the foot of the mountains behind Toledo. The snow on the peaks is blown into the most wonderful shapes, feathers, knives, by the wind—and when the sky is a crushing blue overhead and the rocks sparkle in the sun with their edgings of snow & you can see from Segovia to Toledo … No wonder the muse has fled—Embarras de richesse—

On sunny days in the sun it is charmingly warm & drowsy, at other times very chilly—you see Madrid has the bad taste to be up two thousand & more feet & is far too near the snow fields for comfort—

I've received a very funny letter from a man in N.Y. apropos my article—also notes from divers people—I imagine the thing was shocking bunk—still I hope it stirred people up a little; I am writing another to the effect that America doesn't need art & that art is the antidote for the disease of romantic discontent—and we not needing it—are in the position of a small boy being forced by his grandmother to take castor oil for fear the green apples he ate last week'll make him ill. You see, Americans don't eat green apples intellectually—I take as a text Flaubert's "chaque notaire porte en soi les ruines d'un poète"[12]—Americans, quotha, carry within them the ruins of baseball players—You see it'll be generally derisive & abusive—

Although—absolutely seriously—I believe that most of the hope of the Western world lies in us—still I fear it'll take many a generation of pummelling to bring anything out of our unyeasted dough. Americans are so damn crude—We show up horridly in Spain,—I feel continually mortified at myself—Spain is really wonderful, Phen——ean[13] [Phoenician] Spain, Roman Spain, Moorish Spain, Parisian Spain rub elbows in the most marvellous way. A man in Roman sandals with moorish features, dressed like old Mediterranean figurines—driving a prehistoric ox cart, with a creak as of the 'squeaking & gibbering" of many ghosts, which two massive oxen pull sullenly with that processional gait I've noticed on greek vases, and bom-bom-bom a shiny auto scoots from behind him & vanishes into dust—like a noisy & smelly premonition— Even the beggars interest me, and rather thrill me—the death's head at the feast[14] sort of thing—and the damned Americans are constantly clamouring about them—also the advanced Spaniards—People have no appreciation of the macabre—of contrast—the fact that death & ugliness are the most important part of life and beauty and that without them life would be blank & beauty colorless

But really, I must stop

Ecrivez mon enfant[15]

Dos

Love to the Gazelle[16]—Send me the Monthly—all the numbers—or else just your articles & Paulding's[17]   to whom salut[18]

The letter is in pencil through paragraph three—and Dos Passos' breakfast. Beginning with "Alas," it is in ink.

1. [Sp.] "Coffee with milk."

2. "The Puerta del Sol . . . the largest and most animated plaza in Madrid," commented Karl Baedeker's *Spain and Portugal,* "derives its name from an old gateway, which . . . commanded a view of the rising sun. . . . No fewer than ten streets end in this plaza." 4th ed. (Leipzig: Karl Baedeker, 1913), p. 61.

3. *Actual* (adj.) in Spanish means "present-time."

4. Properly *panecillo* [Sp.], "roll."

5. Dos Passos is creating his own word for *roll.*

6. Amy Lowell (1874–1925), the American poet.

7. The Sweeney family, whom Dos Passos described in his next letter. See also narrative on p. 127 below and photograph on p. 128 below. Dos Passos became friendly with the family and corresponded with Mrs. Sweeney.

8. [Fr.] "Who annoys me."

9. [Sp.] "Lunch & main meal."

10. David Teniers, the younger (1610–90) and Jan Breughel (1568–1625), Flemish painters. Cf. Dos Passos' comment in Letter 44 below: "You shall temper my ardor with the cool hand of the classical temperament." Dos Passos' "brrr" is probably a response to the quality of coolness, or self-possession, which along with the qualities of detail and precision, appealed greatly to McComb.

11. José Giner Pantoja. See Letters 41–45 below.

12. [Fr.] "Every lawyer carries within himself the ruins of a poet." Flaubert wrote *débris,* not *ruines. Madame Bovary,* part 3, chap. 6.

13. Editor's dash. Part of the word *Phen——ean* is written over and is illegible.

14. Cf. Herodotus 2. 78. William M. Thackeray, *Denis Duval,* chap. 2 has "His appearance . . . was as cheerful as a death's-head at a feast."

15. [Fr.] "Write, my child."

16. George Locke Howe.

17. Charles Gouverneur Paulding. See Letter 5, n. 5 above.

18. "To whom salut," wedged at an angle into the lower right corner of the page, is joined to "Paulding's" with an arrow. Salut [Fr.], "greetings."

10

Alicante   Jan 4th [1917]

Arthur

First: Your letters are an unmitigated joy, so ply the pen — ¡Hombre! as one exclaims in Spanish —

Second: I'm in a black mood this evening — so don't expect much of this letter.

A high cream colored mountain with a castle — two churches with dark blue domes, pale blue sky, dark blue sea — that is Alicante — more or less messed up by an Avenue of dusty date palms of which the inhabitants are inordinately proud, a busy harbor with nice lateen-sailed fishing smacks, and a Riviera-looking row of dingy hotels —

Maurice Barrés Contemplating Toledo with the air of a contemptuous camel amused me excruciatingly — I love Toledo and I don't see why the gentleman shouldn't be left out —

(say this to the Zuloaga-o philes[1] it'll shock them).

Your immediate peace letter I have in my hand — my God man, let us have it; but how?

Every day the misery, the grinding horror of it is ground into me more and more until it seems almost blasphemy to propound our glib pacifist schemes. They're so damn simple, so almost infallible — if we could only once, for five minutes get a sane point of view.

I love Spain — and things Spanish and I am furiously trying to overcome my colossal ignorance with regard to it — but I cant get the grotesque sight of the one-legged men in Bordeaux out of my head — and the hospitals — everywhere hospitals.

And then the grotesque, sublime silliness of officialdoms — the censorships, the patriotic porridge so assiduously stirred, the mummery, and all the while with machine-like promptness, with absurd alacrity, the war seizes on the populations, one after another, on the graceful things, the mellow things, the things that have made worth while the creul whelter of life, covers them with a pompous noise of drums and trumpets, with the sham hocus-pocus of a juggler amusing a Christmas

Ignacio Zuloaga's portrait of Maurice Barrès. Dos Passos called it Barrès contemplating Toledo "with the air of a contemptuous camel."
Musée Historique Lorrain à Nancy

party,—and presto—there they are—blackened, scarred, hating: a stench of dead bodies and stupid rows of little wooden crosses, and widows in black—resigned—and every body resigned—

That's the most damnable of all, the resignation of people—

What perfect bosh—! but you see, Arthur, I'm getting to the bomb-throwing stage.

Vive Adler.[2]

I honestly see no reason on earth why a society for the assassination of statesmen shouldnt be formed that would promptly and neatly do to death all concerned in any declaration of war "just" or "unjust."

If Anarchists can murder people so successfully, I don't see why Pacifists can't.

Chocolate[3] and bombs forever!

Let that be the watchword of the Eight Harvard Pacifists—[4]

But have I told you about the pension "Boston"—? I must, I leave denunciations, and explanations of Spanish art & letters for another time.

It's noisiness I've dilated on—now it's meals—

At a long thin table one sits; on one side an American gentleman of the lobster-valetudinarian type; his rather charming wife, who totes him about Europe while he dilates on the germs, the dirt, and the beggars. (His only redeeming feature is that he's a socialist), The wife is an authoress and would be clever if she were better educated. Then comes a wonderful little girl of twelve, who draws brilliantly and who is a fascinating person, their daughter.[5] Then come a Portuguese old lady in a lace cap and her daughter a deathly pale woman with a most interesting face, who never says any things Then two noisy Andaluces, young men, journalists, who discuss in very raucous Spanish which irritates the American gentleman exceedingly. Then at the end of the table are three dull Cubans who spit on the floor;—On my side are, the American Vice-Consul, a horrid young man, who thinks he's a gay dog; a delightful Danish gentleman, an architect, who wears the most amazing clothing; myself; and a Don José Castillejo, a man after your inmost heart.

He is an old fashioned, 19th century liberal, the leader of part of the Educational Party in Spain, a very brilliant man and the enemy of all forms of darkness, also a Pacifist of Lowes Dickinson brand, speaks English French & German very well and is thoroughly delightful—

He also has that subtle humanitarian snobbery of all Lovers of Mankind—(I mean, one has to hate a little to be human)

It is so amusing; while Don Lorenzo the proprietor-waiter produces course after course of delicious Spanish foods, a perfect bevy of conversations jostle each other about the table.

The Lady Authoress and the Danish Gentleman speak German.

I speak bad Spanish to the Danish gentleman, who answers in kind, English to the Americans & Señor C., French to the Portuguese ladies; who in turn speak Portuguese among themselves, French to me, Spanish to the Spaniards, who toss a variety of dialects back and forth—To cap the climax, another Dane appeared one day—and Danish was added to the Babel.

So our meals are distinctly polyglot.

Your letter about the Monthly I have reread—amid gales of merriment which quite shook my hotel (fonda)[6] bedroom, where I am writing by the light of one sputtering candle and a very very dim electric light bulb.

Of course I have momentary homesickness for Cambridge and all its delights and intellectual snugnesses — and more the inhabitants thereof — and that amusing sheet, the Monthly; — but I stifle them in the bud as weaknesses of the flesh.

By the way, I never get the Monthly.

Do have the backnumbers sent, as it will amuse me — & moreover I want to read your articles & Paulding's & Dudley's[7] poetry — if any appears.

Give my regards to Gov Paulding.

Tell Hardinge[8] I've written.

Remember me to the Gazelle[9]

Adios

Dos.

1. A reference to Ignacio Zuloaga (1870–1945), the Spanish painter. A major exhibition of his work had taken place in Boston in November 1916 and then proceeded to New York. In the foreword to the catalog the American painter John Singer Sargent called the exhibition "of supreme artistic interest." McComb sent Dos Passos a print of one of the paintings, a portrait of Maurice Barrès (1862–1923), the French novelist, politician, and extreme nationalist. (See reproduction of *Portrait of M. Barrès* on p. 35.) In a comment on this portrait, the annotator of the catalog wrote: "[Barrès] is depicted with a panoramic view of Toledo encircling him on account of the superb descriptive passages dedicated to the city in his book, Greco, ou le Secret de Tolède, a copy of which he holds in his left hand." Christian Brinton, in *Exhibition of Paintings by Ignacio Zuloaga* (New York: 1916), p. 36.

2. Friedrich Adler (1879–1960), Austrian Social Democrat, who disagreed with his party's support of the war. On October 21, 1916, he shot and killed Count Stürgkh, the Austrian prime minister.

3. Probably an allusion to George Bernard Shaw's *Arms and the Man* (1894), in which Shaw's Captain Bluntschli, a veteran soldier, carries chocolate in place of cartridges.

4. A name parallel with Eight Harvard Poets. This editor has encountered the term nowhere but here.

5. The Sweeneys. See Letter 9, n. 7 above.

6. [Sp.] "Inn." Baedeker's *Spain and Portugal* (1913), p. xxv, said: "The former distinction between hotels and *Fondas* (unpretending houses of a genuine Spanish cast) has practically disappeared."

7. Dudley (Greene) Poore (see pp. 5 and 7 above), a close and lifelong friend of Dos Passos. He will appear prominently in these letters and in the narrative. The son of a surgeon, Poore was born in Cedar Rapids, Iowa, in 1893. After a year and a half of high school there, he prepared for college at Phillips Academy, in Andover, Massachusetts, and entered Harvard in 1913. He met Dos Passos during the 1914–15 college year and became close friends with him the following year. Poore's life centered around the *Monthly* and Symphony Hall, Boston, in 1915–16. Interview with Poore, summer 1971, and telephone interview with him, June 4, 1978.

8. Hardinge Scholle.
9. George Locke Howe.

11

[Letterhead: Café Cardinal,
Bordeaux]
[le] 10 février [191]7[1]

Arthur! Bordeaux always reminds me of you—I mean; it has the same
elegant gloved commercialism, a faint perfume of the romance of traffic
with the sandal-scented Indies, and, in addition, the yearning towards
the Ancien Régime;—the names of the streets, Cours de L'Intendance,
Allées de Tourny, Allées d'Orleans,[2] and the streets themselves betray
it—grey streets of simple graceful houses full of the fastidious gout of
the French Renaissance, houses where people ought live dressed like
portraits by Mengs[3] and drink chocolate out of pink Sèvres.

I am trying to get home to America, most unwillingly—as I dread
the black gloved relations and the discreet shuffle of imitation parch-
ment—wills and all abominations—that will greet me the moment I
land in New York.

If death wasn't such a very simple humdrum thing, even death would
become ridiculous by the tinsel griefs, the red eyes and black crape and
all the silliness of people making themselves miserable because they think
they ought to be.

I arrived here last night to find that there is no boat this Saturday—the
submarines must be rather numerous—so I have to wait about for a
week.

You can imagine me, through misty winter days, chugging in tiny
steamers up the brown sleek river watching the ghosts of poplars glide
past in a changing lacework.

As soon as I have settled matters in America I shall go back to Spain
for a few months to round out my ideas of it.

Excuse a dull letter—

Au revoir—Dos

I'll probably get up to Boston, if I get across the submariny ocean—
Have you a couch?—

1. The dating information shown in brackets is part of the printed letterhead.
2. The streets named are in the center of the city. Intendance: [Fr., hist.], "administration of province." The Marquis de Tourny (1690–1760), intendant of Guienne
(1743–47), greatly improved the architecture and appearance of Bordeaux.

3. Anton Raphael Mengs (1728–79), German painter, b. in Bohemia, and a leading figure in the neoclassical movement. In 1761 Charles III of Spain brought him to Madrid, where he became his premier court painter and an arbiter of taste.

Letters

~

SPRING 1917–OCTOBER 1917

*G*ERMANY RESUMED unrestricted submarine warfare and the United States broke diplomatic relations with her more than two weeks before Dos Passos sailed for New York. Off Fire Island he wrote Walter Rumsey Marvin, a young friend attending preparatory school, about a rumor — which he didn't credit — of a secret treaty between Germany and Mexico, and he commented that the United States must be wildly excited about the war.[1] It was the Zimmermann note that Dos Passos had got wind of (though not accurately), and he landed amid the Senate debate over the country's arming its merchant ships. In New York City Dos Passos stayed at the home of his aunt Mrs. J. R. Gordon,* at 214 Riverside Drive, while he prepared quarters of his own. He had much personal business: settling his father's estate, attending to an anthology *Eight Harvard Poets* which he had undertaken to get published,† arranging to publish an article on Spain in *Seven Arts* — but the approach of war was uppermost in his mind. However much he wanted to return to Europe to witness the conflict, he was infuriated by America's entry and by conscription. On April 10, three days after the declaration of war, he wrote Marvin that he rather thought the harder America fought the sooner the butchery would stop, but this was an uncharacteristic remark. He said nothing of the sort in any of the letters we have to McComb.

McComb was at Harvard, where as editor-in-chief (pro tem.) of the *Monthly* he was trying to publish the next issue and to keep the magazine alive for the coming academic year. The war had disorganized the

---

*Mrs. Gordon, born Mary Lamar Sprigg, was a younger sister of Dos Passos' mother. Her husband was James Riely Gordon, a prominent architect.

†*Eight Harvard Poets* (New York: L. J. Gomme, 1917). It contains verse by Dos Passos, E. E. Cummings, S. Foster Damon, Robert Hillyer, Stewart Mitchell, William A. Norris, Dudley Poore, and Cuthbert Wright.

staff, the magazine had no money, and there were many calls from within and without the magazine for a merger with the *Harvard Advocate*.[2] "There are some who don't want *The Monthly* ever to begin again," McComb wrote Dos Passos on April 26, "and are agitating to have us give up the Sanctum." On May 12 he wrote Dos Passos that the whole place had been sold out, and in his letter voiced despair at the political situation. He found hope only in the recent Russian Revolution.

Dos Passos left for France with the Norton-Harjes ambulance service on June 20. Revolution was so much on his mind when he boarded the steamship *Chicago* that he gave McComb a code word for it. *Nagel* was the word, after Edward Nagel, a student at Harvard who had gotten Dos Passos to read the Russian novelists and infected him with excitement for Parisian avant-garde art, and in whose room Dos Passos had first seen the revolutionary American journal *Masses*.[3] To Dos Passos' outraged amusement McComb was going to Dublin, New Hampshire, a fashionable resort town where his father had a summer parish, to join his parents for the season. This at a time that should try men's souls! When the two youths wrote to each other in July 1917, Dos Passos' address was Sandricourt Training Camp, north of Paris.

That summer Dos Passos took part in the war. When the French prepared an offensive in the Verdun sector, he was with the ambulances that moved up behind the lines. Soon he wrote of watching the troops being brought up for the attack, and on August 27 he wrote of the poison gas. In September the United States government, acting together with a militarized American Red Cross, took over the ambulance service, and the volunteers were told to join the U.S. Army or leave. Determined to remain a civilian, Dos Passos left and in October, after some detached duty, went to Paris. There he waited for a chance to get into one of the volunteer services, and meanwhile enjoyed walking about the city, dining in restaurants, exploring bookshops, looking at gardens, and attending concerts. When a rush call came for more ambulances, he was able to enlist for civilian duty and by mid-November was off amid a string of Fords for the Italian front.

12

[New York
Spring 1917]

Dear Arthur—

I've been hoping to have news of you—or sight of you ... but alas—you seem to have been overwhelmed by the poisoned gases of militarism.

I've decided—

My only hope is in revolution—in wholesale assassination of all statesmen, capitalists, war-mongers, jingoists, inventors, scientists—in the destruction of all the machinery of the industrial world, equally barren in destruction and construction.

My only refuge from the deepest depression is in dreams of vengeful guillotines.

And—I'm going to France with the Norton-Harjes Ambulance as soon as I can take a course in running a machine.

Do come down to New York—And we'll cheer each other up with visions of the gutters of Wall Street gurgling with the bloated blood of ...

Oh but I'm called to dinner[1] and a fine philippic is interrupted.

How depressing to the intellect is food—particularly cold lamb! All my fine frenzy is gone—I can only shake my head or groan without knowing why—   Au Revoir—Dos—

What about Hardinge etc., (particularly the etc.)?[2] Where & how is the Gazelle,[3] and the gentle "B"[4] and the smiling Faylet,[5] and everyone else? Are they all preparing PREPARING?

They say it takes eleven days to die of poison gas.

And what of our belovéd Russian Republic?[6]

With Swinburne I cry "Liberty what of the night?"[7]

Ecrivez—je vous prie.[8]

1. At his aunt's home, 214 Riverside Drive. Letter from Dos Passos to ML, October 1965.

2. Probably a reference to Scholle's marriage, or prospective marriage. Scholle and Elizabeth Klapp were married on April 10, 1917.

3. George Locke Howe.

4. Unidentified.

5. Presumably Arthur Dudley Fay. Harvard, A.B., 1918 (20); A.M., 1927. He joined the board of editors of the *Monthly* in February 1917. Fay later taught at the Fessenden School, in West Newton, Massachusetts.

6. The Czar abdicated on March 15, 1917.

7. "Liberty, what of the night?" is in the nineteenth and final stanza of "A Watch in the Night," in Swinburne's *Songs before Sunrise* (1871). The first stanza begins with the question in Isaiah 21:11, "Watchman, what of the night?"

8. [Fr.] "Pray write."

13

[Cambridge]
April 26. [1917]

Dear Dos:

A thousand thanks for the best review of the Monthly we have had this year! I know I ought to write more, but I am as lazy as Dr. Johnson.

The graduates will give us $50. only[1] also a man is out collecting back debts, the remainder of the $400 must be subscribed for, If you really want to send a small sum I shall be very greatful but I hope you won't feel obliged to. There is no hurry. If you do I wish you would tie a string to it because there are some who don't want The Monthly ever to begin again, and are agitating to have us give up the Sanctum.[2] I mean I wish you would make it conditional on the rest of the amount being subscribed and on the Monthly starting again next fall. The apportionment we expect to work out at about $20. apiece.

I have just been to the printers to see why The Monthly is not out. They tell me they have been trying frantically to get the advertisement dummy from Burry[3] — but in vain — so the thing hasn't even gone to the bindery — it is so hopelessly discouraging — If only there were anyone of last year on the board it would be so different but I can't attend to the whole business myself. I intend however to make a determined effort to have the paper resumed next year.

Dudley[4] says he doesn't know what the war is about but he wants to join the Naval Reserve because he likes the uniform — Tell me your plans. Atmosphere here very depressing — Excuse gloomy note.

Arthur.

1. *only* has been inserted with a caret.
2. Office of the *Monthly,* located high upstairs in the Harvard Union.
3. William Burry, Jr. (Harvard, A.B., 1918), listed as advertising manager, July 1916–February 1917, and as treasurer subsequently. He became a lawyer.
4. Dudley Poore. See Letter 10, n. 7 above.

14

[Cambridge]
May 12th 1917.

Dear Dos,

Thanks for your letter just received. I wrote you a note to 214 Riverside Drive — did you get it? Otherwise admit my negligence. But the situation is so depressing. Ah, my dear friend, I despair of the Republic! These measures of tyranny so alien to the spirit of our institutions! What hope is there? I have become a pessimist. Only in Russia does the sacred flame burn brightly — there they have the courage to really revolutionize and only there (and in Germany) can one talk of peace. I hope Milyukoff[1] is overwhelmed by the forces of radicalism.

All of us here spend the time talking about plans for the future. Gentle "B"[2] and smiling Faylet[3] are drilling "intensively" — also Burry.[4] Gouverneur[5] is still in Copenhagen and intends to remain there apparently.

Dudley Poore, a poet with a love for literature, art, and music, and a distaste for politics.
Courtesy of Dudley Poore

Hillyer,[6] van den Arend[7] and Downes[8] are sailing for ambulance. Allinson[9] and Opdycke[10] still undecided. Graham[11] has gone to Fort Sheridan Illinois, near his home (this through family pull! Oh, democracy and the "equality" of conscription!) Roger Sessions[12] is undecided. Also Dudley P. [,][13] G. Howe,[14] Cuthbert,[15] F. de Wolf,[16] G. Bartlett[17] & myself. Everything is in confusion. Whittlesey[18]—the philosophic militarist has gone to Plattsburg. Mariner[19] remains. Some of us have plans for flight (keep this dark!) to Spain! Oh, unhappy times! What an age! All reason, sanity, light, humanity gone! Forgive the Jeremiad. When I am not in this state, I become a fervid anarchist.

I have saved back numbers of The Monthly for you from the wreckage—(whole place has been sold out). Expect to be in New York Friday evening the 25th. If you can put me up, I shall be delighted, otherwise allright [,] shall see you anyway. Write me a line. Hardinge[20] remains in Cuba—lots of news about him later—

Arthur.

P.S.

Does anyone still believe in the immortal motto of the French Revolution! Why must we have Joffre[21] instead of Robespierre [.] Oh for Marat![22]

1. Pavel Nikolaevich Milyukov (1859–1943), Russian historian and leader of the Constitutional Democratic (Cadet) party. As foreign minister in the first provisional government after the March 1917 revolution, he continued trying to get the Dardanelles and opposed demands for peace without annexations. Forced to resign on May 15, he opposed the provisional government's swing left.

2. Unidentified.

3. Presumably Arthur Dudley Fay. See Letter 12, n. 5 above.

4. William Burry, Jr.

5. Charles Gouverneur Paulding.

6. Robert Silliman Hillyer (1895–1961), Harvard, A.B., 1917. He became a member of the board of editors of the Monthly in April 1915 but resigned in the fall of 1916. Hillyer won the Pulitzer Prize for poetry in 1934.

7. Frederik Francis van den Arend (or "Van," as Dos Passos usually refers to him in his letters here). Harvard, A.B., 1917. A college friend of Dos Passos, he ultimately made his career in the U.S. Foreign Service.

8. William Lowell Downes (Harvard, A.B., 1916), Hillyer's best friend at college. Dos Passos and he had spent time together in Spain during Dos Passos' recent stay. Downes later became an orange grower in California.

9. Brent Dow Allinson, who attended Harvard College from 1915 to 1917. From November 1916 on he was listed as on the board of editors of the Monthly.

10. Leonard Opdycke. Harvard, A.B. summa cum laude, 1917; A.M., 1920. Later associate professor of fine arts at Harvard.

11. Graham Aldis. See Letter 7, n. 2 above.

12. Roger Sessions, the composer (b. 1896). Harvard, A.B., 1915 (16). When the United States entered the war, he was doing graduate work at Yale.

13. Dudley Poore.

14. George Locke Howe, "the Gazelle."

15. Cuthbert Wright (1892?–1948). Harvard, A.B., 1918 (27). During an initial stay at Harvard (1910–13) he became an editor of the *Monthly,* and during a second stay (1916–17) he was again an editor. Later Wright was a writer, a book reviewer for the *New York Times,* and professor of English at Assumption College, in Worcester, Massachusetts. He was a difficult person, and Dos Passos appears to have avoided close relations with him.

16. Francis Colt de Wolf. Harvard, A.B., 1918. He later took an LL.B. degree at Columbia University and went to work for the U.S. State Department.

17. George Hodges Bartlett (1897–1921), Harvard, A.B., 1918. He was a sensitive musician, who managed the short-lived *Harvard Music Review.* A colleague on the *Review* later remembered him as a "shy and quiet spoken" freshman and a person of "rare and winning character." *Harvard Class of 1918: Twenty-fifth Anniversary Report,* pp. 45–46.

18. Elisha Whittlesey. Harvard, A.B., 1918. He was first listed as on the *Monthly* board of editors in the June 1916 issue and as secretary pro tempore in the February 1917 issue. Whittlesey died in 1922.

19. James Theodore Marriner. Harvard, A.M., 1915; Ph.D., 1918. Assistant in English there, 1916–18. Rejected for the armed forces, he entered the U.S. diplomatic service. In 1937 he was assassinated in Beirut.

20. Hardinge Scholle.

21. Joseph Jacques Césaire Joffre (1852–1931). Because of his republican politics Joffre was preferred over other officers as chief of the French general staff in 1911. He was the commander in chief of the French forces on the western front from 1914 to 1916 and victor of the first battle of the Marne.

22. Jean-Paul Marat (1743–1793), a physician who turned to journalism at the start of the French Revolution. He became an extreme radical leader and helped overthrow the Girondins in 1793.

15

[New York
May or June 1917]
Monday

Dear Arthur—

Thanks for your note.

I fear I shan't get to Boston. So many things to do have come up that I shall not stir—alas—from the angularities of New York until I finally embark—

When are you coming down—all the family? Tomorrow? Next day? Do make it soon—

Of course you're passing your exams.

I've been spending my time of late going to Pacifist meetings and being dispersed by the police. I am getting quite experienced in the cossack tactics of the New York police force. I've been in a mysterious police raid, too; nearly piled into a black maria[1]—Every day I become more red—My one ambition is to be able to sing the internationale—

What about Roger Sessions?[2] Did he get arrested or anything?

I think we are all of us a pretty milky lot,—dont you?—with our tea-table convictions and our radicalism that keeps so consistently within the bounds of decorum. Damn it, why couldn't one of us have refused to register and gone to jail and made a general ass of himself? I should have had more hope for Harvard.

All the thrust and advance and courage in the country now lies in the East Side Jews and in a few of the isolated "foreigners" whose opinions so shock the New York Times. The're so much more real and alive than we are anyway—I'd like to annihilate these stupid colleges of ours, and all the nice young men in them—instillers of stodginess in every form, bastard culture, middle class snobism—

And what are we fit for when they turn us out of Harvard? We're too intelligent to be successful business men and we haven't the sand or the energy to be anything else—

Until Widener is blown up and A. Lawrence Lowell assassinated and the Business School destroyed and its site sowed with salt—no good will come out of Cambridge.[3]

It's fortunate I'm going to France as I'll be able to work off my incendiary ideas—"Liberty what of the night?"

San culottely   Dos

Love to all the family and dependents

1. On the pacifist meetings and the police raid, see Dos Passos, *The Best Times,* pp. 45–46.

2. Sessions (see Letter 14, n. 12 above) says that he opposed the United States' entry into the war and probably would have been a conscientious objector at the time. But at a certain point, probably in the summer of 1917, he realized that he wanted the Allies to win and was in a false position. He then tried to get into the U.S. Army but found that his eyes were not up to standard for it, nor for the British army. Telephone conversation with Roger Sessions, December 9, 1972.

3. First sod for Widener, Harvard's bulking main library, was turned in Dos Passos' freshman year, and the books were there and ready for use about the beginning of his senior year. Harvard's business school was not much older. A. Lawrence Lowell's voice had been decisive in establishing the business school in 1908, the year before Lowell became president of Harvard. The school "met with strong opposition on the assumption that it was to be a mere school of successful money-making . . ." (Samuel Eliot Morison, *Three Centuries of Harvard* [Cambridge: Harvard University Press, 1965], p. 472). In Dos Passos' freshman year the business school had 120 students, in his senior year it had 190, and when he wrote this letter it had 232.

16

[Letterhead: A Bord de "Chicago"]
[New York]
June 20th [1917]

[To McComb]

   on a brazen hot afternoon—tied up "it may be for three years,
It may be forever"[1]
   at the foot of fifteenth street—N.Y.

I have a stateroom with three unknown parties and much luggage. The poor old Chicago—a typical one-class boat—has quite the appearance of a transport, being laden with fear, patriotism and young men in uniform—

We were to have sailed at ten, at noon, at four—and now it is five and still the winches sing.

But Arthur—I was disappointed to hear about the fiasco.

Dublin N.H. and the world crumbling!

Dublin N.H and liberty enslaved!

Dublin N.H. and the fair form of free speech spat upon!

Dublin N.H. and the offices of the New York times undynamited!

Dublin N.H. and Civilization drowned in stupid blood—Oh who is to apply artificial respiration?

Cant you imagine the above bein spouted from a soap box at a street corner on second Avenue

À la lanterne[2]—à la lanterne—

But at least you must write—all of you—long letters to the New Republic—long articles in the Masses—

At the Socialist Party's registration places—where people sign the petition to repeal the Conscription Act—twenty thousand have already signed in New York—That's in two days.

Courage.

This sounds like an exhortation of St Paul's when starting out on one of his many voyage—Alas—when I fell down before the the Damascus Gate and felt the light dawn and the Dove flutter at my breast, and the taste of cocoa in my mouth[3]—I fear that I too imbibed some of St Paul's less pleasing characteristics.

My address is

c/o American Red Cross Ambulance

7 Rue François Premier, Paris

Please write often—as I shall really need cheering up—I expect dark days. My only hope is that something'll happen in France and Austria. But it's a slim one—Oh God how long? But anyway write—read my letters carefully as I may try to transmit censurable news. Nagel[4]—the name—will stand for chances of revolution and all the psychological fringe thereof.

I've heard that things are very near the breaking point, in France particularly. Of course—Spain is likely to Flare at any moment—and the influence should be important.

Make the delightful "G"[5] write me a line now and then—Tidings from any of the family will be more-than welcome—Tell Hardinge[6] I'll write him from Bordeaux.

Adios—Dos

["Adios—Dos" appears amid Dos Passos' cartoon *A Revolutionist's Vision of Fifth Avenue,* which fills an entire page.]

1. "It may be for years, and it may be forever!" (from song "Kathleen Mavourneen"). The words, attributed to Louisa Macartney Crawford, may be found in Edmund Clarence Stedman, ed., *A Victorian Anthology, 1837–1895* (Boston: Houghton, Mifflin and Co., 1895), p. 301.
2. [Fr., in the Revolution] An excitative cry by the people to hang someone. "To the lamppost!" or "String him up!" Dos Passos might also have been thinking of a popular song of the Revolution, "Ça ira," which had a call "Les aristocrates à la lanterne!"
3. Acts 9:3–6. "Dove" refers to the Holy Spirit and "taste" to the Eucharist. "Cocoa" refers to the "Cocoa Press," a term then applied to certain Liberal pacifist newspapers in England. They were believed to be controlled by Quaker producers of cocoa.
4. See narrative, p. 41 above.
5. Probably "Gazelle," George Locke Howe.
6. Hardinge Scholle.

17

[Aboard the S.S. *Chicago*]
June 28—[1917]

Dear Arthur—

Grey opal clouds, grey opal sea and a complete nirvana of soft drowsiness. I've never enjoyed a passage so much. Until yesterday I neither thought a think or cracked a book. I lay on deck at the bow, my head pillowed by a life-preserver, and alternately slept, ate and entered into a grey cloudy nirvana.

We've had one submarine scare—the periscope turned out to be a very barnacly log.

The most unusual ship's company—general troopship atmosphere without the discipline. The military air becomes unbreathably dense through a combination of uniforms, two long guns a colored sergeant and Archie Roosevelt.[1] One sings much about

"God help Kaiser Bill
Oh—old Uncle Sam
He's got the infantry
He's got the cavalry
He's got artillery ....
Then, by God, we'll all go to Germany—
God help Kaiser Bill

and other such joys. The devil of it is that God seems to be helping

A Revolutionist's Vision of Fifth Avenue. Cartoon in letter by Dos Passos. (See Letter 16.)

Kaiser Bill again—by the very veiled and emasculated communiqués we get on the boat.

Again the converted, seen-the-glory-of-the-Lord, Saul turned Paul in me is coming out. I feel that I am going to pen an exhortation to the Thessalonians. Courage, messieurs, courage,[2] there are five socialists on the boat. Imagine among what the steward tells me are jeunes gens des meilleurs familles américains; et les Allemands, monsieur, aimeraient bien les torpiller[3] ... Five socialists!—and there may be more—Glory Halleluja!

By the way—if the Monthly starts up next year at college—it can count on a hundred dollars from me—that is if I'm not dead broke by that time—But by God you must make it whiz. You ought to be able to print one red hot issue before getting suppressed anyway—I almost wish I were back in college—If I only had something to blow off steam in—I'd love to lambaste conscription and the daily press and the intellectual classes and Harvard's attitude—

You see here is St. Paul among us—and I've always thought that Saint Paul was the most unpleasant of that very unpleasant gang, the Apostles.

Overheard from Archie R. (honest)

"But it's not only for Germany"

"〰〰〰 〰〰 － 〰〰〰"

Major R.[4] "No, sir .... when this is over the U.S.'ll be one of the greatest military nations in the world."

A.R.— The greatest

Major R. Then we'll be all ready to ...

Unfortunately I missed the context—but I think I heard enough to chew on for a while. And this from Princes of the Blood.

Nearer Bordeaux

29<u>th</u>

And still untorpedoed

Learn to sing the Carmagnole[5]

Dos

Remember that my address is

   ^{c/o} American Volunteer Red Cross Ambulance, Paris

     7 Rue François Premier

1. Theodore Roosevelt's third son, Archibald.
2. [Fr.] "Take heart, gentlemen, take heart."
3. [Fr.] "Young people of the best American families; and the Germans, sir, would very much like to torpedo them."
4. Theodore Roosevelt's eldest son, Major Theodore Roosevelt, Jr.
5. A well-known song of the French Revolution, with accompanying wild dance.

18

^c/o Miss Belle Greene
Dublin   N.H.
July 30th. [1917]

Dear Dos:

I was very grateful for your letters from the steamer. It was awfully nice of you to be willing to give $100. towards the Monthly—I think that is almost too generous but if I have anything to do with running it, I shall certainly see that it isn't wasted. I shall write you about it in the autumn—I don't think it ought to be started unless it is fairly sure of continuing on its own feet.

You will be pleased to hear that I have not been drafted. I don't know whether you will have got my last letter—I have a horrible feeling that I only put a two-cent stamp on it!

I have no news I am afraid and I presume discussions are out of order. Nevertheless I hope tho' I am not sanguine that the peoples of Europe may be induced to lay down their arms in the not too distant future and return to those peaceful occupations at once more honorable and more profitable which they were wont to indulge in before the present untoward events directed their energy to more disserviceable, and also perhaps more questionable, enterprises. (Is this good 18th cent. sentiment?)

Arthur.

19

Sandricourt Training Camp
Sandricourt   Oise
[France]
July 20th [1917]

Arthur—I've been hoping to hear from you—about the effect of the draft among our friends—It is rumored that Roger Sessions was put in jail[1]—is it so? I rely on you also—for all world-events—We receive no news at all—so please bestir yourself and write me long philosophic—red pacifistic epistles.

But, God, I'm glad to be out of the vast American wilderness—I don't feel now as if I could ever go back, though I know I shall—

Politically I've given up hope entirely—the capitalists have the world so in their clutches—I mean the elderly swagbellied gentlemen who control all destinies—that I don't see how it can ever escape. There are too many who go singing to the sacrifice—who throw themselves gladly, abjectly beneath the Juggernaut. It's rather a comfort to have given up hope entirely—You can take refuge in a pleasantly cynical sullenness, and shake the pack off your back and give three leaps and stride away from the whole human tribe. Of course I have twinges, and shall probably ere long take up again my self-inflicted burden[2]—Till then, let all go hang.

That is the mood the war induces—it is interesting to see it work on oneself. You bob like a cork on top of hideousness and agony and stride debonairely across tragic corpses.—Turn the screws of impressedness too far and you get laughter.

(Many days later—drill of boredom & lovely walks through oatfields red with poppies and the lovely tangled woods that were the shooting preserve of the late Marquis de Sandricourt—Nothing of the war but a faint tattoo on the horizon and frequent aeros slithering across the sky overhead)

Paris was really very interesting. I've never seen so many whores—grotesque most of them, as temptations of St. Anthony. The usual Paris-American wine woman and song air was intensified, full of strange recklessness; Canadian and English officers raising the last hell of their lives, poor devils—a strange sinister joy in the certainty of death.—I don't think this is literary straining after mood at all costs: it may be.

Out here in training camp, we are in an American University—a Cambridge that has no Cercle[3]—no Boston bars to find the stuff of poetry in. One swears and filthifies largely and joyfully. Military discipline plus greasy soup remove all joy of life—One waits with faint hope for the moment of release. For me it approaches, as a section is being formed to fetch some cars from Dijon and take them to some unknown point on the front—then three months—then eight days leave—when Dudley and Bobby & Van[4] and I are going to make a desperate effort to scoot together through the Rhone valley—Avignon—Beaucaire, Aigues-mortes—and sun and grapes and wine .... You should join us.

Of the Great Revolution I hear no more—I believe in nothing.

I am very slowly reading William James' Essays in Radical Empiricism[5]—I wish you'd read it, as most of the ideas I find to be my very own.

Do write often.

I haven't heard from Bobby & Van for a dog's age; I don't know where they are now.

Leave America—Come here—in no matter what capacity—Assist at the débacle.

There is a possibility that the Great Awk[6] is going to spread his pinions in this direction—

I dream of Plumblossoms and trivial ladies in silk in Japan—or Korea—let it be Korea—Love to G. Bartlett[7] etc.

Dos

1. A false rumor. See Letter 15, n. 2 above.

2. "I meant the burden of telling the truth about the world." Letter from Dos Passos to ML, March 26, 1970.

3. The *cercle littéraire*, Dos Passos' immediate set of literary friends at Harvard. It included Mitchell, Cummings, Hillyer, and Poore.

4. Dudley Poore, Robert Hillyer, and Frederik Francis van den Arend. (For van den Arend, see Letter 14, n. 7 above.) Poore was doing ambulance work in France as a volunteer in the American Field Service.

5. Published posthumously (ed. Ralph Barton Perry), 1912.

6. Less informally, perhaps, "Great Auk." The problem in transcribing *Awk* is to decide where Dos Passos' handwritten *u*'s end and his *w*'s begin. Dos Passos' reference is to Stewart Mitchell (1892–1957), Harvard, A.B., 1915; A.M., 1916; Ph.D., 1933. Mitchell was listed as on the board of editors of the *Monthly* in April 1915 and as editor-in-chief from July 1915 to June 1916. Of Mitchell as editor, Dos Passos wrote later: "We called him the Great Auk. . . . He was a little older than the rest of us and a great deal better read. He laid down the law to us in that half-comic, half-pompous way he had." Dos Passos, "In Memoriam: Stewart Mitchell," *New England Quarterly* 30 (December 1957): 513–14.

7. George Bartlett. See Letter 14, n. 17 above.

20

August 22d 1917.

My dear Dos,

I was delighted to get your letter in which you spoke of dreaming of plum-blossoms! The other day at Smith & McCance[1] I picked up the Seven Arts in the hope that your article might be in it. It was—in the sainted company of Amy Lowell, van Loon,[2] Randolph Bourne and John Reed. I promptly bought it and re-read your Young Spain[3] (I don't remember it having that title when you read me the Ms. in New York.) I must say I think it very enlightening (I don't know whether you will think this a compliment or not) and on second reading still seems fresh. Roger[4] is quite safe and attacking the pragmatists and the "New Republic." You had better write to him and start a discussion on "The Essays in Radical Empiricism" [.] I am, as you know, somewhat more doctrinaire than our friends the "constructive liberals."

I can't play the chronicler as well as I could when you were in Madrid—partly on account of Monsieur the Censor.

I can only say that I am very much bitterer than I was—the administration has proved a failure intellectually, more so even than I feared. We have sold ourselves to the Imperialists out-and-out instead of supporting the Russian democrats and giving the German liberals a weapon against the Junkers. This was our strategy as advocated by the <u>New Republic</u>. It has not been a success. It was far too subtle to survive the war-fever, but had some chance of success under neutrality armed or otherwise.

The business of keeping a little Liberty for ourselves is becoming daily more difficult as we become more determined to force our version of it on the rest of the world. Anyway the leadership has now gone to Russia. We have handed the torch of freedom to her (if indeed we ever held it very securely in our own hands!) That elusive emblem cannot live in this stifling air.

So much for international politics—a dismal science at best—and yet now all-compelling.

I envy you all going to the south of France. But I cannot at present leave this curious, perplexing country. I shall be through with college in February if I wish—then I know not. Hardinge, you know, is coming back after all as an <u>unc.</u> and will graduate half a year late.[5] I am afraid I do not see nor know way of starting the Monthly. I am going to talk with the Awk (if I may thus designate so judicial and imposing a character as R.S.M.)[6] about it. But many people will be away and there is a universal apathy—no interest in anything but the great futility (which indeed holds all our attentions in different ways) and Cuthbert[7] is so impossible and will try to wreck it if he can and advertising is doubly hard to get and altogether the outlook is most discouraging.

I don't know what college will be like—but there may not even be a 47 workshop[8]—sad thought for Hardinge—who, by the way, is bringing his wife and establishing himself opposite the Cock Horse where the redoubtable Cohn[9] used to live.

George Bartlett and George Howe will of course be back and Francis de Wolf and we may muddle through somehow but shall miss you all dreadfully.

A determined attempt is being made to boost Vermeer of Delft. I bought an Art Magazine (I know nothing more futile) the other day which had a leading article on him. But I found that I could have written a better one myself!

Are you really staying over for the rest of the war? Don't. Come with me to some quiet tropic place—Java for choice—and raise cocoabeans.

Let me hear from you. I shall be at Westmorely 41. (It sounds horridly plutocratic, but I shall feel myself, without egotism as a speck of light on the dark Gold Coast.[10]

Arthur

P.S.

My love to Dudley, Van & Hillyer[11] if you see them. Tell them to write me a post-card occasionally—I am so glad to hear from any of them.

1. Bookseller, 2 Park Street, Boston.

2. Hendrik Willem van Loon (1882–1944), American writer and popular historian, b. in the Netherlands. Although he condemned German military outrages, his defense of Dutch neutrality antagonized some Americans in 1915.

3. "Young Spain," *Seven Arts* 2 (August 1917): 473–88.

4. Roger Sessions.

5. *Unc.*: perhaps "unclassified student." If so, McComb may not be using the term in its proper sense. Scholle was a third-year student in 1916–17 and again in 1917–18. He entered the army as an enlisted man in December 1917 and later served as a U.S. Army intelligence officer in Honduras. Discharged from the army in June 1919, he was an out-of-course student at Harvard in 1919–20 and 1920–21, graduating in 1921 as a member of the Class of 1918.

6. Robert Stewart Mitchell. He dropped the *Robert* from his name in 1919.

7. Cuthbert Wright. See Letter 14, n. 15 above.

8. Professor George P. Baker's workshop in drama, an outgrowth of his graduate course English 47.

9. Edwin Joseph Cohn (1892–1953), the protein chemist. He was a graduate student at Harvard from 1915 to 1917. Cohn later fractionated blood plasma, so that its components could be used individually and stored for long periods; planned and directed blood processing during World War II; and, in 1949, became Higgins Professor at Harvard.

10. "Gold Coast": a term for the "private dormitories" on and near Mt. Auburn Street, south of the Harvard Yard. Westmorly Court was among the more ornate buildings on the Coast.

11. Dudley Poore, Frederik Francis van den Arend, and Robert Hillyer.

21

July 31st [1917]
(In a small & pleasant
Village in Champagne)[1]

Dear Arthur—

I must write you a line.

The devil's own good luck! Bobby & Van den Arend[2] & I are in the same section—section sixty

We wish you were with us.

The military hubbub is more ridiculous than I ever expected it to be, and less meaningful. Some day vast laughter will sweep through the world and all the Smug foundations will crumble and the horror will laugh away into thin air, and people will start to live again.

But France in agony of misery is far more liveable than America in orgy of patriotic bunk—Think that I tolerated it all so long.

Imagine me now—in <u>uniform</u> with my hair clipped entirely off and a flea bite on my cheek—seated in the sodden rain-lisping garden of an erstwhile inn (where we are quartered in the dance-hall) in a leaky little arbor—you know the kind—where you see champagny wedding parties of peasants on summer afternoons ...

There are many seedy arbors, large and small—with shrubbery beds about them, edged with the round buttocks of old wine bottles, arranged in tasteful rows.

Life here consists of waiting until <u>They</u> send orders—<u>They</u> are strange invisible creatures, gods or demons—that move behind the scenes—inventing futilities and "flapping from out their condor wings Invisible woe."[3]—But one can't be woeful, horror on horror pile up into delirious grotesquerie.

But the French add saving grace ... At the automobile base where we were last Sunday—the commandant had just been decorated, and every one had a delightful fete. The barracks were decorated with evergreens, and all the tables in the mess hall were covered with wild flowers—and we all sat down to a delightful dinner and ate vastly and drank toasts in an extra portion of white wine—all laughed and took off our coats and sweated jovially, (for it was very hot) and slapped each other on the back—Liberté, Égalité, Fraternité! Really, they exist in France—

And the decorated gentleman—and the general who decorated walked through the mess hall arm in arm and drank a toast at each table and made a little speech about "bonne santé et toute la France une seule grande famille"[4]—That night we got our first taste of <u>alarums</u>— The siren warning for aeroplane attacks blew and we heard bombs dropped in the distance and all piled out and looked at the brilliantly star covered sky and heard imaginary hummings of Boche avions—but nothing happened.

But write me—Arthur—I'm so anxious for news & opinions—particularly the latter—Don't be skimpy—

You should have seen Bobby Hillyer as I saw him this afternoon on his back in the mud under his car, garbed in blue overalls, a gob of grease on his nose, and a black and grimy bolt uplifted in his hand. In the evenings we sit in the arbors and drink a mixture of strong white wine and grenadine—most delicious—

I've not been so happy for months There's a rollickingness about it all that suits me. Dumas[5]—glorious Dumas—rises in a chant of wine and women and death amid the dull stupidity. Poor humans—how damned adaptable we are. You cant down us—except by heaven. Hell, by God's a stimulus—Noble patriotism etc—is the most detestable part of war. The gory details are almost enlivening—Love—Dos.

1. Dos Passos' diary has him in "St. Martin-les-prés," near Châlons-sur-Marne, on July 31.
2. Robert Hillyer and Frederik Francis van den Arend.
3. From "The Conqueror Worm," by Edgar Allan Poe. Stanza 2 reads:
> Mimes, in the form of God on high,
>   Mutter and mumble low,
> And hither and thither fly—
>   Mere puppets they, who come and go
> At bidding of vast formless things
>   That shift the scenery to and fro,
> Flapping from out their Condor wings
>   Invisible Wo!
4. [Fr.] "Good health [a toast] and all France one big family."
5. Alexandre Dumas (1802–70), Dumas *père,* author of *The Three Musketeers.*

22

[Letterhead: The Pines,
Annisquam, Mass.]
August 30 1917.

My dear Dos,

Your letter from "a pleasant village in Champagne" most welcome. I hope you got one I sent you to Sandricourt a few days ago. The other day Stewart[1] who is in Gloucester with his aunt came to lunch. We talked and talked for hours. I hadn't seen him since our talk in Downes' room[2] at the end of your senior year. We discussed the follies and futilities in which men are wont to engage.

You say the sacred revolutionary trinity finds its expression in France. But I should say that nowhere in all the world to-day could that glorious formula be uttered without hypocrisy—except perhaps in parts of Russia—more & more I feel she is the hope of the future (if indeed the future holds any hope at all) But I agree with you that there are few countries more dead than our own, more hopelessly sluggish.

The little decorating ceremony you described was interesting—in a pitiful sort of way. With these things they buy the souls of men. Distrust them. Distrust all insignia, all pageantry all pomp and the apparatus of heroism. "La France peut être une seule grande famille"[3] but I distrust the family—it, too, is an institution and I profoundly distrust all institutions. Nothing in all the world matters but that actual men, women & children should be happy. It would be undue optimism

to suppose that they are at present in this condition. The French Revo-
lutionists have certainly been vindicated now in their theory that it was
institutions whence spring all human woes. . . .

The Pope made what I thought a very decent & reasonable peace
offer.[4]

"And the first grey of dawn filled the east"[5] but alas, alas—they had
not yet had enough bloodshed—

Write soon—
Arthur.

1. Stewart Mitchell.
2. Possibly *rooms*. Downes is William Lowell Downes. See Letter 14, n. 8 above.
3. [Fr.] "France may well be one big family."
4. For the text of the proposal by Pope Benedict XV, see the *New York Times*, August
17, 1917, p. 2.
5. Quotation unidentified. McComb may be using it to represent the hackneyed pre-
ludes of thousands of accounts of military attacks, etc.

23

[Érize-la-Petite
France]
August 10th [1917]

[To McComb]
Stage Setting: A small village behind
                     the lines
A delicious pine wood whose gleaming needles brush softly the blue
sky where wonderfully soft clouds skim across—on a hill overlooking
a valley through which runs a very famous road[1]—below our little
village—a collection of yellowish ruins—with all the green plots
obstructed by motortrucks or by the regular ranks of the pale green
ambulances of Section Sanitaire 60—

In the distance, above the sough of the pines is heard the grind of
a camion clanking up the road—and the deep measured snoring of the
big guns on the front. Way off to one side in the direction of a town
famous for its jam a battery must be taking pot shots at German airo-
planes that are taking their afternoon spin, for you can here a sound
like someone tapping impatiently on a table with a pencil—

Personages:

Dos—seated on his haunches writing to an old goop[2] of an Arthur
McComb, from whom he has received no word since leaving Paris.

Bobby Hillyer—lying on his tummy among the pine needles—versi-
fying.

Frederik Van den Arend: asleep in a little dell.

In toto a most idyllic scene.

Arthur — the war's a damned farce — not only ridiculous philosophically, but practically. I've built myself a snailshell of hysterical laughter —

Bobby & Van & I — who by marvellous luck all landed in the same section 60 have been having a wonderful time. So far we have done nothing more strenuous than take our cars from place to place, holding them at the disposition of various army corps who don't want either them or us — and invariably send us travelling again, en convoi — (twenty cars followed each the other like elephants marching into Barnum and Bailey's)[3] down pleasant French roads to spend nights in pleasant villages.

Our major occupations are trifold —

1. Searching for latrines

2. Searching for omelettes and wines.

3. Searching for pleasant places in the fields & woods where to lie and read & write and sniff the dear soil of France

France has manifold advantages over America; even in these distressful times. The omelettes are as varied as ever, though eggs are f .25 apiece — and you hear no jibber about the glory of war; everybody is quite frank about things, amazingly so.

I've not met one militarist of the American 'mine eyes have seen the glory of the coming of the Lord type'.

Of Nagel in France — remember what I told you[4] — there are increasing indications. I'll tell about him in the next note.

I've come to firmly believe that the only thing that can save America is Nagelism there — King Alfred's patrimony[5] is the baleful deus ex & in machina of the who bloody mess — as much as the Hun. Bobs[6] & Van & I talk most excitedly of going home to Junius letters[7] & that sort of thing — seriously & a outrance[8] — Would you chuck reason to the winds and join?

Dont tell anyone about Nagel as he might be offended if his plans were known — and also The Colossus[9] might find out about it. The cat also must remain in the bag through the mails.

Bobby & I are writing a novel — doing alternate chapters & much amused — dont tell Cuthbert[10] — I dont know why you shouldn't; but I'm trying to cultivate a clamlike secretiveness.

Van & I often talk of you and wish like the devil that you were with us. Better hell among the pine woods than the shadow of the papier maché colossus —

However we may come back brimfull of plans for a united clamor & progression of parties at the Bourse[11] & <u>elsewhere</u>.

But for the Lord's sake write, man —

If you'd seen the other night.

We were seated in a little tiny garden on the highroad, drinking a glass of white wine with an old schoolmaster & his wife — delightful people who owned a charming & winsome brown eyed cat — We were all a little embarrassedly making polite conversation when the first camion came by — From that moment for hours and hours — with thunder of wheels and grind of gears the attacking division went by us towards the front. Huge trucks packed with young men, all drunk and shouting and exciting and waving their canteens, or else silent and sullen — looking ghastly as dead men in their shroud of white dust

And all the while — though the[12] and the drunken voices drowned everything we could here our hosts — nervously taking refuge in phrases as people will in extremity —

The husband would say 'Ah ce n'était pas comme ça en dix neufcent seize. Il y avait plus de discipline... Regardez ils détruisent les toits des camions"[13] —

And the wife would answer "Mais les pauvres petits, ils savent qu'ils vont à la mort"[14] — Then she'd hug the little cat to her convulsively and kiss it —

Over and over again they said it, and we sat there not knowing what to do — with our wine-glasses in our hands — while camion after camion roared by and the white dust settled chokingly over the large roses and the zinnias of the tiny garden

Arthur I'm in despair about it all ——

Love

Dos

1. La Voie sacrée. It got its name during the Battle of Verdun (1916), when it was virtually the only route by which the French troops could receive supplies.

2. "Boor." From Gelett Burgess' *Goops and How to Be Them: A Manual of Manners for Polite Infants.* . . . (1900).

3. Barnum and Bailey's circus.

4. See Letter 16 above.

5. Great Britain.

6. Robert Hillyer.

7. "Junius" was the pseudonym of the author of a series of bold, eloquent letters which appeared in the London *Public Advertiser* between January 1769 and January 1772. The author sought to discredit King George III's ministers, call attention to the king's political influence, and bring together the opposition. His comments were scathing, his identity a secret.

8. [Fr.] "To the utmost."

9. Presumably the U.S. government.

10. Cuthbert Wright.

11. The Café de La Bourse, at 5½ Broad Street, Boston, a choice, elegant, and expensive French restaurant. The *Monthly* people had been fond of dining there.

12. One or more words are missing here, words that Dos Passos had in mind but did not set down. In the manuscript there is a page break between "though the" and "and the drunken voices."

13. [Fr.] "Ah it wasn't this way in nineteen-sixteen. There was more discipline ... Look they are destroying the covers of the trucks."

14. [Fr.] "But the poor little ones, they know that they are going to their deaths."

24

[Letterhead: The Pines,
Annisquam, Mass.] U.S.A.
September 6th — 1917.

Dear Dos,

I got one of the most delightful letters I have ever received from you a few days ago. The one from a village in Champagne describing the trucks leaving for the Front and you drinking white wine with the old schoolmaster & his wife.

I want you to know, sir, that I have written quite a number of letters and all long ones, to you & if they have not all reached you, it must be due to the mails or the censor. I am so sorry.

I am delighted to know you are all coming back in January. We need you. What you say about Nagel is interesting. He is really quite impossible in this atmosphere—the air is so stifling, as you may imagine.

Brent Allinson[1] is "called to the colors" for September 19th—he will adopt the pragmatic attitude! The "New Republic" is convinced that "all is for the best in the best of all possible worlds" I am not precisely of their opinion.

When I read Stewart[2] about your "égalité" supper party, he remarked, with that splendid air of ironic detachment that "it was curious how a little wine helped along the sentiments of Fraternity and Equality."

We must have many parties at the Bourse and you, Dos, must not bury yourself in New York but come and help illumine the self-styled new Athens.

Galsworthy has a new novel "Beyond"—but it is rather tiresome & erotic like the "Dark Flower."[3]

As for the Junius letters plan—of course something of the sort must be done.

The other day I saw a charming little garden overlooking the sea and the masts of Gloucester fishing-boats—it was devoted solely to the cult of the dahlia. . . .

I have recently been enjoying the cool green-grays of Matthew Arnold, something remote in him from our meaningless strife.

Stewart suggests that you, he, I, Du. Po. and Hillyer[4] buy up some old magazine and amuse ourselves with it—This was before your letter about Junius arrived. Remember me to these and Van den Arend[5] & be sure & write & tell him to.   As ever

Arthur.

P.S.

I am spending the week-end with Roger[6]—we shall discuss the "New Republic," I expect!

Love

A.

1. See Letter 14, n. 9 above.
2. Stewart Mitchell.
3. The latter was published in 1913.
4. Dudley Poore and Robert Hillyer.
5. Frederik Francis van den Arend.
6. Presumably Roger Sessions.

25

[Verdun sector
France]
Aug 27 [1917]

Dear Arthur—

Van[1] & I were sitting side by side in a pitiful forsaken garden we spend our hours off duty in, and he was just opening your letter when a shell shrieked over our heads & exploded with a vicious pang! in the hill behind us. Of one voice we cried 'how ridiculous'. Isn't it damned absurd that one of your serene epistles redolent of eighteenth century abbés peeing in their gardens after their morning cup of chocolate off flowered Sèvres and thinking sonorous cadences of liberty and the world enlightened, should be opened to the accompaniment of a bursting shell

But absurdities are so multiplied in this macabre world of our day that the grotesque loses its gargoyl-force and all flattens out into one dull despair—

Oh Arthur can't we do something, we who still have eyes in our heads & thoughts in our minds? Can't we stop this wailing over the dead?— Our life is a wake over the corpse of an elaborately garbed Liberty that I suspect was purely mythical anyway. Like the Jews at their wailing place the Liberals cover their heads with their robes of integrity and wail, wail, wail — God — I'm tired of wailing. I want to assassinate.

The joy of being on the front is that one is away from the hubbub of tongues, from the miasma of lies that is suffocating the world like the waves of poison gas the French & Germans in this sector reciprocally honor each other with. Then too, the excitement of it is splendid — for us to whom it is new; it'll soon wear off, however, into the utterest routine.

"Pensez", said a stifled mule driver that lurched into a dugout we were lying in during a gas attack one night, 'Qu'il y a des gents qui boivent le café sur les boulevards"[2]

The French are invincible. They don't chatter — they are utterly charming and much more concerned with the ravitaillement[3] than with the German attacks & every man jack of them realizes the utter futility of it all. They have ceased to argue; they merely suffer & shrug their shoulders —

Like the Greeks the poilu has reached the sublime heights of despair — In him the classic is vindicated. For one for whom there is no hope, only the rhythmed fittness of tragedy, death and pain are conquered eternally.

Some of the essays in Brandes' The World at War[4] are very good — The old critic makes a rather superb figure — and, God, how few they are, the prophets of reason — There is no sound of their voices heard amid the babble of the priests of Baal[5] —

I shall never forget the frightened eyes of the horses — choking of gas, standing beside their overturned gun carriages, waiting for the shell that will finish them —

And the drunken troops we saw go by in camions towards the front, camion after camion passing with grind of gears amid the the white powdery dust, while the old schoolmaster in whose garden we were sitting (it was in a town far behind the lines) kept saying "Il n'était pas comme ça en dix neuf cent seize. Il y avait du discipline... Il y avait du discipline[6] —" and his charming wife, hugging a kitten closer & closer to her, her black eyes full of tears — answering, "Mais mon cher que voulez vous, ils savent qu'ils vont à la mort, les pauvres petits, il savent qu'ils vont à la mort"[7] —

Yea verily — ils savent qu'ils vont à la mort — And the only joys left in the world are alcohol & tobacco — I'm not joking: I mean it.

And all that I leave unsaid — I shall have to come home — to heave

"Oh Arthur can't we do something, we who still have eyes in our heads & thoughts in our minds?" Dos Passos to McComb, August 27, 1917.
Courtesy of Lois Sprigg Hazell (Mrs. Joseph W. Hazell)

'arf a brick[8] into the temple of Moloch[9] if nothing else — at least to disturb with laughter the religious halo of the halocaust. Will you join?

Love

Dos

1. Frederik Francis van den Arend.
2. Dos Passos may have intended: [Fr.] "Just think" . . . "that there are people [*gens*] who are drinking coffee on the boulevards."

3. [Fr.] "The food supply." Cf. Dos Passos' probable allusion to *Arms and the Man* in Letter 10 above.

4. Georg Morris Cohen Brandes (1842–1927), Danish literary critic. The book, consisting of essays by Brandes translated into English, appeared in 1917.

5. 1 Kings 18:26–29.

6. [Fr.] "It wasn't this way in nineteen-sixteen. There was some discipline ... There was some discipline—"

7. [Fr.] "But my dear what do you expect, they know that they are going to their deaths, the poor little ones, they know that they are going to their deaths."

8. " 'Arf a brick": a common expression in England. Thus Dos Passos might have heard it while he was a schoolboy there. The earliest *OED* citation (*OED* Supplement, s.v. " 'arf") is from a *Punch* cartoon in 1854 (vol. 26, p. 82) titled "Further Illustration of the Mining Districts." Two workmen regard a well-dressed man in top hat:

"Who's 'im, Bill?"

"A stranger!"

" 'Eave 'arf a brick at 'im."

9. Moloch *or* Molech: in the Bible, a fire god to whom children were offered as sacrifices. Thus Leviticus 18:21 reads: "And thou shalt not let any of thy seed pass through the fire to Molech. . . ."

26

Sept. 25. [1917]
Westmorely 41
Cambridge Mass. U.S.A.

Dear Dos,

. . . Well, here we are back if you please, amid the dust and red tape of Cambridge. Hardinge & his wife[1] have appeared from Havana. . . . I am going to take Laski's brilliant course in Political Theory. I hope too many political idols won't be shattered by the end of it. I think perhaps not as he is more or less of my own individualistic persuasion.[2] Brent Allinson is conscientiously objecting and I think he will get alternative service.

To think that my letter to Van should have arrived in such distressing circumstances—I feel almost grateful to you, though for comparing me to the eighteenth century abbé! Ah, serene age, compare it to our vulgar, strident clamor of the present, the shrieking ugliness of this twentieth century, compare it to the mellow beauty of the other (so felicitously coupled with a radiant hope.)

Return, elusive spirit (I refer to you, not the 18th cent.) and let your wit play about these ghastly dogma which send men to death.

I have recently read that hard, brilliant work of Mrs. Wharton's "The House of Mirth"[3]—it was relentless and splendid. When you arrive you must spend much time in Cambridge and eat good food (at ever-increasing prices)

Love
Arthur.

1. Hardinge Scholle. On his marriage, see Letter 12, n. 2 above.
2. Harold J. Laski (1893–1950), later a professor of political science at the London School of Economics and a British Labour party leader. He taught history at Harvard between 1916 and 1920. McComb's comment reflects Laski's early views.
3. Edith Wharton (1862–1937). She published the novel in 1905.

27

Sept 12 – [1917]
Remicourt – a small
village in Argonne

Arthur –

The government has us in its clutches – picture the scene: An automobile full of gentleman with large jowls and US army uniforms – Richard Norton,[1] courtly in a monocle – in front a large crowd of ambulance drivers – behind them a much shrapnel-holed barn like structure, our cantonment – The section dog by name "P2' wanders about uneasily. An occasional shell screeches overhead, makes the fat jowled gentlemen duck and blink and crashes on the river bank opposite, making much dust fly but causing no apparent damage. Mr Norton has just finished his very modest speech ending with the wonderful phrase, "and as gentlemen volunteers you enlisted in this service, and as gentlemen volunteers I bid you farewell"___

What a wonderful phrase – "gentlemen volunteers"! particularly if punctuated, as it was, by a shell bursting thirty feet away which made every one clap on their tin helmets and crouch like scared puppies under a shower of pebbles and dust – Thereupon, too, to be truthful, the fat jowled gentlemen lost their restraint and their expression of tense interest (like that which is often seen in people about to be seasick) and bolted for the abris[2] –

But all this is merely to announce that I have sworn solemn vows – to remain for the rest of my days a gentleman volunteer –

Let us all be gentlemen volunteers in life – and rollick through it mindless of the insane gibberish talked about us, of the musket barrels they threaten us with –

Doesn't the phrase make you think of the bands of gentleman-volunteers; gentleman-adventurers, who swaggered over to the continent in the time of Elizabeth to fight for liberty of conscience in the Netherlands—They drank and roistered and whored their way through the wars to the consternation of their allies and to the great edification of posterity—We of the Norton Harjes ambulance are much like that— we refuse the yoke and it is rumored and hoped that a new organization is to be formed in Italy—to carry wounded across the Alps or through the Lakes!

[Sketch of a Red Cross gondola which two figures are propelling between war zone and hospital]

Do you remember the Chinese court that in one of the Mongol invasions refused to fight, but went on, in the gardens of a walled town, carrying out its avocations, writing poems and painting pictures and deciding contests of singers until the invaders broke in and slaughtered them all?[3] Theirs was the true courage, the courage to disregard all in life that did not suit their tastes, to prefer extinction to giving up what they considered worth while—

I am sitting beside Van[4] at a board table—By the aid of an intensely smoky lamp I am writing you and he is reading Georg Brandes, 'The World at War"—a chapter entitled Belgium-Persia[5]—significant connection of names!—

We are en repos in a village by the name of Remicourt, where they make the most delicious cheeses mortal ever ate—Camemberts by creed, but young and chaste and tender and reeking with an ozoone of clover and cows and placid contemplation. Van & I, apart from a few trifling military duties, such as trying to induce the very lazy French mechanics to repair our cars—spend all our time sitting under a haystack reading and contemplating and eating the aforementioned cheeses through Elysian September days—"season of mists and mellow fruitfulness".[6] In the evenings we go to a café in the next town and drink infinities of café au lait or white wine and syrop de groseille[7]—while poilus about us sing and mutter revolt and shrug their shoulders or say on les aura[8] (according to their mental complexion)—and we are all very angry and hurt and surprised when at 8:30, by military law, the café closes and throws us out into the starlight, Then we wander home and watch the reflections of starshells on the front behind the horizon—or hear the guns popping at a Boche avion that's bombarding a certain unfortunate railway station behind us—

Red Cross gondola. Dos Passos' sketch in Letter 27.

And what, Arthur, about you? Before you get this letter you'll have wandered back—in your philosophic ancien regime fashion—to Cambridge, our Cambridge of long russet avenues leading through factory land to Boston, and sunsets lingered over on Beacon hill and tea—oh how blessed to me now would be an ocean of Cambridge tea, with little cakes from the Food Shop!—But what, oh drinker of tea in a pale crepe robe de chambre, oh peeper down from the clouds out of olympus— are you going to do when in February, licenciate, you leave the metaphorical groves of Academe?—

Wartime France is very much pleasanter than peacetime America—
and what war time America is—brr—je m'en fiche.[9] The thing is that
if there is the remotest chance of your coming to Europe—as per
schedule—there are many capacities—interpreter, Quaker reconstruc-
tionist etc—I, and probably Van, would would exert all fair means and
foul to join you or to have you join us—

I am torn between a desire to eave 'arf a brick into the middle of
things over there, and to penetrate a little deeper into the tragic farce
that has projected them.

If you knew how anxious I was for news—you'ld write more frequently and at length and circumspectly—Gare au loup![10]—give me
an account of all things pertaining to the Kingdom of Heaven [*and the*
crossed out] peace that passeth all understanding[11] (yea verily!)

Love to the Gazelle & G.[12] and the Family in general and in particular—

Respectful salutations to Cuthbert.[13] May he grow and wax strong
in muscular Christianity

Eat for me aux Italiens[14]

Love—Dos

1. See asterisked narrative note, p. 17 above.

2. [Fr.] "Shelters."

3. Several historians were unable to identify the events described by Dos Passos.
Consequently, although Chinese history is a vast subject, this editor believes that Dos
Passos' account, like a few others in his letters, is distorted or fictionalized. The reader
may wish to compare aspects of the account with some in the career of the Sung dynasty
painter-emperor Hui Tsung (1082–1135); with events during the Mongol conquest of
the Southern Sung dynasty (the capital city, Hangchow, fell in 1276); and with events
during the Manchu conquest of a retreating Ming court at Nanking (1644–45). Two
of Dos Passos' early poems are on the same China theme as that in his letter: "That Garden
of Sedate Philosophy" (in manuscript among his papers at the University of Virginia)
and "There was a king in China. . . . ," a section of "On Foreign Travel," in *A Pushcart
at the Curb* (pp. 176–80).

4. Frederik Francis van den Arend.

5. "Belgium-Persia" is the title of Brandes' chapter or, rather, essay. The four following words are Dos Passos' comment. Brandes compared England's aggression against
Persia beginning in 1907 with Germany's against Belgium.

6. John Keats, "To Autumn" (line 1).

7. [Fr.] Red currant syrup.

8. [Fr.] "We'll get their [the enemy's] skins."

9. [Fr. expletive] "I don't give a hang."

10. [Fr.] "Beware of the wolf!"

11. "The peace of God, which passeth all understanding." Philippians 4:7.

12. George Locke Howe and, probably, George Bartlett.

13. Cuthbert Wright.

14. [Fr.] "At the Italians." A reference to one or more Italian restaurants. See Letter 29
below.

28

[Postmarked September 1917]

Arthur—

This to announce change of address—

The government has taken over the Red Cross with the usual noisome results—Write me hereafter to Morgan Harjes & Cie[1] 31 Boulevard Haussman, Paris. What to do to escape the net of slavery drawn tighter and tighter about us, I don't know. I can't believe the war will end until people end it, by force, or by annihilation. Why we who don't believe in it should be made miserable by the cowardice of our fellows—I can't see. I am beginning to desire to m'en ficher[2] of the whole affair and escape to Siam—but it's at war—God! everywhere is at war—And you really cant realize what that means till you've seen the utter blundering stupidity of it—Its unbelievable that the world doesn't dissolve in shrieks of delerious laughter—

But the ridiculous horror of war's actuality is less hateful than the lies, the gibbering hatreds, the outworn fanatisms, the greeds of the world that talks instead of fights

Love—Dos—

1. A bank.
2. [Fr.] "Wash my hands."

29

Westmorely 41—
Cambridge—Mass. U.S.A.
October 13th—1917.

Dear Dos,

There has been no steamer for three weeks, but at length one has arrived bearing exchange-professor Cestre,[1] and what is more to the point, a long letter from you. I sit down immediately to reply.

By all means let us be "gentlemen volunteers"—there are terms indeed upon which life is not worth the living—to the acceptance of those terms no external authority shall bend us. Of our dignity and our independence they shall not rob us!

Since you and Van (to whom love, and thanks for his letter which shall soon be answered) recommend Brandes' book, I shall certainly read it, but I have been trying as far as may be to get away from the war. . . .

I long to have you back and feed you little cakes from the Food Shop.

Do come in January with Van, for I do not think I shall go over there. I confess I shrink from scenes of violence and confusion. . . .

If you come back we could all form a colony here and shut out, at least for the time-being, with a Chinese Wall, the hopeless reality. . . .

The news of the Naval mutiny in Germany is splendid.[2] Drink to the German Republic! Drink also some silent toasts.

I have just finished Mrs. Wharton's The Custom of the Country.[3] I am in the mood at present for just such relentless criticism.

I don't think I shall eat vicariously for you aux Italiens, just at present. I am not now in the mood for spaghetti nor Chianti nor any externalities whatever. For the moment the spirit of some Puritan ancestor must have chosen to inhabit my mortal frame (or is it the effect of reading Milton?) for I long, not for your "sun and wine and grapes" but to be among a people thin-lipped and austere, their eyes fixed on the inner light.

Love
Arthur.

1. Charles Cestre, exchange professor of English (from France), 1917–18.

2. For reports in the *New York Times,* see the newspaper for 1917: October 10, p. 1; October 11, pp. 1, 2; October 12, pp. 1, 2; October 13, p. 1.

3. Published in 1913.

30

[Paris]
Oct 18th [1917]

Arthur!

Sitting in a high window in the Hotel Continental,[1] in a room of which the bed is covered with a champagne-colored silk comforter— Dudley[2] has just slept there in all grandeur. He is in town with a broken poll from a Ford accident—not serious however—merely a 'bonne blessure'.[3] We are overlooking the dull green & russet trees of the Tuileries,[4] talking dolefully. We feel mice in a cat-world, or as if we had just received billet doux from Caligula suggesting that we open our veins into the bathtub.

Love from both of us—Dos

1. Listed as a "hotel of the highest class" in Baedeker's *Paris and Environs* (1913).

2. Dudley Poore.

3. [Fr.] "Good wound."

4. Jardin des Tuileries: garden on the east side of the Place de la Concorde.

Letters

≈

*A*FTER A SCENIC TRIP south through France and then along the French and Italian Rivieras, Dos Passos reached Milan on about December 7. On Monday, December 10, he wrote McComb that he would leave the city Thursday. Sitting beside Frederik Francis van den Arend (Van) in a Milan hotel that Monday and watching him writing letters to friends, Dos Passos jotted an anxious thought in his diary:

> Have I the faculty for making friends? I wonder—I seem in my life to have made exactly two—which is little for one so greedy as I.[1]

He did not name the two, but his anxiety about making friends—over six years after his unhappy entry in his Choate diary—is arresting.

Dos Passos felt a strong dislike for Milan, but he had to remain there when his section left, as his automobile needed repairs, and he was still there two weeks after his arrival, having been overly optimistic in his letter to McComb. Soon he quit the city and was quartered in a villa on the Venetian plain behind the Piave River, waiting with his section to move to the front. On December 30 he walked to the end of the causeway connecting the mainland with Venice and looked at the city across the lagoon—merely looked, for the men were not allowed to enter Venice without special permission. He was reading Shelley ecstatically at the end of 1917, including two of his poems composed nearby: "Lines Written among the Euganean Hills"[2] and "Julian and Maddalo."

That winter and spring Dos Passos was in the Alpine country northwest of Venice. "In Bassano, where the River Brenta flows from out of the Dolomites round the flanks of Monte Grappa, we saw some service," he wrote in his memoirs. "Our advance posts were in picturesque spots in steep mountain valleys. The roads were occasionally

Attention! Dos Passos (fourth figure from left) in Fontainebleau, heading for ambulance service in Italy.
Courtesy of Sydney Fairbanks

shelled by the vicious Austrian eighty-eights, but neither army had stomach for combat. Most of our cases were dysentery and frostbite."[3] In March he had fourteen days' leave and spent it traveling and walking about Italy. With Dudley Poore, Van, and John Howard Lawson (a Williams graduate whom he had met in the Norton-Harjes service) he went south by train to Naples, stopping in Bologna and Rome on the way. Then he, Van, and Poore walked and rode on to see the coastal scenery and the Greek and Roman remains near Naples. In April he had forty-eight hours' leave, which he spent back in uncongenial Milan.

The previous fall E. E. Cummings and his friend Slater Brown, both in Norton-Harjes Section 21, had been arrested in France, largely because of remarks Brown made in his correspondence. (Cummings' imprisonment in La Ferté-Macé later became the subject of his *The Enormous Room*.) From Milan Dos Passos wrote Cummings' mother on December 16, 1917:

> Can you tell me anything new about Estlin? Ever since his arrest last Fall I've been trying to find out about him — but have been unable to get at anything definite, either through Mr. Norton, or members of section XXI, or French army people I've talked to about it. . . .
>
> I sympathized with him so thoroughly, and my letters being anything but prudent, that I expected I'd be in the same boat; but the censor evidently didn't notice me — so I'm still "at large", as the blood and thunder militarists would say of us. . . .[4]

But soon Dos Passos was himself in difficulty with the authorities. So also, according to his memoirs, were Poore, Lawson, and Van. When their enlistments expired at the end of May, all four were advised to speak about future assignments to the American Red Cross officials in Rome. In the Italian capital, the memoirs say, Dos Passos' three friends talked themselves out of trouble; however, he was in deeper than they, for he had written a pro-Allied friend in Spain, José Giner Pantoja, to try to keep his country neutral.* Seeking to explain that he had a right to express his opinion, Dos Passos went to Paris that

---

*Dos Passos, *The Best Times*, pp. 67–69. Poore says that he did not have to talk himself out of difficulty, as he was never reproached (letter from Poore to ML, January 10, 1978, and telephone interview with Poore, June 4, 1978). Whatever Poore's experience, his constant association with Dos Passos must have made him suspect, despite his distaste for politics. A contemporary transcription-of-sorts of an intercepted anti-war letter from Dos Passos to José Giner Pantoja (a letter including Dos Passos' recommendation of McComb to Giner Pantoja) survives. Following the transcription is a message headed "Bates to Lowell," in which Bates declares that Dos Passos and his friends in Rome hold pacifist ideas.

June. He spent part of the summer trying to clear himself of the taint of disloyalty, anxious to enlist in some army unit now—but it was no use, and that August he took the *Espagne* to the United States.

A letter he wrote McComb aboard ship on August 19 has some lines excised. Perhaps a censor cut out references to horrors which Dos Passos described much later in his memoirs:

> A few days before sailing I got my last sight of the bloody side of war. There had been an American offensive. I guess it was Château Thierry. The wounded were being evacuated directly on Paris. An urgent call was sent out from the rue Ste. Anne for Americans on leave or on duty in the city to volunteer for service in a nearby base hospital. The night I particularly remember it was my job to carry off buckets full of amputated arms and hands and legs from an operating room.[5]

And perhaps the carnage served as an immediate impetus. Aboard the *Espagne* Dos Passos wrote a fourth part of "Seven Times round the Walls of Jericho," the novel on which he and Hillyer had worked the previous year. In part four he put his chief character Martin Howe, or "Fibbie," through the experiences he himself had undergone on the Voie Sacrée in 1917.[6]

Once back in the United States, Dos Passos received help from various people and managed to get into the Army Medical Corps. That fall he was in a company of casuals at Camp Crane, in Allentown, Pennsylvania, cleaning windows and sweeping barracks and grounds while he waited for a promised waiver of the eyesight requirements. Finally it came. He encountered a top sergeant named O'Reilly, a veteran of the gentlemen volunteers, who was getting together Ambulance Section 541 for overseas duty. When O'Reilly heard that Dos Passos could type he made him acting quartermaster sergeant. On the day of the armistice Dos Passos sailed for Europe, and he later spent about two months in Alsace. By March he was studying in Paris as a member of the army's Sorbonne detachment. But before his discharge from the army he had the misfortune once again to find himself in casuals, now at Gièvres, and did torturous busywork moving scrap iron. He got out of the army in July and went for a visit to England, where he looked up publishers.[7]

For much of this time McComb was in Spain. He arrived there in March 1918, planning to study the country informally. Landing in Cadiz, he stopped in Seville and then went to Madrid, where in July he took a clerical job at the American consulate. From Madrid he wrote Dos Passos of Spanish art, manners, and politics and repeatedly urged him and Poore to join him in Spain.

In the course of their correspondence McComb and Dos Passos exchanged comments on the Bolsheviks. Although many of Dos Passos' letters are missing, we get some idea of their nature from McComb's side of the correspondence. Like Dos Passos, McComb had been caught up in the excitement of the Russian Revolution, so much so that in March 1917 he welcomed it in a *Harvard Monthly* editorial.[8] On May 12, 1917, we have seen, he wrote Dos Passos that he hoped that Milyukov, the leader of the Cadet party, would be "overwhelmed by the forces of radicalism." That November the Bolsheviks attained power. But their actions so disgusted McComb that when on October 5, 1918, Dos Passos wrote him that he thought one sees clearly from the bottom, McComb disagreed, citing the Bolsheviks as an instance of what lay on bottom. When Dos Passos sent him part four of "Seven Times round the Walls of Jericho"—the final section, that ultimately became *One Man's Initiation—1917*,[9] McComb condemned its sympathy with revolution. The argument about Bolshevism went on by mail, as over a year passed before Dos Passos was able and ready to come to Spain. By then McComb was planning to go to northern Europe, but he changed his plans so that he and Dos Passos could be together.

31

> Westmorely 41 —
> Cambridge Mass U.S.A.
> November 21st 1917.

Dear Dos,

In spite of the fact that I haven't heard from you for ever so long—I take up my pen. Let me begin by asking for any news you may have of E. Cummins or W. Brown.[1] News of their minor tragedy filters through but rarely. I suppose you know through Van about Cuthbert. He bears it as best he can, but his description of Ayer[2] causes me to pace the room fuming uselessly. I have been urging you to return, but even this selfishness of mine must have its bounds and I can no longer do so. One beats one's hands impotently against a fog of hypocrisy, cant and stupidity of every conceivable variety. Besides (re-enter the selfish motif!) I may myself appear shortly on the other side of the Atlantic and it would be gloom unutterable to find you & the others gone. Of this more in my next letter. The plan is only in its initial stages at present.

I am going to New York this coming week-end and shall see among other things the very fine exhibition of Italian paintings at the Kleinberger galleries. Also go to the theatre and do the usual things. But I am very unsettled in spirit and want to go anywhere from this suffocating atmosphere — only outwardly now my calm self! . . .

Love — Arthur.

P.S.

I went to an amazing intellectualist tea at Mr. Laski's[3] the other day. He very kindly offered to help get something of mine into the <u>New Republic</u>.

a.

1. E. E. (Edward Estlin) Cummings and William Slater Brown. In September 1917 they had been arrested by the French and imprisoned, Brown's offense being writing letters critical of the war, and Cummings' being chiefly his friendship with Brown. Cummings was not released until December 18 or 19, and Brown not until February 1918. Charles Norman, *The Magic-Maker: E. E. Cummings* (New York: Macmillan, 1958), pp. 77–107; Richard S. Kennedy, *Dreams in the Mirror: A Biography of E. E. Cummings* (New York: Liveright Publishing Corp., 1980), pp. 144–63.
2. A Massachusetts town twenty-eight miles northwest of Boston, Ayer was the site of a camp for thirty thousand conscripts. Cuthbert Wright later went to France as a private.
3. Harold J. Laski.

32

[Letterhead: 330 Park Avenue
New York]
December 21ˢᵗ 1917.

Dear Dos,

I was touched beyond measure to get post-card of beautiful creature holding a crucifix, with message on the back signed by Three Scoundrels: a pantheist, an atheist and a cynic. Oh là, là! . . .

Mi querido amigo,[1] I have so much to talk with you about and want to see you — but I suppose I shan't for at least several months. When you are through with the ambulance why not join me in Sevilla or Malaga or elsewhere? We could have a charming time. Dudley[2] too must be longing for quiet — I go about seeking it — a hunted spirit!

At last the Anthology[3] has come out [,] very nice in grey cover and well-bound. I shall discuss it in my next letter.

The Baedeker[4] which you lent me will come in very handy. I have just finished Theodore Dreiser's <u>Sister Carrie</u>[5] — quite a fascinatingly gloomy work with good psychological analysis, more particularly in the matter of human weaknesses of course. I am now reading Mrs. Wharton's <u>Summer</u>[6] which seems not to be as poor a work as the majority of the critics think.

I have on my list <u>Sonia</u> by Stephen McKenna[7] and <u>La Dame qui a perdu son peintre</u>, satire on B. Berenson by Paul Bourget.[8]

Cher ami, I am really very sad and depressed and cannot write a cheerful letter — as for Cambridge, it is breaking up entirely. Thank you for several post-cards recently received — They are a joy . . .

Adios

Love

Arthur

1. [Sp.] "My dear friend."
2. Dudley Poore.
3. *Eight Harvard Poets.*
4. Probably *Spain and Portugal* (1913). McComb, in his unpublished memoir "A Foreign Dye," wrote later that it was "the one we all used in my day."
5. Published in 1900 but deliberately not promoted by Doubleday, Page, and Co.
6. Published in 1917.
7. Stephen McKenna (1888–1967), English novelist. His novel *Sonia* appeared in 1917.
8. Paul Bourget (1852–1935), French writer. The volume of *nouvelles* named *La dame qui a perdu son peintre* (the title is that of the initial piece, a short novel) appeared in Paris in 1910. On B. (Bernard) Berenson, see Letter 68, n. 5 below.

33

[Letterhead: Hôtel Cavour, Milan]

Dec 10, lunedi.[1] [1917]

Arthur!

It's an age since I either heard or wrote — except for a sprinkling of post-cards. The news in George Bartlett's last letter to Van is desperate. Cuthbert sent to the Bagno[2] and the noose tightening about everyone's neck —

God! I feel like a dirty hound for being here in Italy instead of trying to do something at home — But it is so hard — without money or influence, or even with it — still it would be worth doing just to show the damn tyrants that we aren't all cowards.

Milan is a place of gloom and ponderous palaces and chilly rain — and marrow-corroding cold — In Sant' Ambrogio[3] there are three brown skeletons of saints in gold crowns and embroidered slippers. In the cathedral there is a bronze candleabrum where a gentleman & lady perform the act of sin in the Renaissance manner. In front of the Cathedral there is a great criticism. A fussy gentleman on horseback is statued there. The horse is shying in wild affright. He has just seen the cathedral.

Beyond that one eats cold spaghetti in dank restaurants at ponderous prices — and all day one works in a beastly garage delving into the cold and greasy innards of motors being prepared to go to the Piave.[4]

We're leaving <u>Thursday</u>.

Van — luckily — is still in the same outfit, i e Section 1. Dudley Poore is coming in Section 4. And you and George Bartlett are coming in section what number?

Van just cabled G.B. about it today.

You must both do it at all costs — for a thousand reasons — For God's sake dont give up even if it seems a thousand times impossible. It must come to pass.

And Arthur, I shall be sixty times sixty times glad to see you — Be sure to play as your trump card with the Red Cross the fact that you know Italian — speak it as fluently as a condittiere — George B. does too — Also — there's no time to be lost.

Ecrivez mon cher

Dos

1. [It.] "Monday."

2. Bagno [It.], "prison" (from "bath"). According to McComb's gloss to the letter, the "news" about Cuthbert Wright was a false rumor.

3. Church, parts of which date from the fourth century A.D.

4. River in northeastern Italy. After the Austro-German breakthrough at Caporetto in October 1917, the Italian army drew back to the Piave.

34

3507 N. Charles St. Baltimore U.S.A.
Thursday, January 17th 1918.

Dear Dos:

Since writing you last I have received a most welcome letter and two post-cards from you at Milan but you gave me no address so I continue to send my letters to Paris. I dispatched to you a few days ago "The Twilight of the Souls"[1] — I thought you might like to know the latest adventures of the creatures.   Owing to coal shortage, proceeding from transportation disorganization in the Eastern states my steamer is delayed Indeed it is now one whole month since I was due to spread my pinions for other climes! . . .

Well, mon ami, Cuthbert[2] continues to flourish under the military régime. George Bartlett has graduated, having written an absurd thesis for the odious Schenk[3] about the royalism of Shakespeare or some such subject. Did I tell you that Hardinge[4] had a job in the Ordnance department in Washington? This is really all the news of the select. I have been doing a fair amount of reading in the last weeks. . . . Yo tendré cosas más interesantes á escribirle á Vd. la proxima vez. Vd. ve—ahora sé yo el español![5]

de Vd. afmo.[6]

Arturo.

1. By Louis Couperus. See Letter 7, n. 8 above.
2. Cuthbert Wright.
3. Frederic Schenck, instructor in English, 1914–17; tutor, 1915–19. He received a Ph.D. in history from Harvard in 1918.
4. Hardinge Scholle.
5. [Sp.] "I shall have more interesting things to write to you next time. You see—now I know Spanish!"
6. [Sp.] "Most obediently yours."

35

[Dolo (on the
Venetian plain)
December 31, 1917]

Arthur;

Hear the growl of a gasoline stove cooking water for tea in a curious alluminum cannikin and see seated about a pink lace covered table that once belonged in somebody's boudeoir Van, with a grouchy air in a T shirt, a certain Jack Lawson,[1] a dramatist, smoking a pipe of unexampled stench, and myself, with a bland air and a bronchial cough. The stove, whose name is Hope-Deferred-Maketh-the Heart-Sick, is also warming faintly the cold air of a dingy untidy room, with sheetless beds and a confusion of cots and duffle-bags—The sun is preparing to set and getting a chilly tin foil wrap ready to retire into—at which moment the dull Venetian plain will turn from a brightish mauve-grey to a lowering slate color.

Van is reading Anna Karenina [in crossed out] French, Lawson is writing a future Broadway success, I am reading Julian and Maddalo—a poem that I am sure you love. I am wild over it at the moment—

I've written you about the rejoicings over the cable Van received announcing your arrival in January in Madrid and Bartlett's arrival in Italy in February or soon after—But we are most anxious for explanations

What in the name of Heaven is your pretext? Diplomacy? I fear so. Still it will be interesting for a while—a horridly parasitic existence, however, where real intelligence can't exist for five minutes amid the chitter-chatter—At least I don't think it can.

But who looks where they are going when they are fleeing from the City of Destruction?[2]

I admit that I'm frightfully blue about things—

—Before I forget I have not any news at all of Estlin & Brown. I've written all sorts of people, and I know a man in Paris[3] who is trying to find out all he can and who will let me know—

Diversion—tea with Cordial Campari[4] & condensed milk & toast toasted over our second stove (named Fafner)[5] & entrances & exits—a dark-bearded Christy looking man—Fairbanks,[6] erstwhile of Harvard has come in & is reciting verse in an English voice .... —

To return—I am blue as the seven sad sleepers. Life here in our Italian & ugly villa where we are indulging in a sort of protracted houseparty without any thought of the front—You see the Italian government considers the A.R.C. ornamental but not useful—so here we languish well treated, well fed, gazing sentimentally at the Euganean Hills, and wandering to the border of the lagoon to gaze at Venice—where we are not allowed to go, for some subtle reason. Oh God the ennuie of our rather gilded slavery—It chokes out ones energy terrifically.

A wild air raid last night with the brilliant sky full of throbbing aeroplane motors and shrapnel bursting like rockets and in the distance the crashing snort of explosing bombs—rather cheered me up—Modern war has its exciting side as have football games and subway rushes and other things—and danger does make your blood dance about as if you were a properly alive human and not a symbol of repulsion—

I hate the negative attitude of utter detestation I get into. It is stupid and monastic. But bitter hate is the only protection one has against the cosening influences of a world rampant with colossal asininity.

—Oh Arthur—let's all find a retreat in the heart of Spanish mountains somewhere, in sight of the sea, among vineyards and there all go and solemnly renounce the world and make cordials and engraved bookplates through all futurity—

Do tell me all news—

Love

Dos

I am closing this letter hours later after a walk through sunset and starlight and crisp night air. The moon rose clear—so there'll be air-raids again to night. I'm in fear and trembling for the Arena Chapel where the Giotto frescoes are[7]—as that city gets a terrific lot of bombs.

It's hours later—but the gasoline stoves are still roaring for tea—and the same company sits writing—By the way in an hour or so, the seventeenth abortion of an abortive century will have passed into the musty storehouse of history where all the bales of stupidity and greed and misery are finally bundled away—for the edification of that golden future that is always behind the curve of time——

The water's boiling over—a cup 'o tay to ye!

Love Dos.

1. John Howard Lawson (1894–1977), who later became known as a playwright, screen writer, and drama and film critic. B.A., Williams College, 1914. Dos Passos and he rapidly became close friends. Both enthusiastic experimental playwrights in the 1920s, they associated in founding the New Playwrights Theatre in 1926.

2. An allusion to Bunyan's *Pilgrim's Progress*.

3. Estlin and Brown: E. E. (Edward Estlin) Cummings and William Slater Brown. The man in Paris was "Mr. [Lewis] Gannett," according to Dos Passos' letter to Cummings' mother on December 16, 1917.

4. Campari: brand name of the apéritif.

5. Fafnir: in Scandinavian mythology, a dragon slain by Sigurd.

6. Sydney Fairbanks (third figure from left in the photograph on p. 74 above). Harvard, A.B., 1917 (20), LL.B., 1925, Ph.D., 1936. He became a teacher at St. John's College, Annapolis, Maryland.

7. The chapel, in Padua, contains a series of thirty-eight Giotto frescoes, most of them scenes from the histories of Mary and Jesus.

36

Cádiz
España
el 10 marzo 1918.

Dear Dos,

. . . I did not get off till the morning of the 22$^{\underline{d}}$ (You will admit the appropriateness of leaving the Republic on the birth-day of the father of his country!). . . .

You will be glad to hear that I read Nostromo and the Secret Agent of your Conrad.[1] I thought "Nostromo" very fine in its way but I think it is only the realist in him that makes the romance go down! And even then it doesn't really; the Italian family might have come out of a novel of Merimée's.[2] His sceptics are the most convincing of his characters—in Victory[3] Heyst; in Nostromo Decoud.

I have just finished a volume of short stories of Mrs. Wharton's called "Xingu". I am really a worshipper at Mrs. Wharton's shrine and whenever I get hold of your elusive self shall stuff you with that lady's productions. I have also just finished her translation of Sudermann's Es Lebe das Leben which I thought an inferior play—theatrical and thin.[4] But "The Madras House"[5]—I am quite fascinated by it. . . .

. . . How long do you expect to remain in pastry-less Italy? And then where? You know of course where you ought to set your course for — but I shall not preach. I am dying to see you — ça va sans dire.[6]

. . . Poor Cuthbert has been transferred to a camp in the south and that means France very shortly. He is the only unlucky one of us all, I shall write again in a very few days. I hope this address will reach you all right. It is Van's so ought to be yours. Write me ᶜ/ₒ Crédit Lyonnais [,][7] Calle de las Sierpes 87 Sevilla España, I shall reserve impressions of Spain for my next letter — as yet too confused

I forbear to mention my American fellow-passengers. They were incredible caricatures — American business men. If this is what the Industrial revolution has done I shall never mention it again without a blush.

Love

Arthur.

1. Published in 1904 and 1907 respectively.
2. Prosper Mérimée (1803–70), French man of letters.
3. Published in 1915.
4. *Xingu and Other Stories* was published in 1916. Edith Wharton's translation of *Es lebe das Leben,* by Hermann Sudermann (1857–1928), the German playwright and novelist, was published in 1902. It bore the title *The Joy of Living.*
5. Harley Granville-Barker's play (1910).
6. [Fr.] "That goes without saying."
7. A French bank originating in Lyons.

37

ᶜ/ₒ Crédit Lyonnais
   Sierpes 87.   Sevilla España
                                   el 14 marzo. [1918]

My dear Dos,

I found your letter of the 4th of January awaiting me at the bank this morning. I was delighted to have news of you, though rather old news! I am afraid one of your letters has gone astray as I did not get the one you mentioned announcing receipt of cable. I shouldn't wonder if some of mine had been lost too. I hope you got the one I sent from Cádiz.

I remember Fairbanks very well — a delightful person — muy inglés.[1]

I note your suggestion about monastic retreat in Spanish mountains, making cordials and book-plates! — but you see I don't want exactly to renounce the world — find it charming enough wherever it isn't too noisy.   I don't know "Julian and Maddalo" Qué es?

No, I am not a diplomat, a simple estudiante, mon cher, — only not studying anything at present except the manners and language of this delightful people.   Of course I cannot help being quite undiscriminatingly enthusiastic about everything. Well, I shall not bore you with adjectives but what I have seen of Spain has won my cold, northern heart.   Anyway, the entire complex multiplicity of sensations that one enjoys on landing in Europe, have not yet worn off. The ease of living is so apparent and I am afraid I am something of a sybarite—a parasite, too, for the time being, but you have no idea what a state your dear country was in, when I sailed. The day after arriving here I spent á l'américain—true tourist. I climbed to the top of the Giralda,[2] whence a sufficiently fine view, walked through the cathedral—cool, dim, Gothic and "did" the Alcázar[3] and the gardens of the same where roses and orange-trees were in bloom.

Yesterday I went to the Museo Provincial where Murillo reigns[4]— nothing really good—a passable El Greco.

In the evening I went with a Dutch-Spanish steamer acquaintance to see the "eminente bailerina" Carmelita Ferrer (no relation of the anarchist) dance and Emilia Piñol, apparently a popular favorite here, sing. You may have heard of them.

My plans for the future are nebulous. Let me know yours. I read a paper called "El Liberal" but I think in Spain I am something of a conservative   You see I am getting quite unmoral. Take care of yourself—you mustn't have bronchial coughs, you know (when writing this I feel like Paul in the "Small Souls"!)   Is there anything I can do for you in the realm of Don Alfonso? Command me. Arthur

1. [Sp.] "Very English."
2. Prominent tower, originally a minaret.
3. Spanish royal palace, originally built in Mudejar style on the site of a Moslem citadel.
4. Bartolomé Esteban Murillo (1617?–1682) was born in Seville and spent most of his life there. His reputation was at its height for much of the nineteenth century.

38

[Art postcard reproducing a painting in two parts. The painting is called *The Virgin Reading in Her Room* and is attributed to J. van Eyck. On the picture side of the card, McComb has crossed out J. van Eyck, written "wrongly attributed," and added an additional message.]

[Madrid
Spring 1918?]

[To Dos Passos]
Madrid is a nice town—not unlike any other large European capital, though. It is easy to find one's way around after the complexity of

Sevilla. I like the yellow trams. I am looking up R. Jackson[1] but of course he may not be here this year—do you know?

Love

A

Wrongly attributed—ought to be the Maître de Flémalle.[2] The Prado is overpowering. I go and gaze every morning. El tercera "crisis" del mes ha interrumpido el correo—no importa[3] Write—it will get to me some time

Love A.

The work reproduced on the postcard is the Werl Altarpiece, left and right wings (Prado). The woman reading is St. Barbara. See Erwin Panofsky, *Early Netherlandish Painting*, 2 vols. (Cambridge: Harvard University Press, 1966), 1:173 and 2:Plate 97.

1. Roland Jackson, Harvard, A.B., 1916 (15), a talented pianist who wanted to compose music. Dos Passos during his stay in Spain had spent time in his and Lowell Downes' company. Though Jackson was inclined towards pacifism, under pressure from his father he returned to the United States around the summer of 1917, entered the army, and went to France as a second lieutenant. He was killed near Château-Thierry on June 6, 1918. See "The Reminiscences of Gardner Jackson," Oral History Research Office, Columbia University, 1959.

2. Innovative Flemish painter, whose identity has been controversial. Some scholars have considered his work early Rogier van der Weyden (see Letter 42, n. 1 below). It is now more often identified with van der Weyden's teacher Robert Campin (1378–1444).

3. [Sp.] "The third 'crisis' of the month has interrupted the mail for me. It doesn't matter."

39

[Art postcard]

Madrid 11th Abril. [1918]

[To Dos Passos]

Qué hay, chico? Por qué este silencio? Yo te he escrito dos cartas y algunas tarjetas á la dirección milanese. No sé si han llegado. Ésta la envio á París con esperanza de mejor suerte. Escribe! hombre! escribe![1]

Arturo "de Tenoya"[2]

1. [Sp.] "What's new, young fellow? Why this silence? I have written two letters and some postcards to you at the Milan address. I don't know if they have arrived. I am sending this one to Paris with the hope of better luck. Write! man! write!"

2. There is a Tenoya on the island of Grand Canary, one of the Canary Islands. After the discovery of the Canaries, classical Romans often identified them with the Fortunate Isles or Isles of the Blest. Medieval legend had the mortally wounded King Arthur conveyed to Avalon, "the island . . . called Fortunate" (quotation from *Vita Merlini*, attributed to Geoffrey of Monmouth). If we have interpreted McComb's self-designation correctly, it expresses his bliss at being in a neutral country.

40

Madrid España
May 3$\underline{d}$ 1918.

Dear Dos,

At last the long silence of three months broken by a post-card dated April 1$\underline{st}$! I was so glad to know that you were still in this foolish world, but beyond that and your adress the postal gave me no news and I do want news very badly of you first of all and of Van and Dudley and Italia! However the question you asked will take a letter to answer. . . .

Of conditions in Spain, I think I told you they were excellent, though prices of foodstuffs are somewhat dear for the poor. . . .

I have not yet been to Toledo so cannot speak of El Greco authoritatively, but it seems to me that none of the portraits in the Prado equal that in Boston of Fray Luis Palavicino. I am bound to say that I don't entirely follow your cult of the Cretan mystic.[1] He seems to like to strike a note (an interesting note to be sure) rather than to paint from nature. This is only a roundabout way of saying that he is too subjective ... Ribera I dislike, stark light and shade. Atmosphere of Jesuitical Neapolitanism.[2] Nor does the ectstatic Zurbarán[3] win more than his bare meed of praise from me. Nor yet the romantic Goya, except at moments. But, en revanche,[4] all the brighter in his superior loneliness, shines the star of the immortal Velázquez bright with the coldness of perfection yet burning inwardly with the passion for truth—what I would give for those small views of the Villa Medici. I rather like that strange coronation of the Virgin, too (it is not in the Sala Velázquez—why not?) I have written you I think of the Flemish primitives. I am getting to admire the Avignon School[5] very much—partly the result of reading a French book by Élie Faure[6] which emphasizes it, partly result of seeing an excellent Virgin (portrait) in the Prado.

I wish to end a long-standing dispute with you. I will admit that morality is a matter of taste—this brings the whole matter under the convenient rubric "de gustibus etc".[7]—this makes harsh judgments impossible, while at the same time allowing room for preferences!

I close with customary exhortation: Write. Better still: Venga a España[8]

Love—Arthur.

P.S.

If you want to send me a letter to that nice educationalist D$\underline{n}$ José Castillejo[9] I shall be very glad—but don't put yourself out. They say

the son of the Chinese envoy doesn't go out in 'society' but spends his time taking courses at the Universidad — oh, wise celestial!   a.
. . . .

1. El Greco was born in Crete. The portrait McComb mentions is that of Fray Hortensio Félix Paravicino, in the Boston Museum of Fine Arts. In the handbook of the museum (1915), the subject is named Fray Feliz Hortensio Palavicino.

2. Jusepe de Ribera (1591–1652), Spanish painter. He spent most of his life in Naples, which belonged to Spain.

3. Francisco de Zurbarán (1598–1664), Spanish painter.

4. [Fr.] "In compensation."

5. The papal court removed from Rome to Avignon in 1309 and remained there until 1377. Avignon thus became one of the routes by which fourteenth-century Italian art reached France. In the fifteenth and early sixteenth centuries Avignon was the center of a school of painting combining Flemish influences with the surviving tradition from Italy.

6. French art historian (1873–1937), best-known for his multivolume *History of Art,* published between 1909 and 1921.

7. Latin proverb: De gustibus non est disputandum, "There is no disputing about tastes."

8. [Sp.] "Come to Spain."

9. See Letter 10 above.

41

[Milan
April 22, 1918]

Arthur — I sit in the Arcade at Milan — a large place resonant with the well known hum of industry and the paean of trade & the giggle of prostitution and other wellknown sounds. Milan is an aridity — a modernity — rather like Denver Col. except for the Cathedral which is much uglier than anything in Denver, I am sure. Milan believes in being the brightest busyest & best business center in Italy. It is. About the Arcade; the architect on the eve of the opening ceremonies climbed up the scaffolding and promptly tumbled off and was most excellently killed in the middle of the inlaid marble pavement. He must have had one of those sudden moral awakenings that occur in Russian novels of the Tolstoi school

I'm eating an ice the color of the hat of the lady of pleasure that struts up and down in front of me out beyond the tables exposing herself for sale — or rather rent — with the conceited little steps of a guinea fowl. The ice is nasty and magenta colored.

O Arthur write me often from Spain. Its as if an evangelical minister should receive letters from Cotton Mather elaborately describing the City of Zion.

In about three weeks I shall probably be out of this particular Red Cross Service. What I shall do I have no idea. You may have a visit — chi lo sa?[1] But I have no hope of any good luck —

By the way the next time you are in Madrid look up Señor José Giner Pantoja[2] — Calle Miguel Angel 5 — out near the international school. He's one of the most delightful people imaginable — a little man with a black beard who knows Spain and Spanish art and literature like the palm of his hand. I'm writing him to tell him about you — and I am sure you'll find him charming. Horrid as it is going to see people one doesn't know I think Pepito Giner is worth making an exception for —

But write about Spain — after May 1 — to Morgan Harjes Paris

31 Boulevard Haussman.

I grovel on the ground like the Emperor Heinrich at Canossa[3] before my desire of Spain —

Adios   Dos
April 22

1. [It.] "Who knows?"
2. Dos Passos described him in *The Best Times,* pp. 30–31.
3. Henry IV (1050–1106), Holy Roman emperor and German king. Seeking withdrawal of Pope Gregory VII's excommunication against him, he journeyed to Canossa, in north-central Italy. There according to a famous medieval story he stood barefoot in the snow three days before being admitted to Gregory's presence.

42

Madrid España
el 13 Mayo 1918.

Dear Dos,   I was delighted to get your letter of the 22$^{\underline{d}}$ which arrived the day before yesterday. By now you will probably be on your way to Paris. I entirely agree with your impressions of Milan from what I can judge of a hot summer day I spent there in July 1914.   Before writing any more let me insist on your coming to Madrid — it is essential that I see you and as you are finished with your work in the Italian Ambulance, it is no less than a <u>duty</u> on your part to visit me here. I can promise that as far as Spain is concerned it will be a pleasure for you to come. You shall be fed on sugared things which you must have gone so long without, and you shall see the Prado and we shall do many things. You may take me to Toledo to see the El Grecos and I you to the Escorial to see the v. d. Weyden![1]

Yesterday I had such a good time — went with friends to the Sierra — we walked about 20 kil. in the sun and wind which cured a bad cold

I had—Beceril was the first Spanish village I have seen at close quarters—low, heavy stone houses with tiled roofs, treeless, bitterly arid landscape and behind the village the snow-covered "Maliciosa"[2] (which appears by the way in the background of Velázquez' portrait of Don Baltasar Carlos on horseback) Well, I needn't describe all this as you know it better than I, but you must be tempted ..... We were a strangely cosmopolite party at lunch (potato omelette, oranges, cheese, nuts, hard bread) a Parisian lady, an Irish-French-Canadian, an Arab-jew-catalán, and a charming German-Swiss girl, the sister-in-law of Aranquistain [Araquistain] who is an editor of the weekly review "España" and perhaps the cleverest of the pro-allies here.[3] Someone would begin a sentence in one language, finish it in another and be answered in a third!

I have so many things to talk to you about, books and so on, but they will wait till you arrive. Wire me your arrival to Lagasca 48 3º and I will meet you at the station.

Hasta la vista—que sea luego![4]

Love Arthur—

P.S.

Thanks for the introduction to Giner Pantoja [.] I shall look him up some day soon hoping he speaks something besides Spanish! Better still, we shall go together to visit him—I insist you come here where you are needed more than anywhere else   Life is cheap   venez[5]—

1. Escorial: monastery and palace built near Madrid by Philip II, king of Spain from 1556 to 1598; Rogier van der Weyden (c. 1400–64), major early Flemish painter. McComb was probably referring to his very large masterpiece *The Descent from the Cross,* now in the Prado.

2. [Sp.] Literally, "The Malicious One." The village is Becerril.

3. Luis Quevedo Araquistain (1886–1959), writer and political figure. A right-wing Socialist, he was the Spanish Republican government's ambassador to France in 1936 and 1937.

4. [Sp.] "Until I see you—may it be soon!"

5. [Fr.] "Come."

43

[Italy]

May 6th [1918]

Dear Arthur—

I've just received a postcard from you saying you've received no letters —I've written at least three—& since Seville have received none of yours.

Your letters I've been hugely anxious to get—I want to hear a full account of everything   I am absolutely morbidly delighted by the slightest crumbs from your Spanish feast

Today particularly I look towards Spain as people in the Biblical hell looked towards Abraham in the bosom of God & Isaac in the bosom of Abram (how do you spell him?) and Jacob in the bosom of Isaac[1]

Chico qué estoy más aburrido![2]

Today I am sitting inside a Ford Ambulance while it rains outside and camions go by on the road, spraying high the dun colored mud—Italy land of the sun! And the car has got itself overheated and I shall probably be forced to feel its oily pulse and delve into its slimy evil viscera—

O but I hate automobiles.

And you, thank God, are doing the grand in Spain.

By the way on your wanderings take note of any small cheap cottages you see that might at some future not very remote be inhabited by a band of outcasts, fugitives from injustice, pariahs, a cottage where one could live of olla & huevos revueltos[3] and follow one's natural avocations of making an ass of oneself on paper and on canvas, in ink, in pencil, in oils, in pastel in print—and let the bally world go hang—

Pero, querido amigo mio, escribe, escribe, cartas, cartas coloradas, bermejas, cartas del sangre del fuego d'España torrido.[4]

Read Azorin—I think you'll like him. Also La Dame Errante' & Ciudad de la Niebla' of—how funny I can't think of his name now—anyway he's the leading Spanish novelist of the day—a damn leading one, too, I think.[5]

O to be away from the stink of armies and hospitals and mules and automobiles—particularly the oily burning smell of a Ford with indigestion—Alas I smell it now—

Apropos—the enlistment expires about June—After that, I shall take a permission and travel about Italy a little—then to Paris. There is a chance that meanwhile the will be a chance somewhere to do something interesting—possibly to go to Greece in the ambulance service—If nothing turns up I shall take the ultimate course—you know what that is.[6] I shall take it in the end anyway. So be it soon or be it late on se reverra.[7]

Look, write me at once a letter of colossal length about everything in Spain. Write this once to Milan & afterwards to Morgan Harjes Paris

31 Boulevard Haussman
Love
Dos

A bientôt ¿Quien sabe?[8]

By the way—In my last letter I told you about a friend of mine in Madrid—José Giner Pantoja—Miguel Angel 19—whom I should like you to look up—He's a regular authority on Goya & Greco and one of the pleasantest people I ever knew.

I am writing him about you—

1. Abram: cf. Gen. 17:5. "Neither shall thy name any more be called Abram, but thy name shall be Abraham; for a father of many nations have I made thee." On "Abraham's bosom," see especially Luke 16:22–23.

2. [Sp.] "Man, how very bored I am."

3. [Sp.] "Stew and scrambled eggs."

4. [Sp.] "But, my dear friend, write, write, letters, red letters, bright red, letters of the fiery blood of torrid Spain."

5. Azorín: pseudonym of the Spanish writer José Martínez Ruiz (1874–1967); *La dama errante* and *La ciudad de la niebla* are by Pío Baroja (1872–1956). For some of Dos Passos' later comments on Baroja, see his *Rosinante to the Road Again* (New York: George H. Doran Co., 1922), pp. 80–100.

6. The ultimate course was "to report as a conscientious objector." Letter from Dos Passos to ML, March 26, 1970.

7. [Fr.] "We'll see each other again."

8. [Fr.] "See you soon." [Sp.] "Who knows?"

44

[Bassano]
May 7. [1918]

Dear Arthur—

Again I throw a leaf to the winds of the postal service and the world-wind of the censorship. A card of April 23. has just reached me, and I stop in the midst of a paragraph of Chap II Part III of a certain novel-thing[1] to write you again. I'm sitting at a table with Van, Dudley reading the Bible in wonderful vein at intervals, and a bottle of ink. Outside is the yellow swollen river, the town climbing its hill with towers and the grey streakings of the rain.

But soon there shall be a migration of the tribes and many trials on sea and land, and, if things work, ¿quien sabe?

No I believe no more in the gospel of energy—One thing the last year has taught me has been to drop my old sentamentalizing over action; action when it is anything at all is a foolish running about, a sheep-like scurrying from the wolves, or a wolfish snarling stalking of the sheep; let us have none of it. A voice of one crying in the wilderness,[2] rather ... I still believe in that. To turn ones nose to the moon and bay—To blow trumpets and have the walls of Jericho crumble.[3] To call loud till the gods come back from hunting, like the Priests of Baal[4]—and perhaps in the end to help Judith place the nail in the forehead of Holofernes—at least, out of cryings and bayings and laughter to forge the nail that some future Judith will use to transfix the august stupidity of Holofernes's brow.[5]

[Censor's erasure]

And if I refuse to act on my own hook I obviously shall refuse—to the last firing squad if need be to drag with the chain gang.

So much for that.

I have a new avocation in which I commit the most shocking assininities and shall I fear to the last day. I go forth with Dudley to the landscape and put pencil to paper and commit graven images[6] thereon— Then worse yet, I come home and with a box of pastels, commit further indiscretions on a large scale on sheets of brown paper, so that the people in the section probably think that this is another case of insanity caused by the war.

When, in the course of the revolving ages, I get to Spain again I shall go in for drawing, nay even for painting—in a frenetic manner and see what comes of it—as I am awfully het up on the subject. You shall temper my ardor with the cool hand of the classical temperament.

What do you think of Goya's portraits of Carlos IV? Aren't they the most colossal epics of human stupidity ever perpetrated? And the marvellous one of the Royal Family! And Toledo—have you been to Toledo?—Where are you staying in Madrid? Do you frequent the Calle de Toledo and the Market region? Do you wander about on the Castillana?[7] Have you found any of the very excellent and rather recondite restaurants that exist in odd corners? I'm so anxious to have details of your wanderings.

By the way—as I've said in my other letters—at Miguel Angel 19 lives an enormously pleasant little man with a black beard—Señor José Giner Pantoja—I've written him about you—and although I know it's horrid going to call on people you don't know—I think it would be worthwhile calling on him and leaving a note or something with your address—He's really an authority on Goya and El Greco and knows Spain like the palm of his hand—But just as you like ...

It's raining harder than ever so that the campanile nearby and the towers of the town are nearly lost in grey. Au Revoir—Write one letter ᶜ/₀ American Consul—Milan and the rest to Paris—

Have you been to Segovia yet?

O how I envy you.

Love
Dos

Dudley wants to find out all he can about the pottery works of Daniel Zuloaga[8] at Segovia—Have you heard anything

1. "Seven Times round the Walls of Jericho."

2. "The voice of one crying in the wilderness, Prepare ye the way of the Lord, make his paths straight." Matthew 3:3; Mark 1:3; Luke 3:4. See also John 1:23; Isaiah 40:3.

3. Joshua 6:20.

4. 1 Kings 18:26–29.

5. A conflation of the stories of Judith and Holofernes in the Apocrypha (see Judith 8:1–14:1) and of Jael and Sisera (see Judges 4:17–22). Judith cut off Holofernes' head; Jael drove a nail into Sisera's temple.

6. "Thou shalt not make unto thee any graven image. . . ." Exodus 20:4. The command is part of the Decalogue.

7. Calle de Toledo: a wide street, one of the chief traffic arteries in the southwestern part of old Madrid. Baedeker's guidebook describes it as passing on the east side of a large covered market (formerly the Plaza de la Cebada). From the Calle de Toledo, the guidebook says, "dirty lanes" lead east to the Rastro, "one of the largest rag-fairs in the world." Castillana: the Paseo de la Castellana, a wide avenue running north and south in the central section of the city. The guidebook describes it as a northward prolongation of the "shady" Paseo de Recoletos and says that together the two form "the most fashionable promenade of Madrid." Karl Baedeker, *Spain and Portugal* (1913), pp. 84 (on promenade), 92, 103–4 (on the Calle de Toledo and its environs).

8. Ignacio Zuloaga's uncle Daniel (1852–1921), a potter and painter. The nephew's large group portrait *My Uncle Daniel and His Family* attracted special attention during the Ignacio Zuloaga exhibition in the United States.

45

Madrid Spain
May 25. 1918.

Dear Dos,

Your letter of the 7th of May reached me this morning. Two lines of it were censored and the Italian censorship put in a green slip of paper urging correspondents to write clearly and 20 lines to the page and not more than 4 pages. I think the first was your offense!

I want to urge again how much your presence is needed in Madrid — bring Dudley too. I have been waiting for your arrival before doing lots of things such as going to Toledo, and Segovia. If you come (it is essential you should) we could take rooms and live on oranges, cakes, tea and milk chocolate and you could paint and I could keep you from dangerous tendencies to futurism by ... (I don't know just how, but I would.) No, I have not hunted up quaint restaurants and you know it perfectly well! — particularly in hot weather — it would be quite impossible for me to penetrate into Lower Madrid. I am a fresh air fiend and keep to the respectable part of the city! Would you believe it I am staying in a small pension kept by an Englishwoman. I came here because I was tired looking around and now I am too lazy to change, particularly as I have a room with a balcony at the back of the house and looking over trees toward the Calle Velázquez (the house itself is Lagasca 48 — corner almost of Goya) — a quiet situation which is a blessing.

Unfortunately I don't get as much Spanish as I should like, but I am exchanging lessons with a Catalan.

After writing you to send me a letter to D$^{\underline{n}}$ José Castillejo,[1] I wondered why I did it—it terrifies me to go and visit new people alone— still I shall pluck up courage to visit Giner Pantoja as your description sounds very fascinating.

Tell Dudley I am sorry I can't tell him about Daniel Zuluaga's pottery works at Segovia as I really know nothing about them. Remind him that I am no great enthusiast over the Zuloagas, the cult of those gentlemen is indifferent to me. I admire Sorolla[2] much more. However you can tell Dudley that the other day a brick fell on Uncle Daniel's exhibition at the Plaza Oriente[3] and smashed most of the paintings-on terracotta. I am glad you have given up the gospel of energy and the cult of M. Barres[4]—I, for my part have been doing iconoclastic, ruthless things in the realm of economics. Of that splendid edifice (I cannot even now think of it without emotion!) the praises of which used to ring in your ears on long walks by the Charles River, only the firm belief in free-trade remains—the rest is as dead as my once elaborate faith in Rafael Sanzio[5] and Rafael Mengs.

I await your arrival with impatience—I have as much to say as would fill volumes

As ever—

Love

Arthur.

1. See Letters 10 and 40 above.

2. Joaquín Sorolla (1863–1923), Spanish painter, b. in Valencia. A conservative impressionist, he was internationally known for his luminous, brightly colored landscapes and somewhat romanticized scenes of ordinary life in his province.

3. The Plaza de Oriente, the largest plaza in Madrid.

4. Randolph Bourne wrote in September 1914 that Maurice Barrès was "acknowledged in all circles as the most influential writer of the day in France" (Bourne, "Maurice Barrès and the Youth of France," *Atlantic Monthly* 114 [September 1914]: 395). In considering McComb's remark, it is important to recall that Dos Passos had disparaged Barrès in his letter of January 4, 1917, to McComb (Letter 10 above). On Barrès, see Robert Soucy, *Fascism in France: The Case of Maurice Barrès* (Berkeley: University of California Press, 1972).

5. Raphael Sanzio, called Raphael. Cf. McComb's comment in Letter 7 above.

46

[Art postcard]

Madrid   May 27. [1918]

Dear Dos: In further answer to Dudley's question tell him that D. Zuluaga's works are in an old church in Segovia & his two daughters help him. Tell him also, that if he will come here with you, we shall all go to Segovia & I promise to be polite about the Zulugent!

A.

47

[Art postcard]

Madrid   May 31. [1918]

[To Dos Passos]

Your letter of the 6th received—They are pouring in fast, but where are all mine gone—I have sent infinite numbers of cards and letters to Paris, Milan, American Ambulance, etc. You will get them all some day. Meanwhile, don't go to Greece [.] Come here—there is a 'villa' in Zarauz[1] to let——

Arthur McComb

1. A quiet, fashionable bathing resort on the Bay of Biscay, near San Sebastián.

48

[Art postcard]

Madrid   12th June. [1918]

Dear Dos: I got a letter from Arthur Fay[1] to-day in which he said Robert Littell[2] had taken him to see Esthlin Cummings[3] who, he says, "lives in a furtive and squalid manner on the 3d floor of a house in Christopher Street and who has just been summoned for for physical exam. Schofield Thayer[4] and 3 other Jewish & unpleasant creatures were there! If this is Bohemia— — — —" I thought this might interest you. Await your arrival with impatience

—adieu à bientôt
Arthur McComb.

1. See Letter 12, n. 5 above.
2. Robert Littell, a member of the Class of 1918 who attended Harvard from 1914 to 1916. Listed as on the board of editors of the *Monthly* in February 1916, he succeeded Dos Passos as secretary in July. A writer and editor, he later worked for the *New Republic, New York Post, New York World,* and *Reader's Digest.*
3. E. E. (Edward Estlin) Cummings.
4. Scofield Thayer (Harvard, A.B., 1913; A.M., 1914). He was on the board of editors of the *Monthly* when Dos Passos began publishing in the magazine. After leaving Harvard, he studied philosophy at Oxford. In 1916 he married Elaine Orr (later Cummings' wife). Thayer and James Sibley Watson, another past editor of the *Monthly,* launched their influential, avant-garde *Dial* in 1920.

49

[1918]

[To McComb]

O dear—I am frightfully bavard[1] this morning—I must tell you about my curious novel-thing.

You know that Bobby[2] and I last summer, at the front, began writing alternate chapters of a novel that was to be trivial and Rabelaisian—well—Bobby went home and left the thing on my hands—I was to send it to him when I'd finished a couple of dozen chapters—The upshot is that the wretched thing has wormed itself into all sorts of ideas and made me discharge a shocking lot of ammunition prematurely. It is a history of a young person named Martin Howe, nicknamed Fibbie for his habit of telling yarns in his youth. There are chapters at Prepschool at Harvard in New York—and finally the orgy of lies culminates in the war in a sort of whirlwind and all will end at the blue bottom of an inkwell. I'm most anxious to read it to you—The best thing in it is the chorus that happens every five or six chapters of the butler the cook and the chambermaid in Fibbie's mother's kitchen. There is a shocking lot of eating and drinking in it and considerable fornication—so I fear I shall have to translate the poor thing into French to get it published.

I want it to be a gas bomb thrown at the head of the American public—I fear it will remain a stink-box smouldering in my own pocket—¿Quien sabe?

Love, again,

Dos

Possibly a fragment of a letter. Note Dos Passos' close "Love, again."
1. [Fr.] "Talkative."
2. Robert Hillyer (see Letter 23 above).

50

[Northern Italy]
May 21—[1918]

Dear Arthur—Although, just the day before yesterday I sent off a fat and even violent epistle Spainwards, the arrival of some mail from you—a letter of the thirteenth, has made another scrawl inescapable. Indeed the stern daughter of the voice of God[1] urges me to Spain—mais, chico, si tu penses que c'est aussi facile que d'éplucher des petits pois[2]... And O how I long for Zion.

You tale of going to the Sierra nearly drove me wild. Next time you go, climb to the top of the next mountain over from la Maliciosa towards the west and there deposit a wreath in my honor. I spent one of the most wonderful afternoons ever conceived there winter before last, looking at la Maliciosa. There are no mountains on earth like the Sierra. How they flame with color with ochre and orange and scarlet and purple—and their fragrance! As for news—I shall probably be in Italy till the middle of June, then go to Paris—¿y despues?³

I am now at a post in a charming valley in the mountains, very high on the slope of a certain famous peak—one of those grassy parklike valleys with fir trees climbing solemnly up to the rim on one side. In the bottom, like evil-looking lizards big guns squat and spit.

At the post is a certain ecclesiastic, Dom Pietro, who looks exactly like the early portraits of Philip IV. I've never seen anything so striking as the resemblence.

A bientôt—au revoir
John R. Dos Passos

Why I signed in this elaborate and imposing manner I cant imagine. A gun made a nasty large noise in my ear at the moment I was doing it, which may account for the effect—Love—Dos

1. "Stern Daughter of the Voice of God!" Line 1 of Wordsworth's "Ode to Duty."
2. [Fr., except for *chico*] "But, young fellow, if you think it is as easy as shelling peas."
3. [Sp.] "And afterwards?"

51

c/o Crédit Lyonnais
Madrid   Spain
June 24th 1918.

Dear Dos,

A letter of May 21st has just arrived. You mention one written on the 19th which I have not yet received. The last I got was dated May 6th which arrived about a week after one written on the 7th! Thus the mails!   I note you expect to be in Italy longer than you thought [,] so I am sending this there—though in the meanwhile I have written a great deal to your Paris address.

I was fascinated to hear about your half-finished novel—I remember the famous Philip¹ with pleasure but from your description realize that this latest is of quite a different 'genre'. I am most anxious to have it read to me—an additional reason for your coming here.

Yesterday I went to San Fernando—I don't know whether you know it or not—a spot of verdure in this arid Castilla, a place of eclectic scenery [,] English lanes and streams, rows of Flemish poplars with a gossamer-like foliage, an avenue of Italian cypresses cutting a deep blue sky. And also all sorts of intimate, domestic things like honeysuckle and wild roses and poppy-fields and cherry orchards (oh, we ate and ate the most delicious cherries) then bathed twice in the river.

In a few days I am forsaking my pension—I am delighted. I go to live on Lope de Rueda in an appartment with French friends of anarchistic tendencies—but like all real anarchists lead a tranquil life, and work at regular hours and love books. Incidentally I shall have such luxuries as shower-baths and be able to sleep out on a terrace— considerable advantages now that Madrid is getting like a furnace.   As they are going away for August (and I shall probably have to stay sweltering here for I have been offered a job at the American Consulate (—hours 9–1 and also often 2·30–4. which is not bad) the Consul has to telegraph to Washington, the matter is not decided) I invite you to come and live with me for that time, knowing you will not mind extreme simplicity (we shall get our own meals) so if after this you don't immediately apply for your passport, je me fâcherai.[2]

The other day I went to an exhibition of Spanish portraiture—there were two interesting primitives, but I am bored by the Coellos[3] and the Madrazos[4] etc.

I devour every scrap of news from Italy and am quite willing to decipher your handwriting but I think the censor would prefer clearness—at least he has put little green slips in twice to that effect.

Love,
Arthur.

P.S.

I am bound to say that I think your novel would show more of what they call "unity" if you didn't have Bob Littell[5] as a collaborator. The gentle A. Fay[6] has recently seen B. in New York.

A.

P.P.S. Haven't you a typewritten copy of your novel, you could send me on loan?   A.

1. Dudley Poore remembers "Philip" as a stunningly good piece of fiction, approaching a short novel in length, which Dos Passos wrote at about the time of his senior year at college, possibly after his graduation. It was about a young boy's relationship with his parents and seemed to Poore to be transmuted autobiography. Interview with Poore, summer 1971, and telephone interview with him, October 3, 1976.

2. [Fr.] "I'll get mad."

3. The best-known painters with the name are Alonso Sánchez Coello (1531?–88), court painter to Philip II and distinguished portraitist, and Claudio Coello (c. 1635–93),

Spanish baroque painter, considered the last great painter of the seventeenth-century Madrid school.

4. Reference to a family of Spanish painters. José de Madrazo y Agudo (1781–1859) studied under Jacques-Louis David. Both he and his son Federico were directors of the Prado.

5. See Letter 48, n. 2 above.

6. Arthur Fay.

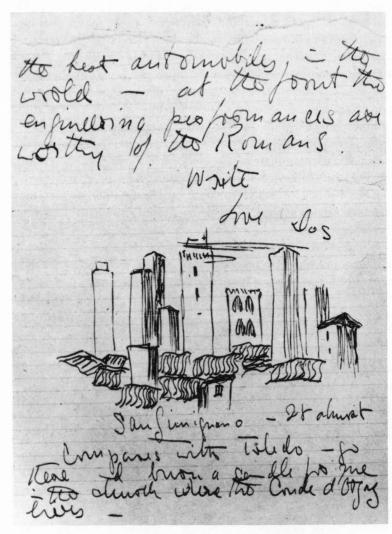

Towers of San Gimignano. Sketch in letter by Dos Passos. (See Letter 52.)

52

Rome—June 9. [1918]

Arthur—

Rome is still enormously wonderful—Dudley and Van & I are seated in a café about to have tea—just returned from a long walk out the Via Appia—a wonderful broiling walk of sunshine and azure and sun rusted ruins—the great aqueducts stretching dark across the pale plain, the mounds of countless crumbling tombs and here and there along the road, a funny row of Roman ladies and gentlemen with lichen on their noses—

We are in Rome pending all sorts of things under the ridiculous accusations of being pro-German ... but I think we are managing to prove our innocence to the Red Cross officials. The whole affair is wonderfully absurd and rather diverting. But it shows that the canker is growing—O tempora[1]

On our way down from the front we managed to stop off at Pistoja —Lucca, Pisa, San Gimignano, "Saint Fina's town of the beautiful towers"[2]—Siena and Orvieto—My ardor for early Italian fresco-work has been fanned to fury—it is unbelievably wonderful. I am marvellously anxious to hear from you—In Milan I'll probably find letters— Of my plans of course I can say nothing—but remember that however long it may take to get there—I have a goal—

When it gets too hot in Madrid where will you go?

Do write me all about your entourage—Who and what sort—and why have you met them?—It is so interesting to be as you are, in a position where one has to start making one's circle over new with new strange material.

Italy—away from the front—is enormously interesting—everywhere traces of an old life fervid and vigorous and fecund—But—except for spots I infinitely pefer Spain—In Spain I always feel at home—and things have a curious significance—subtle and profound rather than picturesque that they have nowhere else on earth—Spain is overcivilized to the point of death and rawly savage at the same time. And Spain is nowhere dead—things are âpre[3] and and vigorous and have a tang of life about them—Modern Italy is so fatuous.

—Of course the Italians are delightful people—they are so enormously sweet and well-intentioned—and kindhearted and so wonderfully hard working—I mean the peasants—And so gullible when anyone, as d'Annunzio[4] said in his first war speech—"makes a heroic gesture"— They do things with their hands wonderfully—to this day they make superb ironwork and the best automobiles in the world—at the front the engineering performances are worthy of the Romans.

Write

Love

Dos

[Sketch of towers of San Gimignano]

San Gimignano—It almost compares with Toledo—go there and burn a candle for me in the church where the Conde d'Orgaz lives—[5]

1. "O tempora, o mores!" [Lat.] "What times! what customs!" Cicero *In Catilinam I* 1. 1–2, and other works by him.
2. San Gimignano: a hill town in central Italy remarkable for its medieval appearance. Saint Fina, who died at fifteen, is its local saint. Baedeker's *Italy . . . Central Italy and Rome* (1904) cites the Italian appellation "San Gimignano delle belle torri."
3. [Fr.] "Rough."
4. Gabriele D'Annunzio (1863–1938), Italian writer and nationalist leader.
5. The Church of Santo Tomé in Toledo. It contains El Greco's *Burial of the Count Orgaz,* depicting a legendary miracle during the count's burial there.

53

[Paris]

July 12 [1918]

Dear Arthur—

I keep thinking of how I can manage it.

I shall be in Paris a long while about this affair—my procés[1]—as I am trying to get the Red Cross to swallow its words and its dishonorable discharge all of which were based on nothing but rumor. The extreme lack of decency, of small obvious humanness, in people comes out more every day. They are preposterous. I refuse to take them seriously.

I want to retire to a village among high mountains,—Shelley's Caucasus[2] will do—and there live among paint pots and white paper and work in a vineyard for a farthing a day. Je suis desenchanté.[3] If monasteries were the thing nowadays I should have been in one long ago.

Let's found one on the end of Finisterre.[4]

Maybe I shall try to get into the American ambulance service and be ditched forever—but my eyes are so bad that I doubt if I should be accepted.

In the Red Cross—c'est finis.

By the way—have you a copy of Eight Harvard Poets? I wonder where I can get one. It seems to have come out some time last fall.

What is Arthur Fay doing?[5] When you write him, will you ask if he knows John Walcott's address.[6] They were at the R.O.T.C. together in Kansas. I suppose they are both lieutenants or captains or something.

It was Bobby Hillyer, you chump, I was collaborating with—I haven't seen Litell since 1916.

Does anyone know anything of the whereabouts of Stewart Mitchell?[7]

O how our poor Olympus is scattered. The muses are driven from Parnassus. The world hurries on its course to idiocy. Dies irae, dies illa[8]—

Addio[9]—Dos

1. Procès [Fr.], "case at law."
2. Percy Bysshe Shelley, *Prometheus Unbound;* also his "Alastor," lines 353, 377.
3. [Fr.] "I am disillusioned."
4. Cape Finisterre, a rocky promontory, the westermost place in mainland Spain.
5. Fay went to France as a first lieutenant in infantry on July 26, 1918.
6. John Walcott (1893–1936) had been at Choate and Harvard with Dos Passos. After getting his A.B. from Harvard in 1915, he attended Harvard Law School until the war interrupted his studies. He received military training at Fort Leavenworth, Kansas, went to France as a second lieutenant in infantry, and was promoted to first lieutenant. He later became an investment analyst.
7. An enlisted man in a field artillery unit, Mitchell spent many months at Camp Sheridan, in Alabama, before he sailed for Europe in late June 1918.
8. "Day of wrath, that day," first line of Latin hymn on Judgment Day, generally ascribed to Thomas of Celano (fl. thirteenth century).
9. [It.] "Good-bye."

54

[Letterhead: Embassy of the
United States of America]
Madrid, July 29th, 1918.

Dear Dos,

Your letter of the 12th received to-day. I feel somehow that you are more accessible now that you are in Paris instead of Italy. But I am distressed to hear about your procès—are Van and Dudley engaged in one too? It is absurd! I am particularly sorry that it is going to keep you in Paris for some time and so delay your eventual arrival here. If you have any difficulty about passport visas let me know and I will do what I can—probably not much!   I entirely agree with you—people are quite obviously preposterous.

I wish, my dear Dos, you wouldn't give me nervous jumps—first about your going to Greece, now about the American Ambulance. On the contrary, you are to come here—you have not yet answered my invitation (perhaps you never got it!) to spend the month of August with me in my Apartment. I mean this quite seriously.   Unfortunately I gave away my last copy of Eight Harvard Poets before leaving the U. S. Otherwise I would send you my copy. Why not order one from America? It was really very well got up—I think I wrote you about it at the time.

You certainly told me it was Littell you were collaborating with[1]—under the circumstances you can understand my polite surprise!   I know nothing of the whereabouts of the incomparable Stewart—the last I heard of him he was in the Y. M. C. A. in Montgomery, Alabama. I spent some delightful days with him in Gloucester last summer.

I shall try to find the address of John Walcott. Yesterday, Sunday, I spent a day of mourning for our scattered Olympus! Oh, the infinite sadness .... when I think of our years 1914–5, first of our evenings at the Little Theatre[2] and midnight walks back to Cambridge where we eat oranges before going to bed .. and then the Monthly and the Pagan number[3] and teas in your room at Thayer[4] .. ... oh ... oh!

I wrote you a letter of criticisms on Spain a while ago—disregard the spirit of it—I was feeling grumpy at the time—in relity I am devoted to Madrid.

As ever, Love,
Arthur

1. Cf. Letters 23 and 49 above.
2. Presumably the Toy Theatre, in Boston. Harvard's 47 Workshop ordinarily presented its plays at the Agassiz House theater, Radcliffe College, Cambridge.
3. The Harvard Monthly of January 1916 consisted of works involving or touching on pagan or classical matter.
4. Thayer Hall, in the College Yard. The university catalog listed Dos Passos as living in Thayer 29 during his senior year.

55

[Letterhead: A Bord de "Espagne"]
August tenth—[1918]

Arthur, dear, come for a moment out of your ivory tower and then go back in and throw away the key. Really you have an excessive faith in the proprieties of the Liberal party in the eighties.

I was notified that if I attemped to go to Spain or Switzerland I should be arrested, and as it is I am given the choice between going back to America and being deported.

I have several friends who will possibly be able to get the matter cleared up for me in Washington and I may be able to come back. But you see I'm now one of those dreadful people ...

Dudley & Van are working with the Quaker Reconstruction people in France[1] — and I wish to goodness I were there too.

Whatever happens I vow I shall not stay in America.

My plans are dreafully complicated by the fact that I am notwithstanding everything very anxious to see as much of the war as possible.

Some day though I shall appear and climb in through the back window of your ivory tower and accept your invitation ... Mais mon enfant, tu ne peux pas te figurer[2]... Righteous indignation is one of the most unpleasant things one can suffer from. Its rather like neuralgia.

Mournful epistles will start coming from America soon.

Love

Dos

1. Dos Passos' statement seems to have been anticipatory, and it was inaccurate. Dudley Poore remembers that the Quakers offered him a job, but also that he didn't accept it. We don't know whether van den Arend worked for the Quakers in France. He was extremely worried in Paris that August and soon returned to the United States. From Boston he wrote Dos Passos on September 20, 1918, that he had written the Quakers a long letter and hoped that they would accept him. After van den Arend left Paris, Poore went to Tours and there entered the U.S. Army. The army sent him to Paris, where he worked in its Overseas Courier Service. Letters from Frederik Francis van den Arend to Dos Passos, February 2 and April 1, 1919; interview with Poore, summer 1971, and telephone interview with him, June 4, 1978; letter from Poore to Dos Passos, October 29, 1918.

2. [Fr.] "But my child, you can't imagine."

56

[Letterhead: A Bord de "Espagne"]

[le] 19 aout [191]8[1]

Dear Arthur—

There are more ways of killing a cat than by skinning it.

I am having a pleasant crossing which I am enjoying hugely though every day brings me nearer to manifold unpleasantnesses. I spend my time reading the Confessions of Rousseau and finishing up my novel and avoiding my fellow passengers. When I get blue I solace myself with Rabelais—You must read the inimitable adventures of Panurge and Pantagruel and Frere Jan. I swear that there is nothing so fine under the sun, with the exception of the Knight of the Doleful Countenance, Don Quijote de la Mancha. Tell me what you are reading in Spanish.

O Arthur I have so many baroque adventures in Paris to tell you of. The world is mad, mon cher, stark staring madness, and its not a jolly lunacy either. Apropos [Several lines have been cut from the page here.]

In America my address is 214 Riverside Drive[2]—New York City. Pray God its not for long—Love

Dos

1. The dating information shown in brackets is part of the printed letterhead.
2. The residence of his aunt, Mrs. J. R. Gordon.

57

[Letterhead: U.S.A.A.S. Section]
Camp Crane
Allentown
Penn
[September 29, 1918?]

Arthur!

Me voici[1]—I am in the Y.M.C.A. hut at a training camp writing with Y.M.C.A. ink on Y.M.C.A. paper ...

I live in a curious limbo known as Casuals where I am neither flesh fowl or good red herring; I am waiting there for a waiver of the restrictions on eyesight or else a complete discharge. In the first instance I shall probably be put into an Ambulance section and go back to my old job—which would please me immensely. If I'm discharged I shall make every effort to return to France with the Quaker Reconstruction.

But who knows?

There's a lovely poem somewhere of Charles d'Orléans where he speaks of his gay companions Idleness and Ennui and Melancholy[2]— With them ever beside me perhaps I shall manage to live through ...

Will the war last one year—or five or fifty?

At present I sit here in Camp waiting—and the hours slouch by o so slowly, hours with creaking shoes!

Write me long letters full of Spain and Spanish cookery—full of oil and pimiento and strong wine of Jerez-de-la-Frontera.[3] Have you read the Romancero del Cid?[4] A wonderful collection of ballads—Have you read Bertrand Russell's newest book Logic and Mysticism?[5] I hear that it is excellent—nay more—inspired.

Still—I am glad that I got myself into the medical corps into camp into boredom. I shall learn lots and be able to thunder the louder for it.

I am so anxious to hear about you—The Int. Department[6] in Paris was very nasty about you when I was having my séances with them.

Do keep me notified of what goes on—

Particularly now do I need your letters.

You cant imagine the simple and sublime amiability of the average American soldier—Here is clay for almost any moulding. Who is to be the potter? That is the great question.

My address is

    214 Riverside Drive

     NY City

Love

Dos

1. [Fr.] "Here I am."

2. Charles, duc d'Orléans (1391–1465), French noble and poet, who was captured at the Battle of Agincourt and held prisoner in England for twenty-five years. In his solitude he put such companions as Care, Ennui, and Melancholy into many of his poems. This editor found no poem corresponding exactly to Dos Passos' description, in which *gay* is, of course, used ironically.

3. City in southwestern Spain. Sherry derives its name from an older form of the word *Jerez*.

4. The collection of Cid ballads. (Not to be confused with the Spanish twelfth-century epic *Cantar de Mío Cid*.)

5. *Mysticism and Logic* (1917), first published in 1910 under the title *Philosophical Essays*.

6. Department of Interior.

58

[Letterhead: Embassy of the
United States of America]
Madrid   Spain
October 30, 1918.

Dear Dos:—   Your letter of September 29 from Allentown. . . .

I think the end of the war very definitely in sight and afterwards we must meet somewhere in Europe. (I choose Holland!) to talk and feast as in other days we were wont. I do not even attempt to write you letters with the flavor of "strong wine of Jerez de la Frontera—(you could do it so much better yourself)—and you will have, I fear, each time to swallow a more homely mixture somewhat resembling Quaker Oats![1] . . .

. . . No, I haven't read Mysticism and Logic—it's impossible to get good English books here. But I have been reading as much Schnitzler[2] as I can get hold of—I really delight in him. If Couperous' 4th book of

Small Souls[3] comes out, do send it to me. I sent you the 3$\underline{d}$ volume about a year ago   did you ever get it? I don't do as much reading as I should like, as my work at the Embassy takes a good deal of time — but in a short while I expect to have more. I am not doing any Spanish reading at present ... don't scold .... I really don't feel myself in the proper sort of communion with these people. In a sense I am a very interested sojourner in a very strange land — and I am glad to be in Spain and to know it as an observer may, but at bottom I am not and never can be of these people — they are really primitives and I love civilization too much perhaps. To Northern Europe in a sense I belong, to England and Holland and France — but in these Mediterranean countries I am only a spectator. I will not say the rôle is disagreeable, but I should not choose it for always. Write me on this and often —

Love
Arthur

P.S.

I hear often and most delightfully from George Howe[4] who is in Queenstown — he was one of the rarest of the spirits of our little society —

a.

1. Oatmeal (a brand name).
2. Arthur Schnitzler (1862–1931), Austrian playwright and novelist.
3. See Letter 7, n. 8 above.
4. See Letter 8, n. 4 above.

59

[Letterhead: U.S.A.A.S. Section]
Camp Crane
Allentown
Oct 5 [1918]

[To McComb]

A green paling fence and three strands of barbed wire — was Lucretius' phrase fulgentia moenia mundi?[1] — anyway three strands of barbed wire and a green paling fence is the rampart of my world —

Therein — are long unpainted buildings here and there including what were once the mirthful edifices of a country fair ground. Signs like Poultry And Pigeons — Long Horned Cattle Exhibit — Soft Drinks — Bar Still stick out among the multitudinous uniformity of barrack windows.

A strange Inferno — of enforced labor — and many degrees, from where the prisoners under guard shovel coal in dirt and ignimony to where the chosen lounge in Headquarters—making out to tap type-writers, to copy orders—drowsed into bliss in the coils of red tape—

In this Inferno is a Limbo—by name Casuals—where, as my luck is always with the unclassified,—I languish, waiting a certain paper from Washington and a chance for <u>Over there</u>: Overseas service—as we say in the army—.

Organization is death. Organization is death—as I sweep acres of floor space and wash windows many as the grains of sand in the Lybian Syrtes[2]—I repeat the words over and over in anagrams, in French, in Latin, in Greek, in Italian, in all the distortions that language can be put to. Like a mumbled Ave Maria, they give me comfort.

O for a beaker full of the warm South[3]—

O Arthur—write me a letter full of Spain. Go into some corner cen-turies deep in Spain—into a tavern on the edge of some small white town in Castile, at the door of which one can stand and look long at russet hills and ochre, and a white winding road going towards a mesa that stands up suddenly—purple in the distance against an olive green sunset. Drink the air and tingling wine from the earthen pot, exchange long courtesies in excellent Castillian with the inn keeper—order a dinner of huevos revueltos con tomate and riz con carne[4]—and while the black raftered room's wine-scented air thickens with the drowsy weight of olive oil and garlic write—write—write

Did I tell you that the novel-thing[5] had ceased. It is finished. Half of it lies in Paris—half in New York—When the Millennium comes—half baked as the worm is, I shall try to join head and tail and publish—

Arthur—are you writing?

I hope to goodness you are—you have far too good a mind to waste on polite incredulity. And, God, there is strife to come—there must be much sharpening of pens—the Dark has conquered and will conquer eternally until the little round world crumbles to dust.—In the scornful trumpets of the light that dies—in the lunge of the beautiful drowning swimmer amid the muddy waters—in the fires of the starving host within the city that burns itself on a great pyre rather than fall slave—is all the beauty that we can have in this shaggy world—The lamp that flickers and goes out is greater and more beautiful in the moment's inten-sity of flare than all the eternity of dark that follows. Let us flare high in our small hour.

I'm glad I'm here even if I seem to grumble. I've always wanted to divest myself of class and the monied background—the army seemed the best way—From the bottom—thought I, one can see clear—So, though I might have escaped behind my sacred eyes I walked with the other cattle into the branding pen—

Van—God bless him—is C.O.ing—I'll write you details—nothing has happened thus far—He has just received his questionaire and has not yet descended into the flaming fiery furnace.[6]

Write me—I hope to get over very soon to France as an Ambulance Driver or Stretcher Bearer—But ¿quien sabe? Until I let you know you had better write me at 214 Riverside Drive [,] Care M^{rs} J R Gordon New York—

[Self-portrait cartoon of Dos Passos in uniform—stiff, spectacled, saluting. The caption reads: "How one feels."]

Love

Dos

Go, a misty autumn day for me to Aranjuez and give my love to the Tajo and its rustling wiers.[7]

1. "Flammantia moenia mundi," "flaming walls of the world" (Lucretius *De rerum natura* 1. 73). Dos Passos has "shining walls. . . ."

2. "Numerus Libyssae harenae," "the quantity of Libyan sand" (Catullus *Carmina* 7. 3). "You ask how many of your kisses are enough, Lesbia? As great a quantity of Libyan sand is found in Cyrene. . . ."

3. John Keats, "Ode to a Nightingale," stanza 2.

4. [Sp. except for *riz* (Fr.) and Eng. words] "A dinner of scrambled eggs with tomato and rice with meat."

5. See narrative, p. 76 above.

6. Daniel 3:6–26: "burning fiery furnace."

7. The town of Aranjuez, about thirty miles south of Madrid and on the Tagus (Tajo) River, is the site of palaces and gardens.

60

[Camp Crane

Allentown, Pennsylvania]

Oct 21 [1918]

You'ld better write me care <u>Morgan Harjes</u> my <u>official</u> address till the judgement day—

Arthur, your letters are such a comfort—I hadn't heard for so long that I was in despair when I got a note written exactly a month ago.

Valencia! First read the Romancero del Cid—you'll be disappointed in the city, but the Silk Hall[1] there is superb and there are many bits worth looking at.

"How one feels." Dos Passos' cartoon, in letter from U.S. Army. (See Letter 59.)

I got there by going through La Mancha to Murcia—the Africa of Spain. The town of Murcia is charming—oh such color and such cosy awning covered streets full of chatter, with the jolliest of baroque and gothic mixed all over the place in wild confusion. I suspect it of being rather like Damascus, with its palms and thick growth of canes beside glittering ditches. Then I went to Cartagena—loving the name, but there is nothing much to see there—narrow mauresque streets loud with the songs of cage-birds; then to Alicante, dull; then walked up one of the loveliest coasts imaginable to Denia, stopping for the night at a certain Villajoyosa. Dont miss Denia—it is Greek—it is Cretan—it is indescribable—The very name makes me drunk. Thence I took the funny little train, sitting on top of a third class coach, to Valencia across a plain full of orange-gardens—Near Valencia is Sagunto which has ancient ruins—Then Tarragona, further up the coast is charming, has the most beautiful cathedral in Spain—and excellent chartreuse and old walls and an aquaduct and a so-called tomb of Scipio. I went from there to Zaragoza via Poblét [Poblet]—but I think I should advise you to go to Barcelona—why dont you go out to the Balearic Isles from Valencia? You could go back by sea to Barcelona and return to Madrid via Tarragona.

O Arthur I'm almost crying as I write these names. Imagine a soul in the dullest, dustiest of hells thinking of the Rosetti damozells[2] whose names were seven sweet symphonies—I presume you remember the ladies, with very pre-Rapaelite hair![3]

In Valencia I remember I had a very funny picaresque adventure—landing in a whorehouse instead of in a hotel. I hope the same fate wont befall you.

But to return to my woes—I procured an induction into the medical corps and was sent to Camp Crane—a dreary spot where I have been waiting a month already for the US army to decide whether it wants to keep me or not. When the innumerable papers return from Washington I shall probably be sent to the front as an ambulance driver. Now I watch the blank wasted days drift by with bored misery. The camp is under quarantine on account of the terrific epidemic of grippe espagnole and for a month I haven't stepped outside the green picket fence that shuts the camp off from the world. I am nearly frantic with inanition.

By the way—I just remembered Játiba a superb old town not far from Valencia—well worth going to, I assure you—In the very ancient Mozarabic church on the hill you will find the tomb of a chocolatero, a chocolate maker, and of his wife, touching testimonial to the ashes of a true benefactor of humanity.

To return to my woes. My scandal was hushed up. I probably told you, through the exertions of a heroical aunt. I got into the army voluntarily — as my eyes kept me out of the draft — because I am very anxious to see things through and think them through, in actual experience rather than hearsay.

The redeeming feature is in the men I run into here. It's like discovering a new country to be completely cut loose from ones class and their habits of thought.

In Washington I saw Hardinge and Betty and Mehitabel, the baby.[4] and the elder Scholles all very charming and very prosperous. Hardinge hopes to be appointed assistant military attaché in Switzerland.

I had a heavenly four days with Ed Massey[5] in Cambridge, and wandered in the rain about Boston with Van and the amiable George.[6]

The Gazelle[7] is in Queenstown

Van is working with the Committee for Democratic control, is objecting to the hilt, but has not yet be dragged into the torture chamber. He hopes to be allowed to join Quaker Reconstruction in France — Ecris mon chère

Dos

1. The commercial hall in the Lonja de la Seda (Silk Exchange), a Gothic building erected late in the fifteenth century.

2. damozell——. The last letter is illegible.

3. Parts of Dante Gabriel Rossetti's poem "The Blessed Damozel" read: "the stars in her hair were seven" and "the groves / Where the lady Mary is, / With her five handmaidens, whose names / Are five sweet symphonies." Beneath Rossetti's two oil paintings *The Blessed Damozel* are predelle portraying the earthly lover, in a wood, beside a river, reclining and looking up.

4. Hardinge Scholle and his wife, Elizabeth (see Letter 12, n. 2 above). They had a daughter, Margaret Lillian Scholle, on August 17, 1918.

5. George Edward Massey received his A.B. degree from Harvard in 1915 and did graduate work in theater there in 1915–16. Dos Passos in *The Best Times* (p. 131) speaks of a "special triangular friendship" between Wright McCormick (see asterisk note on p. 5 above), Massey, and himself. Massey committed suicide in 1942.

6. George Bartlett. He and van den Arend were good friends.

7. George Locke Howe.

61

[Letterhead: Embassy of the United States of America]
Madrid España
November 15th 1918.

Dos:

Your letter of October 5.

Well, it is all over now — the last five days I have been trying to realize all that means, first that men can take the broom and sweep the mess tidy and then begin to live again with tranquility and joy, relieved from the racking tension and the noise and the fury of it—to dream again generous, hopeful dreams, to create beautiful things undisturbed by that unthinkable background of hate and intolerance.

I suppose now you will not come to Europe in a military capacity— but I may at least expect you soon after peace is signed. Do promise. Keep me informed of your plans.

I learned from George[1] that Van had also returned to America. I see he is still the same doctrinaire socialist as ever, and we would still have our ancient arguments but I like people to be true to type—so good luck to him!

These things I like about Spain—the "bargueño",[2] the "burro", the Castilian plain in the very early morning. En plus, all the things it has in common with the rest of Europe—and the Prado. But the people I like less as time goes on. It will be the subject of a discussion between us when we meet. (Too long a topic for a letter). . . .

The Fall is charming here—skies of a blue unfathomable and the Retiro[3] so laden with autumnal gold. I shall indeed go to Aranjuez for you and walk pensively in quiet paths to the gentle sounds of the slow-flowing Tagus and of fallen leaves, thinking of "autrefois"[4] in Cambridge.

I am waiting with infinite interest your novel. I have been so indolent and have not written as I should—I sink too easily into a routine and the atmosphere of chancelleries is not good for literature. (That is just an excuse .... when I think of the junk I wrote for the Monthly!)

Some of us cannot "flare high in our small hour" as your admirable phrase has it—but must burn discreetly, dimly, like shaded candles until we are snuffed ... — —

I do not quite agree with you that one sees best from below—it is hard to attain a serenity of spirit, without a certain background, and money enough to dissolve the petty ennuis is almost an essential part of that background. Stoics can do without, of course. But how hateful, fanatical and violent the "simple common man" can be is shown by the Bolsheviki. My class, your class, the Liberal Bourgeoisie was never guilty of these things. Till later—Love

Arthur

1. George Bartlett.
2. [Sp.] "Carved, inlaid desk."
3. A 353-acre park in Madrid.
4. [Fr. adverb] " 'In former times.' "

62

[Letterhead: American Embassy,
Madrid]
December fourteenth 1918.

My dear Dos,

A letter from you and the first manuscript of yours I have seen since Cambridge days arrived together. It was a great treat. And I am not insensible to the compliment involved in making me at once a critic and a guardian!

This letter is going to be all about your novel.[1] First of all I want to say that as a piece of work, it is nothing less than admirable. I read some of the passages to an intelligent friend of mine here and he was most enthusiastic [,] compared it with Barbusse[2] and on the spot offered to translate it into French for you! — Now please don't let it sleep. You should get a publisher, in London perhaps, as soon as possible. I want in advance to read the first part. Who has it in Paris?

Two things I particularly liked were the descriptions of the garden of the "salmon-colored villa" (p. 93) and of the Abbey (p. 43) These were splendid morsels. The closing-page is good — well, I won't enumerate — in general it gives a fine impression of a hateful reality and is mightily worthy of publication. I won't conceal that I think the tender moral susceptabilities of the American public will be offended by Part IV chap. V. It has of course the air of reality and ought to do the same public a lot of good! — but you will have to pick a publisher with care. Chapt. V as a matter of fact is one of the very best, I decided, on second reading.

A minor point: — I can't admit the neologism Rabelaisianly[3] (p. 49)

The whole thing is very like you, of course, but it marks a decided step I honestly believe, in advance of your Monthly days. It really seems more mature and there is much more feeling in it than in many of your early things — more power — a broader sweep and a better hold of your material. (These remarks sound so platitudinous, but I mean them quite seriously)

I should be inclined perhaps to extend the discussion in the penultimate chapter. Of course in a general way you are Fibbie. May I ask if Randolph is drawn after anyone specifically? — it doesn't much matter to know of course as the type is usual enough.

After having said so many nice things about the literary character of your novel, I am going to quarrel entirely with your general philosophy and more particularly with your apparent conclusion. You can say of course that you were only giving an objective picture, but I think

I detect the revolutionary tinge and for me it is no solution at all. If anything I am more of a "moderate" than when I last saw you. I am entirely undeceived about the Bolsheviki revolution which has turned out to be that most hateful of tyrranies—the arbitrary rule of undisciplined and facile theorists of the lower classes. However we shall discuss this more on our meeting—may it be soon!

Meanwhile my compliments go to you, for a most excellent work. Write soon—

Love
Arthur.

. . . .

1. Part four of "Seven Times round the Walls of Jericho." As noted earlier, this final part became One Man's Initiation—1917.

2. Henri Barbusse (1873–1935), French writer. The comparison is with his wartime novel Le feu (1916).

3. Dos Passos kept it. See his One Man's Initiation: 1917 (Ithaca, New York: Cornell University Press, 1969), p. 89.

63

Carmen de Mata-Moros,
Granada, Spain
Feb. 9, 1919.

Dear Dos:—

I hope you got my letter from Málaga. Shortly after writing it I came here—8 hours in the train past olive orchards and almond trees in blossom, the ploughed earth quite red as we neared Granada. Granada itself is nothing but the Alhambra Hill[1] is fascinating. I am at a little villa-pension recommended to me by Mrs. Sweeney.[2] Very good indeed—it is kept by a Scotch spinster—the food is quite a pleasure with its absence of oil and grease and the raucous klang of ugly Spanish voices is spared us. There is a charming old garden with clipped myrtle and cypresses and a fountain—a high wall on one side and on the other a gorgeous view of the snow-covered Sierra and all Granada and the vega[3] below where the Duke of Wellington's beet-sugar factories steam away! (You will laugh but of course its' meant what prosperity there is for Granada!)

Of course I went immediately to the Moorish palace—a delightful place in spite of some damage and restoration. I liked it better than I thought I would, expecting too much polychromy. But I found the general-tone cream-colored and restful. I go now almost every-day, peering around Ruskin-like, discovering admirable azulejos[4] and fine-cedar-wood ceilings and lovely designs on plaster and wood and delicious views through graceful ajimez[5] windows, and quaint little takâs or recesses for water and odds and ends, quiet little patios with orange-trees and cypresses. The whole delights me infinitely.

And of course I have climbed many towers (all of them have marvelous legends connected with them but I doubt if modern scientific history has left one of these intact) and seen many many gardens, each one more enchanting than the last (including the famous Generalife[6] about which a dusty law-suit is pending since the 15$\underline{th}$ cent.) and seen the "Alhambra vase"[7] which merits the praise generally bestowed on it and the Renaissance palace of Charles V, which would be intolerable where it is right next to the Moorish palace, if it were not in some measure excused by the Italian purity of its architecture.

I can't tell you all I've seen and almost all worth seeing—a tiny private mosque by a quiet pool, a wonderful little collection of modern painting (Seargent [Sargent], Rusiñol[8] etc.) owned by a man who sells tobacco and stamps and who was presented with them all by the artists in question as a token of friendship—a dear little church way down by the Darro[9] in the shadow of the Alhambra Hill with a delicately executed portal (Renaissance—Bädeker is more precise and says "plater-esque") with a campanile with azulejos (what funny and sometimes effective combinations of style the Spanish seem to have liked)

I went in search of some Flemish primitives in the chapel where Ferdinand & Isabella are buried but the light was too bad. Really they shouldn't have good pictures in a church at all. One can say what one likes about the modern museum but at least one can see what one's looking at.

Well this you see is the way I have been passing my time here—in a few days I return to Madrid for a while.

How are you getting on with German in Alsace? I am sure you will find it well worth the trouble. I myself have been reading quite a lot recently to brush it up and when your post-card was brought to me I was in the midst of "Schreie auf dem Boulevard" by René Schickele,[10] a young Elsässer,—you may have heard of him,—quite admirable essays about Paris from the standpunkt[11] of someone subjected to the influence of the two civilizations.   Love   Arthur

1. Hill on which the Moorish fortress palace stands.
2. Mrs. Mildred Sweeney. See Letter 9, including n. 7, and Letter 10, including n. 5, above.

3. [Sp.] "Fertile plain."

4. [Sp.] "Glazed tiles."

5. Ajimez [Sp., arch.]. An arched window with a supporting pillar in the center.

6. Garden of the Generalife. The Palacio del Generalife, near the Alhambra, is the former Moorish rulers' summer residence. It is celebrated for its terraced water gardens.

7. Baedeker had it in the Room of the Two Sisters, in the Palace of the Alhambra. "In one corner of the room is the famous two-handled Alhambra Vase . . . , which an ancient tradition avers to have been found in the palace filled with gold. It is 4 ft. 4 in. in height, dates from 1320, and is exquisitely enamelled in white, blue, and gold. The animals figured on it are apparently meant for gazelles." Baedeker, *Spain and Portugal* (1913), pp. 358–59.

8. Santiago Rusiñol y Prats (1861–1931), Spanish landscape painter and writer, b. in Barcelona.

9. A stream in Granada.

10. German writer (1883–1940), b. in Alsace. *Schreie auf dem Boulevard* was published in 1913.

11. [Ger.] "Point of view."

64

ᶜ/ₒ Crédit Lyonnais
Madrid   Spain
Feb. 22 1919.

Dear Dos,

Your letter of Jan. 31 from Saussheim[1] gratefully devoured. About your not getting my letters the trouble is that up to the end of January I was still sending them to America. Since then however I have written you from Malaga and I think also from Granada. I have been back in Madrid a week—most pleased with my trip but finding I have a curious affection for Madrid as "home" and the centre of things. Don José[2] has introduced me to the library of his Junta and I go there to study—faint reminiscence of Widener! I see a good deal of the Sweeneys who supply me with the Atlantic Monthly and clippings from the Transcript[3]—so that I keep in touch with the centre of things! . . .

As for your own novel I had it in my hand all sealed and ready to mail to you as you asked, when it occurred to me that perhaps you hadn't thought of the risk of mailing it in these times—is it the only copy? . . . You musn't take my outbursts against the Spanish too seriously—at times they are so supremely irritating though and I do think them inferior on the whole to the northerners. Still I like quite well living in Spain!

Let me know if and as soon as you get the wished-for furlough. When and if you do get it come immediately to Spain if possible. Why do you particularly want to study anthropology (though perhaps I can guess!). I am afraid the Assembly of the Chosen cannot be got together much before the signature of peace but there is no reason why we should not form the nucleus before then! . . .

The addendum to your letter shone with a light luridly red! My own will seem palely greenish beside it but Je constate les faits suivants:[4] — The Liberal Bourgeoisie (to which I have the honour to belong!) has always protested against the outrages and atrocities in the Congo, China, Persia etc. It has alas been only lacking in power. It has formed the most educated, the most dignified and on the whole the most disinterested group in every country. I know of course that unfortunately the direction of public affairs has been in the hands of another section of our class more greedy and revengeful. My arraignment of this spirit would be you know as severe as your own. But surely we have seen enough of revolutions to know that only those accomplish anything which are performed by at least a relatively educated people. And think of the Commune! I really don't believe that the Group Spartakus[5] and the Bolsheviki are a solution of anything. Propagating the gospel by the fire and sword has never seemed to me a humane or decent pursuit whether done in Central Africa or in Central Europe.
I think I am not intolerant and I know that they are! They want to reduce me to their level by force. Well, I don't want to be levelled.

My class, your class, stands open to all who merit a place in it and I at least know no distinctions except those of intelligence and taste.

I am quite willing to stretch my hand across the barricade but you will not find me on the other side of it. I was born into a class and I prefer it to any other, in spite of its manifold faults and narrownesses. I shall not go over!

Love—
Arthur

P.S.
Write soon. Forgive the "manifesto" style of the above!

. . . .

1. In Alsace.
2. Don José Castillejo. See Letters 10, 40, and 45 above. McComb discussed him in his memoir "A Foreign Dye."
3. The Boston Evening Transcript.
4. [Fr.] "Let me call attention to the following facts."
5. Led by Karl Liebknecht and Rosa Luxemburg, the Spartacists (formed in 1916) were a radical group of German socialists who opposed the war. Demanding a dictatorship of the proletariat, they resorted to sporadic violence late in 1918, officially turned themselves into the German Communist party at a December 30–January 1 meeting, and on January 5 attempted to take Berlin. The revolt was short-lived, and Liebknecht and Luxemburg were arrested and murdered in mid-January 1919.

65

Madrid Spain
March 6th 1919.

Dear Dos:—   Yesterday a letter came from you dated Feb. 23. According to it by this time you ought to be at the Sorbonne—I hope so for your sake. George Howe writes he is trying to make arrangements to go there—you may meet him but still I haven't much faith in meetings between members of the 'cercle"—they seem destined to remain apart—there is no chance of my going to Paris for instance.

Yesterday I called on José Giner Pantoja[1] and at last found him in. We have arranged to meet again and perhaps go to Segovia together. He was most pleasant (but then of course they are all that!—in a way) I will write you later about him. Since writing I have also been to a tea of Don José's[2] at "Freddy's". . . .

I am quite anxious to read the first part of your novel. Can you spare it? The two parts must certainly be soldered together and triumphantly published. Let me know the course it pursues.

I enclose a serious article about the Bolsheviki which I hope you will meditate. You ask me what I know about them except what I read in the newspapers. Well first of all—their constitution an infamous document which I have studied carefully, secondly extracts that appear in the press from time to time quoted from their own newspapers such as the Vladimir Soviet's official Gazette etc.[3] thirdly the spirit of their defendants here of whom I know a few and the utterly unpardonable acts of the Group Spartakus their imitators in Germany of whom we do get adequate accounts. "Out of their own mouths ......" And I would not disdain the judgment of a man like Bourtzeff[4] who suffered for freedom in the prisons of the Tsar and in those of the Bolsheviki. Lastly we know something of the Paris Commune[5] and of the earlier Terror. So there is something to go by besides the newspapers which are not very reliable.

You mention the "foaming at the mouth" of the Girondins.[6] Well, and were they not right after all? The more I read history the more I am convinced that there is never salvation anywhere outside of moderation. A year ago I was beginning to coquette (mentally) with socialists and others of the extremer sort [;] now I am every day more of a bourgeois liberal in the pure historic tradition. As for the outlook I am none too hopeful ......

I was glad to get news of Dudley and Mitchell.[7] I never knew them as well perhaps as some other members of the Monthly but admired them both immensely in their different ways. . . .

—Love
Arthur.

1. See Letter 9, including n. 11, and Letters 41–45 above.

2. Don José Castillejo. See Letters 10 and 40 above.

3. Vladimir, 110 miles east of Moscow, was a historic town notable for its cathedrals, but it had a soviet of some power. "Extracts" from alleged Bolshevik sources could be authentic material or anti-Bolsheviks' fabrications.

4. Vladimir Lvovitch Bourtzeff (1862–1942), Russian historian, editor, and publicist. The Czarist government again and again imprisoned him for revolutionary activity. When the Bolsheviks won power they too sent him to prison, because he was hostile to their regime. Released in the spring of 1918, Bourtzeff fled to Paris and from there went on opposing the Bolshevik government.

5. The insurrectionary municipal government of Paris in March–May 1871, after France's defeat by Prussia.

6. [Fr.] Members of a group of legislators who played a major role in the French Revolution. The Reign of Terror followed soon after their fall.

7. Dudley Poore and Stewart Mitchell.

66

^c/o Crédit Lyonnais
Madrid España
el 30 de abril 1919

Dear Dos,

Yesterday on Recoletos I met Mrs. Sweeney.[1] She was in town for the day from Escorial[2] where they are living temporarily. She gave me the very welcome news that you had written (for it is almost 2 months since I have heard from you except for that exchange of telegrams in March) and said you were expecting to come to Spain in June. You don't know how this set me agog. Is it really true? Be sure & let me know ahead. . . .

I have done nothing interesting recently [,] no reading even except the daily "El Sol" which I consider one of the most admirable newspapers in Europe. A recent piece of news that cheered me was the reported alliance between Roumania and Ukrainia against the Bolsheviki. Someday I hope three nice strong ropes will hang the three "comrades" Lenine, Trotzky and Bela Kun![3] These people make me "hot under the collar." . . .

Write soon.

Love—
Arthur.

122 / DOS PASSOS—MCCOMB CORRESPONDENCE

1. Mrs. Mildred Sweeney. McComb encountered her on the Paseo de Recoletos, the fashionable avenue. See Letter 44, n. 7 above concerning the avenue.

2. Village near Madrid, on a foothill of the Sierra de Guadarrama, and site of the monastery-palace. Escorial was a favorite summer resort of Madrid inhabitants.

3. Béla Kun (1886–1939?), dictator in the Hungarian Communist republic of March–July 1919.

67

c/o Crédit Lyonnais
Alcalá 8, Madrid, Spain
Friday, May 15th, 1919.

My dear Dos,

For some time I had been depending on Mrs. Sweeney for news of you but at last your letter of May 6 arrived. It pleases me much to think you are not giving up the idea of coming to Spain but why England first and have you some assurance that you <u>can</u> get here because if not it might cause me to alter my plan of remaining. I'm glad the novel arrived all right but am sorry the whole doesn't make a unified work. Is there any particular reason for this? . . .

As for the great subject of our debate — I am, and I suppose I always shall be, by temperament a Girondin. I like those people in public life (if there are any) who weigh the full consequences of a line of action before embarking thereon and those who listen to calm counsels. No matter how bad a state of affairs (and our present state is very bad indeed) I prefer to mend it by appeals to reason than by appeals to passion. No enduring good is to be got by fusilades en masse[1] and suppressing your opponents opinions. But then I don't at all want the sort of society these advanced work-people dream of. I like the sort of people who live on Louisburg Sq. and Brattle Street,[2] though I often don't agree with them. I like their good manners and their quiet dining rooms with old silver on the sideboards and their tranquil libraries full of good books, shutting out the garishness of the modern world. I like distinction and distinctions and the freedom to differ. And I don't like to be levelled by a ruthless tyranny from below. So my sympathies are <u>not</u> with the revolution — they are white rather than red.

Something may be done with a government based on law; nothing can be done with cranks and fanatics [,] with people whose ill-trained minds revolve around a fixed idea which they have never properly examined.

Surely you will see that they are the enemies the good life — at least as I conceive it — to be lived with dignity and measure.

Well, all this I suppose will seem thin to you. We shall have it out some day in conversation, I hope.

Have you read "The Shadow Line"[3] of Conrad. I have just finished it but it doesn't compare with some of the longer ones. "Dr. Adriaan"[4] is out at last, you know.

I have long entertained an ambition to retire to the Principality of Liechtenstein—now the last relic of the Holy Roman Empire. Would you consider joining me!

Adios and write soon—
Arthur.

1. [Fr.] "Wholesale shootings."
2. Louisburg Square, on Beacon Hill, Boston, has been notable for the social distinction and wealth of its homeowners. Brattle Street, Cambridge, was known as "Tory Row" in Provincial days. Longfellow later lived in a colonial house there.
3. Published in 1917.
4. By Louis Couperus. See Letter 7, n. 8 above.

68

$^c/_o$ Crédit Lyonnais
Madrid   May 31st 1919

Dear Dos:—

Your letter of May 24th cheered me inasmuch as it seems practically certain that you will come to Spain in about six weeks. Although it had been my secret intention to make a flight if possible to a northern neutral in the late summer, your coming will alter that as I want so much to see you and also to bear you off with me perhaps to Granada when it gets a little cooler. You may therefore take it as certain that I shall be in Spain but just whether I shall go north this coming month or where in Spain I shall be is uncertain. But you will always get me at the Crédit Lyonnais and I shall let you know of my movements as you will let me know of yours I hope. . . . I hope you succeed in your English mission but don't let the lovely English summer seduce you. There will be a temptation in the English countryside! Still you seem these days to burn with so ardent a light that our cruder Spanish tones may have their attractions for you! Forgive me. Indeed I can rest from argument for I am winning. Admiral Koltchak[1] is about to be recognized by the Allies. The latter at last have a constructive Russian policy. They are bargaining well—will force democratic guarantees from the Admiral in exchange for recognition. They will withdraw their own troops while lending money & supplies to him. This is all very sane

4.

from my point of view and I approve of
the Allied Russian policy as heartily as
I disapprove of Their policy in other
quarters! Don't say anything against
my friend General Mannerheim, ex –
germanophile. As a leading anti –
Bolshevik beaucoup lui sera pardonné!
Seriously the maximalist tyranny is
such a mean, narrow, envious
Thing that I am astonished at a
person of your generosity of spirit
. . . . well at least admit it
has none of the glorious dash and
high magnanimous flights of the
French Revolution. Of course I will
admit I prefer the old world to
the new – if this is the new! a

". . . I prefer the old world to the new—if this is the new!" Page from McComb's letter to Dos Passos, May 31, 1919.

and commendable from my point of view and I approve of the Allied Russian policy as heartily as I disapprove of their policy in other quarters! Don't say anything against my friend General Mannerheim,[2] ex-germanophile. As a leading anti-Bolshevik beaucoup lui sera pardonné![3] Seriously the maximalist[4] tyranny is such a mean, narrow, envious thing that I am astonished at a person of your generosity of spirit .... well at least admit it has none of the glorious dash and high magnanimous flights of the French Revolution. Of course I will admit I prefer the old world to the new—if this is the new! A thousand times I prefer 1913 to 1919 but neither is the world of my dreams,—but perhaps one shouldn't indulge in political dreams at all.

Enough!—I feel—or at least I have been mulling over in my mind writing something on the Prado—something different from all the stale, general, guide-booky stuff that has been turned out, something intimate and personal not pretending to cover the field or discover new artistic personalities à la Berenson,[5] but something simply the result of affections and reflections. What do you think? It would be quite a labor but perhaps worth trying. I should center the thing round half-a-dozen paintings as mid-points. . . .

Write soon—

Arthur.

1. Aleksandr Vasilievich Kolchak (1874–1920), Russian admiral and counterrevolutionary who gained power in Siberia after a coup d'état in November 1918.

2. Baron Carl Gustaf Emil Mannerheim (1867–1951), Finnish military leader and statesman. In his country's civil war of January–May 1918 he led the White Guard, which was aided by German troops, to victory over the Red Guard, which was supported by Soviet troops. Mannerheim became regent of Finland in December 1918, holding the position until his defeat in the presidential election of July 1919.

3. [Fr.] "Much will be forgiven him."

4. Maximalist: ". . . an alternative name for a Bolshevik. Also, a member of any similar group outside Russia." OED Supplement, s.v. "Maximalist."

5. Bernard Berenson (1865–1959), American art critic, scholar, connoisseur, and writer. A Lithuanian Jew by birth, he came to Boston with his parents at the age of ten, and from 1884 to 1887 attended Harvard College (where, incidentally, he became editor-in-chief of the Monthly). His teachers Charles Eliot Norton and William James strongly influenced him while he was at Harvard. Walter Pater's books Studies in the History of the Renaissance and Marius the Epicurean seem to have influenced him even more.

Long before McComb's comment, Berenson had become the world's most widely-known authority on Italian Renaissance art. As a result, his attributions greatly affected the market values of the paintings. From around 1907 to 1937 Berenson was the expert in his field for the art dealer Joseph Duveen. At first he was paid sales commissions, later a retainer plus frequent shares of profits for his authentications. The relationship made Berenson wealthy.

Berenson's greatest achievement as an art historian was his two-volume The Drawings of the Florentine Painters (1903). His other works before 1919 included four short critical books (1894–1907) on the Venetian, Florentine, Central Italian, and North Italian painters of the Renaissance, respectively. All four had indices of Berenson's attributions, as well as of the locations of the artists' paintings. In making the indices, Berenson and his companion (later his wife) Mary Costello combed Italy—churches, small museums, municipal buildings, and private residences. He enlarged his lists with successive editions of the books. The lists, says Berenson's biographer Ernest Samuels, ultimately formed "a guide without parallel for any other period or country." See Samuels' *Bernard Berenson: The Making of a Connoisseur* (Cambridge: Harvard University Press, 1979). The quotation is on p. 296.

Letters

ॐ

$\mathscr{F}$REE TO LEAVE for Spain, Dos Passos telegraphed McComb asking him to meet him in Santander and to arrange invitations in Spain for Dudley Poore, perhaps to help Poore get his passport visaed. Dos Passos himself carried credentials as a reporter for the London *Daily Herald*. He and Poore traveled together from Paris to Biarritz, near the Spanish border. But there Poore faced a few days' delay in getting his visa, as the Spanish government had closed the border temporarily because of labor trouble. Dos Passos had gotten his visa in Paris, and in order not to keep McComb waiting, he decided to precede Poore. On August 12 he met McComb in Santander, and the two had supper and a long talk. The next day they came upon Poore wearing a Basque beret and seated outside a café. Rather than wait he had waded into Spain over the Bidassoa River. Together the three young men went into the little fishing village of San Vicente de la Barquera, where they met the Sweeneys —Peter, Mildred, and their daughter, Margaret.[1]

Peter Sweeney was a man in his mid-fifties, the son of an Irish immigrant who had made a great deal of money in real estate in Lawrence, Massachusetts. Dropping out of public school when he was about fifteen, he went to work in the furniture business. At thirty-one he did some belated wandering—traveling to Alaska and from there to Japan, where he remained for three months, studying Japanese art and history and journeying into the countryside. In 1903 he married Mildred I. McNeal, a teacher and poet. They sailed for Europe with six-year-old Margaret in 1911 and soon developed a nomadic style of life, moving about and settling down as they pleased—for Peter had enough income to live comfortably in Europe and was happy where people had time to sit down and talk. The Sweeneys were in love with Spain and had been everywhere, even in the most remote places.[2]

"Los 3 de Sweeney." This was Dos Passos' appellation for the expatriate American family who befriended him in Spain. Here Peter, Mildred, and their daughter, Margaret, are in Valldemosa, Mallorca, in September 1920.
Courtesy of Alice and Nora Sweeney

Before going south, Dos Passos, McComb, and Poore saw some of the nearby country. Besides stopping at San Vicente de la Barquera they spent a day visiting Santillana del Mar and the nearby Caves of Altamira. "Imagine Dudley and Arthur M⁵C. and I," Dos Passos wrote Stewart Mitchell, "scrambling down slimy ledges in deep and prehistoric caverns, Arthur firmly grasping an umbrella the while."[3] After the three returned to San Vicente de la Barquera, Dos Passos and Poore went for an excursion in the Picos of Europe, walking and climbing through them for about four days. Meanwhile McComb, who did not like climbing or strenuous walking, went on to Oviedo. He did some sightseeing there and in the environs and waited for his friends to join him.[4]

From Oviedo all three went to León and Valladolid, taking in the sights there before proceeding to Madrid. Their plan was to travel together or separately, as they might wish. Poore, who had never before seen Madrid, stayed on in the capital, but Dos Passos and McComb were there only briefly and then went on to Granada by different routes. McComb was in Granada by September 14. Dos Passos had come and traveled on some days before, but he was there again by September 17. And Poore was there by September 23.[5]

McComb persuaded the other two to stay at a pension near the Alhambra, the Carmen de Matamoros ("kill moors"), high on the hill above the town. It was run by a Scottish spinster, Miss Laird, who had a friendly-hostile relationship with Mrs. Wood, an elderly Anglo-American widow and a permanent guest. Although Dos Passos was opposed to staying at a British pension, he came around when he was told that he could live and write in its summer house, which stood in the hillside garden. Here he busied himself with writing *Three Soldiers*. His friends were also working purposefully that autumn. McComb was reading art history, politics, and literature, and Poore was writing poetry, which later appeared in the *Dial*.[6]

Soon after Poore arrived, Dos Passos left for Portugal to do some reporting, and he was gone until October 14. On the way back he got soaked in a rainstorm, and the day after his return he came down with rheumatic fever. Suffering great pain, he had fits of delirium, and required round-the-clock attention. Poore recalls that he wired the British hospital in Gibraltar and got an English nurse. About the time she came, late in October, McComb moved on to Madrid. There he consulted an able German physician and sent Dos Passos the medicine he recommended. Possibly McComb was glad to get away from the distressing situation, for he remained in the capital. The medicine helped greatly, as the physician told him it would. But it was Poore who nursed Dos Passos back to health.[7]

Granada was growing colder, and Dos Passos and Poore, who lacked overcoats, asked McComb to go to a tailor in Madrid and get them two Spanish cloaks. McComb inquired about tailors and, on recommendation, went to a certain Scandinavian one. When Dos Passos and Poore heard of the choice, they were dismayed at McComb's Nordic bias.[8]

Dos Passos didn't go out of doors until November 16, and then he was still very weak. But the atmosphere at the Carmen de Matamoros angered him, and he wanted to get away as soon as possible. In a letter he wrote to McComb the pension became the Carmen de Mata Todos ("kill all"), its British atmosphere led to his derogatory description "the mangy lion," and Mrs. Wood became "Sovereignty." Mrs. Wood had a niece, Miss Dillon, who was also a guest at the pension[9] — of these two and Miss Laird, Dos Passos wrote to Walter Rumsey Marvin on November 17:

> . . . in the midst of jolly preposterous Spain to be caught in an atmosphere of moral malignancy and Scotch parsimony. . . . My friend and I have our meals with three old hags who sit and hate the Huns and make moral judgements on the Spaniards.

By December 6 Dos Passos and Poore were in Madrid, lodging together in a properly Spanish place, while McComb again stayed at a British pension. The three spent the winter with one another in Madrid, conversing, dining, attending the theater, visiting art exhibitions, cathedrals, and churches. Over food and drink they read aloud — from their own writings, from letters, once from a new book by Amy Lowell. Every day Dos Passos worked on *Three Soldiers* and in mid-afternoon read his work to his two friends. Poore recalls McComb's protesting that *Three Soldiers* wasn't the rounded truth. "Photography from a point of view" — so Dos Passos described his method, and he thought of the book as portraying the army from the underdog's point of view.[10]

One can see clear from below, he had written McComb on October 5, 1918 — but McComb had disagreed, citing the Bolsheviks. What was Dos Passos saying about the Bolsheviks during these months when he was with McComb? We know what he wrote Marvin on October 15, 1919:

> Theoretically you are perfectly right about Marxian socialism, of which I am intensely suspicious. In fact I am much more interested in guild-socialism so called — In letting the state get as weak as possible and letting industries organize themselves according to the standard human method of doing things — doing them in common. But you speak as if the other system worked. It doesn't. And it is transforming itself fast into a new feudal aristocratic state with an aristocracy and its parisites exploiting a vast mass of workers kept down by force as in the old slave empires of the orient. That condition must go. Any alternative is better. Of course things haven't really come to a cleavage point in America yet. But the tragic Condition of the rest of the world is inconceivable.

To Mitchell he wrote on December 8:

> Dudley and I at present inhabit in Madrid a rather sepulchral little chamber. . . . We tea with . . . Arthur McComb — who has taken stride

after stride to the right and laments the good old times before the war. He's a positive Jaimist for conservatism, a partisan of Noske.* He has washed his hands and feet for ever of the U.S., for which one can hardly blame him; and is going soon to dwell among the chaste shades of departed liberals in Geneva.

I, on the other hand, like Walt Whitman still cry Allons Democracy, I have not deserted you ma femme—up camerados! Even am I moved to attempt to live there for a while.

Dos Passos' views on Bolshevism were not settled. Compared with his comments to Marvin on October 15, 1919, those he wrote him on January 2, 1920, were much more favorable:

> . . . about Bolshevism: one has to remember that all that is published in the press is propaganda, that the Bolcheviki are the moderate social-revolutionaries, a political party, and the Soviets are a system of government based on the idea of "pure democracy" (—so called in the textbooks on gov't.) that every man shall take direct part in the government of the country—which is arrived at by industrial representation through the heirarchy of soviets, and that much the same system would be in vogue in America—(geographical instead of industrial units) if Hamilton and the rest had taken the New England town-meeting as the unit of government instead of importing Montesquieu's ideas. . . .
>
> As to atrocities, what do you think of General Dyer's little shooting match in India?†

When McComb and Dos Passos discussed politics, Poore was silent, believing that it admitted of no rational solutions.[11] There may have been times when Dos Passos agreed, for he recognized that his hope contained an element of romanticism; at a tea on January 11, 1920, according to McComb's diary, Dos Passos spoke of the "chilly sanity" of McComb's view.‡

As spring approached, Madrid palled on Dos Passos. Working on *Three Soldiers* at the Ateneo (Athenaeum), he felt himself "frantic to

---

*Don Jaime (1870–1931), Carlist pretender to the Spanish throne; Gustav Noske (1868–1946), German defense minister who suppressed the Spartacist revolt in January 1919.

†The massacre at Amritsar, April 13, 1919, by soldiers commanded by the British Brigadier General R. E. H. Dyer. After riots in which Indians killed a number of Europeans, Dyer's soldiers opened fire without warning on an illegal assemblage of Indians, killing at least 379 and wounding well over 1,000.

In the above quotation, Dos Passos wrote the word *Bolshevism* with the letters *c* and *s*, one superimposed on another, following the letter *l*; he had been encountering the word in several languages.

‡For McComb's entry in his diary, see Letter 88, n. 5 below.

do something wild" and wanted to get together with John Howard Lawson and Frederik van den Arend. Madrid was "an amusing town," he wrote Lawson, but it lacked an "ocean or large river—to wash away ones morbid introspectings." March saw him in Barcelona, still busy with *Three Soldiers* and attending from afar to the publication of *One Man's Initiation—1917*. Poore remained in Madrid. But McComb was in Barcelona too, prior to taking a boat for Italy. He was planning a career in art history and intended to proceed to western Europe to study some of the art there. On March 17 Dos Passos came to the dock to see him off on the S.S. *Capitán Revuelta,* bound for Genoa.[12] The two did not meet again until each, after separate travels, had returned to the United States.

Disembarking from the S.S. *Capitán Revuelta,* McComb stopped in Genoa and then—despite Dos Passos' expectation that he would look at a problem painting of Tobias and the Angel in the Museum of Turin—went on to Basel (Bâle) by way of Milan. From the Hotel Bauer-am-Rhein in Basel he wrote thanking Dos Passos for the picture post-cards and art reproductions he had sent, and enclosing cards from the Basel Museum—one of them showing a reproduction of the museum's painting *Bildnis eines unbekannten Herrn* (Portrait of an unknown gentleman) by Hans Holbein, the younger; he also wrote of having seen Erasmus' tomb. After a fortnight in Basel, he went to Geneva, and wrote from there that the thought of going home for a summer in Dublin, New Hampshire, appalled him. If he did go, he said, he would first have "such a 'fling' as never was in Italy." He remained in Switzerland until May 19, 1920, and then left for Italy. That country was experiencing economic turmoil, and McComb must have retained strong memories of its revolutionary atmosphere as well as of its art. As he moved about that spring and summer he sent Dos Passos cards or letters from Bergamo, Verona, Padua, Florence, Udine, Vienna, Venice, Genoa, and Naples. In Naples he boarded the S.S. *Canopic* on August 6 and sailed for Boston.[13]

Less than two weeks after McComb left Barcelona, Dos Passos took a trip of his own. His room overlooked the city's harbor, and nearly every evening, as he paced about, a boat left from under his window for Mallorca. He was looking forward to going there when he met John Howard Lawson's family—though not Lawson. Kate Drain Lawson, whom Dos Passos had known in Paris in 1917, before she became Lawson's wife, appeared with their baby and with Lawson's sister Adelaide. John Howard Lawson had come from New York to Europe with them, but had stayed in France for medical attention while his wife and sister went to Spain. Dos Passos suggested that he and the family all visit the island.[14]

After several days there, Kate, Adelaide, and the baby went on by boat to Alicante, and Dos Passos went back to Barcelona, where through an exchange of letters he arranged to meet John Howard Lawson.* But he was without money to travel, as pesetas awaiting him at a bank had somehow been deposited in the name of "Carlos Dos Passos," and the bank refused to release them. The Sweeneys saved the day with a loan, and he went by train to Tarascon and met John Howard Lawson there in mid-April. Together they toured southern France and from Marseilles went north to Paris, arriving there by May Day.[15]

Dos Passos expected Paris to be "dead," but he found himself caught up in the artistic activity there: Copeau's Théâtre du Vieux-Colombier, the Théâtre des Arts, the Russian ballet. Encountering Poore in Paris was another surprise. Poore was there prior to his helping his parents debark in England in June and staying with them in Paris. He remembers taking the manuscript of *Three Soldiers* to the typists, who were so interested that they crowded around to read it.[16]

When the manuscript was all typed, Dos Passos traveled to England to try to get it published there.[17] He also had to deal with new troubles over *One Man's Initiation—1917*. The British printers, legally liable for indecent literature, were refusing to proceed, and he had to make more changes. From England he sent McComb cards showing paintings by Sir Edward Burne-Jones, William Blake, and the Master of Flémalle, whom McComb found fascinating.

Back in Paris he enjoyed a good deal of Poore's company that summer. At about the same time that McComb was sailing from Naples, Dos Passos took the *Espagne* from Saint-Nazaire to Havana, Cuba, by way of Santander and La Coruña, Spain. "Arthur dear—So we will be together on the briny, separately," he wrote. He was back in New York at the end of August, after a voyage from Cuba in a dilapidated and wheezy Ward Line steamer.[18]

---

*Van den Arend had expected to meet with Dos Passos and the Lawsons in or near Marseilles in early spring. He was going to Madagascar, where he would work for the import-export firm Childs & Joseph, 60 Wall Street, New York, and he intended to leave from Marseilles and proceed by way of Port Said, Aden, and Zanzibar. Much to his chagrin, the firm sent him by way of Capetown rather than Suez. Letters from Frederik van den Arend to Dos Passos, January 31 and December 1, 1920; letter from Dos Passos to J. H. Lawson, February 27, 1920.

69

[Paris
July 21, 1919]

[To McComb]

= en route voulez vous me rencontrer a santander les premiers jours d aout repondez envoyez a dudley poore une invitation visiter votre villa adresse 21 rue valette paris demandez aux sweeney une invitation aussi a cause des passeports : john dos passos =

[Fr.] Translated, with capitalizations and punctuation added, the telegram says: "Ready to go. Will you meet me in Santander in early August? Reply. Send Dudley Poore an invitation to visit your villa. Address 21 Rue Valette, Paris. Ask the Sweeneys for an invitation too, on account of the passports. John Dos Passos."

70

Nov 10 [1919]
("Rule Britannia," Granada)

Arthur you wretch—

Our fury was unexampled when we heard that you'ld gone to a Scandinavian tailor! Of course I realize now that it could not have been otherwise. I await the result with terror not unmixed with awe. In retribution Dudley seriously contemplates appearing in Madrid in a hat dit de torero[1] and with a guitar under his arm. Really you'll be the death of us with your Scandinavians! For God's sake hurry it as I need something to cover my nakedness.

I am up, swathed in blankets, coddling a brasero.[2] The weather is grey and cold, like yesterday's boiled potatoes. The incident of the late unpleasantness is nearly closed. But, oiga,[3] I am tied to the brasero, venomous and ill smelling affair that I loathe, until the cloak comes.

A thousand thanks to you and the Sweeneys for moneys and books and all the trouble you have taken—Remember me to the Sweeneys
à bientôt—Dos

1. "A so-called bullfighter's hat." Dit de [Fr.], torero [Sp.].
2. [Sp.] "Brazier."
3. [Sp.] "Listen."

71

> Carmen de Mata Todos
> Alhambra
> Granada
> Saturday
> [November 1919]

Dear Arthur —

Another cargo of the blessèd Atophan[1] arrived today; thank you ever so much. I put my nose out of doors for the first time today and was greatly edified by the contemplation of the Alhambra Palace Hotel.[2] Dudley tyrannously keeps me wrapped in blankets and sends me to bed at six thirty every night. As a result I daily increase in wisdom and stature, and feel less like a scarecrow.

The anxiously awaited cloaks have not yet turned up.

A delightful letter from Van appeared which I'll read you in due time. He seems to be becoming a spice merchant and is likely to be off to samarcand for a load of cloves and poppy seed at any moment.

What is dagusca 48? or is it Langosta[3] 48?

> Love
> Dos

1. A drug, then used for arthritis.
2. Baedeker's *Spain and Portugal* (1913), p. 332, described that nearby hotel as "new, with fine view, lift, and central heating."
3. Langosta [Sp.], "locust; lobster." On Lagasca 48, see Letter 45 above. According to McComb's memoir "A Foreign Dye" the street was named after a Spanish botanist.

72

> Carmen de Mata Todos
> Sunday
> [November 1919]

Arthur —

A fine day. I have had a walk and sniffed all the spicy smells of autumn. The cloaks have come, and indeed, o much abused Arthur, you are to be congratulated. I kiss you on both cheeks. Dudley and I can do nothing but preen before the mirror. We have determined to be buried in them. But before that we will fly away in them — I am sure they will serve as excellent parachutes — And indeed we must fly.

Sovreignty[1] is insupportable.

O vomitose![2]

Never again. O irony of fate to have caught us here and manacled us hand and foot to the mangy lion.

But the cloaks, the cloaks, o Arthur, they breed voyages, Avila, Segovia, Abyssinia: they solve the housing problem. You should have seen me strutting in the sun. They render torero hats unnecessary.

And mealy-mouthed Lloyd George is about to beat his forehead on the ground before Lenin.[3]

The Dillon has exploded like a charged jelly.[4] The sepulchres have peeled off like ripe bananas and there is no more whiting on them.[5]

Dont be alarmed if we telegraph wildly for money. We'll pay it back the moment we arrive in Madrid. But we may have to evacuate the Carmen de Mata Todos at any minute. I'm expecting money hourly, but it may not come—Best wishes to Los 3 de Sweeney O buyer of beautiful cloaks!

Hasta la vista

Dos

1. For Dos Passos' satirical appellations in this letter: "Sovereignty," "Carmen de Mata Todos," "the mangy lion," and "the Dillon," see narrative, pp. 129–30 above.

2. The suffix -ose meaning full of (e.g., verbose, full of words).

3. The British and French governments were supporting the Russian Admiral Kolchak and General Anton Ivanovich Denikin in their anti-Bolshevik campaigns. But there was a report that Prime Minister Lloyd George, in a Guildhall speech on November 8, had hinted at an attempt to negotiate peace with the Bolsheviks. An uproar resulted in Great Britain, and the prime minister later said that peace between his nation and the Bolsheviks was impossible because of the civil war in Russia.

4. Jelly: a gelatinlike explosive.

5. Matthew 23:27. ". . . ye are like unto whited sepulchres, which indeed appear beautiful outward, but are within full of dead men's bones, and of all uncleanness."

73

Madrid—Nov. 18, 1919.

Dear Dos,

I was so relieved to think that you both liked the cloaks—I tried one on before it was sent & must say I thought it very nice, though I know little about such things. I think the moral of this and also perhaps of your stay at Casa Laird[1] is that we should each trust to our own gods!

Well, do come soon to Madrid. And really I hope you will come in a well-heated first class carriage on the Rápido because you mustn't get a chill whatever happens.

I really sympathize with you in the Carmen de Matamoros. I know how you must be dying to get away. A month ago, even I, was at the end of my tether there.

Lagasca 48 is another terrible British place however. I am here simply because everywhere is full, and I had my possessions waiting here. As Mr. Wilson would say "I can do no other."[2] . . .

How wonderful of Van — I too should like to be a spice-merchant — why not all of us? "Dos Passos & Van den Arend" Batavia and Amsterdam — would sound very well.

Your paragraph about sepulchres & jellies leads me to expect interesting revelations.

As ever —
Arthur

1. After Miss Laird, who ran the Carmen de Matamoros.
2. Woodrow Wilson's speech before Congress (April 2, 1917) asking for a declaration of war against Germany concluded: "God helping her [America], she can do no other." His words resembled the conclusion tradition has ascribed, probably inaccurately, to Martin Luther's speech at the Diet at Worms. Luther seems to have concluded: (trans.) "God help me, amen!" A traditional addition "Here I stand, I can do no other" is inscribed on Luther's monument at Worms.

74

[Letterhead: Hôtel d'Orient,
Barcelone]
8:30 P.M.
11-III-[19]20

[To McComb]

And the villain still pursued her — I'll drop in at eight thirty so that we can dine together — and if I dont find you then — at nine thirty — Be in this lounge thing — Dos

75

[Barcelona
March 1920]
Saturday

Arthur — I imagine you are in Torino, probably at this moment looking at the Cosimo Roselli (Piero di Cosimo) — which?[1] —

The weather has remained superb, so I presume that the Capitan arrived in Genoa without being completely revuelta.[2]

In the course of investigations of Spanish syndicalism from the capitalist point of view I have discovered the amusing fact, which will certain give great aid and comfort to all your Manchesterism, that the Catalans are beginning to monopolize the Turkish market in textiles, as in other products, and that the Turks prefer to buy at a slightly higher price from peaceful Catalonian exporters than to take the goods offered at the bayonet's point by the British and French.

I am working on my novel at my large desk. Outside amid the noise of the harbor, a hand organ is playing "The Wearing of the Green". Otherwise, I and indecision still stare each other in the face like the sphynx and the chimaera.

I have found a pleasant and rather romantic little restaurant. Really, in spite of all, I rather like Barcelona. The flowers on the Rambla[3] grow increasingly lovely.

Mallorca? Ya veremos.[4]

I'm anxious to hear from you. After months of such pleasant communal existence, Solitude is rather solitary.

Here are the reproductions.

Love
Dos

And yet my opinion of the Andaluces goes up daily.[5]

1. Cosimo Rosselli (1439–1507) and his pupil Piero di Cosimo (1462–1521), originally Piero di Lorenzo, both Florentine painters. (The latter adopted his master's name.) McComb's note to Dos Passos' letter explains: "Cosimo Rosselli: a painting of Tobias and the Angel in the Museum of Turin, which had excited D P's [Dos Passos'] interest when he had seen it in 1917 on his way through Turin. . . ."

2. [Sp.] "Turned over." Thus, huevos revueltos, "scrambled eggs." McComb had sailed from Barcelona on a ship named the Capitán Revuelta.

3. The main street of the old town in Barcelona, shaded by plane trees and extending almost three-quarters of a mile, with the different sections bearing their own names. It was continued by the Rambla de Cataluña.

4. [Sp.] "We'll see."

5. McComb's note here is that the Andalusians and the Catalonians are held to be opposites in temperament. He gathers that Dos Passos had his preference for the former reinforced by his sojourn in Barcelona. On McComb's annotations, see Letter 6, n. 8 above.

76

Hotel Bauer-am-Rhein
Bâle, March 30, 1920.

(Write to me here)

Dear Dos: —

Your letter & Dudley's enclosed together with Tarrassa[1] post-cards and the reproductions all arrived to-day, the first word I have had. . . .

Enclosed you will find some cards. The selection at the Museum is rather small—I chose those you would be least likely to know & that I thought the most interesting. . . .

. . . I am in such a state of mind—I should like to be with you in Cataluña & in Paris and here all at once while as for Italy—oh, dear I am afraid I shall be irresistibly drawn back—though I have no money—

The Catalans & the Turks—nothing could be more to my taste.

My admiration for Mr. Nitti[2] grows daily. He has that admirable flexibility and tolerance which will save Europe yet if it can be saved. He sees realities without heat and must appear irritatingly reasonable alike to the French Govt. & to Mr. Serrati[3] & Co. I begin to have some hope if the Rev. can be staved off & we can have Ebert,[4] Nitti, Hoover[5] & Asquith[6]—drab figures if you will, but perhaps for that very reason the greatest hope for us all.

The Cosimo Rosselli—Piero di Cosimo pleito[7] is still on. I avoided having to give a decision by going via Milan.—oh tact! . . .

Love—Arthur

1. Tarrasa: town with Romanesque churches, about fifteen miles north-northwest of Barcelona.

2. Francesco Saverio Nitti (1865–1953), Italian liberal who was premier of Italy in 1919 and 1920. On the Adriatic question, he condemned chauvinist campaigns by both the Italian and Yugoslav presses and favored an effort to come to a direct understanding with the Yugoslav government. In March 1920 he urged rehabilitating Germany economically and called for establishing normal relations with Russia.

3. Giacinto Menotti Serrati (1876–1926), Italian Maximalist leader and successor to Mussolini as editor of the Socialist newspaper *Avanti*. He was important in the history of the Italian left before Mussolini came to power.

4. Friedrich Ebert (1871–1925), first president (1919–25) of the German Weimar Republic. A Social Democrat, he supported Germany's war effort, opposed abolition of the monarchy, and suppressed efforts by the Spartacists and by reactionary rightists to seize power.

5. Herbert Clark Hoover, who in 1920 was a prospect for the Republican nomination for the U.S. presidency.

6. Herbert Henry Asquith (1852–1928), Liberal leader and (1908–16) prime minister of Great Britain.

7. [Sp.] "Dispute."

77

[Picture postcard: "Bern—at the Clock Tower"]

Bâle   March 30. [1920]

Dos: This is what Bern is like. I have seen the Erasmus tombstone. It is placed against a pillar of the Münster[1]. . . . Protestantism here makes weird & unpleasant impression[2] on me after 2 yrs. in the most catholic country. —In the münster there is no altar & the seats (benches) are placed facing <u>west</u> so that the participants can worship the organ if they like.[3] One is forbidden to walk around during service. —There are fat gentleman with silk hats—oh dear. —

Love

A.

I must apologize for my incredulity—Solothurn[4] Museum <u>was</u> shut & I <u>did</u> get it open!—So you were right.

1. [Ger.] "Cathedral."
2. *impressions*? The final *n* is crowded against the margin.
3. In Roman Catholic cathedrals since perhaps the sixth century the custom was for the priest and participants to face east; the altar was at the east end of the basilica, and the priest stood before it with his back toward the participants for much of the Mass.
4. Swiss town, nineteen miles north of Bern.

78

[Art postcard]

Bâle, April 1<u>st</u> 1920.

Dos—I wish I had you to talk to. —I have found out the proper technical Berensonian name for your Master of the Life of St. Vincent. In a work in the Library here he is referred to as Jaime Vergos II.[1] What do you think of that way out of the difficulty?—I have been doing great things— got a Poussin Bacchanal brought out of the store-room for me to look at!—Bad sort of Titianesque work—much plagiarism.—How about your water-colors? When you have finished novel come to Bâle & read it to me instead of going to P. de M.[2]

A McC.

1. Probably a reference to paintings from the parish church of Sarriá, a suburb of Barcelona. The church was dedicated to St. Vincent the Martyr, and the nine extant panels of its retable contained scenes from his life. Chandler Post wrote in 1938 that the panels were in the Museum of Catalan Art. Jaime Vergós II was a painter who flourished in Barcelona during the fifteenth century. Post does not attribute any of the panels to him, but assigns a majority of them to his contemporary Jaime Huguet and his "immediate atelier." Chandler R. Post, *A History of Spanish Painting*, 12 vols. (Cambridge: Harvard University Press, 1930–47), 7: part 1, pp. 46–47, 122–30; part 2, pp. 414–17, 490. See also Baedeker, *Spain and Portugal* (1913), p. 243.
2. Palma de Mallorca.

79

[Mallorca
April 1920]

Arthur: You should indeed have come to Mallorca. I keep thinking of Jan VerMeer. In the first place I have never seen such passionate cleanliness: imaculate white walls, immaculate grey-tiled floors, imaculate little mouse like women with beautiful shawls in greys and suave browns, with kerchiefs on the back of their heads and their hair in a long plait down their backs. The brilliant light, the exuberant orange and lemon trees, the purple mountains and the wine dark sea are all attuned to the soft clear colors of a Vermeer interior.

I am a[1] Lluch—the sanctuary of the chief virgin of the island—a monastery, where you can spend the night between delicious sheets of rough linen, and hear little choirboys in blue sing allelulia under your window when you wake.

I came over four days ago with Kate[2] & Adelaide Lawson and the infant. Palma is delightful, of a rusty apricot color, and quiet, quiet. The island is overflowing with a silence as brilliant as the soft honey-colored sunlight. From Palma I walked to Valldemosa, where Chopin and George Sand had their little escapade. Then round a piece of coast where hovered the shadow of an archduke ... An Austrian Archduke Louis Salvador, who built a lot of foolish little pavillions, made a superb collection of majolica ware, called the lot Miramar,[3] and died, as Archdukes must. (Days later) I saw in the basement of the mansion a touchingly awful white marble monument in which the Archduke's secretary, a certain check (I spell it phonetically),[4] a plump undressed man with a carefully trimmed moustache, is being awakened by the recording angel. The archduke left everything to the heirs of the dead check, and in their house, which I happened upon through a set of ingenious chances, I saw a portrait of the archduke, an excessively fat red faced man in a yachting cap leaning against a seascape. At a town named Deyá I shook off the archduke; the coast lost its Riviera look and the real fun began. Later, at Sóller, on a cliff over the sea, at sunset, I fell in with three jolly Catalans, with haversacks, cameras, spyglasses and a guide of the Baleares. No, but they turned out to be most excellent and delightful Catalans, full of enthusiasm for walking, eating and drinking. We all went together over the high mountains to Lluch, and on the next day to Pollensa, where in a valley glittering with greens and blues and purples, the fattest Catalan sat on a rock. On getting up it was discovered that a whole landscape in creamy oil paint adhered to the seat of his trousers. Later we heard that Anglada[5] had been painting in that valley; so at the next exhibition at the Orfeo Gracienc[6] all of independent Catalunya may admire els pantalons bonics[7] of our fattest Catalan. From the port of Pollensa we took ship, sea being blue, mountains purple and the sky indigo, for Alcudia, a burnt siena town with crumbling walls and a bay on either side and many windmills. From Alcudia I returned to Palma, with eight bad watercolors and a sunburned nose. And now all things have come to pass. Kate, Adelaide and Co. have left for Alicante; and tomorrow I go back to Barcelona, where I hope to find many epistles from you, Arthur. Erasmian episodes, snatches of Holbein, letters of Dürer.

Love
Dos

Write Morgan Harjes—
15 Place Vendome—

1. [Catalan] "At."
2. Kate Drain Lawson.
3. "The domain of Miramar, a creation of Archduke Louis Salvator of Austria (of the house of Tuscany; b. 1847)" (Baedeker, *Spain and Portugal* [1913], pp. 275–76). Dos Passos' tone conveys his impatience with sentimental legends about the archduke, and about royalty in general.
4. Czechoslovakia had been created only in 1918. The word *Czech,* as McComb points out in a note to the letter, was not as familiar as it later became.
5. Hermenegild Anglada i Camarasa (1872–1959), Spanish painter, b. in Barcelona, who worked in Spain and Paris and exhibited often in Barcelona. For a time he settled in Mallorca, where he painted "innumerable" landscapes of the island. *Diccionario biográfico de artistas de Cataluña* (Barcelona, 1951).
6. [Catalan]. *Orfeós* were nationalistic choral and cultural societies which sang Catalan songs and engaged in other activities. *Gracienc* (adj.) is from a place name. The Paseo de Gracia was a wide, tree-shaded boulevard extending northwest from the Plaza de Cataluña (at the end of the old Rambla) in Barcelona. Beyond it lay Gracia, Barcelona's most important suburb.
7. "Catalunya" is the Catalan spelling; els pantalons bonics [Catalan], "the beautiful trousers."

80

[Barcelona]
April 9—[1920]

Dear Arthur—

Back in Barcelona—in my same room. As I am permanently anchored here (relatively) without money, due to one of those fetching equivocaciones[1] in the cable by which my money came to un tal Carlos Dos

Passos,[2] I have hopes of making the esfuerzo[3] necessary to finish up that thrice damned novel.

But I must steal a moment to thank you for the delightful Bâle letter and the cards. When I write my "History and Significance of the Human Nose" 18 vol. 4° gilt-edge, library edition—I swear that the Bildnis eines unbekannten Herring will be the frontispiece. Somewhere, probably in Italy, I once saw a face exactly like it. It's enormously fascinating; and the gloves and the concert-program, and the bit of plump neck. The Sir Nicholas Carew is splendid, too.[4]

The proofs of "One Man's Initiation" came, with deliciously funny expostulations in pencil on the margin. On reading the thing over I felt so disgusted with it, that I sent it back telling them to cut out what they damned please, but for Heaven's sake to let me have a wooden crucifix addressed with an uncapitalized "you'.

Barcelona, after Palma, is stupid and heavy and full of grinding noises.

I have no news of Dudley, so I dont know whether he's in Madrid or Seville or Cordoba.

I'm going to meet Jack Lawson in Carcassonne on the fourteenth, and I suppose will gradually go Americawards. I'll write you each phase of my indecision.

We must all go some day and spend a month and a day in Mallorca. It's not exactly in the grand manner, but of such a rare perfection, that my week there seems like a glimpse through an open doorway at a quite green garden, in the middle of a dull purposeless walk down dusty streets.

Write me lots about Erasmus. I am in a moment when I need the fillip of stories of great people who died very long ago. Its cruel how easily one's supply of salt runs out, and life unsalted, is not a success. If I can ever shake off the weight of that wretched novel ... O where is the huge salt-cellar wrought out of yellowish glinting silver by Cellini into pans and saints, cupids and cherubim, hermaphrodites and virgin martyrs, into which I can delve deep with my two hands?[5] But the novel, the novel ...

Adios.
Dos.

write Credit Lyonnais here until I let you know.

Bauer-am-Rheim[6] is a delicious name for a hotel, makes me think of blonde and bulbous ladies drinking Rhenish out of Bavarian glass flagons in arbors by the waterside, of gentlemen in flapping broad brimmed hats playing bowls on bright green lawns, while a fat man with a Tyrolean cap lolls at a table crowded with preposterous porcelain beer mugs and pipes and sings the Lorelei in beery bass, and fat little birds warble among the willow trees.

1. [Sp.] "Mistakes."
2. [Sp.] "One Carlos Dos Passos."
3. [Sp.] "Effort."
4. References to *Bildnis eines unbekannten Herrn* and portrait drawing *Sir Nicholas Carew,* both by Hans Holbein, the younger, and both in the Kunstmuseum, Basel. On *Bildnis . . . Herrn,* see narrative, p. 132 above. The symbol 4° means *quarto.*
5. Dos Passos' imaginative construction: a play on the Renaissance sculptor's fanciful virtuosity, and a display of Dos Passos' own virtuosity. Cellini's famous saltcellar, made for Francis I in gold, enamel, and precious stones, is 10¼ inches high and has different figures.
6. Bauer-am-Rhein [Ger.], "Farmer-on-the-Rhine." See Letter 76 above.

81

[Paris
May 1920]

Arthur: forgive my long silence: and thank you for Lais and the Funk.[1] Lais is delectable.

As to my itinerary: It was rather mad. I left Barcelona furnished with fluid by the dear Sweenies, as my galleon was lost at sea, but had not enough of the jingling to stop off anywhere, except over a train, accidentally, at Narbonne, a poky little town with a pleasant archepiscopal castle, now an art gallery full of fake vieux maitres.[2] Then Tarascon— dusty, with a lovely romanesque and gothic church, a beautiful bridge, the one Tartarin[3] walks over when he shakes the dust off his feet for the last time, a castle of the roi René,[4] and la Tarasque[5] of blessed memory. (Food bad, dear and prix fixe)[6] Beaucaire, across the Rhone, is a grey damp town with a lovely ruined castle full of irises and pale memories of Aucassin and Nicolette.[7] In Tarascon I met Jack Lawson. From there we went to Arles—St. Trophime[8] and dullish Roman leavings—From Arles to Aigues Mortes and Grau de Roi—marshes, the sea, glittering piles of salt, and unscathed walls some Genoese put up by contract for St. Louis, (or to be exact for Louis le Bel)[9] Anyway St. Louis went on a crusade from there to annoy the Tunisians. Aigues Mortes to Nimes—delicious town where the delicate artificiality of Le Notre[10] blends imperceptably into the courtly grace of the early caesars. The Maison Carrée is a bonbonnière, so light and of such exquisite proportions that when you look at it you feel as if it were resting in the palm of your hand.[11] Jack nearly bought a villa on the hill beside a fat Roman tower on the strength of it. Nîmes to Les Saintes Maries de la Mer, where there is a fortified Romanesque church like a high galleon beached on the sands among the little clustered houses of fishermen. It seems that Salomé and Mary and Martha, daughters of Jacob, and Mary Madgalene and Sarah, their servant, the patron of gipsies, took ship with Lazarus and other notabilies and landed on this spot in the marches of the Rhone delta; a wonderfully savage desolate place.[12] Some movie actors were doing a wild west picture on the sands. From there back to Arles. From Arles afoot to Les Baux, stopping at Montmajour, very beautiful ruined monestary that overlooks the roofs and towers of Arles. A day of furious mistral—gorgeous. Les Baux, ruins of a mediæval and roman castle and of a renaissance town, perched among fantastic crags among the Alpilles.[13] From Les Baux to St. Remy—roman monument and arch—St. Remy to Tarascon & Arles. Arles to Martigues, on a great lagoon full of fluttering little sails. The town straddles the inlet from the sea, and everywhere is full of green water and fishing boats and jolly brown fishermen. Martigues to Sausset-les-Pins on the coast west of Marseilles. Then by train to Marseilles—bawdy, seething, spinning Marseilles. It is not for nothing that one holds the gorgeous east in fee.[14]

We were about to embark for Tunis, when Jack had to go back to Paris on account of his complications, and I took up again the sad predestined path. So here I am. The cycle is complete. In a room on the Quai d'Anjou[15] I have lived and written in many times before, where memories grin and stick out their tongues at me from among the fly-specked irises of the wall paper.

Anyway the first part of Three Soldiers is in the hands of a stenog.

The Luxembourg[16] is open, a crowded room of impressionists, full of delights a dull new room and much Bouguereauism,[17] and the same unspeakable statuary.

In the Arts Decoratifs[18] I found three Gaugins of great interest; and upstairs a complete bunch of Barbizon people[19] except Millet, and some lovely Manets.

Did I say France was dead? I eat my words. I have been to the Vieux Colombier[20] and seen an incredible performance of of play called le Paquebot "Tenacity".[21] Superb. Also a vie militaire play of St. Georges de Bouhelier at the Theatre des Arts, Les Esclaves,[22] a play of such emotional power as to be almost insupportable. Set with unimaginable

"The Maison Carrée is a bonbonnière, so light and of such exquisite proportions that when you look at it you feel as if it were resting in the palm of your hand." Dos Passos to McComb, May 1920.

beauty and simplicity. The Theatres des Arts is run COOPERATIVELY by the Societé des Auteurs. Makes my poor little three soldiers sound like Dr. Watts.[23]

I'm sending you Lululi[24] Romain Rolland's war satire which is excellent. I've never read anything written with such cold flame of scorn.

Vive la France!

Dos

Arthur: I'd love to go to Bâle to see you and Erasmus's ghost walking arm in arm beside the Rhine—but I haven't a cent. I've been living on charity ever since Barcelona. And then, too, I must finish the accursed doughboys before I move anywhere.

All our erratic wanderings in Provence were a search for somewhere to settle and work for a while. Now I am settled and working and moderately content in a bovine way. Shan't we see each other in England? Dudley has started negociations to go there as his mother and father arrive there very soon. By the way, coming into France from Spain the passport business was purely formal (no card catalogues as of yore). They even let one Englishman go in without a visé, after a little grumbling. I think that you ought to come through France to see the Vieux Colombier—but as you will. Still it's much more important to go to Paestum,[25] to say nothing of the Uffizi.

Love

Dos

1. Laïs: the name of several courtesans in ancient Greece. McComb had sent Dos Passos a card of the portrait *Magdalena Offenburg as Laïs Corinthiaca,* by Hans Holbein, the younger, and a card of *Portrait of a Young Man* by Hans Funk (b. in Zurich towards 1470, d. 1539).

2. [Fr.] "Old masters."

3. Chief character of three tales by Alphonse Daudet (b. in Nîmes in 1840, d. 1897), the first being *Tartarin de Tarascon* (1872).

4. King René *or* René of Anjou (1409–80).

5. A monster from which St. Martha is said to have delivered the town.

6. [Fr.] "Standard menu."

7. Lovers in the thirteenth-century French romance *Aucassin et Nicolette.* Aucassin is the son of the count of Beaucaire.

8. Church of Saint-Trophime.

9. St. Louis: Louis IX of France (1214–70). Louis le Bel (the Fair).

10. Cathedral of Notre-Dame et St-Castor.

11. "The Maison Carrée, Nîmes (16 B.C.) . . . is the best preserved Roman temple in existence, and is externally complete. It represents the ultimate of Graeco-Etruscan design interpreted in monumental Augustan architecture . . ." (Sir Banister Fletcher, *A History of Architecture.* 18th ed. Revised by J. C. Palmes [New York: Charles Scribner's Sons, 1975], p. 276). Thomas Jefferson wrote from Nîmes in 1787 that he was gazing at it "like a lover at his mistress."

12. We quote from a standard tourist guide: "The legend tells how the three Maries

(St. Mary, sister of the Virgin, St. Mary, mother of the Apostles John and James, and St. Mary Magdalen) landed there c. 40 A.D. in company with their servant Sarah (represented as an Ethiopian), Martha, Lazarus, and Maximinus, having fled from persecution in the Holy Land. The first two Maries and Sarah were buried here and their relics were discovered by King René in 1448 and enshrined in the upper church. . . .

"The spring pilgrimage is especially curious on account of the influx of gypsies, who come from all over Europe to honour the shrine of their ancestress Sarah." *Southern France* (Blue Guide), ed. Findlay Muirhead and Marcel Monmarché (London: Macmillan and Co., 1926), p. 116.

13. *Or Alpines.*

14. "Once did She hold the gorgeous east in fee. . . ." William Wordsworth, "On the Extinction of the Venetian Republic," line 1.

15. Embankment, with houses, on the Île Saint-Louis, Paris.

16. Musée du Luxembourg, in Paris. Baedeker described the museum thus: ". . . a collection of modern art belonging to the State. The paintings and sculptures exhibited here are generally transferred to the Louvre, or sent to provincial galleries, ten years after the death of the artists." Karl Baedeker, *Paris and Environs* (Leipzig: Karl Baedeker, 1913), p. 323. In the 1924 edition the description is identical.

17. Reference to Adolphe William Bouguereau (1825–1905), a highly successful French academic painter. After impressionism gained favor, critics attacked his work severely.

18. Musée des Arts Décoratifs, in Paris.

19. A group of French landscape painters active c. 1830–70.

20. Théâtre du Vieux-Colombier (at 21 Rue du Vieux-Colombier, in the Latin Quarter of Paris). Jacques Copeau in 1913 founded this repertory theater, which offered plays from many periods, including the modern. In his stagings Copeau was an anti-realist, whose devices influenced theater in Europe and the United States.

21. *Le paquebot Tenacity* (S.S. *Tenacity*), a three-act play written by Charles Messager Vildrac (b. 1882), and produced March 20, 1920.

22. Saint-Georges de Bouhélier, pseudonym of Ludovic-Stéphane-Georges de Bouhélier-Lepelletier (1876–1947); Théâtre des Arts, at 78 bis Boulevard des Batignolles, Paris; *Les esclaves* (The slaves), written in 1906, first performed on April 25, 1920.

23. Isaac Watts (1674–1748), English clergyman and writer of hymns.

24. *Liluli*, a play first published in June 1919, in Geneva.

25. Ancient city, originally Greek, in southern Italy. Paestum is noted for its fine and well-preserved Doric temples.

82

Paris—May 13 [1920]

Arthur—

A delightful letter from you—a note rather—with a Cuthbertian[1] news item—And quotations from The secret Agent—O irrepressable Arthur.[2] And you say you have no buckler—aere triplex,[3] mon cher!

I'm delighted you are going to Italy—Perugia, Assisi, Orvieto, San Gimignano and Siena must not be missed.

I write this in Dudley's[4] room, a low room on a back street near St Germain des Pris.[5] The other day I met him strolling on the Quais. The name of the hotel is du Cardinal; the stairs are steep and ancient and make me think of Manon;[6] the bed is grand and sleighlike. The mustiness of the eighteenth century, that pervades everything would delight you.

But I know Paris too well. Memories grin at me from street corners. I don't know if I'm in this year or last year. One can nearly always go the present, but to meet the past at every turn with its eternal infernal mirror ... I hate it.

Did I write you about the Vieux Colombier? The Ballet Russe[7] is with us; would shake even you out of your anti-theatre mood. There are concerts, and on the Butte one eats fraises des bois with crème d'Isigny[8] as of yore. The wheel of Karma. The wheel of Karma—

Love
Dos

1. Reference to Cuthbert Wright.
2. Dos Passos was replying to McComb's letter of April 20, 1920, from Geneva. Although McComb's letter is too badly marred for transcription, some summary and quotation are possible. McComb wrote of reading some of Conrad's works recently, and he described and quoted from Conrad's *Under Western Eyes* (1911), a novel dealing with anarchism and revolution. McComb also quoted from Conrad's *The Secret Agent*. "How Dos," McComb asked, "can I arm myself with the buckler of self-righteous purpose-in-lifefulness? . . . [most of a line illegible] If I try, inevitably the [possibly *thing*] will magically turn into a . . . [one word illegible] or a volume of Mr. James ... or something & there I will be revealed in all my futility."
3. Horace's *Carmina* 1. 3. 9 reads: "illi robur et aes triplex." Extended and translated, the passage reads: "That man had courage and triple bronze was around his breast, who first committed a fragile boat to the wild sea." Robert Louis Stevenson has an essay "Aes Triplex."
4. Dudley Poore.
5. St-Germain-des-Prés. A very old Parisian church, on the left bank of the Seine River.
6. The novel *Manon Lescaut* (1731), by Abbé Antoine François Prévost.
7. Sergei Diaghilev brought a company of Russian dancers to Paris in 1909 and founded the troupe. It revolutionized and gave new life to ballet and dominated it for twenty years.
8. Butte: Butte Montmartre; fraises des bois [Fr.], "wild strawberries"; crème d'Isigny [Fr.], "cream from Isigny [a village in Normandy notable for its butter]."

83

Bergamo, Italia, 21$^{\underline{st}}$ May 1920.
Dos:—

A note of yours of the 13$^{\underline{th}}$ reached me before I left Lausanne. . . .

Italy is stiflingly hot, but as wonderful as ever. Bergamo is the town of the great Morelli[1]—the inventor of the Berensonian system of art criticism. Unfortunately his admirable little art collection is closed till next month. . . .

To-morrow evening I leave for Brescia.

———

Oh, but no, Dos, the past is delicious. Secretly I have nursed a scheme to return to Madrid some years hence and visit all our haunts when you & Dudley shall not be there & steep myself in gentle melancholy.

Love—
Arthur.

Write Geneva as usual.

. . . .

1. Giovanni Morelli (1816–91). His emphasis on the primary importance of studying pictures themselves (as compared to documents, etc.) and his attention to small anatomical elements (e.g., fingernails) in an artist's work revolutionized art attribution.

84

[Paris]
[May 1920?]

Dear Arthur—
The Rubens is fine so's the Leonardo alack and lackaday.—You should come to the Louvre and see the Triumph of Marie de Medicis;[1] that'ld cure you—
So it's till June 1st is it? Very bad—I fear there is a lotos grows in Giacosa's—or is it a Calypso? A twelve o'clock cocktail Calypso?[2]
It's rained cats and dogs ever Since I've been back in Paris—never seen anything like it—
Remember me to the Scholles—
Mrs S. complains of the dirt in Spain, also of the prices, indolence, dust, etc—Speaks of 'Sparkling Geneva' O tempora o mores—Dos
Thanks for the cheque—Cant seem to remember to get it cashed— but it will save my life some day when I'm broke

Bien a toi[3]

1. Rubens' series of twenty-one paintings *The Life of Marie de Médicis*. The series ends with *Triumph of Truth*, in which Louis XIII is shown giving Marie, his mother, a crown.
2. Lotus: in Greek legend a plant whose fruit when eaten induces contentment and dreamy forgetfulness. In the *Odyssey* some of Odysseus' men eat the fruit and lose all desire to return home; Giacosa: a good pastry shop, with tea room, at Via Tornabuoni 11, Florence; Calypso: (capitalized) in the *Odyssey*, the name of a nymph who detains Odysseus for seven years; (uncapitalized) the name of a terrestrial orchid.
3. [Fr.] "Yours ever."

85

Padua   28$\underline{\text{th}}$ of May 1920.

Dear Dos: —

. . . .

I got through the Confessions and Ave, and then decided I could have nothing more to do with Mr. Moore[1] for at least a year. The irritating vulgarity of his manner and that odious I — I repeated to nausea were not compensated for by any supreme artistic value in the works. Let him leave us alone — with his puerile temperamentalizing — bah! — After this, as a penitent unbeliever might be taken back into the bosom of the Church, I returned with bowed head to Mr. Henry James. In his drawing-room I was at least sure of being courteously received. I was duly rewarded by Washington Square [,] The Pension Beaurepas & A Bundle of Letters [,] all in the master's first & most happy manner.[2]

Then I read one vol. of Heures d'Italie by Gabriel Faure,[3] much talked about these days, but apart from some pleasant quotations from Dante I failed to discover why the book had been written. Our friend Élie Faure has a short novel La Roue[4] which I venture to recommend to you for the interest it possesses in connection with our discussions in Madrid. The hero is a pacifist who goes to Switzerland at the outbreak of the war. Later to Italy where the sombre Palazzi[5] etc. convert him to Élie Faure's peculiar philosophy of harmony & rapture & new harmony, struggle etc. Placid Switzerland with its hotels, peace & comfort is the negation of all this, is real pacifism. He realizes he is not a pacifist, that if there were a revolution, he would be at the barricades etc. Logical result: he returns to fight for France. There is one Clotilde in the book who becomes the hero's mistress (for a night, I think) — she is drawn after Michelangelo's Night.[6] The whole thing is highly intellectualized (and of course not properly a novel at all) — I was very interested — you will be more so, perhaps. It astonishingly approaches your own philosophy. Its intellectualized disregard for all merely average human emotion may (I write without asparagus) appeal to you. I have a feeling that M. Faure would agree that most people "lead incomplete lives" & send them to die for — nothing. (I admit to a little bitterness creeping in here — a little impatience with you & M. Faure (forgive me!) — enough therefore of this). . . .

Amid a profound discouragement with modern German literature, & a feeling that I should after all not be able to answer your & Dudley's question "What is there to read in German?" satisfactorily, I came upon v. Hofmannsthal's Elektra[7]. . . . The whole thing is a superbly concentrated & beautifully wrought piece of work.

By the way, would you in second-hand places look for Élie Faure's Velazquez[8] if you remember. I think it would interest all of us.

Love & write again
Arthur.

. . . .

1. George Moore (1852–1933), Anglo-Irish writer. *Confessions of a Young Man* (1888) and *Ave* (1911) are among his autobiographical works. The latter is the first volume of his *Hail and Farewell*.

2. *Washington Square* (1880), "The Pension Beaurepas" (1879), and "A Bundle of Letters" (1879). Together they formed the contents of a two-volume English edition (1881).

3. French writer (1877–1962). His *Heures d'Italie* appeared from 1910 to 1921.

4. Published in 1919.

5. [It.] "Palaces."

6. *Night,* in the form of a sleeping woman, is one of the sculptures in the Medici Chapel.

7. Hugo von Hofmannsthal (1874–1929), Austrian dramatist and poet. He wrote the play *Elektra* in 1903.

8. Published in 1903.

86

London   June 8 [1920]

[To McComb]

Consternation

[Cartoon of irate woman brandishing umbrella]

Mother Grundy in the form of a British printer refuses to print One Man's Initiation, though it's all set up. Indecent! So I am swallowing my bile and making changes.

You are franker than most, you know—saith the publisher.

Demoniac laughter from offstage—

Dos

87

[Art postcard: H. Holbein, the younger: *Dorothea Offenburg as Venus with Amor*]

Florence June 18—1920.

Dear Dos:—A companion to the other, which I had forgotten to send.—Looking at my record I see I have not heard from you since May 17

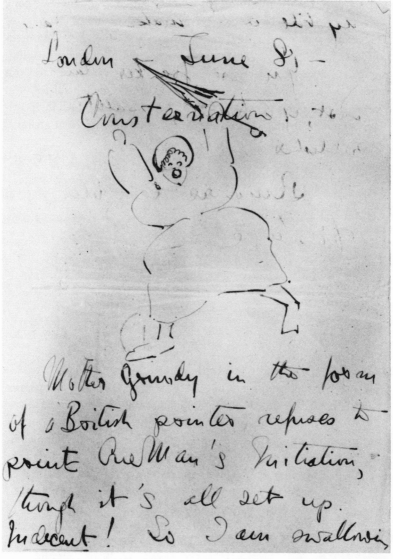

Mother Grundy. Cartoon in letter by Dos Passos. (See Letter 86.)

at Ouchy, & the dreadful thought strikes me that you may have gone already to America. The Books arrived, have been read & returned. — The Faure was wonderfully stimulating in its absence of sentimentality—in its hardness. What a Nietzschean!—Liluli[1] less thrilling, though v. adequate. — All the Angelicos have been transported to Convento S. Marco which is one of the most purely delightful spots in Florence. One gets a v. good notion of F.A. as a painter. All the Botticellis' are now in the Uffizi—the Accademia[2] having been stripped bare —

Love   A. McC—

. . . .

1. See Letter 81 above.
2. Accademia di Belle Arti.

88

[Art postcards]

[Italy?
June? 1920]

Dos: —

. . . You are not quite fair to the Faure.[1] The trouble of course is its incredible intellectualisation   When he gets down to making dates of artists births coincide with wars, he falls to the level of Bag Fuller.[2] I suppose Cézanne is the product of the Crimean war. Working on the same principle one would cheerfully dispense with both the Napoleonic wars & the artists born at that time. This is mere foolishness. But the Nietzscheanism underlying is perhaps the only intellectual defence of war that can properly be made. Though disagreeing with the work I thought it stimulating—the general problem of the relation of art & thought to suffering is of the first importance,—but É. Faure seems to have overlooked or slurred the point that as our sensations grow more complex the capacities for drama grow also & that it really may be time to do away with the mere physical waste & cruelty. The realist novel, if nothing else has shown that the "intensest" situations & the most thrilling can exist [,] do exist, in the most commonplace surroundings & are the more "exciting" for that very reason. But one can't discuss these things on a post-card. In Liluli the Chœur des Intellectuels[3] was delicious—one could with imagination, see the figure of M. Faure himself—a little apart rejoicing in the "bruit confuse qui monte"[4] etc. &

thinking to himself how he would enjoy the bas-relief which might be the result!

But I should like to point out that E.F. specifically agrees with you, in the rightness of sacrificing other people's lives for one's ideas. (The "unconscious" people are merely part of the harmony.)—If I seem to hold this idea (memorably developed over the tea-table at Molinero's,[5] against you, it is because it struck me as the most monstrous ever formed by such a civilised soul as yourself. But I expect a recantation. . . .

The incident of the printer is grotesque. The publishers remark is perhaps the richest of the whole episode—"you are franker than most, you know!"—I have been smiling to myself the whole afternoon about it.

But do write more details. . . .

Love—
Arthur.

1. Élie Faure. See Letters 40 (including n. 6), 85, and 87 above.

2. Benjamin Apthorp Gould Fuller (1879–1956), historian of philosophy. Instructor in philosophy at Harvard, 1906–10, 1913–20.

3. [Fr.] "Chorus of the Intellectuals."

4. Bruit confus qui monte [Fr.], "mounting din." See Romain Rolland, *Liluli,* deuxième édition (Paris: Librairie Ollendorff, n.d.), pp. 137–41. For the English translation, see Romain Rolland, *Liluli* (New York: Boni and Liveright, Modern Library, 1920), pp. 112–14.

5. A very fashionable, upper class tearoom in Madrid, much beloved by McComb. Dos Passos went there under protest (telephone interview with Poore, October 3, 1973). McComb's "Notes" (diary) for January 11, 1920, contains the following entry, already mentioned in our narrative (p. 131 above): "Tea at the Old Molinero; a philosophic discussion on means and ends à propos of Dos' New Society. The Red and the White of the case. Dos' final verdict of 'chilly sanity' on my view."

89

[Art postcards]

Wien, Deutschösterreich
13 July—1920.

Dos:—The cards from Hastings (20·6·) have arrived. The Burne-Jones' so typiques,[1] the Maître de Flémalle so nervously fine, the Blake simply detestable. . . . I have been in Vienna since the 1st & return to Italy to-morrow. My sailing has again been changed to the 1st from Genoa 6th fr. Naples. Alas the date matters little—the fact of departure is inevitable. I learn from Cuthbert[2] that you have returned to Paris. . . .

I rejoice at your rejection of Leonardo—have always been in full accord. (And then he's in a sense responsible for all those terrible Lombards—remember that) Glad you liked the Hals—don't know him enough to say anything myself, but from reproductions, he seems a gain on Rembrandt. I have seen many of the latter recently. They will not do. They will not do, I say. I've given up all the Dutch (except Vermeer & Ter Borch)[3] bag & baggage & all the Flemish after Gherardt David.[4] Why this fuss about Brueghel in the Harvard Fine Arts Camp? Rubens at his best here still remains what he always was & will be:— veal.

Love
A.—

P.S.

Its so good to hear from you. You must let it be often now that I must face that cheerless America.

A.

1. [Fr.] "Typical." Sir Edward Burne-Jones (1833–98), English Pre-Raphaelite painter.
2. Cuthbert Wright.
3. Gerard Ter Borch or Terborch (1617–81), genre and portrait painter. His pictures of Dutch upper middle class life are memorable for craftsmanship, serenity, and elegance.
4. Gerard David (c. 1460–1523), painter, b. in Holland, who established himself in Bruges. He is considered the last great artist of the Bruges school. David's work shows dependence on such painters as Jan van Eyck and the Master of Flémalle.

90

Venezia   July 20—1920.

Dear Dos:—An 'assorted' series of National Gallery cards from you— date June 30. Many thanks. I also sent a few cards from Vienna. The enclosed I selected from a bunch sent by the Sweeneys, as most likely to amuse you & Dudley. . . .

The Nation[1] has hideous accounts of the White Terror in Hungary, apparently from irreproachable sources. It never gave us realistic details of the Red Terror,—a very biased sheet, but still, more reliable than the Press. Bertrand Russell has an admirable article in the Liberator[2] which I will send out. Its intellectual honesty is exceptional—He sidesteps nothing. An honorable opponent. No sentimentality or heroworship.

It looks as if there were to be peace with the Bolsheviki. A good thing.

I wonder if that special gang (Trotzky etc.) will be able to maintain itself in power. Nothing more undesirable than a set of fanatics with guns and any number of dupes behind them ready to die for the "revolution" (realistically: to keep the gang in power) [.] The hope lies from my point of view in their having their angles rubbed off by contact with a corrupt world. If they can be reduced to a sort of "Diréctoire",[3] so much the better.

The Italian mission (Serrati etc.) have returned from Russia and don't seem as enthusiastic as good obedient revolutionaries should be.

Some French workmen went to the U. S. recently. When their ship, returning, stopped at the Azores, they expressed their pleasure at "being in a civilised country once more."

America—Russia, the two hateful extremes. How aesthetically delightful is moderation. If people would only use the Liberal Fiction (or Lie, if you like) instead of resorting to Capitalist & Socialist logical truths, I think it would improve their tempers.[4]

I would like to apply ice-bags to the fevered heads of Judge Gary[5] & Comrade Trotzky.

I write of politics—not worth this rather nice paper, when all is said & done. Why have I not written of Venice? And this evening was so wonderful—Palladio's white marble façade of S. Giorgio Maggiore rising sparkling out of slate-blue water—and music on the Piazza,— but I've been reading these wretched Nations the Sweeneys sent.

What are you going to do or write now?

Love—

Arthur.

1. The New York journal, edited by Oswald Garrison Villard.

2. The *Liberator,* edited by Max and Crystal Eastman, and published in New York. Russell's article, "Democracy and Revolution," appeared in two parts: *Liberator* 3 (May 1920): 10–14, and *ibid.* (June 1920): 23–25. The article was written before Russell's visit to Soviet Russia (May 11–June 16, 1920). After his visit Russell wrote the short book *The Practice and Theory of Bolshevism* (1920). In the article he had viewed international Bolshevism with optimism and some favor but expressed the belief that English moderation would allow Great Britain to attain its own form of socialism "without armed revolution." In the book he condemned Bolshevism strongly but said that its methods were probably unavoidable in Russia.

3. Le Directoire [Fr., hist.], "The Directory," the five-man body that held the executive power in France from 1795 to 1799, under the constitution of 1795.

4. Moderation: McComb was probably thinking of Russell's comments in the *Liberator* (see n. 2 above); Liberal Fiction: Russell had written: "Liberal ideals, in so far as they were genuine, depended upon a certain degree of forbearance as between man and man, a certain unwillingness to push things to extremes. Religious toleration, democracy, free speech, free press and free trade, were all of them ideals implying that the differences between different groups were not irreconcilable." The war, Russell said, had resulted

in "a confrontation of plutocracy and labor, capitalism and socialism." Russell, "Democracy and Revolution" I, *Liberator* 3 (May 1920): 10.

5. Elbert H. Gary (1846–1927), head of the U.S. Steel Corporation from 1901 to 1927. His opposition to collective bargaining led to the nationwide steel strike of 1919 in the United States.

91

[Letter and two art postcards]

Genoa, 28th July 1920

Dos,

I am very pleased with you! First, you have sent me The Rescue[1] which was exactly what I wanted. Second, you are going to Cuba & Mexico, which in itself is an admirable thing to do and in addition has the merit of being quite imprévu [;][2] lastly I shall see you in the U.S. . . .

My American address is the Rectory, Dublin N.H.[3] — write me there. The Canopic my fate is in the harbor, looking very furbished up & new, but only to-day I heard an elderly Italian gentleman say he had known her as a child.[4]

At last the Italian bourgeoisie is taking my advice and doing the "out of their own mouths" stunt. Genoa is plastered with extracts from Serrati's report on his return from Russia. The report is significant enough to make a sceptic, even of you.

The only other line to Mexico is the dear old Compañía Trasatlantica of clerical (jesuit) tendencies. From Santander. Expensive. . . .
About Vienna conditions I can't really speak with authority, having lived rather superficially there & spent much time in the galleries. But as for food even I who was rich in Austria, was glad to get back to Italy. It isn't that there isn't enough but absence of fruit & milk is amazing. Paper napkins everywhere. Table-cloths shamefully soiled. Sheets not as well cared for as one would expect. Many beggars & wounded. Much slouching & dragging of footsteps noticeable. The Jewish question shockingly in the foreground. Inflammatory posters of the Christian Socialists. — Incidents like the following common. A Jewish member of the Town Council went with his family to — — — a small place near Vienna for summer holiday. On arrival was refused a room on the ground of being a Jew, finally got one for the night it was very late — only got a plate of soup for dinner & had to return to Vienna next day.   The small country places are apparently all in the hands of the Christians who pay no attention to orders of the central gov't. — A great many Hungarians of all liberal & radical shades live as refugees

& conduct campaigns[5] in Vienna against the white gov't of Budapest. One sees their pamphlets in every book store window. One realizes V. is the gate of the East, when one hears the newsboys crying "Az Est" — "Magyar Aszág"[6] etc. The one thing I <u>did</u> do was to read the Press attentively. — the country lives utterly hand-to-mouth. — the people are immensely sympathique.[7]

But one is conscious of the break-down in small things, e.g. the facchino[8] of my hotel couldn't clean my white shoes (he hadn't any polish) — I see you laughing at me! — but such a thing would have been impossible in German Switzerland. Here are two people, both South German, living side by side & the one having been a belligerent, the other neutral, has made of them two distinct worlds. (The Viennese of course have it "all over" the others in the essentials — literature [,] theatre etc. — An abnormal number of works on erotics. a Freudian paradise. — One was given me by a Viennese to read. It was by Blüher, the founder of the Wandervogel movement.[9] The whole question centering about this movement is complicated & interesting. Perhaps you know about it. If not I'll explain in my next. — I could go on chattering for ever about Vienna. . . .

. . . You & I almost cross each other at sea. We are due Ponta Delgada[10] 12$\underline{th}$, —

Love
Arthur.

1. Conrad's new novel, published in book form in 1920.
2. [Fr.] "Unexpected."
3. See narrative, p. 41 above.
4. The British White Star *Canopic* was built in 1900.
5. Campaig——. The concluding letters are rendered by a squiggle.
6. *Az Est* and *Magyarország* (the latter one word) are Hungarian respectively for *The Evening* and *Hungary* (literally "Hungarian Country"), a morning paper.
7. [Fr.] "Likable."
8. [It.] "Porter."
9. The Wandervogel movement was begun by *Gymnasium* schoolboys in a Berlin suburb in 1896 or 1897, and it spread rapidly through Germany and Austria. Two of the motives behind it were enjoyment of nature and temporary escape from the severity of the Gymnasium. Hans Blüher (1888–1955), a German writer and philosopher, wrote several works on the movement, including a history of it (1912) and a book described by its subtitle as "a contribution to the understanding of sexual inversion" (1912).

Of this author, Roy Pascal says: "Hans Blüher was to extend his investigations of the positive role of homosexuals in the Wandervögel movement to the whole of history, and in his *Die Rolle der Erotik in der männlichen Gesellschaft* [The role of the erotic in male society] (1917–19) was to attribute to male organizations and homosexual ties the chief creative energy in Western society. Blüher's position is extreme, and represents a current more powerful after the war than before, for his book is a general onslaught on liberalism, on the equality of man and the liberation of woman. . . . Though not an anti-semite (he acknowledged a debt to Freud), and enough of an intellectual to be aware of the obsolete absurdity of the student corps, Blüher can approve their anti-semitism and that of the Wandervögel as a sign of a healthy anti-rational and anti-democratic national instinct. His book anticipates, in its sexual as well as political radicalism, the epoch of National Socialism." Roy Pascal, *From Naturalism to Expressionism: German Literature and Society, 1880–1918* (London: Weidenfeld and Nicolson, 1973), pp. 246–47.

10. Seaport in the Azores, and the largest town there.

92

[France
Summer 1920]

Arthur dear—So we will be together on the briny, seperately. Did I tell you that my boat goes to Santander, Coruña?[1] I hope it takes weeks. From Habana I shall take ship immediately to New York.

I expect to be amused and delighted by God's country, I dont know exactly why. As soon as I get there, I shall bend what few energies I have towards Persia. Anyway I cant accomplish anything in Western Europe at present—except genial and genteel stagnation. America may prove a stimulant, who can tell?

A lovely letter from you from Bergamo about the curator of the museum at Brescia[2]—parlate discretamente italiano,[3] now?

I envy you Italy.

Habana will, I imagine be a scream.

Love
Dos

We may collide in mid-ocean—Here's hoping—
address in God's Country—
214 Riverside Drive
Newyork
(Care Mrs J.R. Gordon
phone Riverside 7979

1. La Coruña, seaport in northwestern Spain.
2. McComb's letter of July 26, 1920, now damaged and not legible enough for use in this edition.
3. [It.] "Do you speak Italian fairly well. . . ?"

Letters

∽

*B*ACK IN THE UNITED STATES Dos Passos spent most of his time in New York, busying himself on a play, essays and articles and awaiting publishers' decisions on his novels.[1] He visited Cambridge in the fall of 1920 and saw friends there. McComb, who was finishing his B.A. degree at Harvard, had asked him to bring the completed manuscript of *Three Soldiers*. Dos Passos did so, and on November 20 McComb wrote him an enthusiastic letter about it. He also gave him news the Sweeneys had sent about Dudley Poore, who was still in Europe, and news of his own doings at college. Replying, Dos Passos expressed hope that he and McComb could get together around Christmas; McComb would be coming through New York on his way to Baltimore to see his family, and Dos Passos would be visiting Washington, where he had relatives. Writing again at the end of January, McComb said he had arranged to take next semester's courses in the graduate school and, taking note of Dos Passos' plan to visit Constantinople, suggested that Dos Passos meet him in Italy the next August.

By early spring Dos Passos was well launched on a writing career. His efforts to find a publisher were largely successful (though he couldn't find anyone to take "Seven Times round the Walls of Jericho"). Doran, Inc. had now accepted *Three Soldiers* and *Rosinante to the Road Again*. Allen and Unwin had published *One Man's Initiation—1917* the previous October, and Dos Passos' essays and articles already had appeared in six national periodicals: the *New Republic, Seven Arts,* the *Liberator* (successor to *Masses*), the *Dial,* the *Freeman,* and the *Nation.* When he left the United States, intending to make his way to the Near East, he had commitments for articles from the *Metropolitan Magazine* and the *New York Tribune*.[2]

In March he and E. E. Cummings boarded the Portuguese freighter *Mormugão* in New Bedford and sailed, via the Azores and Madeira, to Lisbon—a three-week-long voyage. McComb had given him Henry and Brooks Adams' *The Degradation of the Democratic Dogma* to read on the way, Dos Passos later recalled, and the book proved irritating fare:

> Cummings and I read chapters by turns. We hated the book, each for a separate reason, Cummings because it offended some Emersonian streak in his early training . . . and I, because it went against the Walt Whitman-narodnik optimism about people I've never quite lived down.[3]

After pauses in Portugal, Dos Passos and Cummings traveled about in Spain, then crossed into France, where they climbed in the Pyrenees. Later in Paris Dos Passos saw Dudley Poore again. Dos Passos worked on *Rosinante to the Road Again* in Paris, and in July he left from Venice for Constantinople on the Orient Express.[4]

Dos Passos spent part of that month in Constantinople, amid reports and scenes of starvation, fire, and assassination—and in a minor difficulty of his own. He was low on money, as the *Metropolitan Magazine* had gone out of business. Paxton Hibben, a friend who was with the Near East Relief, tried to get him a job with the N.E.R., and when unsuccessful smuggled him onto a boat bound for Batumi. From there Dos Passos went by train to Tbilisi, where he spent a week at the N.E.R. station but again could get no job with that organization. Somehow he met a Persian physician who was returning from Germany, and Hibben's Bolshevik acquaintances authorized the two of them to travel all the way to the Persian border in a railway freight car. From there Dos Passos and the physician had a wild ride by four-horse phaeton to Teheran, and from Teheran Dos Passos made his way by automobile and train to Baghdad. There he spent weeks arranging to join a camel caravan to Damascus and then waited for it to start on a trek which, after more than five weeks, reached its destination about January 1, 1922. *Three Soldiers* had been published the previous September, and the reviews were waiting for him in the Levant.[5]

After Dos Passos had sailed with Cummings in March 1921, McComb completed the school year and then left for a summer's work in Italy. Writing Dos Passos from Rome on July 8 that year, he expressed distress at missing him before he left for Constantinople and explained that it had happened through a misunderstanding. From Siena he wrote on July 20, saying that he was continuing work on a book on Francesco di Giorgio, whom he thought "the most original of the later Sienese." What were Dos Passos' plans? "If you are returning to Paris viâ Vienna," he wrote, "why I have hankerings after the city of Mozart & Schnitzler & might deflect my course thither 'if sufficient inducement offers.'" And on August 10 he answered a letter Dos Passos had sent him from Constantinople and voiced fears "in true American fashion" over Dos Passos' being in the midst of typhus, cholera, and revolution. "At any rate I fear I shan't see you in Europe," he wrote, "but the Soviet* at Cambridge will always receive you. There is an extra bed you know if the Masseys fail you." McComb visited Spain and Portugal in late August and September of 1921 before embarking for the United States.[6] There he spent a semester at Harvard completing work for an M.A. degree in fine arts. When on January 2, 1922, he wrote that he hoped for a meeting in Italy before Dos Passos returned to America, Dos Passos was still in the Near East.

———————

93

> ^c/o Mrs J. R. Gordon[1]
> 214 Riverside Drive
> N.Y. City.
> [August 31? 1920]

Arthur—

O the dear familiar taste of water in the mashed potatos.

Habana was great.

Lovely letter from you.

Are you near Boston? I may be in Cambridge in a week or so for a while—Shall write

> Dos—

1. Dos Passos' aunt.

94

> [U.S.A.]
> Sept. 16. 1920.

Dos:—

Good news! I shall be thrilled to see you in Cambridge in October. I was there one evening recently & looked up the Masseys[1] but they

———

*A house where McComb and some other elegant Harvard men lived. For a fuller description see Letter 100, n. 16 below.

were out of town. Cambridge is shocking. My address is 7 Holyoke Place. Don't forget it & look me up on your arrival. . . .

Please bring for my pleasure all your verse manuscript that you have done since our parting at the Tayá.[2]

Three Soldiers is in the agent's hands I suppose. If ever a complete type-written copy appears, you may remember I expressed a wish to read it. The last part I don't know. Much of what I said about the looseness of the first might have to be modified, if I got a chance to read it to myself. I was and am, such a bad listen. By the way, candidly, I think you might improve the title. . . .

. . . The Scholles are steeped in conjugal felicity, — Mehitabel, Methusaleh (the macaw) et al.[3] Flourishing. They are 'dears' and they are graceful in their way, gliding over the polished surface of things. . . .

A rivederci
Arthur.

1. See Letter 60, n. 5. above.
2. Tayá Line S.S. *Capitán Revuelta.*
3. See Letter 60, including n. 4, above.

95

7 Holyoke Place
Cambridge · Nov. 20. 1920.

Dear Dos: —

Soon I shall send back your novel. It really is an advantage to read it consecutively. I think myself that some typographical or mechanical division of the thing into 3 parts would enable the scheme to be clearly grasped at the outset—I mean the three points of view do form convenient divisions, but you may not agree. I still think the Andrews[1] part the most interesting. With regard to the the[2] end I expected you were to have him get to Spain. I would have been interested in the re-actions of someone thus suddenly transferred to peace & liberty. I'm not pleading for a 'happy ending' of course. The present one is v. effective in its way but for a moment reminded me disagreeably of Galsworthy's Justice.[3] But really the thing is superb—you must write me about the publishers.

The Sweeneys have heard from Dudley[4] who seems to be planning Italy. . . .

I am now engaged on a paper on that fascinating person the Maître de Flémalle. I'm making a real "contribution to learning", because I'm going to talk for the first time about that primitive that the Bynes[5] discovered near Burgos and which that little man Angel Sanchez-Rivero[6] wrote about in España and which shows unmistakeable Flémalle characteristics though also puzzling in some ways. I expect Sachs[7] will be pleased. . . .

It was very good to see you. I expect to be in N.Y. in one mo.

Love

A.

1. John Andrews, the major character in *Three Soldiers*. At the end of the novel, military police seize him as a deserter from the U.S. Army.

2. "regard to the" inserted with caret between "With" and "the end."

3. John Galsworthy's play, published in 1910.

4. Dudley Poore.

5. Arthur Byne (1883–1935) and Mildred (Stapley) Byne (1875–1941), an American couple living in Spain who wrote many books on the Spanish arts. McComb's "Notes," i.e. diary, (December 12, 1919, and January 16, 1920) records his having tea with them in Madrid.

6. Perhaps Angel Sánchez Rivero (1888–1930), author of *Los grabados de Goya* (Goya's engravings) (Madrid, 1920).

7. Paul Joseph Sachs (1878–1965), art teacher and collector of drawings. He retired from Wall Street banking in 1914, and was assistant professor of fine arts at Harvard, 1917–22, and later professor there.

96

[New York

November? 1920]

Cher Arthur—

Merci[1]... (why I start in French I dont know)—Thanks for sending Drei Soldaten[2] back so soon.

What do you mean—exactly by a typographical division—? Different colored inks! 1 & 2 to make <u>first</u> part + 3 <u>second</u> and 4, 5, & 6 <u>third</u>. That is an idea. Maybe I'll do it. Still I dont want to emphasize personality too much.

Those autumn days in Cambridge were very pleasant to me—walks by the river on the banks of which the immortal Lief son of Erik built his house in Vineland—goings into town—nibblings of toast in your charming room in the company of you and your gentle fair haired roommates. When I got back I felt like a ghost yanked back to his coffin by the decree of Rhadamanthus[3] after a pleasant wandering in a half forgotten Elysium.

After all Harvard is much like a dusty superannuated Elysium—the corner of a garden somehow left when the park was cut up into lots—, and the dwellers in it ghosts of ghosts.

Tell Hardinge & Betty[4] how very delightful I found them and their house and their Methuselah and their improbable infant and their Guatemala primitive and all things appertaining to them. I think of all the people I know they are the most <u>perfect</u>.

Write me about the Maitre de Flémalle. O Arthur I think that you too have found your harbor. Guirded about with primitives—not wrack nor ruin nor Bolsheviki nor Rockerfellers can disturb your equilibrium. γνοθί αυτοῦ.[5]

New York is vapid and grimy. Still there are seals in the Aquarium and a Syrian restaurant near the battery where I eat every noon eggplant mashed in sesame oil, and a brownish omelet with nuts in it— Love to the Gazelle[6]

Shall see you soon—

Love
Dos

I expect today a pronouncement from Huebsch[7] on TS. Have a hunch that he'll turn it down—
I shall be going up to Washington a few days before Christmas   When do you go through New York? We'll see each other here and also I hope in Washington—as its only an hour from Baltimore[8]—
Have broken into the Nation[9]—

Dos

1. [Fr.] "Thank you."
2. [Ger.] "Three Soldiers."
3. [Gr. mythology] One of the judges of the dead.
4. Scholle.
5. [Gr.] "Know thyself." Properly written γνῶθι σεαυτόν.
6. George Locke Howe.
7. B. W. Huebsch, the New York publisher.
8. McComb's father was canon of the Cathedral of the Incarnation in Baltimore from 1916 to 1922.
9. "America and the Pursuit of Happiness," *Nation* 111 (December 29, 1920), 777–78.

97

2174 Wyoming Ave
Washington D.C.
[December 1920?]

Arthur—

I must see you cher connoisseur en les ennuies pales et douces, en les maitres de la peinture siennoise et en les jardins silencieusement abandonnés aux mousses parfumées de la futilité[1] — 1   to see you and talk   2   because there are buzzings of departure in the air. Isn't it ridiculous? I may go half against my will to Ireland — then great intrigues Persiawards are under way.

I am in Washington at the above address — Shall come to Baltimore to see you Sunday — or will you come here. Also you must stop a short time in New York on your way back. I have part of an apartment.

Drop me a note —

Dos

Best wishes to Carroll[2] & his mother —

1. [Fr.] "Dear connoisseur of pale and soft anxieties, of masters of Sienese painting, and of gardens silently given over to the fragrant mosses of futility."

2. Archer Latrobe Carroll. A.B., Harvard, 1918. In the 1920s he was a free-lance writer, a translator, and an editor for *Liberty Weekly*.

98

[New York?
January 1921?]

Dear Arthur —

It was pleasant to get your note.

I haven't written because I am newsless.

Shall probably fly the coop in a month or so.

The publication of [Ideograph of three soldiers follows.] is not a whit nearer.

Chances of publishing a collection of essays on Spain seem fairly good — Ya veremos.[1] Rosinante to the Road Again — is the title.

Irish business all up the flue.

Maybe I'll see you in Urbino — some time. Do write a difinitive opus on Francesco di Giorgio.[2]

Write me. It's hellishly cold these days.

Have started a short novel[3] — that advances with snail slowness.

Love
Dos

Love to the perfect Scholles — tell them how much I admire them.

1. [Sp.] "Well, we'll see."

2. Francesco di Giorgio (1439–1502), painter, sculptor, architect, engineer. He was one of the major Sienese fifteenth-century artists.

3. *Streets of Night*.

Dear Arthur –

It was pleasant to get your note.

I haven't written because I am newsless

Shall probably fly the coop in a month or so.

The publication of [ideograph] is not a whit nearer.

Chances of publishing a collection of essays on Spain seem fairly good. Ya veremos. Rosinante to the Road Again — is the title.

Ideograph of *Three Soldiers*, in letter by Dos Passos. (See Letter 98.)

99

[Cambridge?]
January 29ᵗʰ 1921.

Dos: —

I was glad to get your note and on visiting the Masseys yesterday I found myself treated to a further scrap which specified Constantinople as your objective. I'm rather glad you're not going to Ireland, after all. The whole problem there is tiresome and Constantinople is still Mahommedan and has a glamour. Why not make a grand tour and meet me in Urbino — (there are wonderful Uccellos you haven't seen)¹ in August? — What of Dudley, his plans and address? . . .

I've been reading Berenson's attack on Leonardo.² I recommend it especially to you. He leaves only the unfinished Adoration in the Uffizzi for admiration — dwells on Leonardo's responsibility for these disastrous things, chiaroscuro and contrapposto,³ which ruined European Paintings. Also B.B.'s little book "A Sienese Painter of the Franciscan Legend"⁴ — a comparison of Giotto's treatment with that of Sassetta,⁵ much to the deserved advantage of the latter — is very worth while.

Rosinante and the Road Again — let me know of its Progress. Far and away the best title you have found for anything yet. I like it much. What's the new novel about? — and I haven't read the end of "The Moon is a Gong."⁶

I've arranged most beautifully my courses for next half-year in the Graduate School. . . .

Well, to you in the outside world all this must seem childish. I stop. Let me know about your publishing experiences and the steamer you are going on etc. —

Love — A.

. . . .

1. Paolo Uccello (c. 1396–1475), Florentine painter. See Letter 114, n. 12 below. McComb is referring to Uccello's predella *The Profanation of the Host,* which is, alas, revoltingly anti-Jewish. In one of its six scenes a Jew and his family, including a little child, are being burned alive.

2. Bernard Berenson, "Leonardo," in his *The Study and Criticism of Italian Art,* Third Series (London: G. Bell and Sons, 1916), pp. 1–37.

3. Berenson in "Leonardo" (see n. 2 above) defines *contrapposto* [It.] as "the turning of the body on its own axis."

4. Book by Berenson published in 1909.

5. Painter (c. 1400–1450) of the Sienese school.

6. Play by Dos Passos first produced in 1925. It was published, with the title *The Garbage Man,* in 1926.

100

The Fumador[1] of the Mormugão
[March? 1921]

[To McComb]

—Monday—Grey sea—sopping southerly wind—dolphins—a Catalana[2] of a certain age plays la Paloma[3] with many trills on the piano in the senhoras[4] room next door—

Card playing—discussions from the intellectual set in the corner

The Mormugão is an extraordinary boat—Started twenty four hours late from New Bedford where we suffered durance vile at the hands of a certain Miss Harris at the Elm Arch Inn—first night out stopped with terrific suddenness during Jantar[5] and began to roll—such rolls I have never seen—dishes cataracted from end to end of tables—wine upset—apples shot about like cannon balls and from outside came a sound of alarums and confusions—cries of mariners—shrieks from the steerage—The little padre at the Captains right who had been stuffing with right red cheeked heroism turned a sad pea green—the captain hurried out—people finished dinner in silent horror—while Cummings & I drank vast quantities of most excellent vinho tinto[6] and called for more of certain excellent little Portuguese pastries—After rolling fantastically for some hours we started up again—there had been nothing to it but go to bed—as one couldn't stand on one's feet—and to this moment the Mormugão has aquitted herself heroically—Excellent and enormous oily meals at 10:30 and 530—(they say those were the Romans' meal hours) coffee in the morning and chá at four and chá de noite[7] at 9—quiet and cheerful little portuguese—everything following the golden mean rather more than I should wish—but still a perfectly good way to transport oneself across the Atlantic.

Have read the Degradation of the Democratic Dogma[8]—a suggestive but I think a very shallow ill written work—marvellously expressive of the semi-education of our "intellectuals" (a pest on them) Lots of excellent ideas taken from other people and thoroughly indigested. Vulgarization again—After all—why this fuss to prove the moon isn't made of green cheese? Adams among the teachers[9] seems to me like a small child trying to frighten his schoolfellows by crying Here comes the bogey-man—I admit that the Second Law of Thermodynamics is a damn good bogey[10]—but why couldn't he have assimilated it— restated in his own terms boiled it down to the dimensions of his world—as it is its use is meaningless and pedantic. The sort of thing one might write as a thesis for the History of Science course of our dear Henderson[11] after hastily snatching a few phrases out of the bibliography—Compare Russell's superb and genuine treatment of the same subject in A Mathematical Philosophy[12]—

I suppose I'll have to read the Education[13]—O the puling timidity of those people—see the miserable little letter[14] to prefix the "entre nous"[15] tone he carries all through his essays. I can here him saying to a reporter—"Now dont you dare quote me as having said that. If you do I'll deny it"—

Best wishes to the Soviet[16]—

Love
Dos

Thanks awfully for the D of the DD. It has stimulated enough discussion to carry Cummings and me on for a fortnight!—

1. [Port.] "Smoking room."
2. [Catalan or Sp.] "Catalonian" (female).
3. "La Paloma": a Spanish song (c. 1859), known in English as "The Dove."
4. Senhora [Port.], "lady."
5. [Port.] "Dinner."
6. [Port.] "Red wine."
7. [Port.] Chá: "tea"; —de noite: "evening tea."
8. Henry Adams, The Degradation of the Democratic Dogma (1919), a volume of his "philosophical remains," ed. by his brother Brooks Adams, who provided the title as well as a very long introduction.
9. The bulk of Henry Adams' material in the book consists of his 127-page A Letter to American Teachers of History. He had printed the Letter at his own expense in 1910 and distributed it to a list of history professors and educators.
10. However, William James (see Letter 19 above), one of the recipients of A Letter to American Teachers of History, had not been frightened. Replying to Henry Adams on June 17, 1910, James argued: "Though the ultimate state of the universe may be its vital and psychical extinction, there is nothing in physics to interfere with the hypothesis that the penultimate state might be the millennium—in other words a state in which a minimum of difference of energy-level might have its exchanges so skillfully canalisés that a maximum of happy and virtuous consciousness would be the only result." The Letters of William James, ed. by his son Henry James, 2 vols. (Boston: Atlantic Monthly Press, 1920) 2: 346.
11. Lawrence Joseph Henderson (1878–1942), assistant professor of biological chemistry at Harvard, 1910–19; later Lawrence Professor of Chemistry. Dos Passos took his introductory course "History of Physical and Biological Sciences" in 1915–16.
12. Bertrand Russell, Introduction to Mathematical Philosophy (1919).
13. The Education of Henry Adams, privately printed, 1907; published posthumously, 1918, the year of the author's death.
14. "The Tendency of History," a reprint of Henry Adams' presidential letter to the American Historical Association (1894), in The Degradation of the Democratic Dogma, pp. 125–33. Henry Adams' letter dwelt on the crisis which discovering the laws of historical evolution would pose. Powerful social organizations which saw themselves threatened would endeavor to suppress the science of history. "If it [the new science] pointed [e.g.] to a socialistic triumph it would place us in an attitude of hostility toward existing institutions." In his conclusion, Henry Adams wrote thus of the dilemma which would be posed when threatened institutions sought to suppress the new science: "If such a crisis

should come, the universities throughout the world will have done most to create it, and are under most obligation to find a solution for it. I will not deny that the shadow of this coming event has cast itself on me, both as a teacher and a writer; or that, in the last ten years, it has often kept me silent where I should once have spoken with confidence, or has caused me to think long and anxiously before expressing in public any opinion at all. Beyond a doubt, silence is best. In these remarks, which are only casual and offered in the paradoxical spirit of private conversation, I have not ventured to express any opinion of my own; or, if I have expressed it, pray consider it as withdrawn. The situation seems to call for no opinion, unless we have some scientific theory to offer. . . ." Quotations, pp. 130 and 133 respectively.

15. [Fr.] "Just between us."

16. "Ironic name for the residence of some elegant young Harvard men." The house, at 7 Holyoke Place, Cambridge, has since been torn down (McComb's notes to his letters from Dos Passos). Poore remembers the house as a big one with many rooms, on an attractive, quiet street, and says that a number of friends must have taken a lease on it (telephone interview with Poore, October 4, 1975). McComb lived at 7 Holyoke Place; so also did George L. Howe, according to the *Harvard University Register, 1920–21.*

101

[Cambridge?]
May 17th 1921.

Dos:—

Its very like you to be in Salamanca. It worried you that Dudley had got there.[1] Berenson when he was here mentioned paintings by Dello Delli[2] in the old Cathedral (?) at Salamanca. Did you see them? . . .

I enclose review in New Republic of One Man's Initiation[3] which you may not know of. It will be good for the Drei Soldaten.

Poor G. Bartlett[4] has been ill with heart-trouble and died suddenly last night. I had not seen him since returning to America. He was such a gentle urbane person. Its too bad, really. . . .

Got an offer to teach at Dartmouth (giving 2 courses in place of Prof. who is taking vacation) but I could not bring myself to it—a detestable forsaken little place full of athletes & 100% Americans, depths of winter in a New Hampshire village—no, it could not be faced, particularly as I don't intend to teach in life anyway. And I have more immediate plans and work I want to do.

Please write me before July 1 [,] c/o[5] Thos. Cook & Son, 1b Piazza di Spagna, Rome to tell me your plans—

Love
Arthur

You musn't forget to tell me about the Azores. I only know Ponta[6] & want your impressions—have always been curious about the others. And I want to know about Paris & its "Monthly" inhabitants, and about any new places you go to. I will repay you with showers of post-cards this summer.

Mrs. Gardner's[7] as usual yesterday. I am getting more & more enthusiastic about Sargeant [Sargent] water-colors, Catalan primitives, Persian miniatures, and Baroque architecture!—The Fogg[8] people tell me I should specially study Sienese sculpture this summer. Probably shall.

Too bad you missed the Monticelli[9] Exhibition and the Morgan miniatures.[10] Monticelli's sultry fantasies have long fascinated me. . . . I've cut down on "outside" reading almost entirely, but one can't afford to miss Strachey's[11] delicious "Queen Victoria" which is coming out partially in the New Republic & later as book.

As for the Deg. Dem. Dog.—I'm glad it provoked discussion & will make you read Education. I looked at it again in light of your criticism and do not agree that its ill-written. The ideas were not meant to be first hand and one can't state the $2^{\underline{d}}$ law more clearly or pertinently. I think he did boil it down to the dimensions of his own world, not to say to the dimensions of the Adams family. I take exception also to your remark "why all this fuss to prove the moon isn't made of green cheese?" Really now the answer is simple. So many people still think it is made of green cheese and its delightfully exciting to think that its really extinct at −270° Fahr.

Don't you think the intellectual fun of the thing worth it?—I think its a creditable way of passing one's time on the planet. And oh dear if you had to read the nonsense and put up with the sandy aridity of American "intellectual" life for any length of time, you'd really find the Adams, absurd as they are at times (in their "family" moods rather delightfully absurd) a relief.

But are you aware that there isn't anyone here, for instance, (since your departure) with whom I am free to discuss certain ideas to their limit—there are always walls shutting out whole fields of speculation over which they never allow themselves to roam?—

But do write me more against the Adams—

Love

A.

Dig out Dudley and tell him I want to see him.

1. After Dos Passos and McComb left Madrid toward the spring of 1920, Poore made a trip to Salamanca, in western Spain, and other towns in the neighborhood.
2. Dello di Niccolò Delli (c. 1404–c. 1471), Florentine painter who worked in Spain and spent most of his life there.
3. W.H.C., Review of the English edition (1920) of One Man's Initiation—1917, New Republic 26 (May 4, 1921): 302. The American edition was published on June 23, 1922.

4. See Letter 14, n. 17 above.

5. Possibly "before July, c/o."

6. Ponta Delgada.

7. Isabella Stewart Gardner (1840–1924), Boston art collector and hostess, and an early patron of Berenson, who became her adviser and agent in purchasing paintings. She built a palatial Venetian-style villa on the Fenway as her home and the setting for her collection. The villa was later willed to Boston as a public museum, with the provision that nothing be changed.

8. Fogg Art Museum at Harvard.

9. Adolphe Monticelli (1824–86), French painter.

10. Presumably J. P. Morgan's collection. Dos Passos' short biography of the financier in *1919* refers to his miniatures. They are among the objects he "stared hard at . . . with his magpie's eyes" and then had "put in a glass case."

11. Lytton Strachey.

102

[Art postcard showing relief of girl playing double flute, from the *Ludovisi Throne*]

Rome. July 8. 1921.

Dos:—Your p.c. & teleg. this afternoon. Very distressed at not seeing you. If I had known you were sailing when I got yr. first teleg. I would have taken Express to Venice. As it is there is no time. . . . Write me your address in Turkey & when you expect to come back through. The Ludovisi reliefs[1] remain the most thrilling sculpture in Italy.—

Love   Arthur.

1. Reliefs on the so-called "Ludovisi throne" (possibly part of an altar), discovered in the Ludovisi Gardens, Rome. They are generally accepted as early classical Greek (c. 460 B.C.), perhaps made in a city in southern Italy.

103

[Letterhead: 7 Holyoke Place
Cambridge 38, Massachusetts]
November 5, 1921.

Cher Dos,

Just before leaving Lisbon I got a long telegram from Dudley saying that he was telegraphing the Red Cross in Constantinople for your whereabouts. It since appears that no answer was forthcoming but an article in the Freeman[1] seems to indicate Batum-Tiflis-Baku as your general direction—Imagine my coming down the Widener steps one night at 10 about a week after my arrival and somebody whom I didn't recognize in the dark saying "hello" and it proving to be Dudley in the flesh. The delightful person had landed that very day at noon in New York. He stayed at the "Soviet"[2] (!) a couple of days and then we found him a room in Farwell Place near the Christ-church grave-yard, not far from the famous Miss Pinkham's but quieter than that lady's establishment.

Dudley is taking 4 Fine Arts courses (I also of course)—we sit together in a back row in Post's[3] "Art and Culture of Spain" (that's the title of it) and have an awfully good time snickering like naughty schoolchildren. We also take long walks into the autumnal landscape. And in general his arrival among us is a blessing from the gods.

The Masseys and I have been collecting clippings about your Three Soldiers of course you know that the hoped-for storm has come (and corresponding sales I understand from Coöp,[4] Dunster House[5] et al.) the only trouble being that people are too engrossed with the controversy to pay the attention they ought to its quality as a literary work. The imbecilities one has to listen to, just because of your book, my dear! The Coöp has an orange-window made up of nothing else than Three Soldiers. One of the Coöp men said to Leonard Opdycke[6] the other day that he knew you when you were in college and "that you didn't seem the kind of feller to write a book like that"—Leonard though disapproves of your work.—March Wheelwright [,] Jack's[7] brother who was in the army started it, thought he wasn't going to like it, then sat up till the small hours 2 nights in succession reading it and the third night went in town & got drunk!—"A damned-good book, but it ought to be suppressed"—What pleased me enormously was to see that the Poems[8] are "in preparation". (I've gone through literary battles about those, of which you know nothing)

Hillyer is here & Foster Damon[9] & Sydney Fairbanks[10] (to the horror of Dudley)—all teaching English a. . . .

Dos, I'm very much thrilled with the Paris part of Three Soldiers— You have an exquisite feeling for Paris and somehow this part of the book connects up with the Monthly things (I mean the descriptive passages) and I enjoy feeling the continuity. The whole thing is tremendously readable, in spite of all I said in Madrid about its disconnected character,—I'm a little ashamed now of most of that criticism.

I'm almost certainly going to Italy in late February & would like to take Dudley along

What about you? . . .

I'm still working on F. di Giorgio. — Am also excited at present about Piero di Cosimo [,] Tiepolo.[11] The Northern primitives are in momentary abeyance.

Fashion, of course, dictates the Baroque. — Bernini & Magnasco[12] are all the rage.

Read Nicolson's <u>Verlaine</u>[13] & V. Wyck Brooks <u>America's Coming of Age</u>.[14] Both worth while.

Be good & come back soon to the arms of capitalism. — Love

A. K. McC.

1. Dos Passos, "In a New Republic," *Freeman* 4 (October 5, 1921): 81–83.
2. See Letter 100, n. 16 above.
3. Chandler R. Post (1881–1959), assistant professor of Greek and in fine arts, 1912–20; associate professor of Greek and of fine arts, 1920–23. Later Boardman Professor of Fine Arts. His writings include *A History of Spanish Painting* (12 vols.), 1930–47.
4. The Harvard Cooperative Society.
5. Dunster House Bookshop, at 26 Holyoke Street, Cambridge.
6. See Letter 14, n. 10 above.
7. John Brooks Wheelwright (1897–1940), the poet. He attended Harvard from 1916 to 1921 and was one of the residents at 7 Holyoke Place.
8. *A Pushcart at the Curb.* See Letter 124, including n. 5, below.
9. S. Foster Damon (1893–1971), Harvard, A.B., 1914; A.M., 1927. One of the people anthologized in *Eight Harvard Poets,* he became a well-known scholar and a professor of English at Brown University.
10. See Letter 35, n. 6 above.
11. Giovanni Battista Tiepolo (1696–1770), major Venetian painter of his century.
12. Alessandro Magnasco (1667–1749), Italian painter.
13. Harold Nicolson, *Paul Verlaine* (1920).
14. Van Wyck Brooks, *America's Coming-of-Age* (1915).

104

Djulfa — Persia
Aug. 27 — [1921]

Dear Arthur —

I sit without my shoes in a little whitewashed room hung with rugs, curtained with curtains that have stripes in orange and saffron and magenta, looking out across a green plain at great eroded pink and purple hills, down which whistes a vast continuous wind out of the east. Yesterday perched on a locomotive I crossed with my friend Dr. Hassan Khan[1] the iron bridge between Djulfa Russia, (I mean Soviet Republic of Adjerbeidjan) and Djulfa Persia. The contrast is so much in your line that I cannot let a day pass without writing you about it. From Tiflis it was an instructive journey — four and a half days in a boxcar — cholera. people dying of typhus on mats along the edge of the railway track—and endless processions of ruined villages, troops, armored trains—all the apparatus of this century of enlightenment—everything hideous, cruel, filfthy—birth pangs perhaps—Then when we climbed down from our locomotive we were received by bowing customs officials and taken into a little clean room with a tiled floor where stout softspoken gentlemen in black cylindrical caps with a slight buldge to them fingered our passports tenderly with brown fingers of which the nails were stained with henna. Immediatly we were invited to lunch by the chef de douane,[2] settled in this room, that opens on one side on the hills, and on the other on a court with a cistern in it. Water was brought for washing and watermelons and we were left to rest in contemplation of a carpet that had a likeness of the Shah on it. Then lunch appeared—things cooked with tomatos and cucumbers and creamy cheeses. Dr. Hassan and the chef de douane and another doctor talked Persian in low voices and I basked in the extraordinary quiet of it—this tumbling out of the strident tremendous present into the low voiced well padded past—In the corner of the room is a little squab who sits peeping contentedly under the astonished gaze of a very languid little kitten stretched out on a patch of sunlight on the carpet. You would like it here: the ceremonial cups of tea, the noiselessness of people's unshod walk—the camels stalking about, the marvellous sense of grooves well oiled, of all emergencies catered for, of a very old and very feeble and very pleasant civilization—

This letter has just been interrupted by the little gentleman of the house appearing with an enormous pale gold watermelon and a plate on which are five different varieties of grapes—each better than the last. The little gentlemen then sits himself down beside us with a very fragrant galian[3] water pipe and starts quoting Saadi[4]—The sun is getting hot and the kitten is wandering about the edge of the cistern as if it wanted a swim—the mountains are brown and grey now across the green plain.

Of the varieties of melons one could write georgics galore—melons pink, red, yellow, white and milky, dense, watery, acid, sweet, musk-scented. You should really be here.

My Odyssey thus far from Constantinople has been the following: S.S. Aventino five days to Batum via Ineboli, Samsoun, Urdu, Kerasonda, Trebisonde, two days in Batum on boat intriguing to be allowed to land. Then Batum to Tiflis in a jolly but buggy and delapidated sleeping car. In Tiflis a week at the Near East Relief Mission—full of counterrevolutionaries & ministers out of jobs. Then in a propaganda waggon from Tiflis to Erivan—the miserable ulcerated capital of

Armenia, then three box car days to Djulfa—with waits in Nachtishiwan and a frightful ruined border town between Armenia & Adjerbeijdan of which I have forgotten the name—extraordinary trip—with Ararat always in view, and people dying of typhus in the next car and being laid out on brightly colored mats beside the track.[5]

Kuma:[6] The Year of the Rabbit,[7] some days before the opening of the month of mourning for Hussein[8] Moharam—A mud village on the road from Tabriz[9] to Teheran. Third day of joggle in an unbelievable barouche drawn by four horses. One feels much like the unfortunate Phaethon[10] as the thing leaps like a flea from crag to crag, flounders like a muskrat through marshes—tears with unexpected success over trackless hillsides, all under a great searing sun that's like a lash in one's face—already my nose is an enormous and tender beet. But after a couple of hours of this tumultuous progress one always comes on a delicious valley full of violent green trees and watercourses and little moist breezes and a sound of birds singing. Then one is ushered into the Khan[11] of the village—a bare room with carpets on the floor and windows on two sides with a balcony in front of them. Then one takes off ones shoes and squats on ones hams and a samovar is brought and small glasses of tea continually refilled. Then a chicken alive and squawking is presented to Seid-Hassan and pinched and hastened to the slaughter. The head of the reformed brigands who guard the road or the mollah[12] or the owner of the khan come and drink tea with us and discuss the fate of Islam until supper appears on a large brass tray. Shilov of rice, a chicken, cheese, yoghourt, honey, butter and great quantities of delicious flat slightly corrugated bread, which serves for plate and knife & fork. Then there is more tea and cigarettes from Rasht and I roll myself up in my striped coverlet and go to sleep on a rug, or if, as is the case tonight there is reason to fear the historic & redoubtable Miameh chinches, on the roof.[13] O a most excellent existence.

Arthur! I conclude this epistle from the basé eminence[14] of the Hotel de France—Teheran. Thirteen days on the Phaeton chariot joggled somewhat of the bloom of my primal enthusiasm, but a day spent alternately in sleeping and bathing has done quite a lot to restore my sunburned fleabitten frame—in this amazing and delapidated oasis of French provincialism

Teheran is a rambling tree shaded well watered town full of little porticoes and extraordinary tile work, overhung by purplish mountains with patches of snow on them. The streets are full of carriages of ancient build in which withered and yellowed dignitaries jiggle like dry peas in a pod, and grand people on horses with flowing manes and long silky tails such as on sees in Japanese prints—and peasants with domed felt hats and their beards tinct red with henna.

Ghoda' hafes shimaum[15]

Dos

Shall probably appear in America round Christmas—What a shame to have missed you in Italy—

1. A Persian physician.

2. [Fr.] "Head of customs."

3. Kalian. Dos Passos probably wrote *galian* by ear.

4. Saadi *or* Sadi (c. 1184–1291), Persian poet and prose writer. His best-known works are the *Bustan* (Garden of fragrance) and *Gulistan* (Garden of flowers).

5. Editor's commentary: the Italian steamer *Aventino*, proceeding east, made stops at the Turkish ports of Inebolu, Samsun, Ordu, Giresun, and Trabzon before it arrived at the Georgian port of Batumi. From there Dos Passos went by train to Tbilisi, the capital of Georgia, and afterwards to Yerevan. When he traveled on southeast, Mt. Ararat was always in view. After waits in Nakhichevan (in Azerbaijan) and another town, he arrived at the border town of Dzhulfa.

6. Possibly Komi, a small village near the town of Mianeh.

7. Astrological term. An American Presbyterian missionary to Persia wrote: "As in ancient Chaldea, so now in Persia, astrology is a flourishing science. . . . They [astrologers] have the years divided into a series of twelve . . . , respectively the year of the mouse, ox, leopard, rabbit, snake, whale, horse, hog, hen, sheep, dog, and monkey. Every year has its special attributes." Samuel Graham Wilson, *Persian Life and Customs* (New York: Fleming H. Revell Co., 1895), p. 222.

8. Hussein (c. 626–80), saint and martyr of the Shiite Moslems, a grandson of Mohammed the Prophet and a son of Ali. During the first ten days of Muharram, the month of Hussein's murder, Shiites mourn his death; they sometimes engage in self-laceration.

9. Tabriz, Mianeh, and Rasht, all mentioned in the same paragraph, are in northwestern Iran. Mianeh is a town (in 1921 it was a small town) ninety miles southeast of Tabriz. Rasht is a city near the Caspian Sea.

10. [Gr. mythology] Son of Helios, the sun god. Phaëton induced his father to allow him to drive the chariot of the sun for a day but was unable to control the horses. He would have set the world on fire had not Zeus struck him down with a thunderbolt.

11. "In the East: A building (unfurnished) for the accommodation of travellers; a caravanserai." *OED*, s.v. "khan."

12. Mollah *or* mullah: "A title given among Mohammedans to one learned in theology and sacred law." The word can be traced back to Arabic. *OED*, s.v. "mullah."

13. On Mianeh, see n. 9 above. The American painter Edwin Lord Weeks, recording a journey made in 1892, wrote of Mianeh: "This is the home of the redoubtable insect of which the bite is believed to be fatal both to men and horses. We were therefore not unwilling to favor the popular superstition by encamping at some distance from the town." Weeks, *From the Black Sea through Persia and India* (New York: Harper and Brothers, 1896), p. 59.

14. Basse éminence, "low eminence," would be an oxymoron in French.

15. [Persian] "May God be your protector."

105

[Art postcard]

[Cambridge, Massachusetts]
Nov. 18.—[1921]

[To Dos Passos]
Ever since your Persian letter I have been seized with a profound dégoût for Cambridge & courses. Dudley is giving up in March & I am preceding him to Europe in February—A horrid feeling in my bones that I shall miss you again. This would not do. . . .

A. K. Mc

106

[Baghdad
November 1921]

[To McComb]
O Gentle Arthur, I sit on Tigris bank and sadly absorb whiskeys and sodas,—nasty drink—and contemplate a silly moon dull as the bihydrochide of quinine[1] tablet I take thrice daily to chase the malaria. Baghdad, outside of certain humorous features and that horrid quality known as picturesqueness leaves me cold. The only virtue in it is that it possesses—Who shall say from what mysterious source?—a store of excellent German beer. See how insidiously the 'orrid 'uns carry on their propaganda in the Orient.

I am tired of wrangling for transport and paying hotelbills and interviewing bigbugs. I am utterly tired of writing articles on political questions. I have decided that journalism and I—even the so-called higher brand—don't jibe, and that I am wasting valuable time writing unpalatable idiocies, when I might be writing idiocies to me, at least, palatable. I am anxious to get back to conversation and good cookery. I shall retire to some quite nook and write long novels an not even be lured to a ride on the subway—travel Bah! Down with the illusion of geography. I'll have none of it. A quiet simple life among one's books ... When a man starts to swear off drinking he's in danger from John Barleycorn.

I have been here two weeks trying to arrange to caravan across the desert to Damascus. They say the route goes through the oasis of Tadmor where are the ruins of Palmyra—Pensez-y![2] But things move with heartbreaking slowness in these parts—before one can do anything one discusses it a thousand times. Then everyone assures me I'll be robbed and murdered, or at best stripped even of my pants by the Bedouins who rule supreme in those parts nowadays. Imagine me clad in a loin cloth of palm fronds riding into the American Consul's at Damascus on a mangy camel. My only real fear is that they will take my glasses. Imagine trying to find an oasis without ones specs—with the mirages too! If that seems too difficult I think the British will be kind enough to fly me over—not oversafe either—to Jerusalem.

Then having bandied about Palestine and Syria a little I shall take ship at Beirut for Marseilles, stay in Marseilles long enough eat an enormous meal of seafood and probably return by the usual prosaic route to the States.

I wonder what has happened to everybody. I haven't had a letter since July in Constantinople. Never felt more out of the world.

Love to the Cambridgites—

Dos

1. Quinine Dihydrochloride (Lat.: Chinini Bihydrochloridum).
2. [Fr.] "Think of it!"

107

[In the Syrian Desert]
Rabi-el-Thani, XIII
A.H. 1339[1]
[December 1921]

Dear Arthur—

I have just been staring at a great burnished moon through the stinging fragrant smoke of the camp fire of the caravan leader, Djassem el Rawwaf. Now I sit in my crimson tent, inset with black torch like decorations and little diamonds of pink and pale blue—and write by the light of a candle—outside is heard the bubbling of the waterpipe of Fahad the cook, and the crunching of the cuds of four hundred camels. We are seventeen days out from Baghdad on the Syrian desert, having been delayed by mud, swollen streams, Bedawi[2] trying to carry off our camels and the compassion of Allah—I have an almost reputable beard & am beginning to be admired by the outfit in consequence. I wear a black handkerchief on my head, held on by a black fillet of camel's hair, and a sort of burnous of brown and white-striped wool— All my life is merged into camels. The water tastes of camel, the rice is flavoured with camel, all night the groaning and bubbling and chewing and crunching of camels crowded about my tent lulls me to sleep, all day I ride a light colored beast named Malek, who has charming eyelashes and who wiggles his ears when I sing to him—her rather— Who could do justice to the excellence, sensitiveness, disdain, discretion, disgust, hauteur, insouciance, disapproval, condescension, snobbishness, gluttony, foiled pride, satisfied ambition, thirst, boredom, arched eyebrows, hushdope—expressed by Malek in the course of a day's slouching long-striding journey—? The whole beast is expressive from the cleft tip of his wobbly lips to the little bunch at the end of his tail. To have known intimately a camel makes worth while any delays, lingerings, supperless days, wet feet I may have undergone in getting myself in on this caravan.

Damascus [January 1922] After a legendary and rather Biblical forty days[3] I arrived in Esch Scham lustful after baths and food and warmth. Since then I have done nothing but bathe and eat, wobbling on chilblained feet, extraordinarily sore in the groin from the pommel of my saddle, from cookshop to cookshop in the bazaars, where I gorge on pastries made of honey and sour cream, and on extraordinary messes of vegitables stewed in deliciously rank-flavored olive oil. Battered but triumphant like the old black bull in the song. Damascus is rather like Granada—full of watercourses and built against a saffron streaked hill. The bazaars are full of great radishes and crisp lettuces and leeks and the moist chilly air has that wonderful tang of winter that Dudley so loves.

The reverse of the medal is the table d'hôte at the Hotel Victoria—where I scowl with what scorn you can imagine at the long row of silent suspicious masticating jowls—after shivering in splendor of a camel's back in a robe embroidered with gold and sky blue and dipping my right hand[4] into the ricepot of many a Bedouin sheikh.

Where are you going to be Arthur—? I am rushing pell mell towards civilization and I hope towards the company of the elect—avid for warm quiet rooms into which through a faint haze from teacups shall seep long violet twilights—and long mornings writing a thundering
    ¡ojalá!
(inshallah)[5] splintering novel against futilitarianism, and messy vehement dinners.

Write Morgan Harjes—

Love

Dos

A note by McComb written alongside the close of this letter says: "This was forwarded by Mother from America and reached me in Vienna end April 1922."

1. Moslem calendar. Dos Passos' date is incorrect, as it converts to December 25, 1920.

2. Bedouins. Dos Passos is using the singular of the Arabic word. Historically the adaptation of the word into Latin and French led to a confusion of singular and plural forms. *OED*, s.v. "Bedouin."

3. Thirty-six days according to his journal.

4. "Many Arabs will not allow the left hand to touch food, because it is used for unclean purposes. . . ." *Encyclopædia of Religion and Ethics* (1908–27), vol. 6, p. 492, s.v. "hand."

5. Ojalá [Sp.], "God grant." Inshallah [Arabic], "if God wills."

108

[Art postcards]

[Cambridge]
2 January 1922.

Dos:—Getting back from New York late on the night of the last day of the year, your letter was found waiting—stamped with the name of a country I had never heard of [.] Iraq indeed![1]—You are taking strides America-wards I must admit. But what is this talk of aeroplanes?—Are there no more magic carpets in the city of the khalif?—You disappoint me. Although I suppose now that the unbeliever has camped in Bagdad things are not as they were. Yet Allah is great.

Your dégout for travel comes at an inopportune moment—your letter heartens the forces of reaction (by which is meant the Hillyer-F. Damon school of "live in Pomfret or Dedham" devotees.[2] "I have no curiosity about Europe" they say [;] hah, indeed—well I have—am sailing actually on Feb. 16 for Napoli. Think of the joy!—Its high time that I left Harvard. Dudley,[3] too, follows perhaps in March. Stewart[4] goes to Italy in the spring. You had better come. Paris is démodée. Sail from Italy for America—you will be returning to fame and riches.

Listen, amigo mio, when you are through with business in N.Y. come back to Italy—lets all rent an appartment or something—come & go as we please, you & Dudley & I & all write furiously. I have to bring out my thing on F. di G.[5]—My address will be c/o Am. Express [,] Piazza di Spagna & in Naples Hotel Continental

Love   Arthur.—

1. The area constituting Iraq was part of the Ottoman Empire at the outbreak of World War I. It became a British administered League of Nations mandate in 1920 and (although remaining a mandate) a kingdom in 1921.

2. References to Robert Hillyer and S. Foster Damon. Dedham is in Massachusetts; Pomfret is in Connecticut. Dos Passos was at this time writing to Hillyer at a Pomfret address, but the letters were usually being forwarded to Boston.

3. Dudley Poore.
4. Stewart Mitchell.
5. Francesco di Giorgio.

109

Beirut—Jan 7—'22

Arthur—

Some letters from you were an amazing comfort among the hideous amount of sheer merde[1] I found waiting for me here. They gave one a feeling of the orderly search after well lighted well modulated spaces. I knew you'll like Palma. Because, Arthur, you're a sort of Mallorca— pullida Majorca[2]—in this idiotic blathering world.

Write me your plans to Paris at once. By gosh I wont miss you this time—

Dos

Make Dudley tell what he is going to do—apply the rack if necessary—From here to Marseille then Paris and New York—

1. [Fr.] "Shit."
2. Pulida [Sp.], "neat; polished." Mallorca [Sp.], "Majorca." Dos Passos began to write "pullida Mallorca," then crossed out *Mallor——* and substituted *Majorca.*

Letters

✑

*A*NXIOUS TO MEET Dos Passos when he returned from the Near East, McComb wrote from America on January 2, 1922, that he was sailing for Naples on February 16. Somehow hopes for a meeting went awry again. Dos Passos was in Paris by February 8, then he went to England, and from there he sailed to the United States.[1] Arriving in New York he found himself a celebrity. *Three Soldiers* had provoked a national controversy about World War I and military service, and the publisher, Doran, Inc., wanted him to make personal appearances. But Dos Passos found the task disagreeable, and as he was working on his novel *Streets of Night* and revising his play *The Moon Is a Gong,* he also found it distracting.

Dudley Poore was at Harvard, having returned from Europe in the fall of 1921 and gone directly there to work for an M.A. degree in art history. When Dos Passos found his life in New York too hectic, he went to Cambridge for several weeks and took a room at 19 Farwell Place, where Poore lived. Later, in the spring, the two were in New York, and it was probably then that Dos Passos wrote McComb his spoof about the discovery of a painter Lugubrio dei Funghi (see Letter 117 below). Poore's parents were renting a house in Skaneateles, New York, near picturesque Lake Skaneateles, one of the Finger Lakes, and that summer Dos Passos spent several weeks there with Poore; and in the fall the two had adjoining apartments at 3 Washington Square in Greenwich Village, subletting them from Elaine Thayer (née Orr), the future Mrs. E. E. Cummings.[2]

When Dos Passos developed eye trouble and couldn't work, he went to North Carolina for a rest and stayed with Frederik van den Arend's, or Van's, family. (Van den Arend had gone to work in the import-export business and moved to Madagascar.) Dudley Poore in January 1923 left the United States to join his parents in Italy, and Dos Passos wrote McComb that Poore was on his way there. His letters made cryptic references to a romance of his own and possible marriage. In March 1923 Dos Passos sailed to Le Havre on the *Roussillon*. His letter to McComb written aboard ship shows him planning to write *Manhattan Transfer* "as soon as everything is sufficiently blotted out." After a stay in France, Dos Passos headed for Rome, and there he, Poore, and McComb spent some time together. Poore was returning to America, but before he went Dos Passos and he walked in the Volscian hills; and then Dos Passos and McComb spent a week looking at art in Florence. Towards the end of April Dos Passos wrote Mrs. Sweeney that he was walking alone in the Eastern Apennines. August found him in Spain, where he visited his old friend Pepe Giner Pantoja; and on August 30 he embarked for New York, intending to work on *Manhattan Transfer*.[3]

110

[Picture postcard: "Afrique Occidentale: Jeune Fille de Dakar." Photograph of smiling native girl with bare bosom]

[Paris?
February? 1922]

Arthur—I'm awfully annoyed at missing you this way—And I am going to stay in America at least the period of the writing of two novels—I'm very much excited about your œuvre. Do knock Mr. B. [Bernard Berenson] into a cocked hat. A delightful old 1st engineer on the S.S. Gergovia gave me this card. Bet you don't know the G's pedigree. she was on her last voyage[1]—Love Dos

1. The *Gergovia* was a 1,981 ton screw-propelled iron steamship with two decks. She was built in 1883 by Scott & Co., in Greenock, Scotland. When she first appeared in Lloyd's Register of Shipping in 1884–85, her owner was the Compagnie Française de Navigation, her port of registry Marseilles, and her flag French. Lloyd's Register reported the same port of registration and flag in 1924–25, when it noted that the *Gergovia* had been broken up. Information courtesy of Lloyd's Register of Shipping.

111

[19 Farwell Place
Cambridge
March 1922]

[To McComb]
Cambridge is full of traces of you, Arthur. Desolate is the Merle,[1] lonely the whispering gallery at the Cock horse,[2] joyless the Soviet.[3] Really

it was too bad that we should have missed each other again this way. It must not happen another time.

Dudley and Van and I were in Naples in March 1918. Do go to Ravello and round the sea road to Amalfi—

My glimpse of Palermo and your two cards of Naples (not the pictures but the text)—have sorely tried my determination to stay for several centuries in this delightful country—Really I've never found it so amusing. Dudley and I have taken to going to burlesque shows and have a wonderful time. And the daily papers are a joy—ladies poisoning themselves amid hilarious supper parties in Back Bay.[4] Millionaire Bootleggers' Thrilling Chase by Police. Ten Drink Shellac. When arrested Mother Macree proved impenitent when branded as a murdress by our reporter. They only paid 49[c.] for it was her only defense.

Milkmaid Disembowelled[5] Latest CrimeWave Development. Jersey City Tragedy. and so on ad infinitum.

I am living for a week or two in a delicious upstairs room at Dudley's place. I sit at a little square table and try to work and my next which has been started for at least eighteen months and deals with a certain Miss Nancibel Taylor and two gentleman friends, proceeds with heartbreaking slowness.[6] Then we'll probably both go down to New York. Have seen the Scholles and your two delightful roommates, also J. Wheelright,[7] L. Apdyke[8] et al. at a teafight at the Soviet.

Am sending you Rosinante.[9]

Do send full accounts of your doings and accounts of the great "Cheko"[10]

O how passionately and overwhelmingly it must be spring where you are

Love

Dos

1. Shop with soda fountain, at 1276 Massachusetts Avenue, opposite Widener Library. One could get coffee and sandwiches at the Merle.

2. See Letter 1, n. 4 above on this restaurant. "Whispering gallery" is Dos Passos' reference to its genteel atmosphere.

3. See Letter 100, n. 16 above.

4. A fashionable Brahmin district of Boston.

5. *Disembowelled* may be the last word of the headline. There is a page break between *Disembowelled* and *Latest*.

6. Nancibel Taylor is a leading character in *Streets of Night*.

7. John Brooks Wheelwright. See Letter 103, n. 7 above.

8. Leonard Opdycke. See Letter 14, n. 10 above.

9. Published March 18, 1922.

10. Possibly a reference to the Soviet at 7 Holyoke Place, Cambridge. (The Cheka was the Soviet Russian secret police from 1917 to 1922.) The quotation marks around *Cheko* make it unlikely that it is a miswriting of *Auk s* (cf. Letter 19 above).

112

Roma   9 March. [1922]

Dos,

I have your card written in Paris about a month ago, I gather. I feel so melancholy at missing you. Particularly because I feel I've been a little out of touch with you this last year. I know about your physical movements but I'd like awfully to know where you are now, politically & economically speaking, after your tour in the unfortunate parts of the world.

And I'd like to know how soon A Puschart at the Curb is expected to be out. Also Rosinante. Also whether you've done anything with

(1) Fibbie.[1]

(2) The Moon is a Gong.

(3) with a novel which Latrobe[2] said you'd started in N.Y.— I suppose two novels at your rate will not take more than a year,—if I have enough money[3] I'll visit America at that time, if not I'll linger in Europe.   I wish Dudley might persuade you to return to Europe. Travel is <u>not</u> an illusion (though it may be in the East.)

I'll be here till May, then I shall go pretty directly to Vienna. Address me here ᶜ/ₒ Cook's. —

My oeuvre as you are good enough to call it is likely to be as dry as an educator cracker. According to the latest it may be published in parts in the Am. Journal of Archaeology—however it isn't nearly finished and I'm too busy at the moment with other things to attend to it.

What do you know of Michelangelo Anselmi of Lucca?[4]—

I suppose you know a lot of Arabic and a deal about Hafiz,[5] the Koran, the Moghul School of miniatures, damasks of Ispahans, the Sufi heresy, the habits of the camel, the Turkish mosques of the VIII c. etc. but Dudley I trust will show you that we, too, have not been idle in the Kultur-competition!

Love

Arthur.

1. "Seven Times round the Walls of Jericho."
2. Probably Archer Latrobe Carroll. See Letter 97, n. 2 above.
3. McComb had a Bacon Traveling Fellowship from Harvard for two years, 1922–23, according to one of his curricula vitae.
4. Italian painter (1491–1554), born in Lucca, who settled and resided chiefly in Parma.
5. Persian lyric poet (d. about 1390).

113

[Art postcard: *Marriage of the Virgin,* by Lorenzo da Viterbo, in the Mazzatosta Chapel, S. Maria della Verità, Viterbo]

Viterbo   March 14.—[1922]

Dos:—You who are so moved by frescoes take note. Lor. da V.[1]—is quite at the height of Benozzo[2]—color even more interesting—extra-ordinary for a provincial. As for Viterbo, I am in reaction against the Fogg worship of small, shabby Central Italian towns (no, the hotel is excellent so it isn't that) and now I'm all for the great centres of Italian life, (following Dudley in this)—I mean Rome, Naples, Palermo, Milan (can't go as far as to say Turin)   Return to Rome tomorrow.
   Be good. Avoid radicals.

A. K. McC.

1. Lorenzo da Viterbo (c. 1437–76), Viterbo's leading painter in the fifteenth century.
2. Among those influencing the work of Lorenzo da Viterbo was Benozzo Gozzoli (1420–97), Florentine painter and student of Fra Angelico. Benozzo painted the *Procession of the Magi* (fresco) in the Medici-Riccardi Palace, Florence.

114

[New York
Spring 1922]

Arthur carisimo[1]—

Indeed it was rotton our missing each other—We must have high festivals before long to make up.
   Now for your questions:
   Pushcart—will come out in August I think.
   The first part of Fibbie—written in cahoots with Robert H.[2] has gone back to him and he is going to make out of it a tale of the spirit world, I believe. The remaining fragments are going to be welded into a new synthetic sympomatic sublimated synchonated syncopated sub-versive symphonic and somewhat subrosally sexual romance of the underworld the midworld and the upperworld possibly to be entitled The Man in the Mirror or something of the sort (put in your orders early) adv.
   The M. is a G.[3] is to be rewritten this summer: There is a little man in Chicago who wants to do it—if he gets together money enough to start a repertory theatre. Doran will probably publish it eventually.

What the novel Latrobe[4] said I had started in New York is I cant imagine—There is a very ancient thing that used to be called Streets of Night on which I am at present working most laboriously—talk about stale flat and unprofitable[5]—its a very garbage pail of wilted aspirations—and largely concerned with that futilitarianism I rejoice to see you abandoning more and more.

3 soldiers has produced 8000 iron men—Never had so much in my life—though I owe about 2500 of it. At any rate it will solve the question of the next trip to foreign parts when that question arises. Also I shant write any more damn fool little articles until I am broke again.

And who is Michelangelo Anselmi of Lucca? Sounds like brown gravy and chiaro[6]-obscured to me.

Dudley I find knows a most dreadful lot about Romanesque sculpture and has pictures of inconceivable things.

We are both at present at 45 Barrow Street in Greenwich Village (but not of it) and live in rapt contemplation of a photo drawing by Antonio Pollaiuolo that's in the Fog.[7]

I spent several delightfully placid weeks at 19 Farwell Place—The Soviet[8] was charming. I had no idea George Roberts[9] was so very much of a person—We dined and wined at the Parthenon the Posilipo and Hung Loo Foo (or some such) a delicious Cantonese place where every dish was as perfect as a poem by Po Chui translated by Waley.[10] Also Dudley and I went to eat private lobster at the old oyster house.[11] It was delightful even if one did feel like a hant and even if everybody talked about the same things they used to talk about seven years ago— New York is grimy hectic and rather thrillingly gruff with springtime.

I envy you Viterbo.

I have registered a vow to learn all about and see all the paintings of the scientists—Pollaiuoli, Ucello [,] Castagna, Masaccio, Buffalmacho and della Francesca[12] & pupils before many years spin round the barberpole. Have suddenly become all reexcited about them—via the Antonio P. drawing.

But I must answer some letters asking me to speak to women's clubs—O qué vita[13]—

Drink down a cup of honey colored Roman sunlight and drive on the via Appia—and sip a glass of gold wine of Frascati for me—

Write fully

Dos

As for I radicali—I can't see 'em for nuts.[14]

1. Carísimo [Sp.], "very dear" (usually in the sense of very expensive). Dos Passos may have had the Italian word *carissimo,* "very dear," in mind. Its use in a salutation is a common Italian expression of affection.

2. Robert Hillyer.
3. *The Moon Is a Gong.*
4. Probably Archer Latrobe Carroll.
5. Shakespeare, *Hamlet,* act 1, sc. 2, line 133.
6. [It.] Chiaro, "light."
7. Fogg Art Museum at Harvard. For Pollaiuolo, see n. 12 below.
8. The Soviet was at 7 Holyoke Place. On 19 Farwell Place, see p. 185 above.
   9. George Brooke Roberts (Harvard, A.B. summa cum laude, 1922), another resident of 7 Holyoke Place. Grandson and namesake of a president of the Pennsylvania Railroad, he became a Philadelphia architect.
   10. Po Chü-i (772–846 A.D.), Chinese poet. Arthur Waley (1889–1966), an Englishman, was an influential translator from the Chinese and Japanese.
   11. Old oyster house, close to Faneuil Hall, by the Boston market. The Posillipo and the Parthenon (both mentioned in the same paragraph as the oyster house) were also in Boston. The Posillipo was an Italian restaurant; the Parthenon was a Greek restaurant, up a flight of stairs. Telephone interview with Dudley Poore, August 15, 1976.
   12. Antonio Pollaiuolo (c. 1433–98), his brother Piero Pollaiuolo (1443–96), Paolo Uccello (c. 1396–1475), Andrea del Castagno (c. 1423–57), Masaccio (1401–28?), and Buffalmacco (first half of the fourteenth century) were all Florentines. Piero della Francesca (c. 1420–92), who did some work in Florence, was from Borgo San Sepolcro. The sense in which Dos Passos uses the term *scientists* suggests Berenson's comments on Uccello's and his successors' studying anatomy and perspective and attempting "to reproduce objects as they are." Bernard Berenson, *The Florentine Painters of the Renaissance* (New York: G. P. Putnam's Sons, 1909), pp. 33–40. The quotation is on p. 40.
   13. Qué vida [Sp.], che vita [It.]: "what a life."
   14. I radicali [It.], "the radicals"; for nuts (phrase used in negative contexts), "at all" (*OED* Supplement, s.v. "nut"); nuts (noun), "crazy persons."

115

Roma, 9 April 1922.

Dear Dos,

After getting post-cards from Palermo and Paris, months old and having no relevancy to anything going on now, it was good to get your note from Cambridge. . . .

I'm green with jealousy of you and Dudley, and I not with you. So glad you're enjoying America—it's a great country. Even in Rome I buy the N.Y. Herald every day to get the tit-bits. I particularly rejoice in the bits on 'sex.'—i.e.

Tornado revivalist predicts next war due to Women's bare knees. . . .

While on the subject of newspapers, I enclose some clippings—the one about Conrad because of its information on what he's doing and the Villard[1] one because it was a sort of camel's straw as far as I'm concerned, in my attitude to American liberals. Of all the fatuous, sentimental patriotic bunk—

I don't go in much for labels in these latter days, but Stewart[2] not long ago used the phrase conservative-pacifist of himself and me, and it isn't so bad. —

Well, I'm afraid Miss Nancibel Taylor[3] & her gentlemen friends sounds rather improper—and delightfully American.

You're a dear to send me Rosinante. The Sweeneys write me they've received a copy from their bookseller.

In a sense the Pushcart will excite me more than anything. You know I regard your verse as the special province of my press-agent activities. Did the Persian journey produce any?

Do get Dudley to publish his garden-poems. (Don't tell him I said so—I worried him about them already)

I'm going to Florence in a few days [,] thence to Vienna. . . .

. . . I'm having a very good time, but the F. di G.[4] is progressing rather slowly. As far as Berenson's list goes, I'm revising it quite drastically.

I'm making a catalogue of the drawings of the divine Parmigianino.[5] Have you seen Liliom?[6]—

Are you going away for the summer and if so where?—I shall be in Germany.

Address me   Hotel Metropôle

Vienna.

Love—Arthur.

1. Oswald Garrison Villard (1872–1949), owner and editor of the *Nation* (New York).
2. Stewart Mitchell.
3. See Letter 111, including n. 6, above.
4. Francesco di Giorgio.
5. Francesco Mazzola (1503–40), major Italian mannerist painter, b. in Parma. The name Parmigianino derives from his birthplace.
6. Play by the Hungarian writer Ferenc Molnár, first produced in Budapest in 1909. The Theatre Guild produced it in New York in 1921.

116

[New York]

April 25 [1922]

Arthur—Such a nice letter from you—Am writing in Dudley's room at the Brevoort[1] where he is living in state. Marvellous clear sunshiny day with fifth avenue roaring under a blue sky. I've never liked this fantastic city so mucho, questo paese sotto sopra as Mario Tambulini[2] used to say last year.

About the Pushcart—really Arthur you dont know how much your admiration of it bucks me up. I've been working over it and am very low in my mind about it—lots of the things seem so fearfully washy and unintense—

Liliom was superb. I saw it in Boston. There is a new O'Niel play

'The Hairy Ape' just moved up town[3] — superb material not entirely solidified — yet very poignant.

I am trying desperately to settle and work but things keep coming up to unsettle and make me loaf — spring, the housing problem, people, publishers, aunts. And poor Miss Nancibel Taylor waits and waits — two young gentlemen have been crossing the Cambridge Bridge for some two or three weeks.

More later —

Love
Dos

1. The Hotel Brevoort, at Fifth Avenue and Eighth Street, in Greenwich Village. Built in the mid-1800s, it became a fashionable hotel noted for its cuisine. In Dos Passos' time, before and after World War I, it was a favorite gathering place for literary people and intelligentsia. It was demolished in 1954.

2. "So much, this upside-down town. . . ." *Mucho* is Spanish, or English with an Italian ending. The rest is Italian, "questo paese" for "this town" and "sotto sopra" for "upside-down." Mario Tambulini is unidentified.

3. Eugene O'Neill's *The Hairy Ape* opened first at the Provincetown Playhouse, MacDougal Street, Greenwich Village, on March 9, 1922. It opened uptown on April 17, 1922.

117

[New York
Spring? 1922]

Arthur — I have forgotten again and again to write you of our most important new discovery among the lesser known quattrocentistas. O[f] course you knew of him already. It was the mereest accident that the name did not come up in our conversation. Everyone well informed on these matters must know of him. But you have already guessed. I refer to the great neglected master Lugubrio dei Funghi (detto Il Sepulchro) whose great tryptich of the three leper saints is still preserved in the little Tuscan town of Peste, unfortunately decay and neglect have lost to us the other works of the master and the once pictured walls of the great camposanto have crumbled to dust and mould. In the existing tryptich we would be struck at once by the intensity of the pigment and the vermiform writhe of the line were it not that owing to Il Sepulchro's habit of using bitumen and mixing embalming fluid with his vermillions the tryptich, — painted on coffin boards, you know — exhibits that uniform greenish hue so cherished by amateurs of the Byzantine.[1]

Dudley and I have a new rite — eating eggs Benedict at the Brevoort (poached on vaguely bacon flavored toast, smothered in a golden sauce, surmounted by a slivver of truffle) in the morning.

Write me about Viena.

Remember me to the Sweeneys.

Love

Dos

1. The non-English words in paragraph one are Italian except when otherwise described. *Quattrocentista* (It. pl.: −*isti*), "fifteenth-century artist." Lugubrio: name derived from *lugubre* (adj.), "lugubrious" *or* "dismal." Dei Funghi, "of the Fungi" *or* "of the Mushrooms." *Detto,* "called." Il Sepulchro, "the Sepulcher (*or* Sepulchre)." Dos Passos may have used *sepulchrum,* a form of the Latin word (or used *sepulchr* from the English word), with an Italian article and an *o* ending. The Italian word is *sepolcro. Peste,* "plague." *Camposanto,* "cemetery."

118

Wien, 25 April 1922.

(^c/_o Cook. Stephansplatz[1] 2.)

Dos,

After reading your article in <u>Asia</u>[2] and hearing rumours of 39 days on a camel I feel glad that you are now using the Subway & the Dudley St. car.

Vienna is such a Weltstadt.[3] There's everything going on, theatres, opera, concerts, Exhib. of Oriental Art, etc. etc.   I saw <u>Reigen</u>[4] last night, so beautifully acted (if it hadn't been for Liliom one would really have forgotten what good acting was like) and so exceptionally naughty. It was the essence of Schnitzler. I actually took Mrs. Sweeney who was very brave and took comfort in its being 'art & truth' but was grateful to me for shaking my head doubtfully when the question of Margaret's going was raised. Though really as that dear jeune fille had just read Three Soldiers, I did not see how Schnitzler could teach her much which she oughtn't to know.

. . . Venice was grey−I had never seen it except in mid-summer weather. Last time I decided its banality was a little against it, but it isn't banal. Perhaps it was because this time I did none of the 'sights' but discovered several things, for one a cloister not in Bädeker, untouched, mouldering away. . . .

Later   26 April−

Since writing above, a letter from my mother arrived enclosing one from you written in Damascus, redolent of camels−gradually your mail is coming through & I realize that you kept us au courant very well or intended to [,] had the post permitted. . . .

I've just seen an article writing up you & your water-colors in the World Magazine.[5] I realize now quite vividly that you're a 'celebrity'—oh dear [—] well I have a sort of comfortable feeling of being on the inside as it were, and it doesn't look as if you would allow them to make you entirely public property. . . .

Sweeneys copy of Rosinante has just arrived. . . .

A. K. McC.

. . . .

1. St——platz. Partly illegible.
2. "One Hundred Views of Ararat," *Asia* 22 (April 1922): 272–76, 326.
3. [Ger.] "City of the world."
4. Arthur Schnitzler's play, written in 1897, first produced in 1920.
5. A. Hamilton Gibbs, "Story-telling in Flaming Colors," *The World* (New York), March 5, 1922, *The World Magazine and Story Section,* pp. 10, 16.

119

[Art postcards]

Vienna   30 April 1922

Dos:—I wrote you the other day but since a letter of yours from N.Y. has come [,] hence this line. . . .

I'm very grateful for all the dope about your literary doings. I won't ask any more questions. Delighted, too, at all the good dollars 3 S. brought in. You are now a capitalist, you know. I greet you, my brother in sin.

Yesterday (I write this ¶ May 2) there was a nice orderly procession of people carrying red flags and singing the Marseillaise. Mrs. S.[1] & I dodged through it on our way to look at the greatest technical achievement of Vermeer Van Delft in Czernin's apartment.[2] This was as it should be.

I send this to Cambridge as George Roberts[3] (I rejoice at your appreciation of him) seems to think your N.Y. address is 6 Patchin Pl. You on the other hand have the impression that it is 45 Barrow St.

My present interests carry me rather far from the wonderful scientists but again, I rejoice at your interest in them. . . .

Before I left Rome I did all the things you recommend—you must know that I have forsaken the Prophet on the question of wine, if only because their names and their colours and the mood of the Italian scene require the sipping of wines—I am now going hectically to dash around in the Germaine countries and look at galleries and then retire once and for all to the enchanted South. I have all the convert's zeal, you see.

I'm interested in your futilitarian novel. I don't know whether I've abandoned the creed as much as you think—it depends on the interpretation one puts on the word—but I <u>am</u> purposeful in so far as it is my desire to know a little something about Italian painting. . . .

I have to go to Dresden to-morrow to see an elderly lady on an errand from my mother. My plan was to push on, but what do you think— Mr. Scholle Sr. & an Austrian Count who are trying to sell things to American museums apparently wanted to have me back in Vienna by mid-May so much to pass on some paintings etc. that they offered to pay the difference in my expenses for coming back from Dresden as well as commission on the things. I accepted feeling flattered & pleasantly important. I've already attributed a Guidoccio Cozzarelli[4] for them. So you see I'm doing the Berenson stunt. All this by the way is 'hush dope.' Everything in the art business always is for that matter. . . .

I continue to move in Ottoman circles. Tea & chatter at the Turkish Embassy yesterday. . . .

Love
Arthur.

1. Mrs. Sweeney.
2. Vermeer's *A Painter in His Studio*. This work has had a curious history, and a not altogether apolitical one. We quote from Ludwig Goldscheider, *Johannes Vermeer* (London: Phaidon Press, 1967), p. 130. "Bought in 1813 by Johann Rudolf Count Czernin from a saddler for 50 Austrian Gulden as a work by Pieter de Hooch, whose name is inscribed on the rung of the stool. . . . In 1860 G. F. Waagen saw the painting in the Czernin Collection, recognized it as a work by Vermeer and also found his signature. —Until 1942 in the Czernin Collection (on loan to the Kunsthistorisches Museum, Vienna). From 1942 to 1945 the picture was in the possession of Adolf Hitler, who kept it at Berchtesgaden.—Returned by the Allies to the Vienna Museum (1946)."
3. See Letter 114, including n. 9, above.
4. Guidoccio di Giovanni Cozzarelli, Italian painter and miniaturist who flourished in Siena during the second half of the fifteenth century.

120

[Art postcard]

Margitsziget, Budapest
Magyarország[1]
27 majus.[2] [1922]

Dos:—Ezer köszönöm[3] for Rosinante. (Paying you back for your Arabic)—I'm enjoying re-reading it—its very good to have something

of yours removed from the controversial atmosphere surrounding Three
Soldiers. —Your Maragall[4] is soaked in the Mediterranean I like that
one particularly—some of the Talk by the Road[5] was quite new to me —
a little I had read in the Nation. . . .

Love
Arthur

1. [Hungarian], "Hungary."
2. Május [Hungarian], "May."
3. Ezerszer köszönöm [Hungarian], "I thank a thousand times," is the expression
probably intended.
4. Dos Passos' essay-chapter on Joan Maragall i Gorina (1860–1911) in *Rosinante
to the Road Again*. (Chapter XII, "A Catalan Poet.")
5. "Talk by the Road": a recurring title for six chapters set in various parts of *Rosinante
to the Road Again*.

121

[New York]
May 28 [1922]

[To McComb]

Well Arthur you old exquisite—how are you? I steal a moment from
Miss Nancibel Taylor, otherwise known as Streets of Night to gossip
awhile.

Dudley is in retreat at Skaneateles—I have a superbly huge room
in the back of a house on Washington Sq. and am tolerably content
and working somewhat. Your letters give me an occasional pang of longing for the fleshpots—but on the whole I find work and New York satis-
fying—N.Y. particularly, if it weren't for the aviary squawkings of the
literary gentry that I cant quite get away from, would be superb. I like
its fearfulness better than ever. I paint and scribble and dine in Italian
restaurants and talk to bums on park benches, and the days fly by like
flocks of ducks—whirr and they're gone—

But Arthur you old sinner do let me hear about "Ottoman circles"
and your ill got gains in the Art Game—I expect to hear at any moment
that you have gone to Angora to act as adviser on the q.t. to Mustapha
Kemal[1] who will have just discovered a Bellini[2] (of N.Y. manufacture)
in the Mosque of the Prophet's Suspenders at Abu Bunkum[3]—But Miss
Nancibel is getting restive—

love
Dos

Best wishes to the Sweeneys etc.

1. Mustafa Kemal (1881–1938), Turkish leader and from 1923 to 1938 president
of Turkey. He took the name Kemal Atatürk in 1934.

2. Gentile Bellini (1429–1507), Venetian painter, brother of Giovanni Bellini. From September 1479 to November 1480 he was in Constantinople, where he painted portraits and did other work for Mohammed II, the conqueror of Constantinople. In 1905 a private collector there, J. R. Martin, bought from an old Turkish family an art album containing scores of works—among these a miniature pen and gouache painting which he attributed to Gentile Bellini. In an article on this picture (which has since generally been attributed to Bellini) Martin wrote: "I now hope that further researches will bring to light not only a single Bellini, but a whole album with the portraits of the courtiers of Mohamed the Conqueror. . . ." Isabella Stewart Gardner bought the painting in 1907. See J. R. Martin, "A Portrait by Gentile Bellini Found in Constantinople," *The Burlington Magazine* 9 (1906): 148–49 (quotation on p. 149).

3. Mosques contain no pictures—a fact which adds to the bunkum in the passage.

122

[Art postcards—subject: architecture]

Florence, Sept 17—1922
c/o Am. Express Co.

[To Dos Passos]
Amigo mío:[1] —

Where, I wonder are you?—I continue to address 3 Washington Sq.—I wait for the Wanderlust to seize you & propel you this way. It is time for palavering—a year & a half must be threshed out. Let me know where you are spending the winter.

Your passage through Pomfret I heard of but do not know whether to assume therefore that Miss N.T.[2] is finished. . . .

Now I'm in the centre of Anglo-Toscana.[3] Yesterday went to the XVII & XVIII c. exhibition at the Pitti.[4] Expected to be converted to baroque painting but couldn't swallow it—the XVIII however was superb—never realized how important Guardi[5] is. Technique dazzling. . . .

I don't know Dudley's address—will you give him the enclosed card. He ought to be interested in the last conversation of S. Benedict with his sister St. Scolastica. What do you suppose they talked about?

I miss you both—wish you'd come & share a flat or something with me in Rome this winter.

Write, if only a line—assuring me of your existence.

Love
Arthur.

If you see Stewart[6] in Gloucester give him my best.

1. [Sp.] "My friend."
2. Nancibel Taylor, i.e., *Streets of Night*.
3. Toscana [It.], "Tuscany."
4. Florentine art gallery, second only to the Uffizi in importance.

5. Francesco Guardi (1712–93), major Venetian view painter.
6. Stewart Mitchell.

123

[Art postcards]

Florence   Sept 18 — [1922]

Dear Dos,

A card from you in N.Y. dated Aug. 21. I wrote you yesterday Have you got various communications from me from Amsterdam, Dresden, Salzburg, Rimini etc. Yes, I got the Lugubrio letter [.][1] I'm afraid I disapprove of him. He sounds neo-Catholic. Seriously I'm sick of the whole monographic activity about these footling minor trecentists.[2] (F. di G.[3] really is not little at all)   After looking at them I feel the extreme necessity of looking at something worth while [,] say an Uccello, a Velázquez a Degas. . . .

I'm awfully eager for news of you. Have I missed any? Your last was dated May 29.

Do put enough stamps on — I'm delighted to pay the 'postage due' but fear some cards may have strayed for want of an extra cent.

Also pray address
American Express
   Florence. —
as by the system I have established all mail sent to Rome has to go to Austria before it reaches me. The systems too complicated to change! . . .

Love
Arthur.

. . . .

There is a sense in which I must compliment you on Lugubrio. He is real enough. When did you find him. After dinner I bet.

1. See Letter 117 above.
2. Fourteenth-century artists or their imitators.
3. Francesco di Giorgio.

124

[North Carolina (near
Asheville)]
Oct 23 [1922]

Arthur! — I'm down in North Carolina with Van's[1] very charming family — whither I fled to attempt to escape a strange series of head aches culminating in my eyes turning to hard opaque pebbles in my head. Damned annoying just as I was battling hardest with that tiresome bitch Miss Nan Taylor. However and hallejah I this morning put the finishing touch on that lady whom I now leave to her own courses toward oblivion. Never have I undertaken a piece of work more anti-patico[2] and I fear less successful.

My apologies to Mr. Adams. The Education is by far the most inter-esting American document I've thus far encountered, and as a source-book for futilitarianism is perfect. Imagine, it took him till he was 61 years of age to discover that woman's sex was a force in the world! The very unspicy pedestrian quality of it is vastly instructive. Have you been reading Yeats's memoires in the Dial? They are marvellous for contrast. And remember H.A.'s terror on meeting Swinburne and Kipling[3] — it's delightfully Harvardian and grotesque. I would have omitted the delightfully a year ago and probably shall a year from now, but at this moment fresh from Miss Nancibel's toils I feel as if I'd put that sort of thing far enough away to smile at it for a breathing space.

Incidentaly Miss N's name is Streets of Night — and your opinion about her is very important — because I cant help but feel that the treat-ment is rather your sort of thing. The subject is less in your line that it would seem at first glance.

What about Rome?

Look you must write me all your winter plans iminidiatly to 3 Wash-ington Square — N.Y. City — because there is high probability of an Italian jaunt — on my part flying — during the winter — as I must go before I spend all my Three Soldiers money as I'll certainly never have a chance again for ages. Dudley is going in January to see his family in Naples. I want to see every piece of plaster a 'scientist'[4] ever put brush to, if I can.

So for heavens sake let's not miss each other again — And let me know at once where you will be when and why and whether Piazza Essedra [Piazza dell'Esedra] is the proper address. I'll send The Pushcart[5] there in a week or two, So write me about it — You know you and Dudley seem to be the only people who pay the slightest attention to my poor little verses, So it's important that fiats be issued about them, for their damnation if need be. I'm so horribly afraid they are just washy —

Remember me to George Roberts if he's about —

O for the wine of Tivoli and Frascati and oily lunches in the trattorie along the appian way —

Yours

Dos

What's M<u>rs</u> Sweeney's address? I owe her a million letters—She's been so kind to continue writing me—

The great Arend himself is at present in Paris—on his way home, his firm having failed for a paltry ten million dollars.[6] La folie des grandeurs[7]—

This letter, which Dos Passos mailed to Rome on October 24, 1922, reached McComb about a year later in New York. (Information from McComb's note written on the letter.)

1. Frederik Francis van den Arend. He is referred to as Arend in the final paragraph of this letter.

2. [It.] "Disagreeable."

3. See Henry Adams, *The Education of Henry Adams* (Boston: Houghton Mifflin Co., 1918), pp. 139–44, 319–20, on Adams' meeting the two British authors. Of his meeting Swinburne (1862), he wrote: "Adams could no more interest Algernon Swinburne than he could interest Encke's comet. To Swinburne he could be no more than a worm. The quality of genius was an education almost ultimate . . . but one could only receive; one had nothing to give . . ." (p. 142). Of meeting Kipling (1892), Adams wrote: "Kipling and the American were not one, but two, and could not be glued together. The American felt that the defect, if defect it were, was in himself . . . but he did not carry self-abasement to the point of thinking himself singular. . . . All through life, one had seen the American on his literary knees to the European . . ." (p. 319). Walt Whitman, whose writings Dos Passos loved, had asserted: "I find no sweeter fat than sticks to my own bones." "Song of Myself," sec. 20, in *Leaves of Grass* (1891–92).

4. Plaster: a reference to frescoes. Pigments mixed in water are applied to freshly plastered walls, and they combine with the plaster. Scientist: see Letter 114, n. 12 above.

5. Dos Passos, *A Pushcart at the Curb* (New York: George H. Doran Co., 1922). The book was published on October 11.

6. See note to narrative, p. 133 above, on van den Arend's job with Childs & Joseph. Stories about the failure of this import-export firm may be found in the *New York Times,* January-March 1922. Not long after these stories appeared, van den Arend wrote Dos Passos that the firm had gone bankrupt for nine million dollars (letter from Madagascar, May 10, 1922). In *Manhattan Transfer,* published three years later, Dos Passos had Blackhead and Densch, an import-export firm, fail for ten million; the partners complain about the disastrous market for what van den Arend in the non-fictional world had bought, beans.

7. [Fr.] "Megalomania."

125

[New York?
December 1922?]

Arthur—

Do send me your actual <u>unchangeable</u> address—Did you get the

Cook's
pushcart? Sent to Rome—also one to send on to M<u>rs</u> Sweeney?

Streets of Night finished. working on two plays—

Then steamships, Paris, Rome? Cape Verde Islands who knows

where, including New Orleans and Cadiz and wistfulness towards Morocco

Dos

126

[New York
January 1923]

Dear Arthur—

So glad you got the poems. If I dont fly the coop soon I'll start massacring the literati in New York. I've seen too damn much of them.

J.G.P.[1] is Pepe Giner with whom I ate a memorable box of sardines and nearly froze my feet in the Puerto de Navecerrada.

By the time you get this letter you probably will have seen Dudley in the flesh wearing a wonderful elephant's breath hat.

As for Juliet who shall say? XXVII[2] works both ways you know. Moon shines tonight

Lua cheia esta noit[3] is in Azores Portuguese and was said in a curiously haunting tone by a man who had been a barber in Frisco and was on the Mormugão going home to Terceira to get him a wife in his own village.

Did you get the second copy to send Mrs. Sweeney?

Shall see you in the Spring d.v.[4] wind and weather permitting Dont get too Anglo-Florentine

Dos

1. A reference to *A Pushcart at the Curb* (pp. 52–3), where a section of "Winter in Castile" is dedicated by initials to José Giner Pantoja. Sections of other parts of the book are also dedicated by initials, to McComb (p. 148), Dudley Poore (p. 74), Roland Jackson (p. 123), and Robert Hillyer (p. 110).

2. Dos Passos was born on January 14, 1896.

3. "The full moon this night," in section XI of "Phases of the Moon," in *A Pushcart at the Curb* (p. 209). Dos Passos' writing *noit,* for the Portuguese *noite,* was a transcription of Azorian speech.

4. Deo volente [Lat.], "God willing."

127

[Aboard the S.S. *Roussillon*
March 1923]

Dear Arthur—

I've just waked up out of five days blissful lethean sleep in a divinely comfortable bunk on the Roussillon (ex-German ship of the China service) New York and divers labyrinthine heart wrenchings and entanglements nearly did me in—I feel like someone escaped from a madhouse into the sane twilight of these grey Atlantic days—There's a huge swell out of the northeast and we roll and creak our way along with sleepy dignity. There are almost no passengers and there are long wet decks to be alone on. Never been so happy in my life—I dont know where I'm bound and I haven't much money but I dont care—

Finished a play called the Garbage Man[1] before I left. Now as soon as everything is sufficiently blotted out—I shall start knocking together a long dull and arduous novel about New York and go-getters and God knows what besides—I'm terribly afraid of the speed with which the years tramp by.

I'll be in Paris a couple of weeks and then make tracks for Italy. This time we mustn't muff our meeting—I'll go anywhere you say at any time.

My aim is see all the works of all the scientists particularly Uccello and Piero della Francesca and any other fresco painting I can pick up en route.

Dudley's in Rome I imagine. Address him Cooks'—

Write me at once care the eternal Morgan Harjes—14 Place Vendôme where you will be—and when.

I'm going to travel cheap and walk a vast deal.

I feel as gay as if I'd never been abroad before and as seaworthy as a Mother Carey's chicken[2]—

"Those of us who have grown tired"—O Arthur—what is weltschmerz for if not to be drowned in white wine of Frascati! All I want is a chance to get tired—

God I wish I'd gone to sea when I was a kid as I always wanted to—

I wrote Ogier[3]—Hope he gets his translation published—

But I must go to sleep again—I want to land in Havre as fresh a chicken just breaking out of an egg—

A bientot

Dos

1. Previously referred to as *The Moon Is a Gong*.
2. Any of certain species of petrels, especially the stormy petrel.
3. Not conclusively identified.

Letters

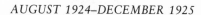

AUGUST 1924–DECEMBER 1925

$\mathcal{P}$URSUING HIS CAREER in art, McComb in 1924 published his
copiously illustrated "The Life and Works of Francesco di Giorgio."
His presentation of this fifteenth-century Sienese artist appeared as an
article in *Art Studies,* a journal edited by members of the Harvard and
Princeton fine arts departments, but it was extensive enough to have
been a brief book.[1] Aside from his writing and traveling, McComb
worked for the Metropolitan Museum of Art, in New York, in 1923
and 1924 and taught at Vassar College from 1924 to 1926. Meanwhile
he acquired a family; he and Constance Atwood were married in New
York in 1923, and in 1925 they had a daughter, Pamela.[2]

Single still and self-employed, Dos Passos was in Europe again in
the summer of 1924. So too was McComb, who probably intended
the irony when he wrote him from Venice in June, "The society columns
of the N.Y. Herald announce your arrival in Paris." (Writing to John
Howard Lawson that summer, Dos Passos expressed irony on the same
subject: "Now I am working in a red plush room at the [Gerald and
Sara] Murphy's* place at Antibes where I'm being 'entertained' as the
New York Herald would say with great elegance and a great deal of
gin fizz.")[3] Dos Passos and McComb continued to correspond with
friendly criticism of one another. After *Manhattan Transfer* appeared
in 1925, McComb wrote a letter of congratulations mingling praise

---

*Gerald Murphy (1888–1964), the painter, and his wife, Sara (1883–1975), both
Americans from wealthy families. In the fall of 1921 they moved to Paris, and there Dos
Passos, according to his memoirs, first met them. For many years, beginning in the late
summer of 1924, the Murphys made their home at their Villa America, at Cap d'Antibes,
on the French Riviera. They were people of taste, means, and graciousness, whose friends
included Dos Passos, Archibald MacLeish, F. Scott Fitzgerald, Fernand Léger, and Pablo
Picasso. See Dos Passos, *The Best Times,* pp. 145–50; Calvin Tomkins, *Living Well Is
the Best Revenge* (New York: Viking Press, 1971).

for the novel with apprehension about his friend's involvement with the leftist journal *New Masses,* which was launched the next year. And from an oasis on the edge of the Sahara Desert, where he had gone trying to avoid another attack of rheumatic fever,[4] Dos Passos answered with mock contrition.

128

Florence, 9th of August 1924

Dear Dos, — I didn't know your more plutocratic sounding new address till Mrs. Sweeney gave it to me.[1] A post-card went to America, another to Morgan Harjes, but to retrieve them is not essential.

And I heard not without a slight pang, of the Pampluna adventure,[2] and am wondering whether you are back and am saddened at not getting a post-card of a cloister or a fresco. I only hear of people through the N.Y. Herald these days — I ask you, do you want to be heard of that way? . . .

I have made no discoveries about painting during the summer, which annoys me. Like going stale. As if one had got all the reactions one could out of Ital. P. for the time. (Must migrate to China.) Tuscan archit: & landscape hold me, but I don't like to hear the word Donatello, (as I did this morning —) The American lady with the tired genteel voice, might as well have said 'Chandler Post.' . . .

. . . Loeser[3] was here, also B.B. [,][4] who referred to the Metro. as the 'Necropolitan.' . . .

Who has turned up in Paris? — Cummings? If Elaine[5] is still there please remember me most warmly.

Love

A K McC

1. Dos Passos had sent Mrs. Sweeney the address "Bankers Trust Company — 5 Place Vendôme Paris." Letter from Dos Passos to Mrs. Mildred McNeal Sweeney, postmarked June 14, 1924.

2. At the Fiesta of San Fermín, in July 1924. Hemingway had attended in 1923, and was there a second time. See Dos Passos, *The Best Times,* pp. 154–56; Carlos Baker, *Ernest Hemingway: A Life Story* (New York: Charles Scribner's Sons, 1969), pp. 112, 129–30.

3. Charles Alexander Loeser (1864–1928), American connoisseur, collector, and non-professional critic of art. He, Berenson, and George Santayana were a trio of friends as undergraduates at Harvard. Santayana's memoirs contain some pages on Loeser as a Jewish friend and frequent benefactor whom he continued to see after college. Contrasting Loeser with Berenson, Santayana wrote: "I felt that he [Loeser] loved the Italian renaissance and was not, as it were, merely displaying it." Between Berenson and Loeser,

rivalry and distrust regarding each other's work caused disputes in Italy, and Berenson came to consider Loeser, much of whose life was spent in Florence, one of his "enemy-friends." McComb in the preface to his *Agnolo Bronzino* (1928) called Loeser "my friend"; and in a Florentine memoir (1966), in which he expressed reservations about Berenson's personality (citing "a distinct compulsion to tease"), he quoted Santayana's contrast between the two connoisseurs. See George Santayana, *Persons and Places* (New York: Charles Scribner's Sons, 1944), pp. 224–31; Samuels, *Bernard Berenson: The Making of a Connoisseur;* McComb, "The Anglo-Americans in Florence," in *English Miscellany* 17, ed. Mario Praz (Rome, Italy: British Council, 1966), pp. 279–310.

4. Bernard Berenson, whom McComb had first met in 1921. During the spring semester at Harvard that year, McComb wrote Dos Passos of having seen and listened to Berenson. When McComb was in Italy in July 1921, he sent or left his card, and the Berensons invited him to lunch at I Tatti, their villa near Florence. Letters from McComb to Dos Passos, March 16 and May 17, 1921; McComb, "The Anglo-Americans in Florence," p. 281.

5. Elaine (née Orr) Cummings. She had married Scofield Thayer in 1916 and divorced him in 1921. She married E. E. Cummings on March 19, 1924, and divorced him on December 4 of the same year. See Richard S. Kennedy, *Dreams in the Mirror: A Biography of E. E. Cummings,* pp. 111, 231, 248, 264 and passim.

129

[Art postcards: the Pollaiuolo *Tobias and the Angel;* two portraits of men, ascribed by the cards to Filippo Mazzola and "Mazzola" respectively; and a portrait of Amerigo Vespucci (a detail from a fresco) by Domenico Ghirlandaio]

Vassar   8 Dec 1925

Dos — Its almost 8 years since you sent me a card of this from Turin.[1] I've just written for the little Cosimo Rosselli Triumph of Chastity[2] which you & Dudley used to talk so much about in Madrid — I found it listed by the photographer as a Botticelli. — Oh,[3] I do agree with you about the scientists [;] there's nothing in Venice of that date at all comparable except perhaps Antonello[4] — But the later manner of Botticelli has begun to intrigue me afresh — if you could see the new Fogg Botticelli Crucifixion — all cleaned, very damaged, but one of the most intense things ever painted — of an exacerbated intensity — one of the few good things I suppose for which Savonarola was responsible.

I hope you did not fail to read the reasoning of the court in the matter of freeing the Fascists behind the Matteotti murder. The Times came out with an extremely sarcastic editorial.[5] The Times also did well on Manhattan Transfer as you perhaps saw — a large-print important-looking review & intelligent at that.[6] I've just finished the work & offer my congratulations. Its so much more convincing than 'Streets of Night.' I enjoyed reading it but of course you're always readable (you may remember I read Streets of Night in two sittings)   M.T. is full of niceties of observation & the total effect is certainly to give one the feel of the wonderful horror (I speak from my own point of view) which is N.Y. And I still stand on my coward's advice of Flee, flee!—I should think the Watch & Ward in Boston may well get after it—& even Sumner. (For the abortions & the fairies I mean)[7]

I was delighted of course with the nautical knowledge displayed. The gaiety was often in that same too high key, I thought, which I remarked in Three Soldiers—your 'parties' my dear Dos, are among the most desolatingly melancholy things in literature—but I am not certain in my mind whether you intend them so. In their curiously un-genuine boisterousness, I feel the regret of an over-conscious 20th c. young man for his lost Elizabethan youth. But those days are over for ever—— I seemed to observe also a growing aversion to that slipshod sort of "thinking" which Utopists, singers of the Internationale etc. go in for & this I was naturally delighted at—so that I regretted to see in yesterdays Times that you were to be associated with the New Masses. Of course if you can get some of the foolish young gentleman's millions—even so I venture to call the price high.[8] That dismal roster of names of agitators—what are you, my dear friend, at the age of 30 doing among them—oh, no [,] seriously I mourn. Already I see in print their re-iterated banal formulae decking out the heavy obvious cartoons of Mr Robinson.[9] Why not go to Tibet & turn prayer-wheels?

— — — — —

Should I send this letter? Oh, well you've stood a good deal from me in the past [,] so here goes!—You won't pay any attention anyway so I feel irresponsible.

    C.[10] wants me to say how much she enjoyed M.T.

As ever
A.

1. Written on the reverse side of the Pollaiuolo *Tobias and the Angel* card. See the reproduction of the painting on p. 209.

2. This painting, which is of uncertain attribution, is also in Turin.

3. Alternate reading "oh." (with period rather than comma following the word) possible.

4. Antonello da Messina (c. 1430–79), Italian painter, b. in Messina, Sicily. He produced major works in Venice and strongly influenced the development of its art.

5. Reference to Giacomo Matteotti (1885–1924), Italian Socialist leader murdered by Fascist hirelings. In releasing three important Fascists, the Court of Public Prosecutions "decided that though they had instigated the kidnapping of Matteotti, the murder was unpremeditated and that, therefore, they could not be held responsible for . . . [his] death. As all political crimes except murder come within the scope of the recent amnesty, the Court ordered their immediate release." The reasoning and the above quotation are in the *New York Times*, December 3, 1925, p. 27. The editorial appeared in the next day's issue, p. 22.

6. Henry Longan Stuart's review. *New York Times,* November 29, 1925, sec. 3, pp. 5, 10.

7. Watch and Ward: New England Watch and Ward Society; John S. Sumner, successor to Anthony Comstock as secretary of the New York Society for the Suppression of Vice; fairies: homosexuals.

8. Charles Garland, a philosophical anarchist, used his $901,555 inheritance to establish the American Fund for Public Service in 1921. The "Garland Fund" provided money to support *New Masses* for three years.

9. Boardman Robinson (1876–1952), American cartoonist, illustrator, and painter.

10. Constance, McComb's wife.

130

[Beni Ounif
Algeria
December 1925]

Arthur—I was just wanting a letter from you and here the man at the post office produces one like a rabbit out of a hat. I read it sitting on a stone outside the mudwall of the gardens while the departing sun strutted like a peacock pulling off trick after trick of meticulously arranged color—At a little distance away were the striped bales left in a circle by the caravan that arrived this afternoon from somewhere in the Sahara. I'm staying at a little town called Beni Ounif de Figuig that is the quintessense of desert.

But Arthur amigo mio I feel rather hurt that you should hesitate for a moment to tonguelash me. I'm used to it, and you must know by this time that I honor your ratings more than most people's praises. They dont have much effect I admit, but there is always time for repentence, saith the Sinner.

Do you know I never realized that the fish Tobias has in the Torino picture was a merluza. You certainly sweetened your lecture, Arthur, with a dainty assortment of postcards. The Mazolas and the portrait of the person who gave his name to our extraordinary continent pleased me very much.[1] I wonder what he would think of his namesake, if somebody glued his bones together and propped him up in his grave.

Figuig is the northern end of the long route to Timbuctoo—occasionally Taureg[2] are said to come here though I haven't seen any yet. Its an oasis of datepalms full of trickling waters among wild mountains with a number of mud villages and a railway station. There's a fine little erratic hotel kept by a very commerçante[3] french woman who feeds me delicious meals. I intend various labors but I dont seem to do anything   I spend my time walking like mad among the mountains. I no sooner get indoors than some new entertainment furnished by

"Your Tobias and the angel filled me with melancholy reflections. . . . Its time I hitched up my pants and mended my ways." Dos Passos to McComb, December 1925. McComb had sent him a copy of the Pollaiuolo painting above.
Alinari

Sahara Inc. drags me out. You can come here in a sleeper. I advise you to do it some time.

Your Tobias and the angel filled me with melancholy reflexions on the falling of hair, the loss of friends, the disappearance of ocean greyhounds and other rather banal thoughts tumbling out like things out of a slot machine.[4] You are quite right. Its time I hitched up my pants and mended my ways. The trouble is there is nowhere much one can settle except into the grave. I might embrace Islam but that would necessitate a painful operation and I cant convince myself that I would be better off without a foreskin than with one. Its much the same with communism or your own romantic tory antiquarianism — The nearing of the end of a year always brings on these idées noires[5] — It is a ridiculous and repulsive spectacle that one offers, I fear, continually scuttling about the world from place to place and person to person like a cockroach running away from a light. I am assailed by wise adages and knowing saws. The trouble is they're all quite true — rolling stones gather neither moss nor information. Here I am suddenly trying to pick up arabic. Its undignified. Its obscene.

But enough of this.

Give my love to Constance — and I'd like to hear about Pamela[6] — I wrote you that Morgan Harjes had also defenestrated me my account and my mail. So Poste Restante[7] Fez or care American Legation Tangier might be good addresses. Also the Murphies[8] — Villa America Cap d'Antibes A.M. France will hold and forward my mail.

Forgive this Lamentation — my morale is actually excellent and my health continually improving —

Yours

Dos

1. See the description of the art postcards on which McComb wrote Letter 129 above. Merluza [Sp.], "hake" (a species of cod), which is widely eaten in Spain. Mazzola is the name of a family of Italian painters. Three, all born in Parma, were: Filippo (c. 1460–1505), his son Francesco, known as Parmigianino (on whom see Letter 115, n. 5 above), and Girolamo Mazzola Bedoli (c. 1500–69), a relative of Parmigianino through marriage.

2. Properly *Tuareg.* A nomadic Berber people of the Sahara.

3. [Fr.] "Business-minded."

4. On Tobias, see the book of Tobit, in the Apocrypha. Tobias and the Angel paintings were numerous during the Florentine Renaissance. They are thought to have been used for devotions to St. Raphael for the welfare of many a young man on a journey. Maud Cruttwell, *Antonio Pollaiuolo* (London: Duckworth and Co., 1907), p. 96. For a highly critical discussion of the theory, see E. H. Gombrich, *Symbolic Images* (London: Phaidon, 1972), pp. 26–30.

5. [Fr.] "Gloomy ideas."

6. Constance, McComb's wife, and Pamela, their baby daughter.

7. Poste restante [Fr.] is the equivalent of U.S. general delivery.

8. Gerald and Sara Murphy.

Letters

𝒩EW YORK CONTINUED TO BE Dos Passos' home for several years, although he journeyed widely. For much of the time he was deeply involved in radical efforts: in 1926 he joined in founding the New Playwrights Theatre, an avant-garde leftist enterprise in which he and John Howard Lawson were two of the five playwright-directors; he was a member of the Executive Board of the newly-established *New Masses;* he journeyed to the scene of the massive textile workers' strike in Passaic, New Jersey, and described his experience in that journal; and he visited the imprisoned Sacco and Vanzetti in Massachusetts and wrote feelingly in their behalf.[1]

McComb's activities meanwhile largely involved research and teaching. In March 1926 he published a comprehensive article on a minor Florentine cinquecento painter Francesco Ubertini (1494–1557), who was called Il Bacchiacca.[2] That summer he and his wife, Constance, did some sightseeing in Europe, spending much of their time in Spain. On July 9 he wrote Dos Passos describing the palace of La Granja de San Ildefonso, which the first Bourbon king of Spain built to remind him of Versailles. From Madrid two weeks later he sent news he had heard about the Carmen de Matamoros. And from Barcelona on August 10 he wrote nostalgically of his sojourn in Spain in 1919–20 and told of his and Constance's having just gone to Mallorca and Gerona. Replying at the end of August, Dos Passos advised McComb against going to Italy. Fascism and class warfare were now very much on Dos Passos' mind.

Probably an experience of his the year before was directly responsible for the warning. While he was on Gerald Murphy's sloop the *Picaflor* cruising the Mediterranean, a violent storm arose and threatened the party. Fortunately a tugboat appeared and rescued them by drawing the sloop into Savona. Writing to John Howard Lawson afterwards, Dos Passos commented on the beauty of some of the towns on the Italian Riviera, but had harsh words about Savona:

Savona is a dead town—do you remember how swell it seemed in 1917—? It was communist and everybody has been killed by the fascisti or chased away. The most fantastically sinister place I've ever been in. We got into the fascist café and had drinks with the leading gunmen. An extraordinary set of thugs. All the time we were there not a soul in the albergo diurno except ourselves, no one in the restaurants, on the streets, around the harbor full of rotting steamers, except for the one café that was full of obscene roistering, overfed bruisers tossing down glasses of crème de menthe, and morbid looking schoolboys, sons of bankers, playing chess and drinking tea.[3]

McComb had a more immediate experience with political violence on his trip. Soon after traveling in Spain he and his wife went to Greece, where General Theodorus Pangalos had recently made himself dictator. On August 22, 1926, Pangalos was deposed in a coup d'état by General Georgios Condylis, who sought to restore constitutional government. However, on September 9 forces wanting a military regime defied Condylis' demand that they hand over their arms. When they marched on Athens, a battle ensued, and both sides suffered heavy casualties before the rebellious troops were disarmed. McComb witnessed some of the fighting in Athens before going on to Turkey.

He stayed in Turkey more than a week. On October 3 he was in Venice, and from there he answered Dos Passos' caution on Italy with praise for Venice's civilized air. For contrasts he cited the atmospheres of two eastern cities: Istanbul, and Moscow, on which he had been reading a French satire.

That winter Dos Passos was in Mexico, which had an atmosphere unlike all three. His desire for a warm climate during the cold months was a factor in bringing him there. But so too were Mexican society and art, and he interested himself in the Mexican revolution and in the mural paintings of Diego Rivera and José Clemente Orozco and later wrote about them in *New Masses*.[4] At the approach of spring he returned home and that year participated in last-ditch attempts to save Sacco and Vanzetti—who were electrocuted on August 23, 1927.[5]

By 1928 Dos Passos was finding work with the New Playwrights Theatre frustrating for a variety of reasons—one being that he was a morning writer, and late theatrical hours meant sleepy mornings. As he felt he needed a change and was full of curiosity about Communism, he embarked for Europe in the late spring and after visiting friends in a number of countries headed for the Soviet Union. Arriving by way of Leningrad that summer, Dos Passos acquainted himself with the city, then visited Moscow, and then went on an exploratory expedition in the Caucasus, returning to the Russian capital in the autumn. His stay in the U.S.S.R., which lasted until December, left him confused and upset by evidences of terror but on the whole favorable towards Soviet society.[6]

It was at a hotel in Leningrad that Dos Passos first met W. Horsley Gantt, a Virginia physician working under Ivan Pavlov. The two Americans walked in the Caucasus together and became lifelong friends.[7] Gantt and McComb were very different sorts of people and appear to have lain outside of one another's orbits.

Dos Passos was back in New York for the rehearsal of *Airways, Inc.,* which the New Playwrights Theatre presented in February. Though he soon resigned from that group, 1929 was a busy year for him. In Key West in March and April he was very much in love with Katharine Smith, and he wooed her that spring and summer. Even before he had left for Russia he was working on the novel that became the trilogy *U.S.A.,* and now he raced to complete volume one, *The 42nd Parallel.*[8] In the midst of all this he found time to keep up with friends—those he had made after college, like Ernest Hemingway and Edmund Wilson, to name only two—and Harvard friends, including Dudley Poore, Stewart Mitchell, and McComb.

McComb had experienced major changes in his career and private life. He had been appointed instructor in fine arts at Harvard in 1927, and was living in Boston, where in 1928 he completed a book on the Florentine painter Agnolo Bronzino (1503–1572). But he had not been faithful in his marriage and was separated from Constance (according to her they were divorced in the spring of 1929).[9] Writing to Dos Passos in late April 1929, he commented that he supposed the refusal of former Governor Fuller of Massachusetts to save Sacco and Vanzetti would prevent Dos Passos from reappearing in Boston—McComb's comment was regretful but not sympathetic or accurate. If McComb followed the plans announced in his letter, he left Boston for a summer in Europe.

That year Dos Passos saw a good deal more of Poore, who lived at the Hotel Lafayette in New York during the winter of 1928–29. In April Dos Passos wrote Mitchell that he breakfasted with him occasionally, and in late June he visited Poore for a few weeks in upstate New York, at his mother's house. He didn't talk much about *The 42nd Parallel* there. (But he later wrote asking Poore whether he knew

Dos Passos and Katharine Smith in Key West, 1928. Waldo Pierce, the painter, is only partially in the picture. Of the fish, Dos Passos later wrote: "They aren't fit to eat. . . . Sheer vanity catching tarpon." *The Best Times,* p. 201. *Courtesy of Marion Smith (Mrs. William B. Smith)*

the words of certain old songs, Poore did library research on them, and some of the lyrics found their way into "Newsreel" sections of *The 42nd Parallel*.) In July Dos Passos was in Chicago, where he appears to have done some library work for the novel.[10]

Dos Passos married Katy in Maine in August. Getting married doesn't seem to have broken the momentum of his work. He got his manuscript to Harpers in October. During much of the fall he and Katy lived in Provincetown, in a house Katy, her brother Bill Smith, and some friends had been inhabiting. He visited McComb at least once in Boston during the fall — and wrote Poore about a lady friend of McComb's, and of McComb's unbending enough to call her by her first name. In December, after Dos Passos had corrected proofs for *The 42nd Parallel*, he boarded the steamship *Roussillon* with his wife, planning "to show Katy old haunts in Europe and to introduce her to old friends."[11]

131

[Picture postcard. Burgos: Sepulcher of Alfonso X]

San I[l]defonso   9 July '26

Dos!   I can't remember whether you were ever at La Granja — my sort of place you will say — very XVIII[e] s. [,] Sitwellian[1] — one rides from Segovia in the cool evening — straight into red-violet hills and finds this courtly little place — Two windows in the delicate rococo palace are open — (for the Principe de las Asturias[2] & the Infanta Isabel have arrived) and reveal lighted crystal chandeliers and yellow silk hangings while below the faithful subjects dance on the gravel to tenuous music. And in the morning the hot sun brings out the smell of box and the palace is seen to be a tea-rose color flushed ever so slightly with pink — — — and the XVIII c. is not a dream!

Very different all this from what is suggested by this postcard [.] I've never seen such tombs as at Las Huelgas & tapestries — but Burgos is a dull town & I'm off all that late Gothic stuff rather. Of course you were completely right about N. Portugal — Coimbra & Oporto, — Lisbon we delighted in especially the food — Salamanca the most perfect place — A

1. XVIIIe s. [Fr.], a form for *dix-huitième siècle*, "eighteenth century." "Sitwellian" is an allusion to an English family of authors: Dame Edith Sitwell (1887–1964) and her brothers Sir Osbert Sitwell (1892–1969) and Sir Sacheverell Sitwell (b. 1897). Osbert

became the fifth baronet upon his father's death in 1943, and Sacheverell became the sixth upon Osbert's death.

2. Spanish equivalent of British Prince of Wales.

132

[Picture postcard]

Madrid   22 July [1926]

Dos—Just back from two days in Toledo where I met a man who had just been to Granada & stayed at the Matatodo's. —Would you believe it—nothing has changed [.] Sovereignty now 87 still walks to Granada & up again and still complains to Miss L.[1]—She now lives in the Casa del Gran Capitán. Was overheard to say to Miss L.: Your boy, your boy Emilio, came into my house in his shirt-sleeves, and more than that, he grinned at me, he grinned at me!!

As ever   A

1. Miss Laird. On her, the Carmen de Matatodos, and Sovereignty, see narrative, pp. 129–30 above.

133

[Letterhead: Hotel Colón, Barcelona]
August 10th 1926.

Dear Dos,

This place, lunching at Miramar,[1] dining at Martin, going to the Arxiu Mas[2] for photographs and so much more reminds me of you and the days we spent here six years ago, before I went to Italy. On the other hand Barcelona doesn't touch one as Madrid does—or perhaps its simply that one never has the same feeling about a place where where one has only been a "transient"—at any rate these memories are pleasant and not too much mixed with regret at the passage of time—though we've wished for your presence more than once.

Madrid on the other hand— —I tried to imagine starting to live there once again. It really would be impossible—impossible to conceive it unless once again I could see you & D.P.[3] in your Spanish cloaks striding down the Castellana[4] or Mr. S. with his hat pushed back on his head and his chair tilted sitting by a marble table at the Vaquería[5] & talking of Clémenceau & other strange dead subjects—or drink thick chocolate at near midnight at the Mallorquina[6]—or sit on winter evenings in the heated Sweeney rooms at the Pension Americana with the beds covered with books & papers—as none of these nor many other pleasant things can ever happen again—it seems to me that my Spanish days are in a sense over & that this rapid visit of two months may be the last for some time.　But if one already knows (at least in the tourist sense) a country—it is rather good fun to visit it rapidly—it puts ones ideas about places in order.　We're on our way to Granada now—back from Palma viâ B. to Madrid & down.

Did I write you what a great success Gerona was?—I don't remember your ever having said that you had stopped there. But I think (as you agree with me about Catalan Gothic) that you would have liked the Cathedral—finer even than the Barcelona examples. The town reminds one at moments of Italy—the river front recalls the Arno, but is "far from a slavish imitation."　The gardens of Mallorca charmed us. We agreed in liking Palma much better than Valldemosa (say it not to the Sweeneys). . . .

Went to the Parque Güell & the Sagrada Familia.[7] Quel theâtre![8] . . .

As ever

A.—

1. McComb entered in his diary for March 13, 1920: "Lunched with Dos at 'Miramar' overlooking the Harbor."

2. Archive of photographs, founded by Adolf Mas i Ginestà (b. 1860) and widely used by art historians.

3. Dudley Poore.

4. The Paseo de la Castellana. See Letter 44, n. 7 above.

5. Mr. S.: Peter Sweeney. Vaquería: reference to a small dairy restaurant where the Sweeneys often went in the afternoon. McComb liked the place, which was not characteristically Spanish, had a tearoom atmosphere, and was on one of the fine avenues. Dos Passos was decidedly not fond of the restaurant. Telephone interview with Dudley Poore, October 3, 1976.

6. A confectioner's shop, with an upper-class clientele. Baedeker's *Spain and Portugal* (1913) gave the address as Puerta del Sol 8.

7. Güell Park and the unfinished Church of the Holy Family, both by the Catalonian architect Antoni Gaudí i Cornet (1852–1926).

8. Quel theâtre! [Fr.], "How theatrical!"

134

end of august [1926] in
a little wood near Westport[1]

Dear Arthur—

Your letters and cards have been extremely pleasant to receive—I feel rather cheap for having nothing of interest to trade for them—I'm exactly as when you last saw me. Fairly content tangled in various doldrums in the environs of New York. I've been working hard all summer

on a play without achieving anything of the slightest consequence—
I'm afraid I feel the demons of navigation brewing.

You and Constance[2] seem to be doing Spain with Sweenian thorough-
ness. It's pleasant to be reminded of those strange seasons in Madrid
and the Vaquería—Somehow I dont feel that they were altogether
wasted—You can imagine my satisfaction on hearing of Sovreignty's[3]
good health—Some things at least may prove to be eternal.

Harpers address is I think 39 East 33rd.[4]

I have sent you a garbage Man[5] care Cooks Madrid

Speaking of Mallorca you speak is if you hadn't gone to Lluch and
Soller and the place at the end of the island of which I forget the name.
I hope you went for the white tranquility and the ensaimada.[6]

What are you up to next? Are you really going to trust yourselves
into Mussolini's shiny imperium. I guarentee you'll find it darned
unpleasant.

Spain's the only place in Europe where the government doesnt matter.

I'm finishing this letter in the little house of one of the Masses editors
beside a gasoline lamp that may explode any minute—it makes a most
dangerous roaring noise. The inevitable moth is just about to singe it's
wings

Do write me more about Europe. I cant imagine it as being of the
slightest interest. Not even the franc is falling any more. At least they've
kicked out one of their damn dictators. Maybe the wops can take a
pointer from the Greeks.

A woman who fainted over Valentino's[7] bier was discovered by the
attending physicians to have an onion in her handkerchief. When
Gertrude Ederle arrived Dudley Field Malone who was running the
parade became indignant because Selectman Hauenstaufer made a
speech about how it was her German virtues that had led Trudy to success across the wild channel waves, and tried to stop the proceedings,
but already the German singing societies from upper Amsterdam Avenue
were singing Die Wacht am Rhien in front of City Hall.[8]

Germaine Championnière[9] writes me that Dudley[10] mysterously
materialized in [The remainder of this letter is missing.]

1. Presumably Westport, Connecticut.
2. McComb's wife.
3. Mrs. Wood, the elderly Anglo-American guest at the Carmen de Matamoros.
4. McComb, writing to Dos Passos care of his publisher, had used the address 49 East
33 Street.
5. Published by Harper and Brothers on July 20, 1926.
6. Ensaimada [Sp.], "light pastry roll or bun."

7. Rudolph Valentino (1895–1926), the film star, had died on August 23. In the biography of Valentino in *The Big Money* Dos Passos later satirized the charlatanry and hysteria at his funeral.

8. "Die Wacht am Rhein": German patriotic song. Dos Passos is giving a fictionalized, satirical account of a recent event. On August 6, 1926, Gertrude Ederle (b. 1906) swam from Cape Gris-Nez, France, to Kingsdown, England, becoming the first woman to swim the English Channel and breaking the existing men's speed record. New York City gave Miss Ederle, a butcher's daughter born and reared on the west side of Manhattan, a tumultuous greeting. In the harbor she was taken aboard the city's welcoming boat, the *Macom,* then given a ticker tape and confetti parade to City Hall, where the Mayor received her, and afterwards given a triumphal procession up Fifth Avenue and on to her home at Amsterdam Avenue and Sixty-third Street.

Dos Passos' burlesque presentation seems to derive from an incident aboard the *Macom:*

> When Miss Ederle entered the cabin for the interview with newspaper men, she was greeted by Magistrate Charles A. Oberwager, speaking for the United German Societies. . . . [He] spoke of the fact that Miss Ederle was the daughter of German parents. . . . Mr. [Dudley Field] Malone [her lawyer, who had charge of arrangements for her reception] told Magistrate Oberwager that he objected to the introduction of the Germanic element into the welcome to Miss Ederle. He informed the Magistrate that all those in the welcome were invited to take part as Americans. Mr. Malone said that those who insisted in making it a hyphenated celebration were at liberty to withdraw. [*New York Times,* August 28, 1926, pp. 1, 3. The quotation is on p. 3.]

9. Mademoiselle Germaine Lucas-Champonnière, a French friend of Dos Passos, whom he had met during the war.

10. Dudley Poore.

135

[Letterhead: Hotel Tokatlian]
[Constantinople-Pera]
[le] 15 Sept. [192]6.[1]

Oh Dos. . . .

There's an exquisite autumnal coolness and a breeze from the Black Sea all the time — very grateful after the dust & heat of Athens — where yr. servant came down with an ignominious disease called sandfly fever and had no sooner recovered than he was the witness of street-fighting when Condylis proceeded à la fois[2] against the royalists & communists & Pangalos' guard. My girondin soul was not ill-pleased at his success. . . .

As ever
Arthur.

1. The dating information shown in brackets is part of the printed letterhead.
2. [Fr.] "At one and the same time."

136

VENEZIA—3 Oct.—'26

Dos—

I was about to write you anyway to relieve my mind of one or two sentiments—when lo, your letter of August 31 (!) finds its way here—but our mail has been in a dreadful state. . . .

The East, as I've written you is Vanity. Not worth it. Our delight to be in Venice!—You wrote me a p.c. from here 5 years ago comparing V. to Coney Island. Caro amico,[1] you are very wrong. Not all the beads, glass factories [,] tourists, singing in lighted gondolas, etc. can cheapen or spoil it. Its fundamental distinction. And after the East, its <u>solidity</u>, its civilised air—these are what impress one.

Have you read Je brule Moscou in Morand's latest (L'Europe Galante)[2]—amusing, yet it adds a little fuel to my re-kindled flame for the West. After one has looked at the truculent visage of Mustapha K.[3] in every shop window for ten days, croyez-moi,[4] Mr. Coolidge shines with a beauty never suspected!! . . .

No we didn't 'do' Spain thoroughly—just the great things for C's[5] sake. Coïmbra, Oporto, **Salamanca, Burgos, *Gerona, *Ronda were the new places for me.[6]

Madrid—the Vaquería wasted—perish the thought—one has learned a little perhaps since but I don't see that that alters it. Those days were good too. I like to be reminded of them though (or because) they're invested with the melancholy of all giorni passati.[7]— —

Yes, we went to Soller, & Estellenchs but not to Alcudia or Pollensa We consumed ensaimadas daily.

At this very moment they've begun to sing Santa Lucia under the window!!! . . .

I close—you'll not want to hear more of this Europe. But Dos, write me a line to the Chatham [,] E. 48 & Vanderbilt Ave. about Nov 6 or 7.—Or call me up.

À bientôt—Love from us both

Arthur.

Don't let the demons of Navigation get you till I arrive. They certainly have got hold of <u>us</u>.

1. [It.] "Dear friend."
2. Paul Morand, *L'Europe galante* (Paris: Bernard Grasset, 1925), pp. 173–213.
3. Mustafa Kemal, president of Turkey.
4. [Fr.] "Believe me."
5. Constance McComb's.

6. McComb is imitating Baedeker's use of asterisks as commendation marks.
7. [It.] "Past days."

137

[Art postcard]

Rome, 26 Jan. '27.

Dos, It was nice to get your card & know you were actually in Mexico City. I really want to go there—in spite of my increasing disinclination for travel.——We lunched in the sun on the Pincio[1] to-day & later looked at Mussolini's lion-cub "Italia" in the zoo. There is a new tea-room on Via Sistina & a new & intelligent English Bookstore opp. the Am. Exp.—On the crowded streets people are told by helmeted policemen to walk on the left hand side. Otherwise nothing new.—I work afternoons at the Am. Academy on the Janiculum[2]—walking down the steps by S. Pietro in Montorio, to the sound of bells in the city below, is very nice.—But I have something of a New World nostalgia—nothing could be stranger—Let me know of your further adventures & when you return to the U.S. We go to Florence about the 8$\underline{^{th}}$ of Feb.

As ever
Arthur.

1. Hill of Rome with beautiful grounds and a famed view from the west.
2. The American Academy in Rome, with a School of Classical Studies and a School of Fine Arts. The Janiculum is another Roman hill.

138

[Art postcard]

Florence
6 March 1927.

Dos, It was a surprise to learn you were still in Mexico City on the day when we came from Rome to Florence. Décidémment[1] Mexico must be an exciting place—in a way there's nowhere I'd rather go.—Italy changes about March 1$\underline{^{st}}$ and does her best to seduce one.—But I shall be back in America about mid-summer.—

But Dos, with me hungry for Aztec heads & Churrigueresque[2] door-
ways, you send me p.c.'s of (1) Brera-Crivelli Madonna[3] (2) O Paco
do Cintra[4] (3) Royal Saloon Carriages L & N W R'y. (4) The "Flying
Scotchman" at Hatfield.[5] (colored!)—Now, I ask you is that fair or
decent, nay rather (as Vernon Lee[6] would say) is it not positevily
malicious?—   Thanks for the kind words about poor little Bacchiacca.[7] At present I'm deep in a volume on Bronzino which ought
to be ready by next fall & which I hope you'll like. When does one
see you again?—

Arthur.

. . . .

1. Décidément [Fr.], "decidedly."
2. Richly exuberant baroque architectural style of late seventeenth- and early
eighteenth-century Spain; also, that style as adapted in Latin America, especially as executed by native workers.
3. Painting in the Brera Gallery, Milan, by the Venetian painter Carlo Crivelli (c. 1430–
after 1493).
4. O Paço de Cintra [Port.], "The Palace of Cintra" (Sintra, Portugal).
5. The London and North Western Railway is the "R'y" indicated in McComb's item
three. *The Flying Scotsman,* in item four, was the London and North Eastern Railway's
famous train between London and Edinburgh.
6. Pseudonym of Violet Paget (1856–1935), English essayist and novelist, member
of the Anglo-Florentine colony, and a remarkably cultured, imaginative, and clever person.
Her villa, writes Ernest Samuels, had in the 1890s already become "a chief meeting ground
for intellectuals and aesthetes of Anglo-American and Florentine society" (Samuels, *Bernard
Berenson: The Making of a Connoisseur,* p. 177). McComb first met her in the fall of
1922.
7. McComb, "Francesco Ubertini (Bacchiacca)," *Art Bulletin* 8 (March 1926): 140–67.

139

[Art postcard]

Boston   17 May '28.

Dos   Thank you for your Key West letter. I was passing through
N.Y the other day & called you up at 9:15 in the morning but you
were not to be found. I hoped we might have lunch together. Hardinge
S.[1] said he had seen you at a theatre [;] otherwise it never would have
occured to me that you would be back so soon. Send me an occasional
p. c. from Europe.—I'm glad you're doing a novel.—I never did like
the theatre anyway, I've decided.—Just 5 yrs. ago, I see from my diary
you sent me The Waste Land.[2]   A.

. . . .

1. Hardinge Scholle.
2. Eliot's poem was published in 1922.

140

[Baku, U.S.S.R.
Autumn? 1928]

Dear Arthur—I always like to write you when I stray from the straight
and narrow and find myself within the walls of the uncontrollable Ritz.
Tumbling off the train here in Baku, after having slept on boards for
weeks (and liked it) crossed three high passes in the Caucausus and
variously transported myself over magnificent mountain roads, on foot,
on horse and in a little and horrible waggon called an arbat, an insidious
oriental took me in a cab to what turns out to be a genuine Ritz—fit
even for you or Stewart¹ to softly rest your bottoms in—fancy beds,
service, caviar, Georgian wine—at Jesus only Knows what cost—and
even baths. You will be glad to hear that it is run by the Hotel Trust
of the Republic of Ajerbeidjan—And that it is the means by which the
republic gets back some of the large salaries they pay their oil techni-
cians—I have just finished a vast dish of caviar and am now eating Mr.
Sturgeon with mushrooms and I expect to sleep like an executed grand
duke.² It difficult for me to finish letters here. I'm now in Moscow,
trying to find a room to live in. The weather's like Madrid in the
autumn. And the town is fine. I think even you would like it. You could
eat your odd little scraps of fodder in vegetarian restaurants and the
theatres are pretty darn fine. There are few automibles, to everybody's
woe, but to the great pleasure of the pedestrian. There are 2 magnificent collections of French painting Cezanne, Gauguin and Van Gogh
by the barrel. And there is a great deal of rather expensive but delicious
fruit for sale everywhere. Incidentally where did that Van Dongen³ come
from? Arthur I hope it wont be Van Dongen after Barrocco.⁴ One thing
leads to another you know. If there was ever a worse painter I'll eat
my shirt.

Didnt manage to see Elaine⁵ when I was in England but I hope to
on the way back. I expect to be here a couple of months more and to
be back for the inauguration of Andrew Mellon⁶ or the Kellogg Pact.⁷
Are your passports ready for the next war?

love
Dos

In Baku—they have air raid drills and everybody has to run around and sirens blow and large cannon-crackers are dropped from 'Anglichani' planes and all the comsomols[8] sport gasmasks. Everybody seemed to enjoy it.

1. Stewart Mitchell.

2. The letter is in pencil up to this point and in ink afterwards—the change corresponding to a change in Dos Passos' locale.

3. Kees van Dongen (1877–1968), Dutch painter who settled in Paris. A member of the Fauvist group in 1906, he became a highly fashionable portraitist at the end of World War I.

4. Probably Federico Barocci or Baroccio (1526?–1612), Italian mannerist painter, b. in Urbino.

5. The former Mrs. E. E. Cummings (née Orr), now Mrs. Frank MacDermot. She had married MacDermot shortly after divorcing Cummings. See Letter 128, n. 5 above and Kennedy, *Dreams in the Mirror: A Biography of E. E. Cummings*, p. 273.

6. Andrew William Mellon (1855–1937), industrialist, financier, and (1921–32) U.S. secretary of the treasury. Allan Nevins called him "the dominant figure in the Harding and Coolidge administrations." At the Republican National Convention of 1928, Mellon supported Herbert Hoover, who became the party's nominee for president on June 14. On Mellon's importance from 1921 through 1928, see Nevins' article on him in the *Dictionary of American Biography, Supplement Two*. The quotation above is from the article (p. 448).

7. The Kellogg-Briand Pact, renouncing war as an instrument of national policy. Delegates of fifteen nations, including the United States, signed the pact in Paris on August 27, 1928, and the U.S. Senate ratified it on January 15, 1929.

8. Comsomols: members of the Communist Union of Youth. The Russian word for which Dos Passos writes *Anglichani* is the noun for "Englishmen"; his spelling is phonetically appropriate, but the word is customarily transliterated *anglichane*. For the adjective "English" one would use *angliskie*. In sentence two of the letter, *arbat* should properly be *arba*.

141

108 Mt. Vernon St.   Boston   27 Oct. '28.

Dos,—It was nice to get the flimsy envelope with the foreign stamp, and inside the variegated scraps of paper written over with the sketchy account of your adventures. The Hotel Trust of Azerbaidjan! I think that would have pained Matthew Arnold, in whom is the only other reference to that country I know. I was relieved to think of you back in Moscow and away from those Black Sea sturgeon. (I converted someone to Kellogg's Corn Flakes not long since)[1]—I also got a card from Moscow from you—your previous visit.—Your Airways, Inc.[2] is on the bookstands. I've not yet read it, as I am, if you will believe it extraordinarily busy—really working for one of the few times in my life. I give four lectures a week & attend to 30 tutees (all dumb-bells). The course seems to be coming along quite pleasantly. I'm just in the middle of talking about Furini.[3] Do you know his stuff? Deep harsh blues and a sultry atmosphere against which very caressingly painted feminine nudes. One of the high points. I want to get hold of you and talk Seicento & Settecento[4] to you, make you listen [—] you won't have to like Domenichino or Guido Reni. But Feti, Strozzi, Magnasco, Crespi, Furini, Guercino drawings[5] — I'm sure with your Florentine scientific bias you've never looked at any of these attentively. I know in advance also that you won't like them, since you admitted once to not really liking <u>painting</u> as such. However I want to talk to you just the same. About Russia too. You are missing the amazing imbecilities of the presidential campaign. . . .

Nov. 6. Election day. This was not mailed, by inadvertence.

Are you going to be back by Christmas so that we can have our annual meal at the Lafayette with Dudley?[6] I'm sailing on the Carmania May 10 for Plymouth.

Love
A.

1. Flaked cereal was originally a health food, developed at the Battle Creek Sanitarium.
2. *Airways, Inc.* (New York: Macaulay Co., 1928). It was published on October 15.
3. Francesco Furini (c. 1600–46), Italian painter, b. in Florence.
4. [It.] Il seicento, "the seventeenth century"; il settecento, "the eighteenth century."
5. Besides Furini, the Italian painters named are Domenichino (1581–1641), b. in Bologna; Guido Reni (1575–1642), b. in Bologna; Domenico Feti (c. 1589–1624), b. in Rome; Bernardo Strozzi (1581–1644), b. in Genoa; Alessandro Magnasco (1667–1749), b. in Genoa; probably Giuseppe Maria Crespi (1665–1747), b. in Bologna; Guercino (1591–1666), b. near Bologna.
6. The Hotel Lafayette, where McComb wanted to dine with Dos Passos and Dudley Poore, was at Ninth Street and University Place in New York. Like the nearby Brevoort, it was noted for its cuisine. The hotel, which acquired its name Lafayette in 1902, was closed in 1949.

142

108 Mt. Vernon Street   Boston
24 IV 29.

Dos, mon ami,   For long I've been meaning to write you. In fact I was going to announce my impending arrival at one of those discreet, those almost sly, Epicurean breakfasts which you enjoy daily with Dudley. Its a horrid disappointment that I shall not, on account of having changed my sailing to one from Boston on May 30. . . .

I wanted to thank you too for Airways Inc. I was delighted to have a copy. I will be candid. I speak here primarily as a bibliophile. (as a collector of your complete works!)[1] I will confess I have never been really fond of the theatre. I think the theatre is an intolerably cramping & artificial medium for getting said the kind of thing I want to hear. (I make an exception for the Chekov sort of thing. And of course for the commercial revue — at least for the Noel Coward[2] kind) But look at James. Look at Conrad. — I'm glad, my friend, that you're getting out of it — not wasting any longer the wealth of your talent on the slut.

I would love to speak at length to your unbelieving ears all these things, over a meal at the Athens. But I suppose the actions of the last Governor of Massachusetts will prevent your re-appearing here. I regret it. I regret it very much. — If you & Dudley had come recently you would have seen a finer French show than Knoedlers.[3] . . .

. . . Send me a card indicating whether you will be in Europe & if so at what address. They tell me you are just back from Florida. — Will there be a Palm Beach–Coral Gables scene in the next novel. I hope so. . . .

As ever
Arthur.

. . . .

1. Parenthetical remark inserted with caret.
2. Sir Noel Coward (1899–1973), English playwright, actor, and composer. He was knighted in 1970.
3. M. Knoedler and Co., international art gallery, located in New York City, Paris, and London.

143

[Art postcard]

Boston   23 Dec. [1929]

Dos, I was glad to hear of your sailing on the Roussillon instead of on the Am. Scantic to the chilly north. — Cuthbert[1] is in Paris [−] his address Hot. des Balcons, rue Casimir Delavigne (near Odéon) — I have just engaged a passage on the DeGrasse for June. — Dudley telegraphs he may come to Boston soon. — I was only sorry to be suffering from that peculiarly depressing middle-aged tiredness due to overwork the one night you were here.

Best to K.[2]

Send me cards

Arthur

1. Cuthbert Wright.
2. Katharine Dos Passos.

McComb in 1931, in Boston.
Courtesy of Robert Lynch

Letters

𝒟OS PASSOS AND MCCOMB remained in touch during the 1930s, although there was never again anything like the long, continual companionship they and Dudley Poore had enjoyed in Spain. Traveling as much as ever, Dos Passos made his home in Provincetown, on the bay. At the time a number of his friends from Harvard days lived in the Boston area: McComb remained at Harvard until 1939 and was in Boston for most of his life; Poore taught English at Harvard from 1930 to 1939; Robert Hillyer taught there from 1919 to 1926 and again from 1928 through 1944; and Stewart Mitchell, who was with the *New England Quarterly* and the Massachusetts Historical Society, lived in the area. Boston was not as accessible as new highway construction made it after World War II. But Dos Passos would be there and see his friends from time to time, and he and Katy would invite friends to visit them.

Most of Dos Passos' friends did not share his politics, a fact which would have surprised a public which thought of him only as the best-known American left-radical novelist of his generation. Although Dos Passos was in sympathy with the anarcho-syndicalism of the I.W.W., he saw the Communists during part of the 1930s as the most active group dedicated to ending capitalism. In 1931 he was a member of the Communist-inspired committee which Theodore Dreiser led into Kentucky to investigate the plight of striking coal miners. And in 1932, the harshest year of the Great Depression, he was one of a group of fifty-two writers, painters, and professional people who publicly supported the Communist candidate for president.[1]

Dudley Poore recalls Dos Passos and McComb arguing about the labor movement some time in the 1930s, while Poore, Dos Passos, and Katy were in McComb's home. Poore has forgotten the specific topic, but says that at some point Dos Passos cried out "Nonsense! Nonsense!"

and McComb turned white and cold with anger and finally made no answer.*

In the spring of 1933 Dos Passos suffered a recurrence of rheumatic fever. Katy had needed her tonsils removed, and he took her to Johns Hopkins Hospital. His friend W. Horsley Gantt now worked at the Johns Hopkins medical school, and they could stay with him in Baltimore. No sooner had Katy vacated her bed than Dos Passos came down with his illness. Racked with pain and short of funds, he took his turn as a patient. It was a good time to have friends, he did, and they rallied around: Gantt got him excellent medical talent (at least some of the treatment was gratis); Hemingway sent one thousand dollars, a great deal of money in 1933; and Gerald and Sara Murphy bought Dos Passos ship tickets so that he could come and convalesce at Cap d'Antibes. The tickets were for the first Atlantic liner with gyro-stabilizers, the 48,502-ton *Conte di Savoia,* which had made its maiden voyage from Genoa to New York only months before.[2] After Dos Passos' crossing, McComb wrote him a sympathetic note which reflected their mutual interest in steamships and their antagonism in politics. He expressed satisfaction that Dos Passos had traveled by the Italian line.

McComb was having his joke. Taking the Italian line was convenient, but it implied no acceptance of Mussolini. In the early 1930s one of Dos Passos' chief motives in sometimes working in tandem with the Communists was to have left-wing unity against the Fascist threat. Believing that monopolistic capitalism led to war and fascism, he looked to leftists' unity to counteract it in the United States and abroad. But the Communists had other ideas. In Kentucky Dos Passos had discovered with bitterness that they were preoccupied with party tactics, not with the fates of individual miners. But he refrained from criticizing them publicly because he valued their vigorous agitation. In February 1934 he was outraged by the Communists' lack of concern for left-wing unity when they broke up a non-Communist rally protesting Dollfuss' armed attack on Austrian Social Democrats; and the next month he publicly accused the Communists of "unintelligent fanaticism."[3] From his correspondence with Edmund Wilson we can see that by the end of the year he had lost hope in Russia because of Stalin's terror.†

---

*Poore says that in Spain the arguments between Dos Passos and McComb had been amicable; now in Boston, although everything was outwardly polite, the argument was "too unpleasant not to remember." He thought that the friendship might be at an end. Telephone interview with Poore, June 14, 1975.

†Dos Passos was repelled by events which followed hard upon Sergei M. Kirov's death. On December 1, 1934, Kirov, a member of the Russian Communist party politburo, was assassinated in Leningrad, probably by Stalin's order. Using Kirov's assassination

McComb in 1934. A scholarly author, he was teaching fine arts at Harvard.
Courtesy of Robert Lynch

Despite all the changes, Dos Passos' views were wide apart from McComb's in March 1935, when McComb answered a long letter Dos Passos had written from Jamaica. We don't have the letter from the island. But McComb's reply indicates that Dos Passos said something slightly disparaging of British society, like what he wrote to Edmund Wilson about the same time:

> Jamaica is wonderful to look at and smell when you're away from any human habitation—but the condition humaine here presents a dreary, and not comic as you'd expect, similacrum of British society in black-face—The climate is wonderful and so are the fireflies and the little chameleons and the hummingbirds, but I certainly shant be sorry to leave this Terrestial paradise. We almost kissed a large party of cruise passengers with rattles, beads, little bottles of rum, souvenir baskets etc that poured into Charley's Bar where we were having a drink today; they looked so much more lively than the local prunefaced mulattos—what a miserable race.[4]

In his reply, McComb described his own feelings about the British Empire and linked them with those of J. P. Morgan. Bringing the finan-

as a pretext, Stalin inaugurated a period of devastating political purges and terror, which lasted until 1939. Dos Passos wrote Wilson, in a letter of December 23, 1934: "This business about Kirov looks very very bad to me. In fact it has completely destroyed my benefit-of-the-doubt attitude towards the Stalinists—"

cier in was probably another dig at Dos Passos, who had attacked "The House of Morgan" in one of the most memorable of the short biographies in *1919* (volume two of *U.S.A.,* published in 1932). With humor, extreme prudence, and some acuity, McComb went on to caution Dos Passos that his left radical politics were not in accord with his self-interest in survival.

144

[Picture postcard: R.M.S. *Aquitania*]

[1933?]

[To Dos Passos]
  BEWARE!
This is to announce the arrival of the ARCH-REACTIONARY on the shores of the Old World. The Plus Ultra double-eagled, K. and K. sous-signant[1] will have as his address (for these are degenerate times) c/o Am. Exp. Florence (But He will alas be unable to perform his devoirs[2] at the tomb of Prince Metternich (R.I.P.)[3]

Dos, I was awfully sorry to hear about your second bout of fever [.] I kept myself informed viâ Dudley[4] and was pleased to learn that you were allowing the Conte di Savoia to transport you to the sands of Antibes.

Here's hoping the gyroscopes had a soothing, as it were massaging, effect.

Best to Kate.[5]

A. K McC.

1. Plus ultra [Fr.], "most extreme"; double-eagled: reference to Hapsburg coat of arms; K. and K.: kaiserlich und königlich [Ger.], referring to the emperor and king of the Austro-Hungarian dual monarchy; sous-signant [based on Fr. present participle *soussignant*], "person undersigning."
2. [Fr.] "Duties." Earlier in the sentence, *But* is inserted before *He* with a caret.
3. R.I.P. [abbrev.]: requiescat in pace [Lat.], "may he rest in peace."
4. Dudley Poore.
5. Katharine Dos Passos.

145

10 March 1935

Dear Dos—It was very nice to get your long letter from Jamaica. To have it lying on my desk was like old times. I enjoyed it. . . .

I thought the natives of Jamaica much more attractive than those of Nassau who seem to have been crossed with Jews. And I rather like their gentle imitation of England. Some mulattos the women in wide straw hats[1] came on board to look at our ship & behaved as if they were going to a garden-party. It was amusing and I liked it. Particularly in contrast to the American tourists (thus I had the reverse experience to yours & Kates)[2] who slapped one on the back, called one by one's first name and asked personal questions.—The Cubans were about as bad, but it did not strike one so painfully because as foreigners there is no reason why they should obey Anglo-Saxon rules of good form.

But I would have liked Jamaica apart from the scenery—I was not there long enough to be bored, though I might have ended by becoming so. Those admirable black policemen with red stripes on their trousers, and pith helmets! Kingston was poor, to be sure, but there was an air of ease about it all. Life & property safe and justice to be had (none of this in Cuba). I confess to a feeling of great security & relaxation on British soil. I am morally at ease in the British Empire (Mr. J. P. Morgan, I believe, feels the same way!) which I suppose is why I like it so.

The climate of Havana I thought near perfection and it's a seductive city. I only wish I could have seen it before 1898. Even in 1915 the sky-line (now ruined) was still unchanged, and the Capitol had not been built.[3] I feel badly at having missed you in Havana.

It would have been pleasant wrangling with you in Charly's Bar. I gave up my chance to go into the Church some time ago!—I admire T S Eliot & think he's logical enough with his insistence on the Church. Metternich (brought up under the "Enlightenment") towards the end began to soften toward the Jesuits. I do not think my lack of religious temperament would be any bar. From that point of view the churches are all 'devaluated'—the only truly religious people to-day being Communists & Nazis. These promise the distant descendants of their adherents pie in the sky. (Jam to-morrow and a nice little Ogpu[4] to-day.)

I should like to urge you, too, to give consideration to your personal situation. If Fascism comes you go into a concentration camp. If Bolshevism, you will be liquidated for "deviation" (i.e. shot in the back of the neck in a cellar, or sent to die more slowly in an Alaskan (?) Lumber-camp.) Under decrepit capitalism, your life is secure & your freedom of movement & opinion unhampered. I therefore urge you to forsake the fashionable intellectual movements of the day and to take your stand, as it were, for God, for country & for Yale.[5]

Let Kate also ponder these valuable words.   When do we see you—summer?

Arthur

Hillyer is giving a dinner for RSM [,] DGP & A McC.[6] on the 21st to commemorate the twentieth anniversary of our meeting. It would be much better if you could be there. A sweet idea the 20th ann. or lugubrious, depending on your temperament.

I must say John Strachey (the Eton-proletarian) writes very well [.] I liked his comparing Dr. Hayek to the Red Queen.[7] Dr. H. has the dope on the economic crisis. Admits the things that would cure it can't be done.

H. G. Wells & Laski[8] have both lost hope recently. You see even our Liberal friends are convinced something is really, really wrong. Poor dears.

A.

1. "the women . . . hats" inserted with caret.
2. Katharine Dos Passos.
3. McComb first visited Cuba in 1915, according to his memoir "A Foreign Dye."
4. The Soviet secret police (1923–34).
5. Final words of Yale's alma mater song "Bright College Years"; also a Yale motto.
6. Robert Stewart Mitchell, Dudley Greene Poore, and Arthur McComb.
7. John Strachey (1901–63), British leftist politician and writer, who had an Eton background. His biographer Hugh Thomas writes: "Between 1932 and 1935, Strachey published three political books which established him as the most articulate spokesman for Marxism in Britain, indeed probably the most respectable English Marxist." In the third of these, *The Nature of Capitalist Crisis* (1935), Strachey devoted much space to *Prices and Production* (1931), by the economist Friedrich August von Hayek (b. 1899). Strachey declared: "It [Hayek's " 'sound' way"] reminds one of the Red Queen's remark to Alice: 'Here, you see, it takes all the running you can do to keep in the same place. If you want to get somewhere else you must run at least twice as fast as that.' In the same severe spirit, Dr. Hayek tells the capitalists that, if they mean to restore the rate of profit without inflation, they must not only cut costs by means of technical improvements as fast as prices fall, but that they must also cut wage costs in order to get ahead of the fall in prices." Hugh Thomas, *John Strachey* (London: Eyre Methuen, 1973), p. 129; John Strachey, *The Nature of Capitalist Crisis* (New York: Covici-Friede, 1935), p. 89.
8. Harold J. Laski.

Letters

$\mathcal{D}$OS PASSOS WAS WRITING continuously during the 1930s, as he did during most of his adult life. Friends in Provincetown remember his routine: at least four hours of intensive, uninterrupted work every morning, with Katy guarding him against intruders. In the afternoon he would take long walks, call on or entertain friends, enjoy drinks, and read. When he went off to do journalistic work he would write in his hotel room, and when he visited friends he would seclude himself mornings.[1] Considering the quality, his productivity was astonishing. *The Big Money* appeared in 1936, and the assembled trilogy in January 1938. With *U.S.A.* he achieved the reputation of being one of the two or three most talented American novelists of his generation.

U.S.A. was a radical leftist work, but by the time Dos Passos finished the trilogy he was finding hope in Franklin D. Roosevelt's administration. In September 1936 he published an article in *Esquire* pointing out the political significance of the German satirical painter George Grosz's emigrating to the United States: Europe had become stifling to intellectual and artistic effort, he wrote, and the United States was now "the refuge of the traditions of western European culture."[2] And in the fall of 1936 Dos Passos was so impressed by the New Deal that he voted enthusiastically for Roosevelt's re-election.[3]

While finding new hope in the United States, Dos Passos remained attached to the Spanish people—though he never saw much merit in their governments. He went to Spain in 1937 to try to help the anti-Fascist forces in the Civil War, and his experience turned him into an outspoken anti-Communist. His trip followed an undertaking by some American writers, including Ernest Hemingway, Archibald MacLeish, and himself to help produce a motion picture which would gain sympathy for the Republican government. In Spain he found that a friend of his, José Robles Pazos, had been executed. Interpreting the execution as due to the Communists' attempt to destroy whatever leftist elements they couldn't control, he soon left Spain and proceeded to denounce the Communists' intolerance, will to power, and murderous machinery. Though still in favor of sending arms to the Spanish Loyalists, he despaired more than ever of Europe and now devoted most of his attention to his own country, stressing representative majority rule, individual liberty, and the need for democracy to permeate American industry.[4]

For Dos Passos and McComb, what conversation there was on politics must have remained vexatious all through the 1930s, despite Dos Passos' disgust with the Communists, for McComb stood politically with Mussolini and Franco. McComb's friends at Harvard and in Boston knew him as a pro-Fascist, though not a pro-Nazi. He was outspokenly pro-Franco during the Spanish Civil War and continually expressed sympathy with Mussolini before World War II—even appearing in a black shirt and saying jokingly he was wearing it in support of Il Duce. But while believing in a strong hand at the helm as an assurance of safety and order, he was nonetheless a gentle person, always an observer.[5]

McComb much later related an incident in which he expressed his pro-Franco sympathies to Bernard Berenson. It took place at Berenson's villa I Tatti, where McComb was often a dinner or tea guest when he came to nearby Florence.[6]

During the Spanish Civil War Berenson was affectionately critical of Mrs. [Edith] Wharton's inevitable attitude and referred to "dearest Edith—a rabid Francoist of course". But although Mrs. Wharton had no particular connexion with Spain, it is hard to see how the friend of Maréchal Lyautey, the inhabitant of the Faubourg, the owner of the Pavillon Colombe, and the possessor of a private fortune could have had, or been expected to have, "Republican" or anti-clerical sympathies. B. B. however, who also had not much connexion with Spain took the conventional views of the popular front, in France and America, for truths. It was the only time I think that I ventured to differ, or rather that I cared with all due deference to express my difference from B. B. I had, as it happened, lived in Spain at an impressionable period of life—the matter was too near the heart to pay B. B. the dubious (in this case highly questionable) compliment of total silence. But my mild reservation in favour of conservative Spain, my ritual bow, as it were, to the traditionalism of the illustrious General, brought out something attractive in Berenson. He did not like argument and always shunned it. (Naturally I too had no wish to argue believing as I do with Eliot that "in our time, controversy seems to me, on really fundamental matters, to be futile", and again Spain was such a matter as Eliot speaks of, and indeed was the litmus paper of the period). When therefore Nicky Mariano, who was present — this was in the drawing-room where the Sassetta hangs — said to me (not I hope believing it, but merely I think to draw B. B. out): "But you say all this intentionally as a pose of contrariness, don't you?" B. B. put in quickly: "No, No, Nicky — it is so, I am afraid. He really means it. But let us not talk of it, because it divides us". I was glad to fall in with this. . . .[7]

A *habitué* of Berenson's library when in Florence, McComb had been working steadily on Italian art since 1920. Harvard University Press published his *Agnolo Bronzino: His Life and Works* in 1928 and his *The Baroque Painters of Italy* in 1934.[8] Scholarly in their tone, with little to allure the general reader, the two books were well received and useful, the former being the only one on Bronzino in English. Despite these and other substantial publications, and a promotion to assistant professor, McComb was not kept on at Harvard. His friends offer different explanations: the requirements were made very stiff at about the time he came up for tenure, he was too independent to engage in academic politicking, and his love affairs hurt him at the university. Bernard Berenson wrote him later: "I fear you have been too un-sensational hitherto in yr. teaching & writing to satisfy the demands of academic salesmanship."[9] Still, with McComb's reputation as a scholar of Italian Renaissance and baroque painting, he could probably have gotten a professorship at some other good university. But he did not care to teach again or to live anywhere less congenial than Boston. He inherited money at about the time he left Harvard and with his European background found it natural to enjoy an independent gentleman's life.[10]

When the United States entered World War II, McComb was living at 94 Chestnut Street, in an apartment with an old aesthetic bachelor-digs atmosphere. The sound of aircraft overhead terrorized and enraged him. Desiring tranquility, he withdrew to Gloucester, Massachusetts, that winter and in the spring of 1942 moved to Asheville, North Carolina, even as he had moved to Spain in 1918. Asheville was more economical than Boston, and McComb now had money problems, but his major motive was to get away from the war. "V for Vichy" he had teased Stewart Mitchell in September 1941, parodying the "V for Victory" slogan that his countryman Winston Churchill was popularizing.

In July 1942 he wrote Mitchell that he was taking steps towards opting for citizenship in Eire (he received it the next year). Writing from Asheville for the *25th Anniversary Report* of the Harvard Class of 1918, he declared that it was "just as well not to have one's convictions, such as they are, on record" in the strange times in which he lived.[11]

Unlike McComb, Dos Passos felt impelled to be with the action, as well as to put his convictions on record every year of his life. Now in his forties, he saw the war as a journalist. He traveled to Great Britain to attend a P.E.N. (International Association of Poets, Playwrights, Editors, and Novelists) congress in 1941 and afterwards published several articles describing wartime politics and society in that country. Remembering that during a war the most important changes are apt to occur at home (a point which he had carefully documented in *U.S.A.*), he spent much time during the next two years talking to farmers, workers, labor leaders, businessmen and government officials in all parts of the United States. These experiences he described in *State of the Nation* (1944).[12]

Early in 1945 Dos Passos was in the Pacific area as a reporter with the American combat forces, and towards the end of the year he was in Germany. In the defeated Reich he observed day-to-day problems of the occupation, the relationship of Russian and American troops, and the onset of the Nuremberg war crime trials. These observations abroad he described in the wide-ranging *Tour of Duty* (1946).[13]

"Thrown into direct contact with all kinds of people," he later remarked, "I found myself praising and blaming men for their skills, for their character, for themselves instead of for their position in the lineup of the Marxist class war. So vanished the last traces of the Greenwich Village radical who saw only certain limited classes of men as socially good."[14]

The wartime years gave Dos Passos a new respect for conservatism; after viewing wartime England in 1941, he wrote that never before had it occurred to him that ritual was a bar to retrogression as well as to progress. To Edmund Wilson he wrote in 1945 of a distaste for "monolithic socialism even of the most benign cast." And in a postwar article in *Life* he publicly rejected socialism, saying that conditions in Europe had changed though ideological names remained the same. Socialism had once seemed to promise:

1. "ascendancy" of an anti-militarist class (the workers)
2. industrial as well as political democracy

3. increased individual liberty

4. substitution of public service for money profit as "the driving motive of human behavior"

5. wider distribution of goods.

Judged by these standards, Russian Marxism had certainly failed.[15] As for British socialism, Dos Passos seems to have favored a good degree of it in 1941, but only in some democratic, participatory, and economically stimulating form. A visit he made to Great Britain in the summer of 1947 left him unhappy with its Labour government;* while it had aided the lower class, he wrote in *Life,* it had restricted individual liberty and virtually barred economic initiative.[16]

His outlook on the United States appeared also to change drastically. Dos Passos had supported Franklin D. Roosevelt for a third term in 1940, but soon the administration seemed to him to be losing touch with the people and failing in its domestic duties. Harry Hopkins' statement to him that domestic problems would have to wait until after the war became a sign of domestic catastrophe for Dos Passos; and he found America's part in yielding large areas of Europe to Soviet domination reprehensible. His novel *The Grand Design* (1949) describes an abandonment of domestic principles by the Roosevelt administration and portrays Communist infiltration into the government.[17]

Jefferson was becoming more and more important to him. In *The Prospect Before Us* (1950) and some earlier postwar writings Dos Passos declared that the contrast was not between "capitalism" and "socialism." Rather it was "between the sort of organization that stimulates growth and the sort that fastens on society the dead hand of bureaucratic routine or the suckers of sterile vested interests." The trend in the United States, he said, was towards control of industry and government in huge bureaucracies—and merger of these into a regime of which the Soviet Union was the extreme example. Warning that the trend was approaching a critical stage, he said that the way to save the republic was to build up the habits of local self-government, strengthen civil liberties, and make economic opportunities for individuals. Jefferson and John Adams, he said, had understood—as Karl Marx had not—that in human society the "struggle for power is more fundamental than any organization of it." The United States had been founded on the "one

---

*Dos Passos probably had low expectations when he arrived in 1947. He had written Wilson two years before: "What worries me about European socialists is that they dont seem to have advanced beyond the bureaucratic state of mind. . . . I dont see any very different mentality among the labor party people in England." Letter from Dos Passos to Wilson, July 19, 1945.

basic truth"—that no human being can be trusted with power over other human beings. In *The Grand Design* Dos Passos saw Franklin Roosevelt's career during World War II as illustrating this truth.[18]

A novel about national misfortune, *The Grand Design* appeared fifteen months after Dos Passos suffered a personal catastrophe. While driving on Cape Cod with Katy in September 1947 he was momentarily blinded by the sun—low on the horizon—and ran into a parked truck. In the collision Katy was killed instantly, her head almost severed, and Dos Passos lost his right eye. Katy's death (especially given the manner and circumstances) was a far greater blow than his loss of the eye. He wrote Edmund Wilson that he had lived fifty-two years without knowing "the existence of these archipelagos of remorse and boundless continents of grief."[19]

Nevertheless he rebuilt his life. Two years later he married Elizabeth Holdridge, who herself had been widowed by an automobile accident and left with a young son, Christopher, or "Kiffy," and in May 1950 John and Elizabeth Dos Passos had a daughter, Lucy. The family made their home in Westmoreland, Virginia, where Dos Passos had inherited a share in his father's farm. (After dividing the farm with his brother Louis in 1948 and selling some non-contiguous property in the early 1950s, he had a tract of about eighteen hundred acres.)[20] And there the family dwelt in a Federal-style brick house by the Potomac.

In the following years the family fell into a pattern of oscillating between Westmoreland and Baltimore. Home was still Westmoreland, where they had grounds and farming operations to look after, the river and bay in which to swim and boat, and space to entertain overnight visitors. Baltimore had the Peabody and the Enoch Pratt Free libraries, which Dos Passos could use for his writings on Jefferson and other historical subjects; it had better and more convenient schools for the children—private schools, which required a good income; and it had W. Horsley Gantt and other friends they met through him, and Dos Passos' cousins in nearby Bel Air, Maryland, and in Chevy Chase. The pattern was strenuous—steady, concentrated writing in the morning as in prior years, with Betty typing and helping in many other ways; a long drive from Baltimore to Westmoreland on Friday, and back again on Sunday afternoon. Friends, old and new, came and were entertained at Westmoreland, and in turn the Dos Passoses visited and enjoyed entertainment on their vacations.[21]

One memorable visit was Edmund Wilson's in 1951. Dos Passos and Wilson had been engaged in a political and literary dialogue at least since the 1930s, when they were both leftists. Once their politics diverged widely, Wilson became for Dos Passos the kind of political antagonist that McComb had been in 1919. After Wilson's visit in 1951, Dos Passos wrote him:

> It was great fun having you — you must come often into our benighted necks. What were the obnoxious political opinions you refer to? I must have been far gone in my glass because I dont remember that you ever gave me a chance to emit a political opinion, you were so busy quoting and demolishing past errors, errors which I very much doubt if I ever entertained.[22]

Advancing age did not diminish the lure of a trip for Dos Passos. He traveled as ever, many a time alone as a writer or lecturer, but more and more as Lucy grew up he went with Betty and Lucy, combining writing with adventure the family could share. Brazil fascinated him as no other country had since Spain in 1916. He had gone there in 1948 during a tour of South America to do articles for *Life*. In the summer of 1958 he returned, now with Betty and Lucy, and gathered material for an article on Brasília. And he went with them again in the summer of 1962, flying from New York to Lima, going on with his wife and daughter to Brazil and then by himself to Buenos Aires to speak at a P.E.N. conference. His book *Brazil on the Move* (1963), based on all three visits, had as a major theme the threat of Communism to Brazil. Describing the challenges in developing the country and people's accomplishments in meeting them, he sought to show that Brazil's growing frontier required individual initiative.[23]

Anxious for more Brazil, Dos Passos, Betty, and Lucy were there again in the summer of 1966. Reporting on the trip in *Holiday* magazine, Dos Passos wrote:

> When people ask us why we enjoy the country so, we find ourselves answering: "Because it is so large." Brazil does represent about half the area and half the population of the South American continent — and so varied. . . .*

On that trip a bush pilot in a sixteen-year-old Cessna flew the Dos Passoses from Goiânia, in central Brazil, to a spot near the Araguaia River. There they took a houseboat and spent a week going downriver, fishing, bathing (where they did not fear piranhas) and occasionally pausing along the way. "There is nothing in the world pleasanter," Dos

---

*"And the people are so easy to take," he added. In his book on Brazil, he had written: "I can't help a sort of family feeling for the Brazilians. Perhaps the fact that I had a Portuguese grandfather helps account for it." Dos Passos, *Brazil on the Move*, p. 14.

Passos wrote in his article, "than drifting down a great, clean, untraveled river where every turn brings some fresh sight into view or some unfamiliar flying creature." The rapid, pale-green Araguaia River brought them to its confluence with the Tapirapé, a sluggish brown one, and the family's last stopping place was an Indian village on the Tapirapé.[24] From there Dos Passos wrote McComb that he had eaten capybara steak.

Dos Passos saw McComb only on rare visits to Boston after the war, for Dos Passos had a busy career and a great many friends, and McComb would not visit him or meet him elsewhere. Now in his fifties, McComb had in fact no money to travel or entertain and lacked the adaptability to earn it. Attempting to increase his modest income, he had invested his money unwisely — so it turned out — and suffered terrible losses.[25]

About 1951 McComb sold sixty-eight of Dos Passos' letters to Goodspeed's Book Shop in Boston, which proceeded to advertise them. Receiving a query from Professor C. B. Tinker, chancellor of the American Academy of Arts and Letters, Goodspeed's quoted a price of $225.00 and stated that it didn't intend to break up the collection. Tinker thereupon bought the letters for the Academy.[26] Their going so cheaply on resale may indicate how badly McComb had needed the money.

He was now living at 84 Charles Street, in a one-room furnished apartment with a closet kitchenette and a fireplace. One witness describes the fireplace as unused, but two of McComb's friends recall his using it when they brought him wood. In the center of the room, amid ordinary-looking maple furniture, stood McComb's desk — a gateleg table stacked high with pictures and books. Pictures of Mussolini, whom he honored all his life, lay there too. The room was dusty and also stuffy, for McComb rarely opened the windows. In the bathroom the lighting fixture had burned out but hadn't been replaced. As McComb clipped or shaved his whiskers by candle light, and not daily, he often looked unshaven.[27]

In such circumstances he would talk about the necessity of preserving privilege. Culture had never been carried forward to the future by more than an elite, he would maintain, and it should be the work of an entire civilization to preserve the existence of that elite — even to its own deprivation. Despite his poverty he clung to certain amenities, especially breakfast at the Ritz-Carlton Hotel. For the rest of the day he would eat lightly — lunch would be at Schrafft's (perhaps scrambled eggs) and dinner at another Schrafft's or at the Café Florian. Although he wore frayed seersucker suits, their Brooks Brothers origin made him feel well-dressed; he had his shirts done at a hand laundry, at a much higher price than common laundries charged, and then wore them four days.[28]

Professor Sydney Freedberg of Harvard, a former student of his, got him summer teaching there; but it turned out that McComb hadn't kept up with recent scholarship. McComb also did part-time teaching at nearby colleges, some authenticating of paintings, and editorial work for Boston publishers.[29]

Part of McComb's problem was that he wasn't one to fit into any organization. Houghton Mifflin gave him work proofreading and indexing but found him a trial as he insisted on using English spelling and would consult only the Oxford Dictionary. This would do for Winston Churchill's writings, but not for American books.[30]

At the Boston Athenaeum he had the job of organizing and classifying the Cooper family's business papers—a task for which Paul Cooper, a descendant of James Fenimore Cooper, was paying the Athenaeum. Cooper was greatly irritated when he discovered that McComb had used file cards vertically.[31]

McComb got into real trouble after Houghton Mifflin gave him an advance on royalties to edit Bernard Berenson's letters. The publisher understood that he would go to Florence and work in the library at I Tatti, where Nicky Mariano and her sister Baroness Alda Anrep, the librarian there, would help him. Dreading airplanes, he went by ship first class and visited England and Switzerland before going on to Italy. He left himself money for only a few days at I Tatti.[32]

During the 1960s McComb spent much of his time with young adults. They had a strong counter culture then, many of them rejecting the money orientation, politics, and hair styles of their elders and using or experimenting with narcotics. Constance Worcester attributes his behavior to his not having had fun in his youth, as his parents were demanding and watchful.[33] McComb boasted of young women's attentions and said he wasn't interested in any woman over twenty-seven. At the Athenaeum one Sunday he brought a girl friend in to be photographed by a statue of a nude Venus. Although the Athenaeum wasn't open to readers Sundays, an official made quite an issue of the incident.[34]

McComb was an attractive man, cultivated and charming in manner and speech, sensitive, with great dignity and insistence on being himself, and an essential part of this self was a disinclination to endure anything unpleasant. Laurette Murdock, who worked as a copy editor

McComb, in a seersucker suit, in front of the Boston Athenaeum.
Courtesy of Robert Lynch

at Houghton Mifflin, recalls him as he walked along Beacon Street on the way to the Athenaeum carrying a book bag—tall, stooped, head leonine. Fierce looking, she thought. (Our pictures suggest a cragged, brooding look.) When he came face to face with you he smiled. Or at least his face seemed welcoming.[35]

Two of Dos Passos' friends from *Harvard Monthly* days, Dudley Poore and Stewart Mitchell, figured again and again in his correspondence with McComb. Poore left his job at Harvard in 1939, and afterwards he did a variety of literary work, including free-lance writing and editing, and translating poetry and fiction. Requiring some economic security, he went to work for the U.S. State Department, in the Department of Cultural Affairs, in 1944. For the next eighteen years he lived in Washington, D.C. After retiring he traveled, and spent intervals at his home, deep in New York State country by the shores of Otisco Lake.[36]

Mitchell was another lifelong friend of Dos Passos, lending or giving him money when he was short, helping him with scholarly problems after Dos Passos turned to writing early American history,* and extending hospitality in his Cambridge apartment when Dos Passos had to remain around Boston for medical attention after his accident. A pro-Loyalist, Mitchell argued with McComb over the Spanish Civil War. A Franklin D. Roosevelt supporter in four elections, he nevertheless voted a straight Republican ticket in 1952—writing Dos Passos that he couldn't stand "the gang in Washington." Mitchell probably respected Dos Passos more than McComb, whom he twitted (and mimicked to Constance Worcester's brother Gurdon). But he saw and dined with McComb often over the years and helped him in diverse ways as they were old friends and fellow Bostonians.[37]

Mitchell enjoyed a standard of living that McComb would have relished, but it had its cost. Before coming to Harvard he had been befriended by his elderly "aunt" Mrs. G. H. Thomas, a widow who was actually the aunt of his deceased half-brother. He became far closer to her than to anyone in his family, enjoying with her a happiness that

---

*A historian, literary man, and editor, Mitchell was managing editor of the *Dial* from November 1919 to November 1920; a member of the editorial board of the *New England Quarterly* from its founding and managing editor for the first ten years; editor of the Massachusetts Historical Society from 1929 to 1939 and director from 1947 to 1957. He had a Ph.D. in history, and his publications included *Horatio Seymour of New York* (1938) and *New Letters of Abigail Adams, 1788–1801* (1947). Allan Nevins called the Seymour book "a truly definitive biography."

he had not known with his mother. He traveled with Mrs. Thomas and for long periods dwelt with her in Gloucester, in a large house with servants. Mrs. Thomas' largess enabled Mitchell to live luxuriously. However, the relationship did not foster social independence or economic self-reliance in him. Dos Passos in a letter to Poore once, perhaps merely in a moment's anger, called her a vampire.[38]

Mitchell's private life in his later years was unfortunate. Aggressively homosexual, he was strongly attached to a young man Richard Cowan —a fact which Dos Passos and Katy accepted, inviting them both out to Provincetown. When Cowan committed suicide in 1939, Mitchell was overwhelmed with grief. The next year Mrs. Thomas died at ninety-one, bequeathing Mitchell the income of a half-million-dollar trust fund so that he could write. Despite the income, his life deteriorated badly. He had other young men, on whom he spent much money, and he became notorious as a rake and alcoholic. On November 3, 1957, he died in a fit of delirium tremens.[39]

Probably McComb hoped for some money from his wealthy friend. But there were problems with Mitchell's will and estate more apparent than any disappointment for him. Whatever McComb's thoughts, he was disturbed when he wrote Dos Passos about the will and asked about his forthcoming memorial piece. Dos Passos wrote a warm appreciation of Mitchell's learning, humor, and freedom from cant (*New England Quarterly,* December 1957), and McComb complimented him on it.[40]

Prior to 1951 the Dos Passos–McComb correspondence had lapsed (we don't know for how long). It resumed after McComb helped Charles W. Bernardin, a biographer of Dos Passos, with materials on the 1919–20 stay in Spain. When in October 1951 McComb wrote Dos Passos of the help, Dos Passos began his answer with: "How nice to see your neat and rational handwriting on a letter again." On politics Dos Passos conceded a great deal, saying "You were certainly right on the negative side," but he was too much the Jeffersonian and Whitmanian democrat (or perhaps merely the historical realist here) to accept McComb's Metternichean orientation.

McComb does not appear to have given Dos Passos notice of the sale of his letters. On June 7, 1961, the American Academy of Arts and Letters wrote telling Dos Passos that it had them and stating: "We have held these letters under the tightest restrictions, allowing only two trusted scholars, friends of yours, to see them but denying them any rights to quote even a sentence." Word of the letters had gotten out, the Academy added, and it asked whether he would allow Robert Elias,

who was preparing an edition of *One Man's Initiation — 1917*, to see
a letter referring to the work. Dos Passos agreed.[41] Later that year
Daniel Aaron's book *Writers on the Left* appeared and, citing Dos
Passos' permission, quoted from the letters. This led the Academy
librarian to write Aaron a letter arguing courteously that he should have
gotten the institution's permission as well.[42] Aaron's quotations also
produced an apologetic letter from McComb to Dos Passos.

Then in October 1962 Bernardin wrote the Academy saying that he
had learned of the letters and wanted permission to see them. Dos Passos
had given him much help over the years, he added, having written him
about a hundred letters, replied to a score of long questionnaires, and
read and commented on chapters of his work. The Academy immediately queried Dos Passos, asking him to signify his answer on an
enclosed carbon copy of its letter. Dos Passos wrote "Permission
granted" on the carbon and sent the original to McComb with a note
partly intended to set him at ease. But some years later he wrote Edmund
Wilson, without mentioning McComb: "I find it aggravating to find
my old letters for sale by the used paper dealers."[43]

There is a season for writing memoirs. Requests for biographical
information already had Dos Passos recalling details about his life and
wondering how well the scholars would understand. When McComb
wrote about aiding Bernardin, Dos Passos expressed a wish that
McComb himself would write a memoir on Spain. While in North Carolina McComb had indeed done one on his school days in England, and
he wrote further memoirs later after his return to Boston. Learning of
all this in December 1962, Dos Passos urged him to continue. To this
urging McComb replied with a wish that Dos Passos would write some
of his own reminiscences, as they would be better than professors' works
and he would enjoy comparing Dos Passos' views of the Spanish period
with his own. At the end of 1964 McComb sent Dos Passos his Spanish
memoir and got back an enthusiastic letter urging him to go on, as well
as a suggestion for a suitable preface.

A year later Dos Passos was at work on his informal memoir *The
Best Times,* which carries his life to the year 1933. As the New American Library had given him a handsome contract for both hardcover
and paperback editions, Dos Passos was anxious to keep the memoir
short enough for a paperback. He wrote it somewhat impressionisti-
cally, perhaps because he didn't want it to turn into a novel. Some time
in the 1960s when Dos Passos had lunch with Poore and the Brazilian
novelist Érico Veríssimo in Washington, D.C., the talk turned to autobiography and how hard it is not to alter or distort material, and Poore

remembers Dos Passos' saying the only safe thing to do is to give a quick look at the past, before you can go to work and fictionalize it.[44]

The letters at the Academy turned out to be convenient for Dos Passos, who referred to and quoted them repeatedly. After the memoir came out, a number of friends wrote him about errors of detail. And biographers will point to omissions and distortions; however, these features are in the very nature of autobiography, and often lead biographers to deep insights. *The Best Times* (1966) is a lively and characteristic memoir by a truthful man.

The same year that *The Best Times* appeared, a part of McComb's memoirs, "The Anglo-Americans in Florence," came out in *English Miscellany,* published in Rome. In a graceful, evocative style, it described Bernard Berenson, Charles Loeser, and Vernon Lee. (On Loeser and Vernon Lee see, respectively, Letters 128, n. 3, and 138, n. 6, above.) McComb wrote that he thought it likely the Florentine atmosphere of "gentle manners" had helped make each of the three seem somewhat more attractive than he would have seemed in, say, Detroit. Elsewhere in the memoir McComb referred with distaste to the "power-driven successful back-slapper . . . so much *en vue* today" in the United States.[45]

That autumn a new publication *The Boston Review* carried two contributions by McComb in its first number. One consisted of eight letters from Edith Wharton to Henry Cabot Lodge, and McComb in editing them recalled with nostalgia the tone of polite society in her day. McComb's companion contribution, "Notes on the Dodo," told the history of the extinct bird.[46]

146

[Picture postcard]

Florence   27th July 1937.

[To Dos Passos]

Your card of the 8th was forwarded and found me (you really might have guessed my whereabouts!) here. So I can't have a dip in that fine cold water but thanks for asking me just the same. Left Boston 20. June spent a week in Gibraltar, then came here viâ P. & O.[1] — Marseilles. Plans a bit uncertain but probably not back till end Sept. — Elaine[2] appears to be in Switzerland. — Best to Kate.[3]   A.

1. Peninsular and Oriental Line.
2. E. E. Cummings' former wife (née Orr), now Mrs. Frank MacDermot.
3. Katharine Dos Passos.

147

[Art postcard]

22/IV/44

ᶜ/ₒ S.M.[,][1] Gloucester Mass.

Dos! I'm back from the South and in and out of Boston a lot, job-hunting.[2] Do call up if you come this way & let us meet. Que tal. Que hay de nuevo?[3] Arthur.

1. Stewart Mitchell. McComb appears to have been his guest.
2. McComb left Asheville permanently around August 1, 1944, having arranged to sell pictures to museums for a New York City dealer. For the better part of a year, beginning that September, he lived near New York or was away on business to a number of other U.S. cities. A letter he wrote to Mitchell on January 30, 1946, shows him back in Boston, living at 84 Charles Street. Letters from McComb to Mitchell, July 28, 1944–June 21, 1945; letter from Mitchell to Richard R. Beatty, June 26, 1945.
3. Qué tal. Qué hay de nuevo? [Sp.], "How are you? What's new?"

148

84 Charles St.
Boston
30 Oct. '51

Dear Dos,

As you know, I've been in touch with Bernardin in connection with the book he is writing about you[1] — A year or so ago I gave him some anecdotes, opinions etc. for his Spanish chapter, and answered various questions. He has now shewn me his chapter (or rather sent it, — I've never seen him actually) He seems polite & appreciative. But I did not know he was going to quote me in those few pages — and a good deal, too. He will send you the chapter of course. I simply wanted to say that if you wish to contradict anything I've said, or expunge it, please do. A footnote could be used for the first of these purposes. It is not a question of the truth or sincerity of my impressions & memories of those days, but merely a question of your wishes — for which no reasons have to be given. I value yᵣ good opinion rather more than being within the covers of a book — having got there somewhat unexpectedly on yᵣ coat tails, too! But perhaps you will like or be amused by what I have said.

I liked thinking over those days in the Spain of 1918–20 — I often recall them in any case. I should almost have liked to have written a 'memoir' of them myself & have tried to convey how dear they were to me — and also, how, without my knowing it at the time — important for my later life. My American years I feel differently about.

I hope all is well with you & your family. I myself have been plagued for 5 years trying to make ends meet — a colossal & all-absorbing nuisance. I am afraid I'm not well adapted to this society and it has little use for me. To be fair, it is long since I have had any use for it! Its morals & manners, its methods & aims do not command my admiration. Its hopes & wishes & dreams are not mine. Tout le contraire.[2] Gadgets & science, war & "democracy" — I dislike them all. But I think it will die of its follies. It cannot be saved (and perhaps is not worth saving).

I've just finished doing the Index for Winston Churchill's book[3] for Houghton Mifflin and have learned about y^r forthcoming book — as it is reminiscential in character, I understand, I shall be particularly anxious to see it.

As ever

Arthur

The only trifle of money I have left is in sterling (blocked)

1. Bernardin had completed "The Development of John Dos Passos" (1949) as his Ph.D. thesis at the University of Wisconsin. On Bernardin's subsequent biographical work, see narrative, pp. 245 and 7 n. above. See also his "John Dos Passos' Harvard Years," *New England Quarterly* 27 (March 1954): 3–26, and his "John Dos Passos' Textual Revisions," *Papers of The Bibliographical Society of America* 48 (First Quarter, 1954): 95–97.

2. [Fr.] "Quite the opposite."

3. Presumably *The Second World War: Closing the Ring* (1951).

149

Westmoreland, Va.

Thanksgiving Day [1951]

Dear Arthur,

How nice to see your neat and rational handwriting on a letter again. I hope Bernardin hasn't made himself a nuisance. He's a distressingly thorough young man. I did my best to explain to him that his function was to follow and not precede the undertaker — but since he insists on continuing with his rash enterprise I've sent him what data I could remember. I can see that your letter was a great help. I'm sure it added a great deal of light — I find myself remembering our conversations at the Lecheria de le Castillana[1] — You were certainly right on the negative side — but I doubt if anything in the order of Metternich could have propped up the decaying social order. What neither of us could have imagined (at your most Metternichian I dont think you forsaw Stalin and Mao[2] (—or Nehru—great God—Nehru)[3] what neither of us did imagine was that the new order would be so much worse than the old for every mother's son—I wish B. had quoted you more directly—in fact I wish you had written the chapter—Write your memoir of that period in Spain. It will be worth a great more than poor B's strainings to comprehend—though as you say he's polite, appreciative and (I add) industrious. Its his industry I find disarming.

I'm sorry you've been plagued by that dreary bedfellow Lack of money—I've known his clammy embrace myself and he's a thorough bore. No wonder you are feeling a little let down: indexing Winston Churchill would let anybody down   Still I'm all for saving the it you despair of. It's all we've got: there isn't any more. Cant Stewart[4] find a warm sinecure in the bosom of the Mass. Hist. Sy for you? Give him my love—

Yrs ever

Dos

Lucy's[5] eighteen months old and very lively   She has blue eyes and is at present very blond (sangre de los godos?)[6] Farming is the only form of gambling I've ever enjoyed. If you ever get to Washington come and see our strange little civilization at Potomac mouth. I got Dudley Poore down last Christmas—completely unchanged, preserved in the State Dep't like a mammoth in ice.

1. Poore identifies the Lechería de la Castellana with the Vaquería (see Letter 133, including n. 5, and Letter 134 above). Telephone interview with Poore, October 3, 1976.

2. Mao Tse-tung (1893–1976), leader of the Communist China state.

3. Jawaharlal Nehru (1889–1964), prime minister of India. He pursued a policy of non-alignment in the cold war between the United States and the Communist powers. Dos Passos' exclamation may have been due to Nehru's lecturing-philosopher's tone, as well as to his policy. See Robert Trumbull's account of an interview with Nehru in the *New York Times*, November 11, 1951, sec. 6, pp. 9, 52–57.

4. Stewart Mitchell, who was director of the Massachusetts Historical Society.

5. Lucy Dos Passos.

6. [Sp.] "Gothic blood."

150

84 Charles St.

Boston   23 XII '51

Dear Dos,

I have been getting my Xmas cards at the Fogg—they are almost entirely Buddhist, Mohammedan and so on, but I seem at the moment

Dos Passos with Lucy and Kiffy at the family farm, in Virginia.
Courtesy of Elizabeth Dos Passos

to have no Ming porcelain ducks, Egyptian cats or Japanese bamboo-shoots on which to send you the wishes of the season, & to thank you for your very nice letter of Thanksgiving time which I much enjoyed having.

I never move for various reasons (including a distinct disinclination to travel, which overcame me some years ago,) but if I should, nothing would give me greater pleasure than to visit you in Westmoreland and I shall remember your invitation.

I was glad to learn something of Lucy and interested to know that her appearance was algo asturiana.[1] And digging Dudley Poore out of the State Dep't was quite a deed!

No, Bernardin was not a nuisance. I was pleased, at his bidding, to recall those days. You are very kind to suggest that I should write my remembrances of them. As a matter of fact I should like to see you do a kind of autobiography, in which that period would form a chapter. —For I doubt very much the rumour that there is much of this in your new novel.

No, I was honoured to do the Churchill. Not that I am a fanatical admirer, not at all. In a way he is a brilliant journalist & something of an adventurer. He is not really my favourite statesman of the day—I think perhaps Salazar[2] is—but he is generous to opponents, he has not always been wrong (as he puts it) and he can write English. This last is really striking.—You will not I hope accuse me of chauvinism if I say that whatever else they do, it does not seem to me that Americans—since the death, let us say, of Henry James & Mrs. Wharton, write English any more. A strange language of stereotypes has grown up which I confess to finding objectionable—nay, unbearable. The Vandenberg Papers[3] (which I am now indexing) are full of what I mean. . . . You are right—there is much we could not have foreseen, including Stalin, in 1919. For myself, I should not have been able to guess the tempo of the subsequent decades. It is true that I knew the direction in a general way was wrong but how many implications nevertheless escaped one!—It would be interesting to review all that some time.

You mention old Prince Metternich. Yes, I must say I honour those who have fought the modern world, & those who delayed & tried to prevent its birth. Francis-Joseph[4] and Pius IX[5] and those who fought at Gaëta.[6]

But I did not mean to write you an essay! Though I may some day!

I still exist in some way. Since you wrote, the Bank of England came to my rescue & released a little money for my use. Imagine!

All best wishes, my dear Dos

Arthur

1. Lucy: Dos Passos' daughter; algo asturiana [Sp.], "somewhat Asturian." After the Moors overran most of the Iberian peninsula, Visgothic nobles retreated to Asturias; it became the starting point for the Christian reconquest.

2. António de Oliveira Salazar (1889–1970), Portuguese statesman, premier (1932–68), and dictator.

3. Arthur H. Vandenberg, *The Private Papers of Senator Vandenberg,* ed. Arthur H. Vandenberg, Jr. (Boston: Houghton Mifflin, 1952). A Republican leader in the U.S. Senate, Arthur H. Vandenberg (1884–1951) supported creation of the United Nations in 1945 and thereafter led in making U.S. foreign policy bipartisan.

4. Francis Joseph (1830–1916), emperor of Austria and king of Hungary. He held the peoples of his diverse empire together during an era of increasing nationalism.

5. Pius IX (1792–1878), pope (1846–78). He refused to recognize the kingdom of Italy and issued the encyclical *Quanta cura,* with a list (*Syllabus*) of eighty of the "principal errors of our times." Article eighty condemned the view that the pope "can and should reconcile himself to and agree with progress, liberalism, and modern civilization."

6. Town in central Italy, formerly part of the kingdom of the Two Sicilies. Piux IX fled there in November 1848, after a revolution in Rome. In 1860–61 King Francis II of the kingdom of the Two Sicilies made a last stand there with twelve thousand men against Victor Emmanuel II's nationalist forces.

151

address during weekdays   552 Chateau Avenue

Baltimore 12 Md.

phone Hopkins 7-6745   Jan 21 [19]55

Dear Arthur,

It was a pleasure to get your card and I thoroughly enjoyed the sad little tale of Mr. Prentis.[1] My those places must have been fun in 1900. It really makes an excellent short story. I've read it several times, each time with more satisfaction

Arthur please drop me a card with your address. Is it still 88 Charles or was it ever? To be sure I'm sending this care the Massachusetts Historical Society via the Great Awk.[2] I wish I could get to Boston one of these days to see you — Of course you wouldnt think of coming this way, or would you?

Bonne année[3] —

Yrs ever

Dos

1. McComb seems to have sent Dos Passos a copy of his article "A Consular Appointment of 1900," which had appeared recently in the *New England Quarterly*. This article quoted the correspondence in 1900 between Secretary of State John Hay and Senator Henry Cabot Lodge of Massachusetts about a new consular post for Lodge's constituent Thomas F. Prentis, who for some reason was dissatisfied with the city of Rouen. After failing to obtain Iquique, Chile, Mr. Prentis sailed to a proffered post in Batavia, and when that turned out to have been promised to someone else, made a second long voyage to another post, in Saint-Pierre, Martinique, only to die when a volcano destroyed that city. In the introduction to his article McComb wrote: "It is unlikely that a correspondence so urbane, so informal, so witty—I had almost said so gentlemanly— would be found in the same connection today." McComb's article is in vol. 27 of the quarterly (September 1954): 382–88.

2. Stewart Mitchell.

3. [Fr.] "Happy New Year."

152

84 Charles St Boston
31 Dec. '55

Dear Dos,

This is just to say that I was so pleased to get a picture of Lucy, clearly a beguiling child, whom I should like to see, but you will not, I suppose be taking her on your travels. And I also wanted to add that I am pleased you are thinking of Boston—remember that I have no telephone & am difficult to get hold of so please give a general alerte so that I shall be on the look out for you. If necessary a message can be left at the Athenaeum where I go every afternoon.

I would like to see you before we depart from this odd—indeed apparently unique—planet. The last day of the year makes one rather over-conscious (?) of time.

I read that Robt. Hillyer was in a motor car accident the other day.—I never step into one—nor into an aeroplane—myself The other day I went in a train as far as Wellesley & was surprised—it resembled no train that I remembered.

Happy New Year—but that only makes sense, if one adds: may it be like some other time than ours.

Yrs
Arthur

153

84 Charles St. Boston
14 November 1957

Dear Dos,

Miss Bruce[1] tells me that you are going to write a Memoir of Mitchell. Normally this would go into the <u>Proceedings</u>[2] which are <u>very</u>

<u>far behind hand</u>, and therefore I wonder if you would be so very kind as to send me a carbon copy of it when the time comes, and I could, after reading it shew it to friends.

If it is not a secret, may I ask who approached you on the matter?

S.M. left a rather curious will—which is being contested—and not much property.

There is a good deal that might be said, but this is perhaps not the moment.

It was the opinion of Santayana that the world, when they were in the hands of "scientific blackguards" would regret gentlemanly English rule. We are now since some days almost officially in the hands of the said blackguards. Regrets will soon be the order of the day everywhere and I should not be surprised if in the future which is being prepared for us, the Armenians might get to the point of regretting my friend Sultan Abdul Hamid II![3]

With this by no means whimsical thought, I take leave of you,

Y[rs]

Arthur

1. Marjorie MacKenzie Bruce, Stewart Mitchell's secretary.
2. Of the Massachusetts Historical Society.
3. Ottoman sultan (b. 1842, ruled 1876–1909, d. 1918), called the Great Assassin and the Red Sultan for his role in the massacre of nearly two hundred thousand Armenians in 1894–96.

154

[December 1957?]

Dear Arthur,

I thought this might amuse you—my unique effort to write in French—its more or less a recollection of a piece I wrote for the Monthly many—well only forty two years ago.[1]

It resulted from my spending a jolly evening—eating scampi and drinking Barbaresco[2]—with some Belgians in Venice.[3] We all became très très belges[4]

A Merry Christmas to you

Yrs ever

Dos

1. Dos Passos' "effort" was "Fragments d'une enfance bruxelloise," in *Bruxelles, ville en forme de coeur*, ed. Jacques Biebuyck (Brussels: Éditions Universitaires, 1957), pp. 53–56. The much earlier piece was "Les Lauriers Sont Coupés," *Harvard Monthly* 62 (April 1916): 48–51.
2. Barbaresco: a strong, red wine from Piedmont; scampi [It. plural]: shellfish much like shrimp. Italians often grill them with olive oil and garlic.

3. The meal was at a restaurant during the 1949 International P.E.N. Congress, in Venice. Dos Passos was a delegate of the American Center. Letter from Elizabeth Dos Passos, June 21, 1976; Marchette Chute, *P.E.N. American Center: A History of the First Fifty Years* (New York: P.E.N. American Center, 1972), pp. 48–49.

4. [Fr.] "Very very Belgian indeed." Elizabeth Dos Passos says that Dos Passos and she did not stay "to make a night of it." See n. 3 above.

155

84 Charles St   Boston
11 Apr. '58

Dear Dos,

Margaret Sweeney recently sent me from St. Gallen a box containing letters I had written to her mother—among them were some from you which I forward thinking you might like to have them. It is all very long ago—I thought it was very nice of Margaret. . . .

Did I tell you that I'd met her husband, Konrad v. Hofmann—an extremely nice man, interesting to talk to, sympathique. When Prinz Rupprecht[1] died, he was one of the honour watch. (Which reminds me: did you know—the Queen sent a representative to the funeral—very nice of her & interesting, as he was the Stuart heir, of course.

I suppose you saw of the death of the Infanta Eulalia[2] at the age of 94. She was not a wise or admirable person perhaps, but how curious that in our time should die the granddaughter of D. Fernando VII![3]

This note gives me the opportunity to say that I read your obituary of S.M.[4]—it was wonderfully well done. You remembered him as he was, & avoided dealing with painful things, which of course would have been out of place. There were a good many of these & my own feelings about him changed more than once in the course of the many years I knew him.

He had a great knowledge of the workings of American politics & could make this dull subject interesting and while not doubting what you say about being able to "talk politics" with him, it was not true of me. I could listen but I could not converse with him on them. For one thing I disliked his American chauvinism. I was not much impressed with his late conversion to Toryism. I do not think he was a Tory (not, at least, if I am one!) I think he liked dividends & didn't like the graduated income tax. I think what he was really converted to was orthodox Capitalism. But all this is a long subject.

I wish you'd come to Boston. We could dine at the Athens[5] & talk about things.

Best wishes
Arthur

1. Crown Prince Rupprecht (1869–1955), eldest son of the last king of Bavaria. According to an obituary: "Some Scottish Jacobites, who claimed the British throne for the House of Stuart, regarded Prince Rupprecht as their rightful ruler." *New York Times*, August 3, 1955, p. 23.

2. Infanta Eulalia (1864–1958), aunt of Alfonso XIII (last king of Spain prior to Juan Carlos I). She defended divorce, introduced American millionaires to her relatives in Europe's royal houses in return for expensive gifts, and attacked the manners of English women. "She spent more time in the headlines of newspapers than in the Court of Spain." *New York Times*, March 9, 1958, p. 86.

3. Ferdinand VII (1784–1833), king of Spain (1808, 1814–33). The years of and between his reigns witnessed French invasions of Spain, Spain's loss of its colonies on the North and South American mainlands, Ferdinand VII's repudiation of the liberal constitution of 1812, and his setting aside of the Salic Law (an action which led to the Carlist Wars after his death).

4. Dos Passos, "In Memoriam: Stewart Mitchell," *New England Quarterly* 30 (December 1957): 513–14.

5. Athens-Olympia Cafe, up a stairway at 51 Stuart Street, in the theater district.

156

Westmoreland, Virginia
Sept 1 1958

Dear Arthur,

On going over my desk after returning from a delightful trip to Brazil, I find your letter and the Sweeney correspondence. Thank you very much for sending them. I know I meant to write but I rather suspect I didn't. Please forgive me if I didn't. Last spring was full of sturm and drang—until we got off to a highly tumultuous tour of the sister republic. I find that I enjoy traveling just as much at 62 as I did at 22. Must be something wrong—Fortunately Betty my wife and Lucy (aet. 8) enjoy traveling too. The trip was poisoned by my having to deliver various lectures—but that was the price that had to be paid. The Brazilians were as delightful as ever—We met Dos Passos cousins in Santos and were nearly stuffed to death by them at luncheon—we all became very Portuguese, in spite of my inability to cope with the intricate little language my paternal ancestors made up; and it was a great deal of fun. We went to Brasilia the new capital and got so involved with the national folie des grandeurs that we came away believing it was all there. There's a lot of marvelous local Baroque and beautiful colonial furniture and their modern "world's fair" architecture is enormously entertaining. Now settling down to the writing of novels again considerably refreshed.

The survival of the Infanta Eulalia is I suppose hardly less peculiar than our own survival into the later half of the twentieth century.

By some miracle a funny little anonymous foundation on the Pacific Coast has come across with a subsidy for me to write a novel on,[1] so

I shall be free—God willing—from the rat race of article writing for a year—perhaps I shall be able to get to Boston. The fact that the Athens still survives is almost as remarkable as the survival of the infanta. By all means let's eat supper there—

Yrs ever

Dos

1. The novel was *Midcentury,* and the help came from the William Volker Fund, of Burlingame, California. It awarded Dos Passos $8,500 for one year, beginning September 30, 1958. A year later he got a six-month renewal, at $4,250.

157

84 Charles St.

Boston

10 Sept. 1958

Dear Dos,

I was very pleased to get your letter with its account of your Brazilian doings. It all sounded quite entertaining—it was quite proper that you should find cousins in a coffee port. I must say Brazil is a country I should rather like to visit [,] though more in 1908 than 1958—I wonder if you were in the north—Bahia and the journey on the Booth Line steamer from Pará to Manaos must be quite special. . . .

I wish to ask you about something that is on my mind. I have—I am not sure whether you know this—been working free-lance for publishers among other things (& I have just finished giving a course at Harvard Summer School)—my steadiest work was for McGraw-Hill doing translations of F.A.[1] articles for their forthcoming Art Encyclopaedia,[2] & I also am in touch with Houghton Mifflin & Little Brown. —At present there is a technical hiatus in the McG-H. work & it is an "off moment" for the others.—What I wonder is if you are in touch with any other publishers who perhaps might have proof-reading, indexing or translating to do—It would be a very great favour to me if you would bear me in mind, or write me a line if you have any ideas—I know that it is a chore to put pen to paper when you have so much other writing to do & if it were not that it is so difficult (for people like myself) to earn even the most modest living in this Eldorado, I should not dream of bothering you.—I remember a similar request long ago & you put me in touch with J. P. Bishop—it was in 1941 I think[3]—

I was delighted for your sake to hear that you are free to write what you want for a year while regretting possible articles on Brazil (?)

In another way everything has an air of unreality as everyone's life is entirely in the hands of Mr. Dulles & his Chinese General[4] ("warlords" they used to be called when they were out of fashion) — a precious pair. — Those whom the Gods wish to destroy ....

Yours as ever
Arthur

1. Fine arts.
2. *Encyclopedia of World Art,* 15 vols. (New York: McGraw-Hill Book Co., 1959–68). McComb was also a contributor, with eleven short biographies credited to him. See vol. 15, p. xxi.
3. John Peale Bishop (1892–1944), American writer and college friend of Edmund Wilson and F. Scott Fitzgerald. In 1941 he was director of publications, office of the coordinator of inter-American affairs.
4. John Foster Dulles (1888–1959), U.S. secretary of state (1953–59). Some of his political philosophy appeared in a *Life* magazine article apparently inspired by him. "If . . . you are scared to go to the brink [of war], you are lost." He used the term "massive retaliation" in reference to the West's reliance on atomic weapons for defense. (See James Shepley, "How Dulles Averted War," *Life* 40 [January 16, 1956]: 70–72, 77, 78 ["brink" quotation], 80.) Dulles supported Generalissimo Chiang Kai-shek, whose government had lost the mainland of China and moved to Taiwan.

158

Westmoreland, Va
Sept 21 1958

Dear Arthur,

We went to Bahia (Salvador)[1] which we found completely delightful — a sort of negro Cascaes[2] — and to Recife and Belem[3] but unfortunately didn't have time to go up the Amazon — Another trip if we can ever scrape up the cash.

The only place I can think of is Doubleday — Next time I go to New York — during the next 2 or 3 weeks — I'll call up some people — may uncover something — and may not — anyway I'll do my best and let you know if any possibility appears

Yrs ever
Dos

1. Bahia is another name for the port city of Salvador, in northeastern Brazil. The city is predominantly Negro and is noted for its African cultural inheritance.
2. A Portuguese resort town (a fishing village originally) fifteen miles west of Lisbon. Dos Passos wrote *Lisbon*, then crossed it out and substituted *Cascaes*.
3. The city Belém, capital of the state of Pará, in northern Brazil, is sometimes called Pará. McComb refers to it thus in the preceding letter.

159

[Boston?]
28 Dec [1960]

Dear Dos—It was strange to run into you—and yet in another way not—at Houghton Mifflin. This belated card will bring you my wishes for 1961—it will be in time for that. Yet truthfully speaking little good—other than perhaps some small personal goods—can be expected from 1961.—

Please look at the postage stamp. An old friend from the days when we used to discuss things in Madrid is none other than General Baron Mannerheim—Who would have supposed that this distinguished ex-Czarist officer—the bête noir of liberals & democrats for so many years would appear on a U.S. stamp as the "Liberator of Finland"—Twice he fought on the same side as the wicked Germans.[1]

Could either of us seated at a café table in Santander have foreseen this apotheosis? It is merely accident that I have the stamp, but how could I not think of you?

Arthur

Dorothy de S.[2] said she saw you off at station. She told you why I was at HM Co no doubt.—As for you, there was rather veiled talk of a novel.

1. Mannerheim commanded Finland's forces in their skillful resistance against the Soviet invasion of 1939–40. Finland's defeat led to a loss of territory to the U.S.S.R. After Germany invaded the Soviets, Finland went to war against the U.S.S.R., and Mannerheim again commanded the Finnish forces. The United States never declared war against Finland. Compare McComb's comments on Mannerheim in this letter with those in Letter 68 above, and see Letter 68, n. 2 on German aid to Mannerheim's White Guard in 1918.
2. Dorothy de Santillana, managing editor (Trade Department) at Houghton Mifflin, and former wife of Robert Hillyer.

160

Westmoreland, Va
January 1   1961

Dear Arthur,

A happy new decade to you. I had caught a glimpse of that Mannerheim stamp, and immediately thought of you. I remember (in Madrid or Santander) thinking he had horns and a tail and your standing up for him. How in the world did he get put over on the U.S. Post Office? I'm sure theres an amusing story of internal intrigue behind it. I wonder

how the present day Finns regard him. It would be amusing if Pravda
or Isvestia took it up as another proof of the reactionary warmongering
of the Eisenhower regime. I must say I'll see Mr. E retire to Gettysburg
without regret;[1] I'm consoling myself over Kennedy by remembering
I refused to vote for Franklin D in 1932 because his platform was so
conservative. Maybe the Kennedy clan will behave as Roosevelts in
reverse.

I'm going to be in Boston Feb 26 27 & 28 in the hands of Anne
Ford of H. M.'s publicity department[2]—Shall make a great effort to
see you. I hope you really are doing the editing on B.B.'s letters.[3] I cant
imagine anybody doing it better. Thanks for the modest little card

Yrs ever

Dos

1. Dwight D. Eisenhower's term ended January 20, 1961; he had a farm outside Gettysburg, Pennsylvania.
2. Houghton Mifflin Co. published Dos Passos' novel *Midcentury* on February 27, 1961.
3. Bernard Berenson's letters.

161

84 Charles St.
Boston
22 Jan. 61

Dear Dos,

I was very pleased to have your New Year's letter. This line is mainly
to say that I'm looking forward to seeing you on your February visit.
About the 15th I'll call Anne Ford and find out yr general schedule. On
the basis of that I'll leave a note either with her or at your hotel (if she
tells me you are staying in a hotel).

I had the same thought as you—who persuaded the Post-office to
honour Baron Mannerheim, an ex-Czarist General who twice fought
(though not with that specific intention) on the German side?—How
strange is time. It seems so much less important that we differed about
M. than that we (unlike any one else hereabouts) know who he was,
and remember something of what he did! I am constantly surprised that
people's knowledge of events & characters seems to go back such a
little distance! I shall have more to say on all this when we meet. All
that I say will probably, like these things, be signs of age!—

Yes, it does look as if I were going to edit BB's letters. The legal details
are almost settled. I'm glad you like the idea & think it suitable. I'll

have to write a preface — not altogether easy, but a chance to say one or two things. My interpretation may be a little different from the customary ones.

> Till soon
> Yrs as ever
> Arthur —

I never hear of Dudley Poore — I hope you'll have some news of him when you come. A.

162

> 1821 Sulgrave Ave
> Baltimore 9 Md
> Feb 23rd 1961

Dear Arthur,

I'll be arriving in Boston late Sunday (Feb 26) afternoon. H. M.[1] are putting me up at the Ritz-Carleton. Shades of poor old Mitchell! That evening I'm taken for dinner, but would it be possible for you to come over for breakfast Monday morning at nine a.m.? Or is that too early for you? I just want to be sure of seeing you   The rest of the time will be taken up in acting "the sedulous ape" for the publishers. In any case call me at that time on Monday

> Yrs ever   Dos

Perhaps you could leave a message for me at the desk — if you cant make breakfast — When you'll be free and at home on Tuesday —

1. Houghton Mifflin.

163

> 84 Charles St
> 18 Dec 1961   Boston

Dear Dos,   This will bring you the best wishes of the season, and the hope of receiving a line from you. I am not sending cards this year, as I would have to go to the Museum or Cambridge to get tolerable ones and do not wish to bestir myself for I am just out of a fortnight in hospital & am "taking it easy". You were here the day of my fracture (Feb. 28) and the year (almost entirely calamitous) ends with 'fibrilation' (an irregularity of the heart beat)   I am restored and feeling very well, though not energetic. I was comfortable & well-treated in hospital & picked up no staphyloccoei (Sp.?)—(I understand resistant strains of these latter live in such places)—There is no reason this thing should recur (Gurdon Worcester[1] has suffered from it on & off for years) but naturally one feels a little as if one had been jostled by a figure in the market place at Baghdad.[2] Enfin c'est de nôtre age.[3]   —This is an appropriate day to write you. Goa.[4] What irony. My favourite Leftist attacks my favourite rightist.[5] Katanga. Once I thought of buying some shares in the Union Minière du Haut-Katanga[6] (it sounds liké something that would be ironically treated in Conrad).—I have been two months in Europe. Aug 31 sailed, back Nov. 8. & was in Sussex [,] London, Paris, Lausanne, Florence, Naples. A familiar round. Our publishers are very annoyed that I am back so soon, although I pointed out that there was no more money with which to stay. They ignored this and alleged that the winter in Boston was apt to be cold. I knew this. The final result is that I am peeved, too, as I dislike being scolded at my advanced age. I wish you "the most" (if that is the correct hipster term)   Arthur

Kenneth Murdock[7] reigns at I Tatti—why I do not exactly know. He said he had seen you & you had spoken of me, but I know little of what you are up to.

A

1. Gurdon Saltonstall Worcester, consulting psychologist, son of Dr. Elwood Worcester, and friend of McComb.

2. Allusion to a speech by Death in W. Somerset Maugham's play *Sheppey*, act 3. John O'Hara took the title for his novel *Appointment in Samarra* from the same speech.

3. Enfin c'est de nôtre âge [Fr.], "After all, it's what you'd expect at our age."

4. Indian troops invaded Goa and two other Portuguese enclaves on the west coast of India early on December 18, 1961.

5. Jawaharlal Nehru was prime minister of India, and V. K. Krishna Menon was defense minister. Salazar was premier of Portugal.

6. The province of Katanga contained most of the Belgian Congo's mineral wealth, and the Union Minière du Haut-Katanga was the largest corporation in the Belgian Congo. Soon after the Congo gained its independence in June 1960, Katanga declared itself a republic. With Belgian aid its president, Moise Tshombe, fought off attempts by the Congolese central government to seize control there. Supported by the Union Minière, he continued to resist Congolese and U.N. forces in 1961.

7. Kenneth Ballard Murdock (Harvard, A.B., 1916, summa cum laude; Ph.D., 1923), a college friend of Dos Passos. He was dean of the Faculty of Arts and Sciences, 1931–36, and became Higginson Professor of English Literature in 1939. In March 1961 he was asked to start and direct a research center at I Tatti, which Berenson had bequeathed to Harvard.

164

[Art postcard of Vincent van Gogh's *Orchard in Bloom*]

[Westmoreland, Virginia
December 1961]

Arthur
A Happy New Year to you
from
Dos

165

84 Charles St.
Boston
2 Aug. 1962

Dear Dos,

I feel impelled to write you a few lines because of things that have come up in the last week.   I suppose you read in the current New Yorker (i.e. the one dated 28 Jy) the Profile on Gerald & Sara Murphy with a lot, too, about Scott Fitzgerald in it.[1] I suppose you must have known S.F. but I don't remember your speaking of him. Everything I read about him by admirers makes me think of the term people in our childhood might have used about him—I cannot read his books— but you may have more knowledge of all this than I.—The Murphys of course loved artistic forme—even so I wonder at their putting up with him. Was there something fascinating?

I was made sad by the death of Raquel Meller[2] at the age of 74—in Barcelona

Finally there is the matter of the quotations from yr letters to me of 1917–18 made by Aaron[3] with your permission in Writers on the Left. It must have surprised you to learn they were in the august institution where they now repose.[4] When I see you I'll tell you the story (too long for a note and in part disgraceful) but for a time I deposited them at the M.H.S.[5] to which I intended to give & bequeath them, as I thought they ought to be preserved for history. This was sub regno Mitchelli[6]—I think you were brave to let Aaron publish what he did, but I should not have blamed you if you'd said no.

I wanted to tell you that I heard in Feb.ᵞ from Dudley Poore in Madrid—after all these years. He was again looking at the pictures we liked in 1919 & mentioned the Maître de Flémalle. I was sorry to learn he'd been suffering from high blood pressure. I myself was again in hospital in April—this time with pneumonia & lung abscess. Sir Alexander Fleming's famed drug[7] brought me round. I hope all is well with you & famille

A.

P.S.

I am not at all on good terms with H M Co[8] —but continue to work under difficulties on the book. I never go near them. —That is a long story too.

A.

I address Virginia but one never knows—you might, I reflect, be in Callao or Lourenço Marques[9]

1. The profile is Calvin Tomkins' "Living Well Is the Best Revenge," *New Yorker* 38 (July 28, 1962): 31–32 and passim to 69; Scott: F. Scott.

2. A fashionable, elegant Spanish singer, whom McComb had enjoyed in Madrid, where she performed before upper-class audiences. Dos Passos didn't like her but enjoyed another woman singer, who appeared in public theaters (telephone interview with Dudley Poore, October 3, 1976). By 1923 Raquel Meller was a favorite in Paris.

3. Daniel Aaron.

4. American Academy of Arts and Letters. See narrative, pp. 241 and 245 above.

5. Massachusetts Historical Society.

6. [Lat.] "During Mitchell's reign."

7. Penicillin.

8. Houghton Mifflin Co.

9. Callao: city and principal seaport of Peru; Lourenço Marques: seaport in far southern Mozambique.

166

Hotel Glória
Rio de Janeiro
August 31 [19]62

Dear Arthur,

You didnt guess too wrong on Callao—We were there early this month—it's now part of Lima, inspecting inter alia[1] the Bata Shoe Factory of all things.[2] The Czechs in exile have built a worldwide empire out of cheap shoes.

To tell the truth I didn't get much 'bang' out of the New Yorker piece. It is factually fairly accurate. I knew Scott[3] quite well, liked and respected him in spite of his maniacal obsession with wealth in the American sense. The Murphys like the man who wrote the piece   So they received it with equanimity.

Send me Dudley Poore's address—to Westmoreland if you have it. I'd love to see him. I've been out of touch with him for many years.

The family returns Sunday to the States (Lucy's school) but I have to stay in these uneasy regions for another month attending to journalistic chores of various sorts. Shall d.v. fly direct home from Buenos Aires in early October. Hope you are all restored from your bout with the hospital

As ever
Dos

1. [Lat.] "Among other things."
2. Dos Passos' cousin-by-marriage Brodnax Cameron was a director of three Bata companies. Knowing that Dos Passos would be in Peru and would be interested in its economic life, he arranged for the inspection. Interview with Elizabeth Dos Passos, July 1976.
3. F. Scott Fitzgerald.

167

[Postcard]

18 Oct 1862   84 Charles St
Boston

Dear Dos: So nice to get a line from you from Rio de Janeiro. I hope you didn't have to go to Brasilia!—Dudley's address was Am. Exp. 3, Plaza de las Cortes [,] Madrid. That was about March 1st He had been there all winter I think staying at the Pension Americana. He was not going to stay the summer but must have left a forwarding address.—I follow the Council[1] with interest but feel more familiar and 'at home' with that of '69–'70. Manning & Newman, Pius IX, Döllinger & Acton[2]—and the breach in Porta Pia[3] seem more real & still more interesting.—I hope you are now safe & snug at home with yr family.

Arthur

1. Vatican Council II, convoked by Pope John XXIII, had opened in Rome on October 11, 1962.
2. Vatican Council I, the council of 1869–70, was convoked by Pope Pius IX and is remembered chiefly for enunciating the doctrine of papal infallibility. Henry Edward Manning (1808–92), the English archbishop (later cardinal), attended the council and strongly advocated such an enunciation. John Henry Newman (1801–90), the English churchman (later cardinal), Johann Joseph Ignaz von Döllinger (1799–1890), the German theologian and historian, and Lord Acton (1834–1902), the English historian, also played parts in the overall history of the council, though Newman and Döllinger were not in

Rome. Newman, while believing in papal infallibility, thought that the council's enunciating it would be inopportune. Döllinger opposed the doctrine, refused to accept it after it was promulgated, and suffered excommunication in 1871. Acton, like Döllinger, opposed the doctrine; however, unlike him, Acton remained in the church.

3. While Vatican Council I was still in session, the Franco-Prussian War began, and France in August 1870 withdrew its garrison protecting Rome. On September 1, 1870, the council suspended sessions. The French Empire was overthrown on September 4. Not long afterwards troops of King Victor Emmanuel II of Italy entered papal territory, and on September 20 they attacked Rome. Pius IX decided to resist, in order to prove himself a victim of force. His resistance brought new notice to the Porta Pia, a gate of Rome basically designed by Michelangelo. When Italian artillery made a breach in the wall near the gate, the pope ordered a cease-fire. Rome was occupied, and in 1871 it became the capital of a united Italy.

168

84 Charles St
Boston
20 Oct 1962

Dear Dos,

I have had a few lines from Bernardin whom I last heard from 10 or more years ago. The Oklahoma Univ. Press is going to do his book in 2 vols. He asks to examine y^r letters to me (having seen Aron's book)[1] I have replied that I have all yr letters of the last 20 years and all post-cards since 1916 — but have not encouraged him [.] He can consult the letters which Aron saw. — This is to keep you au courant.

Another birthday of mine (Hallowe'en) approaches [–] its too appalling to be as old as this. Nevertheless I'd like to discuss Cuba,[2] De Gaulle[3] & Mississippi[4] with you. I can no longer necessarily guess your views as I once could. Mine too I suppose might have surprises. Did I tell you I now have a tel.? CAP 4738.

Yrs in haste
Arthur

1. Daniel Aaron's *Writers on the Left*.
2. Strong tension between the United States and Cuba, and its ally the U.S.S.R., soon culminated in the Cuban missile crisis. Two days after McComb wrote this letter, President Kennedy announced to the people of the United States that he was imposing a limited blockade on Cuba.
3. Charles de Gaulle, president of France.
4. After a Federal court ordered a Negro, James Meredith, admitted to the University of Mississippi, Governor Ross R. Barnett of Mississippi sought unsuccessfully to interpose state authority. Federal troops had to quell riots before Meredith could register on October 1, 1962.

169

[From the American Academy of Arts and Letters]

> [633 West 155 Street
> New York 32, New York]
> October 30, 1962

Dear Mr. Dos Passos:

The enclosed is self-explanatory. Do we have your permission to let Professor Bernardin see your letters to Arthur McComb, which are in our collection?

For your convenience, please signify your answer on the carbon copy of this letter and return it to me in the enclosed envelope.

> Very sincerely yours,
> Felicia Geffen[1]

Mr. John Dos Passos
Westmoreland, Va.

. . . .

The message is on the institution's letterhead paper.
1. Assistant to the president, American Academy of Arts and Letters.

170

[Dos Passos' comment, handwritten on the original of the above letter, beneath the query]

> [November? 1962]

Dear Arthur—

Since these are the letters everybody sees I'll go ahead letting the professors see them. Just to tease the scholars suppose you hold the rest back for a while—? Now at least I know where they are—You probably told me and I forgot

> Yrs ever
> Dos

171

Westmoreland, Va
  is permanent.

> 1821 Sulgrave Avenue
> Baltimore 9 Md.
> Nov 2 '62

Dear Arthur,

While I was in South America the Angel of the Lord has certainly been mowing down our contemporaries. Cummings' death was particularly painful to me.[1] I loved him dearly and had been carrying on an occasional conversation with him since college.

Of course we went to Brasilia; it's a great show—some of the buildings are excellent others wretched—a sort of World's Fair atmosphere that I find exilerating.

In re Bernardin:

2 vols is really appalling—yet he who says "a" must say "b". I foolishly encouraged Bernardin years ago. I dont know that I want him reading all my letters. Suppose I wanted to print them myself? If you can satisfy him with the ones Aron[2] saw it might be sufficient—one or two others maybe—but not too many.

If I get to Boston I shall certainly use your new telephone but Arthur, it must have a fifth number—jot it on a card.

To tell the truth the only painful thing about the approach of old age is time's massacre of my friends—up to now. Plus tard? On verra[3]—

Many happy returns of Hallow'Een.

Yrs ever   Dos

I must say the present Cuban snarl is enlivening. Do you suppose that Kennedy is preparing to "make like a president'? I dont trust any of those boys—particularly not Robert[4]—who seems to me the dominent figure. Still they'll do anything to win an election—even affront Kruschev[5]

---

1. E. E. Cummings died on September 3, 1962, after suffering a stroke at Silver Lake, New Hampshire.

2. Daniel Aaron.

3. [Fr.] "Later on? We shall see."

4. Robert F. Kennedy, attorney general in his brother's cabinet.

5. Nikita Sergeyevich Khrushchev (1894–1971), Soviet premier and leader. On October 28, 1962, he agreed to withdraw Soviet missiles from Cuba. On October 29 the United States announced that the next morning it would lift its blockade of Cuba for two days, while the acting secretary general of the United Nations was in Havana for talks. The *New York Times'* front-page headline on November 1 was: "CASTRO IS BALKING AT INSPECTION; MISSILE REMOVAL ON, U.N. HEARS; U.S. RENEWS AIR-SEA WATCH TODAY." The headline on November 2 was: "CASTRO REFUSES ANY INSPECTIONS, SAYS ROCKETS ARE BEING REMOVED. . . ."

172

84 Charles St.   Boston
Guy Fawkes Day [November 5] 1962

Dear Dos,

I was glad to hear from you & at the same time distressed as to the letter business which in an indirect way is partly my fault.—I do not know Aron[1] nor did he ever communicate with me. Someone said to me recently: "I saw your name in a book" etc. so I looked it up. I was struck with the fact that Aron apparently did not mention that the letters from which he quotes were in the Academy. Of course I knew that he must have seen them there and I naturally went on to assume that he had your permission to publish. I now gather (correctly?) from your letter that he did not.[2] This was altogether improper. (He gave rather the impression that I had lent him the letters)

The legal situation (perhaps you've not gone into it) is as follows. . . .

You were probably puzzled by an oblique reference of mine to the whereabouts of the letters (the Academy was what I meant by writing: "august institution") That was because I assumed you knew. . . .

After I had posted my last letter I realized that I'd not spoken of the death of Cummings. Have you seen Marion?[3] Slater Brown saw her in NY recently & gave a rather harrowing account of her unhappiness. They were very close, I thought—more than most married people—I had not seen him since he gave the Norton lectures in Cambridge [,] which is now at least 6 or 7 years ago (?)[4]—Yes, the death list grows rapidly & it is sorrowful. The immense leisureliness with which life begins, the great speed with which it comes towards its end is extra-ordinary. And yet there is something unbelievable & surprising about each cessation. Time is an Einstein Pixie. I have a good memory for dates and for sequence—yet I swear it is only yesterday that you & I & Dudley[5] were in Madrid! . . .

Yes, Robt Kennedy sits in on all the great decisions (Cuba) & his opinion is considered, perhaps taken. And what does he know about anything except how "to get on." But I am not fond of the figures in Am. Public life. Unlike you (who know a great deal about it) I don't, I've decided, understand the psycho-political atmosphere very well. I'm much better on Europe where I don't even live any more.

As for my telephone number—CAP 4738 is all right. Where P = 7 (as they would say in algebra?) it makes no difference (CA 7-4738) in the dialling. . . .

Yours as ever
Arthur

P.S.
The Cuba affair was at times rather livelier than I liked. These victories of diplomacy (?) do not enchant me. Lord Salisbury never liked them & felt both sides should go away satisfied.[6] It is true that this is not Ld. Salisbury's epoch—hélas[7]

One more thing: I shall certainly not give the letters & p.c.'s here to <u>anyone</u>. I suppose I should bequeath them to the Academy so that everything will be together, though?

A.

Or perhaps just let them be returned to you or y^r daughter, on my departing this little planet. That might be better after all.

A

1. Daniel Aaron.
2. Incorrectly. See Dos Passos' reply in Letter 173 below, and see narrative, p. 246 above.
3. Marion Morehouse (Cummings).
4. Cummings delivered the Charles Eliot Norton Lectures at Harvard during the 1952–53 academic year.
5. Dudley Poore.
6. Robert A. T. Gascoyne-Cecil (1830–1903), third marquess of Salisbury, British Conservative and Unionist leader. He was prime minister from 1885 to 1886, 1886 to 1892, and 1895 to 1902.
7. [Fr.] "Alas."

173

1821 Sulgrave Avenue
Baltimore 9   Md
Nov 18 '62

Dear Arthur,

I'm afraid I overstated my case in my last letter. I really lose no sleep about who reads my letters. I gave all those scavengers permission to read them etc. It's just that I'm occasionally seized with a mischievous desire to hold something out on them. I hope to live long enough to confound their prognostications and to turn their analyses topsy turvy. Bad cess to them. Anon.

Until the angels came for Mrs Woodrow Wilson I had considerable trouble with her legal advisers in the case of a few quotations I wanted to make in the World War I book that is out this week.[1] I'll send you a copy because I'd really like to know how certain things strike you.

The Cuban situation remains rather livelier than I like — the price of past follies. Sometimes it is hard not to believe that there arent Communists in important posts where they — oh hell I'll leave it to the candy manufacturer and his John Birch Society.[2] Everything in Brazil was much less hush hush and the Brazilian press is incomparably bolder than ours —

Yrs ever

Dos

I'll use those phone numbers if I get a chance

1. Dos Passos, *Mr. Wilson's War* (Garden City, New York: Doubleday and Co., 1962).

2. Activist U.S. anti-Communist organization founded in 1958 by Robert H. W. Welch, Jr., a retired Massachusetts candy manufacturer. Its social views were ultraconservative, and its aims included impeaching government officials.

174

84 Charles St
Boston
20 Nov. 1962

Dear Dos,

. . . .

Everyone seems very pleased that De Gaulle is winning [,][1] that Nehru is disillusioned[2] and that Kennedy has won a victory over Cuba. But it is all folly—this civilisation is too fond of violence & war & it will perish. I don't see what can save us all from a run-away technology and a marked suicidal bent. Spengler & Jung—so different—are surely nevertheless both right in their prophecies & fears. As Spengler says: "Caesarism approaches with silent tread";[3] and Jung: a great crime is being prepared."[4]

As ever
Arthur

. . . .

<u>Nov. 21 evening</u>

Dos: The morning after I wrote the above letter it was still unposted and yours of the 18<u>th</u>—19<u>th</u> from Baltimore came. I therefore held it out till now until I had a chance to add to it & also I shall direct it to Baltimore. . . .

. . . I have not yet seen notices of your book [*Mr. Wilson's War*]—I shall be delighted to have a copy as the whole thing (period, theme etc.) interests me very much. Don't you feel that you remember a great deal that other people have forgotten? But I thought Barbara Tuchman (did you know she was old Morgenthau's great niece—the Ambass. in Constantinople) did an extraordinarily good job in 'August 1914' (in America 'The Guns of August') considering she was a baby at the date in question.[5] . . . When and if I see you I'd like to discuss a little literary project of mine to be attended to when the Berenson Letters are done—reminiscential in character (actually about 100 pages are done—it would be a question of taking it up again)

In sending yr book, do indicate on a slip what things (you imply that there are some you want my reactions to) you would like me to note—or on second thoughts, perhaps you'd prefer I read it first as a whole. Either way.

Yours as ever
Arthur

. . . .

1. Gaullist candidates on November 18, 1962, won by a large margin in the first of a two-stage election for the French National Assembly.

2. Communist China invaded India on October 20, 1962, in a dispute over border territory.

3. Cf. Oswald Spengler, *The Decline of the West,* trans. Charles Francis Atkinson (2 vols. in 1 vol. ed.), vol. 2, *Perspectives of World-History* (New York: Alfred A. Knopf, 1939), p. 507. Spengler's work was published in the original German in 1918–22.

4. For Carl Jung's meaning, see his *The Undiscovered Self,* trans. R. F. C. Hull (Boston: Little, Brown and Co., 1958).

5. Barbara W. Tuchman (b. 1912) is the granddaughter, not great-niece, of Henry Morgenthau (1856–1946), U.S. ambassador to Turkey from 1913 to 1916. Her historical narrative *The Guns of August* was published in 1962.

175

[Letterhead: Library of the
Boston Athenaeum]
3 Dec. 1962

Dear Dos,

The book [*Mr. Wilson's War*] arrived several days ago and instead of acknowledging its receipt and thanking you for it, here I've been every evening reading it & absorbed in it. (I've reached the winter of 1917–18. It's perfectly splendid and I'm so pleased to have it. . . .

It's a fine story—in a deep sense more truly meriting the word 'tragic' than 1939–45. You have caught the variations and your method of vignette, dramatic confrontation etc. is of course an excellent [,] eminently readable way of covering that staggering mass of material. You have dug up some fine bits. . . .

I was struck with the great lack of parti-pris.[1] Everything that is done up to 1917 leaves a not totally unsympathetic impression (Bryan & Wilson, too) but as the war goes on you allow yourself some little sarcasm & occasional bitternesses (and this is just as it should be—I mean not only the fact in itself but the slight change which occurs is right and corresponds to the change which so many decent people actually felt). . . .

I hope some time we have a chance to talk about it all. (I have made a few notes on details). . . .

I shall probably be writing you again when I have finished reading.

This very day I sent round my Ms. to Houghton Mifflin. If it ever comes out I'll ask you to read my preface and glance at some of the footnotes which may amuse you.

As ever and again many thanks,
Arthur

1. [Fr.] "Bias."

176

[Letterhead: Library of the
Boston Athenæum]
7 Dec. 1962
(an unpleasant anniversary)

Dear Dos,

The morning after I wrote you last, came that fine p.c. — a church in Viana do Castello — how I wish I could have spent more time in Portugal. Especially in small towns e.g. Braga, or Evora. I am one of the few who like Oporto.   The usual view that Spain & Portugal were in decline in the XVIII c. should be treated with reserve I think. Besides the beginnings of decline often seem quite attractive. Later is often another matter. Still XIX c. Iberia has a strong attractiveness too — at least for me.

I've finished your book — wonderful reading. I do congratulate you. And this in spite of a rather unattractive cast of characters on the whole. In another period your book might well have been entitled:

Mr Wilson's War

or

Facilis Descensus[1]

I am not being flippant, really. I got a great sense of character deterioration as I read along.   I was wrong probably in what I said about sarcasm. As soon as I began to read again, you had resumed your reportorial detachment. But all my old indignations came back again!

You kept consistently to a position which involved placing yourself solidly in America. This gave great unity & a kind of strength to the book, but naturally involved your saying a good deal less about the Central Powers. (I feel they were essentially superior)

There are so many small things I want to comment on — too many for a letter. . . .

Here's a little bone: why do you say Even the Reichstag etc. p. 271[2] — no parliament on the Allied side did as much. I object to that even!!

Are you going to have an English edition? I made a few pedantic notes of a proof-reading kind—not affecting anything really—but if you think they might be of use for 2^d or Engl. ed. I'll make a fair copy & send them on

As to my scheme about which you are good enough to ask: Some years ago when I was in Asheville[3] I wrote a little paper on my English school-days. Then, here at 84 [Charles Street] I wrote some more reminiscences—50 pages on Anglo-Florentine figures of between the wars. Then a little account of a philosophical anarchist[4] whom I knew in Madrid—This was a kind of preface to an account of the attempt on Don Alfonso and Doña Victoria Eugenia on their wedding day in 1906 (from the Spanish transcripts of the legal depositions—which no one else ever seems to have consulted). Peter Gunn, an Englishman who is working on a book about Vernon Lee, knowing that I knew her [,] wrote to ask me for information. I sent him a carbon I had of the section on V.L. and he read it to his wife & they thought I should do more of the same. Perhaps I should, say, Harvard, Paris, Germany—much more on Spain. It could make a vol. and might be published in England—certainly not here [.] I'd love to talk about it with you sometime in detail and even ask you to read a bit to see if you think its really feasible.   As ever   Arthur

Its nice to be in touch with you!

1. ". . . facilis descensus Averno. . . . ," ". . . easy is the descent to the underworld. . . ." Vergil *Aeneid* 6. 126.

2. Dos Passos writes: "Warweariness was the prevailing mood. Even the German Reichstag had passed a resolution urging a peace of understanding and the permanent reconciliation of the peoples."

3. See narrative, p. 236 above.

4. Referred to by name as Marcel Ogier in McComb's manuscript "A Foreign Dye." Cf. Letter 127, including n. 3, above.

177

1821 Sulgrave Avenue
Baltimore 9 Md.
Dec 14 [1962]

Dear Arthur,

Thanks for your letter about Mr W's W. I'm so glad you felt it wasn't a waste of time. I'd be delighted to have your proofreading notes. It has already been pointed out that Karl Muck's Karl got spelt with a C.[1] There's just no way of avoiding these little errors, and I found Doubleday's proofreaders no help at all. I'm afraid Hamish Hamilton's[2]

English edition is beyond the proofreading stage, but it may not be. Anyway, if there is another printing I can get corrections made in Doubleday's plates.

If I ever get to Boston we'll talk about your project. Do go on with it. Do you _ever_ get to New York? I go down there once a month or so, but dont get to Boston except when there's some need to see the Houghton Mifflin people on their home ground. This happens rarely since I usually see Lovell Thompson[3] when he's in New York.

Yrs ever

Dos

1. Karl Muck (1859–1940). Dos Passos says: "The drive against German music culminated in the arrest of Dr. Carl Muck, the elderly and muchadmired conductor of the Boston Symphony Orchestra" (_Mr. Wilson's War,_ p. 300). _Brockhaus Enzyklopädie_ (1966–74) has _Carl._

2. Hamish Hamilton Ltd., publisher.

3. Lovell Thompson, vice president and trade manager of Houghton Mifflin Co. and a friend of Dos Passos.

178

84 Charles St [Boston]

19 Dec 1962

Dear Dos,

. . . I didn't catch Carl Muck.

I felt you might approve my idea, since you'd once urged to do a bit on the Spanish period. I'll try & begin again on it after Jan 1.   No, I don't get to N.Y. — except for stepping on and off a steamer[1] I've not been there (and that was one night only) since Dec. 1 [,] 1946! I thought you sometimes came & stayed with Edmund Wilson in Cambridge, but that's probably only when you are here anyway for Houghton. I wish it were otherwise. It would be nice to talk about things.

Yours

Arthur

. . . .

1. Possibly "steamer [.]"; in the manuscript _steamer_ appears at the end of a line.

179

84 Charles St [Boston]

Sat. 5 Jan. '63

Dear Dos —   All best wishes for the New Year. . . .

. . . My attention has been called to the fact that there is a biography of J. Dos P. by one Wrenn (1961)[1]. . . . I've not seen it. Surely that'll annoy Bernardin!   In thinking about it all, I could not but wish that you'd do, if not a full-dress autobiography, then at least some reminiscences. It would be so much better & more authentic than the works of tutti grandi[2] & besides personally it would entertain me to compare y^r view of the 'Spanish period' with mine—which I've begun—but I began logically enough with Havana with the result that I've only just got to Cadiz and it is March 10, 1918! What do you think of my suggestion?

And I wanted to tell you that Houghton Mifflin wrote in very complimentary terms about my BB[3] thing—so it will be published but not for some time—as everything that matters is of course slower in the jet age.

Yrs
Arthur

1. John H. Wrenn, *John Dos Passos* (New York: Twayne Publishers, 1961).
2. Tutti i grandi [It.], "all the great ones."
3. Bernard Berenson.

180

The Colonnade Club[1]
University of Virginia
Charlottesville Va
2/12/63

Dear Arthur,

Did I ever answer your note of Jan 5? I suspect that I did write you a note during that period but I dont think it was anything very drastic. I've been in a great stew trying to get my Brazilian articles ready for the publisher.

These biographies you speak of are an unavoidable nuisance. I dont think they even sell books because people who read them think now they dont need to read the books. I saw a new one peeking out at me among the paperbacks in the bookstore at Newcomb Hall (the local college union).[2] When senility is sufficiently advanced I'll probably start putting down my own recollections just to confound the confusion.

I'm delighted that the B.B.[3] edition will go through—tell them to send me the bound page proofs when they get to that stage.

I'm spending three weeks in exile from my family at the University of Virginia as "writer-in-residence". Curiosity, the need to scape up a little cash for future (and past) journeys. The professors, particularly in the English department, are a foggy lot. The students much brisker— but I ask myself que diable allait-il faire dans cette galère.[4]

Dos Passos as writer-in-residence at the University of Virginia (1963). Smoking helped him bear up under the questioning and photographing.
Courtesy of the Department of Graphics, University of Virginia

It's been a wintry winter but I heard a dove the other morning and maybe a—black billed?—cuckoo this morning. Its snowing right now—

Yrs ever

Dos

1. Faculty club.
2. At the university, not far from the Colonnade Club.
3. Bernard Berenson.
4. "What the devil was he doing in that [a Turk's] galley?" Molière made this the character Géronte's leitmotiv in his play *Les fourberies de Scapin,* act 2, sc. 7 (1671). Earlier Cyrano de Bergerac had used an almost identical leitmotiv in *Le pédant joué,* act 2, sc. 4 (1654). Molière's words became a familiar French expression meaning "Why on earth did he get involved in that affair?"

181

[Greeting card. Its illustration is of a conventionalized horse, rampant, and the legend reads: "Horse from Pennsylvania German Fraktur, late 18th century." The printed message is one word, "Greetings."]

Spence's Point, Westmoreland, Va
Christmas Eve [1963]

Arthur: How are you? How were you affected by the gory events that closed up 1963?[1] How's Berenson? What prospects for 1964? Anyway good wishes from

Dos

1. President Kennedy was assassinated on November 22, and two days later his assassin was murdered.

182

84 Charles St
Boston
29 Dec 63

Dear Dos,

How nice to see your handwriting. Recently too I had a specimen of Dudley Poore's—in the shape of two cards from Palma & Mallorca (he was, he said, on his way to Rome—I don't understand modern travel) This had been preceded by a brochure apparently mailed in N.Y.—has he been in this country? Have you seen him? . . .

The book will be out, they say, Feb 24. They have thus taken 1¼ years. . . . Extracts from the book (incl. my Intro.) are coming out soon in Encounter.[1] I have just sent the corrected proof of this back to London.   Hutchinson[2] bought the rights to the book for £ 250 —

As to the events of November: I was shocked & sorry of course. Kennedy I liked better than the other figures on the stage of Am. politics — in spite of the Bay of Pigs[3] & his apparent attitude to the negro revolution (both of which I disapprove) there was something intelligent about Kennedy. He thought about things & he read (very different from FDR[4] who was ignorant, revengeful and war-mongering). — And there is no conservatism (in my sense) in America [,] so why not have a rich intelligent member of the Liberal establishments? So my thoughts ran — but essentially I live in the past & I do not care for the technological, permissive, mass-media age (this is my understatement of the year)

I wish you'd come to Boston & we could talk about all sorts of things. We've seen a lot in our day!

My very best wishes to you & famiglia[5] for 1964

Arthur

. . . .

1. McComb, ed. "Some Letters of Bernard Berenson," _Encounter_ 22 (February 1964): 28–40.

2. Hutchinson and Co. (publishers), London.

3. Some fifteen hundred Cuban refugees invading Cuba landed at the Bahía de Cochinos (Bay of Pigs) on April 17, 1961. The United States helped to organize the invasion and gave it a destroyer escort, but at the last minute President Kennedy forbade air cover. The invasion was a disastrous failure.

4. Franklin Delano Roosevelt.

5. [It.] "Family."

183

[Postcard]

[Letterhead: Boston Athenæum]
24 Jan. '64

Dear Dos,   I'm sending you a copy of my BB book,[1] and I hope it reaches you (I'm assuming you're still at home — but is this a safe assumption?) and that it may amuse you to look it over. . . .

I hope all is well with you.

As ever
Arthur

I'm told the P.O. does not forward books, so would you drop me a card whether Balto. or Va. or elsewhere   A.

1. *The Selected Letters of Bernard Berenson*, ed. A. K. McComb (Boston: Houghton Mifflin Co., 1964).

184

[Postcard]

[Letterhead: Boston Athenæum]
3 Feb 1964

Dear Dos,   Thanks so much for your card. I now feel more secure & will send off the book to Balto. to-morrow. I've just heard from Dudley P.[1] strangely enough or else I'd not have been able to give you his address. It is ᶜ/₀ Am. Exp. 38 Piazza d'Spagna [,] Rome. He'll be there till the Spring. I'll send him a copy of the BB book and then any comments you & he care to make on it & its episodes will remind me of conversations in Granada!

Yours ever
Arthur

1. Poore.

185

84 Charles St
Boston Mass.[ts]
22 VIII '64

Dear Dos,
    I have been thinking of you & have wondered what is yʳ attitude to the Goldwater Revolution[1] — I've seen nothing from you in print. Is there going to be? May I have a line of private advice on this? — How I should like to talk to you. (I admire neither side myself, but G. thoroughly frightens me)   I almost expected you might be writing about the Convention at the Cow Palace.[2] I have been reading the English Papers & weeklies. The Economist by a typographical error (later noticed & approved of by the spectator) twice referred to the Con Palace.
    All this in turn brought some other questions into my mind & I then decided I'd write you this note. Did you get in touch with Dudley? In the Spring he was on his way back to Marietta from Italy.[3] Did he then go back to Europe or is he is still in M. — Have you a later European address for him? ——

After you wrote me a card saying to send the BB[4] book to Baltimore I immediately did so. Did you ever get it? . . .

I saw some good reviews of M̲ʳ̲ ̲W̲i̲l̲s̲o̲n̲'̲s̲ ̲W̲a̲r̲ in the Engl. papers. Did it have a good sale? My thing only sold 2600 to June. Curtis Brown Ltd (London)[5] wrote that 6 publishers had turned down my Spanish-Italian Memoir. He listed them. The general verdict was 'charming but perhaps lacks a cutting edge for these difficult times' Wonderful phraseology! I was somewhat disappointed though, as I was much more wrapped up in that than in the B.B.

I hope all is well with you. Do you feel that time is passing madly and that we are in the nature of survivors? — Yrs   Arthur

1. Walter Lippmann, describing Barry Goldwater shortly before the Republican National Convention of 1964, spoke of "his roughriding, devil-may-care readiness to attack the whole central movement of national and of Republican opinion in the twentieth century" (*Newsweek* 64 [July 6, 1964]: 13). On July 15 the convention nominated Goldwater as Republican presidential candidate. In his acceptance speech, he said that "extremism in the defense of liberty is no vice."

2. A cavernous arena for sports, exhibitions, and conventions, located 6½ miles from downtown San Francisco, in Daly City, California.

3. Poore was returning to his home, located by Otisco Lake in a country area. Marietta was merely his post-office address.

4. Bernard Berenson.

5. Literary agent.

186

Westmoreland, Va
Sept 6 1964

Dear Arthur,

I was convinced I had written you about the Berenson letters. I duly received the book and it sits on my shelf in Baltimore. Thank you[1]   I dip in it from time to time. What another world it deals with.

I find Goldwater far less frightening than Johnson and Humphrey[2] — Enclosed is a short account of the Cow Palace events.[3] I must say I found them very enlivening.

I exchanged a couple of letters with Dudley; since then silence. He was coming through Baltimore to Washington and said he would look me up. That was in the spring. Have you his Marietta address? I have it somewhere but have mislaid it. I might try stirring him up again. I'm hoping to see you around Oct 22 when I do a reading for the Jesuit Fathers at Boston U.[4]

The English papers, I find, are moonstruck mad on the subject of Goldwater. They seem to get their opinions from Walter Lippmann.

How do you like the United Nations in the Congo?[5]

"Mr. Wilson's War" sold moderately well—for me.[6] I'm sorry you are having publisher trouble—have you tried American publishers?

Anyway I'm hoping to see you in good health and spirits—almost every day some old friend meets a dismal death. Survivors indeed.

Yrs ever

Dos

1. "Thank you" inserted with caret.

2. President Lyndon B. Johnson and Senator Hubert H. Humphrey. In late August 1964 the Democrats, meeting in Atlantic City, had nominated them as the party's presidential and vice-presidential candidates respectively.

3. Dos Passos, "The Battle of San Francisco," *National Review* 16 (July 28, 1964): 640, 652.

4. Dos Passos read at Boston College (which is the Jesuits' school), not Boston University.

5. U.N. forces battled Katangan forces in December 1962, and Tshombe in January 1963 agreed to end secession. The last U.N. troops left the Congo at the end of June 1964. Though secession had been suppressed, other revolts unsettled the country. In July President Joseph Kasavubu, perhaps from desperation, appointed Tshombe his prime minister. On September 3 the rebel commander in Stanleyville told the U.N. that he was holding all whites there as hostages against air raids by the Congo government.

6. Sales were 22,544 by the end of the year.

187

[Postcard]

[Letterhead: Boston Athenæum]
12 IX 64

Dear Dos,   I was very pleased to hear from you and to know you were coming up about Oct. 22. My number is CA 7-4738 but of course I am out in the day a good deal. Messages can be left at the Athenaeum where I am almost every day [.] CA 7-0270. So do try to look me up & I can always come to the Ritz or wherever you are staying. (I remember the last time was the day I broke my arm [,] 28 Feb 1961)—DGP's[1] address is Otisco Valley Rd. Marietta [.] Thank you for your NR[2] report—interesting—in what I think of as your 'impressionist' manner.

Y^{rs} as ever   Arthur

1. Dudley Greene Poore's.

2. *National Review*.

188

[Postcard]

[Letterhead: Boston Athenæum]
14 Sept '64

Dear Dos, . . . [I] forgot to answer y^r question about the Congo. I despise the new state. But I accept the candidate of the Union Minière du Haut-Katanga, <u>en principe</u>![1] Tshombé hated, is now loved — after all, just like Germany & Japan. Hard not to be scornful. A bientôt

Arthur

1. [Fr.] "On the face of the matter."

189

[Art postcard. A picture of a sailship in tropical waters appears on the illustrated side. On the correspondence side the legend reads: "Oil painting by Robert Salmon of the sloop *Sally,* manned by seamen of the U.S. frigate *Constitution,* cutting out a French ship in Port Plate in May, 1800." McComb underlined Port Plate and wrote under the legend: "Puerto Plata? — Dom Rep? Never heard of this expedition."]

[Boston
December 1964]

Dear Dos,

I have to-day sent you the Ms. (Spanish section) 4$^{\underline{th}}$ Cl. — it will get to you in time. Although it is not much, yet I tell myself that the nature of the subject and the recollection of the time cannot fail to cause you to muse. I wish <u>you</u> would do y^r memories of that period. Best wishes of the season — Arthur

190

[Picture postcard: "State Capitol and McKinley Memorial, Columbus, Ohio"]

[Westmoreland, Virginia]
New Years Day 1965

Arthur — Thanks for the delightful card — that was during the short 'war' with the French under John Adams. I suspect you have the right location. Seasonable condolences—looking forward to arrival of yr. packet—Yrs Dos

191

[Picture postcard: "Boston Athenaeum: the Second Floor." Beside the photograph, McComb has written: "In these elegant <u>1840ish</u> surroundings I work part of each day."]

[Boston]
3 Feb. 1965

Dear Dos,   Dudley[1] & I have been in touch, much to my pleasure. Would you be so good, <u>when you are through with it</u> as to give or send him my Ms. instead of returning it to me?—I was touched by the accounts of Weygand's[2] funeral. Indeed the justice of God is not the same as that of De Gaulle. His family need not fear.

Arthur

Postcard illustration of Boston Athenaeum, second floor. McComb's comment on his surroundings, in his card of February 3, 1965, appears alongside it.

1. Dudley Poore.

2. Maxime Weygand (1867–1965), French general. During and after World War I he was Marshal Foch's chief of staff. In 1920 he went to Poland to help stop the Soviet invaders, and on his return he was called the man who had saved Europe from the Bolsheviks. Appointed France's commander in chief when its defenses were collapsing during World War II, he persuaded the government to seek an armistice. After Weygand died, twenty-five years later, President de Gaulle refused to allow use of the Saint-Louis-des-Invalides military church for his funeral. The ceremony, held at another Paris church and attended by several thousand people, came near to being a political demonstration against de Gaulle. *New York Times,* January 29, 1965, p. 29; January 30, 1965, pp. 1, 2; February 3, 1965, p. 14.

192

1821 Sulgrave Avenue,
Baltimore 9, Md.
Feb 3 '65

Dear Arthur,

I've just stolen an hour from my work to read the first hundred pages of your reminiscences. All I can say is, please, more. I suffered a pleasing nostalgia from your evocation of Miss Laird's.[1] Do you remember how we used to call it the Carmen de Matatodos? It will amuse you to note, that I—who was, if I remember right, pretty snooty about Moorish patisserie in 1919—was bowled over by the romantic beauty of the Generalife when Lucy and Betty and I were there four years ago.[2] It was August, very hot and every cranny was infested with Dutch tourists and Germans, each with four cameras dangling from his or her neck. The crowd was so great that a tourist fell into one of the pools ... and still it was entrancing. In that connection I may add that yesterday afternoon I spent a half hour examining with some approbation the allegorical landscapes of Thomas Cole[3] at the Baltimore Museum.

Saw Dudley a few days ago—quite unchanged after a decade. He says you wrote him that he might look at your hundred pages, so I'll turn them over to him tomorrow when I meet him for lunch at the lower entrance of the Library of Congress. He wants to take it with him to South Miami, where he seems to have a querencia.[4]

Thanks for letting me see it, and forgive me for taking so long. I find the consistency of your attitude posivitely[5] startling. I'm reminded of Doughty[6] in Arabia Deserta. I hadn't thought of you as being so Scotch. When did you formulate this scheme of the world? It was certainly long before we met. A fragment recollected from that moment in childhood would make an excellent preface to the reminiscences as they now stand. You leave me quite breathless to know what went before and what comes after.

Yrs ever

Dos

What was the name of the physician who used to arrive all out of breath when I was sick at Miss Lairds? He wanted my disease to be Malta fever. I used to fear he'd get a heart attack walking up the hill.

1. See narrative, pp. 129–30 above.

2. Late in July 1961 Dos Passos, Elizabeth, and Lucy flew to Spain, where Elizabeth's son, Christopher, was taking summer courses at the University of Santander. Dos Passos came to Spain as a tourist and was not asked any political questions or subjected to any obstacles. He, his wife, and daughter toured Spain and made a short side trip to Portugal. Early in September 1961 they and Christopher flew from Madrid to the United States. Letter from Elizabeth Dos Passos, April 21, 1980.

3. American painter (1801–48), b. in England, a leading figure of the Hudson River school.

4. [Sp.] "Favorite place of resort." See also Letter 193, including n. 4, below.

5. Misplaced insertion of it above typed *posively*.

6. Charles Montagu Doughty (1843–1926), the author of *Travels in Arabia Deserta* (1888) and the six-volume epic *The Dawn in Britain* (1906–07), was an English patriot and Christian in his motivation, demeanor, and literary product. A recent commentator on him wrote that although Doughty was in Arabia for nearly two years, "the Doughty who emerged . . . was substantially the man who entered it. Nowhere in *Arabia Deserta* is there any indication that he is adding to or modifying his intellectual regimen." Thomas J. Assad, *Three Victorian Travellers* (London: Routledge & Kegan Paul, 1964), p. 131.

193

[Letterhead: Library of the

Boston Athenæum]

9 Feb. 1965

Dear Dos,

My postcard & y^r letter (which gave me much pleasure) crossed. It was good of you to read my pages & pass them on to Dudley, and also to comment on them in the way that you did. Nothing could have been more complimentary than that you should have desired 'more'.

Now that you mention it I do remember that we called the villino[1] Matatodos but had momentarily forgotten it. I cannot remember the name of the physician who was in favour of the Malta fever theory — I left very soon, you remember [,] to see Cassell[2] send medicines etc. & Dudley remained on hand & he must have seen more of him & may remember—Perhaps you asked him when you lunched together. I'm glad you found DGP[3] unchanged.   I'm not sure how you are using the word <u>querencia</u>—if a 'favourite spot', I am surprised at S. Miami. But I took it in another sense.[4]

The Generalife—yes, how romantic (and I notice you used the same word that I did)   I treasure your story about the tourist. Yet it is rather grim. It is a source of satisfaction to me that the years 1918, 1919, 1920 must have been the 'emptiest'—of all the years of modern Spain. Dudley & you were perhaps always more tolerant about tourists than I. . . .

I am erratic in my reading & have never opened <u>Arabia Deserta</u> [,] so that I cannot get the full force of your comparison—I don't quite know whether you mean consistency <u>since an early time</u> but I read you to mean that. I myself feel that I've gone through the usual trial & error, but I can see that there may have been less of this than I think. I can't think of anything in childhood which would be a turning point or have dramatically set me on the path to feeling & thinking in the particular manner in which I do. But is very agreeable to me to know that you read a Weltanschauung into the whole thing. Most people are only perfunctory & polite readers, don't you think?

A Scot—that was an interesting comment. I thought about it a good deal. There must be much truth in it. But you know I have never set foot in Scotland—and I suppose I think of myself as 'English expatriate' (though I have in fact no English blood that I know of)   In an analytical mood I should even say that I was the kind of rootless cosmop. which the turn the century quite frequently produced with no 'home' anywhere and 'at home' in Italy—and 4 or 5 other countries. It is symbolically quite right that I should have been born in Paris, whereas all the members of my family were born where they belonged. On the other hand I am not displeased, indeed quite proud when I make out questionnaires, and answer: birthplace: Paris.

A propos of Scotland here are some family notes, since we have never spoken of these matters in all these years. . . .

I would apologize for the inordinate length of this letter & all this talk about myself were it not that <u>its all your fault</u> for raising points of such interest to me!

It was so nice of you to write. You didn't say what you were engaged on, nor where you were planning next to go (for I feel sure you <u>are</u>

planning) I saw a review of your Brazil book in the TLS,[5] but have not read it as yet.

As ever

Arthur

. . . .

1. [It.] "Small villa."
2. The German physician in Madrid whom McComb consulted about Dos Passos' illness in October 1919.
3. Dudley Greene Poore.
4. Possibly the sense of an amorous interest.
5. Anonymous review of *Brazil on the Move* in the *Times Literary Supplement*, January 28, 1965, p. 70. "This interesting roving report on Brazil," the reviewer held, "is spoiled by the naive and obsessive anti-communism which is to be found in so much of Mr. Dos Passos's recent writing."

194

Westmoreland, Virginia.
March 12 '65

Dear Arthur,

A couple of friends of ours, Judge Jacob Moses and his wife, are going through Florence towards the end of April.[1] They are anxious to see Berenson's villa and have learned that it is only open to the public on Wednesday. Is there anybody they could see or write to to get in on some other day, in case they arent there on a Wednesday? Judge Moses is 92, lively as a cricket, and belongs to one of those prodigious Baltimore Jewish families that have for years championed the arts in a population entirely dedicated to spectator sports, crabcakes and rye whiskey.[2]

It just occured to me that you probably know the curator. Drop me a line at Westmoreland, as we are driving down this afternoon for a two week stay, if you find it convenient and unembarrassing to mention somebody's name. Otherwise dont worry about it. How are you anyway?

Yrs ever,

Dos

1. Jacob M. Moses (1873–1968), lawyer prominent in labor and Jewish affairs. He was appointed judge of the Baltimore juvenile court in 1908. Moses' wife (Mrs. Sally Clary) was principal of Homewood School, a day school in Baltimore, when Lucy Dos Passos attended it. Telephone interview with Elizabeth Dos Passos, July 26, 1980.

2. Jewish contributions were outstanding among the holdings of the Baltimore Museum of Art. Of its thirteen major collections (as listed in a book it published in 1955), at least six had been given by Jews. One of the six was the museum's chief attraction to art followers beyond Baltimore, the Cone collection, emphasizing Matisse and early Picasso. The sisters Etta and Claribel Cone, who were friends of Gertrude and Leo Stein, learned of Matisse and Picasso while visiting the Steins in Paris.

195

[Picture postcard: "Kaiserin Friedrich mit Kindern."]

> 1821 Sulgrave Ave
> Baltimore
> Md 21209
> 1/26/66

Arthur

The first question of course is: are you still here?

If so how well?

I've been looking up records etc to get up a memoir of my salad days and find myself using your name a great deal.

Drop me a line

> Yrs ever   Dos

Translated from the German, the printed legend beneath the postcard picture reads: "Empress Frederick with her children."

196

> [Letterhead: Library of the
> Boston Athenæum]
> (Surely it was 33 years ago to-day
> that the Führer came to power)
> Sunday 30 Jan. 1966

Dear Dos,

How nice to see your handwriting. And where do you find those strange nostalgic German cards. Twenty years ago you sent me the Königstrasse in Hannover (as it was in ca. 1900), now the Empress Frederick & her children.[1] I suppose ca. 1888. . . .

. . . To answer: I am remarkably well, really since my bad winter (1961–2)—my fibrillation is 'cured'—i.e. I returned to normal a year or more ago, but I take the leaf of foxgloves[2] daily (the remedy the old woman discovered in Wiltshire in the late XVIII c. —nothing synthetic about it!). I have lost weight which is excellent and am now a very decent 165. Everyone says how well I look but I am conscious, that at our age there may at any moment be an interruption. . . .

Yet I continue, as no doubt you do, as if everything were eternal, I make telephone calls [,] affix postage stamps, go to Schrafft's for luncheon, and even fall in love (ridiculous at my age?)

How are you, my dear Dos? Pray give me an account of your own health. How old is Lucy now & where is she? — I am simply delighted that you are writing your Memoirs — there is nothing I shall look forward to reading with greater interest and I pray I may survive to do so, I shall no doubt have much to say to you about them.

I, by the way, never much cared for Kaiserin Friedrich and my sympathies tended to be a bit with her son.

I've been reading the new (Jenkins) Life of Asquith.[3] I feel a great deal cooler about them all. But imagine: — my 'girl-friend' (highly intelligent and à la page)[4] was not in any way responsive to the name of the Rt. Hon. H. H. Asquith. (She is 26) Oh, Dos! oh Youth! oh, Time!

But I like the young. I have indeed, you will be amused to know, — introduced the latest California slang expression to Charles St. (which is usually very 'advanced' in these matters) Not bad for an elderly Mandarin! Blackmail: You'll have to write if you want to know what it is.

As ever

Arthur

P.S.

By the way, my Florentine Memoir is to be published by Mario Praz[5] in his <u>English Miscellany</u> (Rome) [,] some chapters of the Spanish thing in the Harvard Advocate in the Spring or Fall and the Harvard Press are selling the <u>Baroque Painters</u> to a re-print house. . . . The original edition was only 500 but much more <u>di lusso</u>[6] of course.

I hear from Dudley[7] occasionally, much to my pleasure.

1. See legend on picture postcard in Letter (i.e., message) 195 above. Empress Frederick was Victoria Adelaide Mary Louise (1840–1901), first child of Queen Victoria of England and mother of Kaiser Wilhelm II of Germany.
2. Digitalis.
3. Roy Jenkins, *Asquith: Portrait of a Man and an Era* (1965).
4. [Fr.] "Up-to-date."
5. Mario Praz (b. 1896), Italian university professor, scholar, and critic.
6. [It.] "Deluxe."
7. Dudley Poore.

197

[Picture postcard: "Pirkenhammer b. Karlsbad   Schützenmühle"]

[Baltimore
postmarked February 5, 1966]

Arthur: These are from a cache of ancient p.c.s I found in an old trunk in the attic. I thought they would amuse you. Delighted to have such good news of you. Let's survive as long as we have our wits about us, but, please God, no longer. I too take the juice of the foxglove since a touch of virus pneumonia got into the pericardium last year. Otherwise fine. Now you must pass on your slang expression

Yrs ever   Dos

The picture postcard with Dos Passos' message was published in Prague in 1904. Translated from the German, the printed legend beneath the picture reads: "Pirkenhammer by Karlsbad. Schützenmühle."

198

84 Charles St   Boston
12 Feb 66

Dear Dos,

Pirkenhammer bei Karlsbad[1] 1904—! That year I was much in Saxony nearby. . . .

The slang is the use of the word trip to mean experience.[2] e.g. 'What a trip'. . . .

Yrs   Arthur

Let me know sometime about the progress of y^r book (Memoir)   I am most interested

A

1. See legend on picture postcard in Letter (i.e., message) 197 above. Before World War I Karlsbad, in the Austro-Hungarian Empire, was the most fashionable watering place in Europe. From there a very popular one-hour walk led to the village of Pirkenhammer, where one might dine at the restaurant Schützenmühle.
2. Commonly used for an experience with drugs, especially LSD.

199

[Postcard]

As always a beautifully nostalgic card. . . .

[Letterhead: Boston Athenæum]
8 July 1966

Dear Dos: How good to have a word from you. Brasil again! . . .
You will be baked in leaves in the Matto Grosso[1] as if you were some
Greek dish. Dudley sent a card by the very same mail that brought
yours! He is back in Marietta. — A new review <u>The Boston Review</u> is
publishing some stuff of mine on Sept 15 — its first number. Time moves
inexorably on. I try to surround myself with the young & the beautiful, not <u>mirabile dictu</u>[2] without some success. Fie upon the sad reality
of things

Yrs

A

1. Mato Grosso (formerly spelled "Matto Grosso") [Port.], "thick forest": state in
central and western Brazil.
2. [Lat.] "Wondrous to tell." Vergil uses the expression a number of times in his
Georgics and the *Aeneid. Georgics* 2. 30–31 reads: "quin et caudicibus sectis (mirabile
dictu) / truditur e sicco radix oleagina ligno." "Even when the trunks are cut — wondrous
to tell — an olive-bringing root shoots forth from the dry wood."

200

[Picture postcard: Brazilian native Indian, with feather headdress and
spears]

[Brazil
Summer 1966]

Arthur — We are sweating little horses — at the junction of the Araguaia
and the Tepitaré[1] Rivers. Eaten by nothing worse than gnats. Had capi-
vara[2] steak for lunch —   Saudades[3]

Dos

1. Tapirapé.
2. Capybara, a largely aquatic rodent which at maturity measures about four feet
and weighs seventy-five to a hundred pounds.
3. A peculiarly Portuguese word, not translatable in a word or phrase. "Fond remembrances" gives some of the meaning. *Saudades* conveys nostalgia, sadness, and an existen-
tial longing for better times.

201

[Postcard]

[Letterhead: Boston Athenaeum]
14 Sept 66

Dear Dos— . . . it is an outrageous (if possibly classical) piece of <u>one</u> <u>upmanship</u> to make me look up the confluence of the Araguaia and the Tepitaré[1] As for your caprivara steak, je m'en f——[.][2] Really.— Are your works being reprinted by H M Co?[3] I got 12 gns. from Rome the other day for my Memoir.[4] I'll send you both the Miscellany & the Boston Review when they both appear. Saudades indeed.

Arthur Senex[5]

Senex, but some girls still like me—à mirâcle[6]

1. The confluence of the Araguaia and Tapirapé rivers is in the extreme northeast of the state of Mato Grosso.
2. Je m'en f... (fous) [Fr. expletive]. "I'd rather not talk about it."
3. Houghton Mifflin Co.
4. See Letter 196 above.
5. Arthur, the old man. Senex [Lat.], "old man."
6. À miracle [Fr.], "miraculous."

202

[Art postcard]

17 Nov 1966

Dear Dos, How very nice of you! Nothing could have pleased me more than to have this particular book [*The Best Times*]. I have started it with delight and shall read every word. How little I knew really about your early life. And then the account of your father. Odd, I didn't realize your people were Madeirenses.[1] My plan is to write you a long letter after I've finished the book. . . .

Yrs A—

1. [Port.] "Madeirans."

203

[Letterhead: Library of the
Boston Athenæum]
26 Jan 67

Dear Dos,

A few lines more about your Best Years[1] which I was delayed in reading by the exigencies of the season and a strange increase of demands made on me by various people — And there is little time left!

I was much interested in the account of your father and it surprised me how little about him & y^r family I had known. This & the Persian part were among the best in the book I thought. I was also interested that you had drawn so much from the letters written to me, in all the first part. And y^r description of me (pp. 25–26)!

I was struck with your deliberately choosing a vernacular style when describing your childhood (which upbringing seemed to me very haute bourgeoisie,) and in an educational way, as you recognize, very 18$^{\underline{th}}$ c. Mandarin, indeed. Your one-time radical friends will certainly shake their heads & say that you have merely reverted to your up-bringing. It is certainly more complicated than that & there is much to be said for your own 'underdog' theory.[2] . . .

Your introductory story was wonderful — in itself, and also as revealing an attitude which has always been perfectly clear to those who know you, but the public is now let in on it.[3] . . .

Two unimportant places where my memory (perhaps necessarily!) improves on yours. I came to U.S. to get married in 1923 not 1921 and we met in Santander not in Madrid in 1919 (p. 80) and moreover on the day when the Archduke Joseph overcame the Communist régime in Budapest.[4] We then travelled down together stopping in León and Valladolid.

Dear Dos, what fun, what melancholy [,] to read about all these things.

Thank you again for sending me the book.

Yours as ever
Arthur

. . . .

1. *The Best Times.*
2. See Letters 59 and 61 above.
3. A humorous introduction describes Dos Passos' encounter with a high school senior who complained that he wasn't "acting like a writer."
4. Archduke Joseph (b. 1872), a member of the Hapsburg family. McComb's description of events in Hungary is inaccurate. So also is his identification of the date of the meeting in Santander with the date of Joseph's coup d'état in Budapest.

Coda

$\mathcal{O}$N FEBRUARY 21, 1968, McComb collapsed in Boston at the corner of Berkeley and Marlborough streets and was dead on arrival at Boston City Hospital. Poore wrote Dos Passos about the death and its circumstances, news of which had come to Poore from another of McComb's friends: "On that . . . afternoon he had spent the earlier hours with a girl friend and was proceeding gaily to another rendezvous at Florian's when the blow fell."[1] Before his death McComb had prepared a commentary on his life for the *Fiftieth Anniversary Report* of his Harvard class, concluding:

> . . . I have avoided the wars of the twentieth century — perhaps the only feat of which I am entitled to boast. From a position of relative quiet and safety, therefore, I have followed during these many years, and not without emotion, the Decline of the West.[2]

Dos Passos survived McComb by two and a half years and, though suffering from chronic heart failure by October 1968,[3] continued to travel and write. Two of his experiences and his comments on them belong in our coda. In January 1969 he and Betty flew for a visit to Easter Island, a bit of land twenty-two hundred miles west of Chile where giant fallen statues testify to a vanished civilization. And in May 1969 he was at Cape Kennedy watching the launching of the Apollo 10 spacecraft, which ascended and circled the moon.[4] After the spacecraft was in orbit, the astronauts rehearsed maneuvers for a lunar landing and return. Of the Apollo program Dos Passos wrote in a circular for the United States Information Agency:

> In our century we have seen everything that is hideous in man come to the fore. . . . but now, all at once . . . there emerges a fresh assertion of man's spirit.[5]

At the end of 1969 Dos Passos was in critical condition at Johns Hopkins Hospital, and his physician remained there almost the entire

An area for good conversation over good food. John and Elizabeth Dos Passos entertain in their Virginia home in May 1970. Dos Passos sits at the far end of the lunch table, facing his wife. The man on the left is the Chilean writer Enrique Lafourcade, whose wife and child also sit at the table. The man on the right is Manoel Cardozo, professor of history at The Catholic University of America, in Washington, D.C.

Courtesy of Elizabeth Dos Passos

An area for hard work. Dos Passos sits in his work room in Virginia while Elizabeth looks over his shoulder.

Courtesy of Elizabeth Dos Passos

night of December 31. When Dos Passos' condition improved, he moved to Good Samaritan Hospital in Baltimore, and there he finished the manuscript of his book *Easter Island*.[6] Of his experiences on the island, he wrote:

> Every human group that has accomplished anything leaves behind a lesson for posterity. If we could learn these lessons in time we might find ways to avoid our own destruction.[7]

After Dos Passos emerged from Good Samaritan Hospital, he and Betty flew to Arizona, and that summer they went to Maine; but when his condition grew worse there, they returned to Baltimore, and he again entered Good Samaritan Hospital. Dos Passos died at home in Baltimore on September 28, 1970.[8]

Looking back to Dos Passos' and McComb's childhoods, we are tempted to contrast two memories: Dos Passos' writing: "I do not care what misery I go through now if I can only in the future be great," and McComb's hating the plaque over his bed which read: "I ought, I can, I will."* Considered together and—of course—in retrospect, they seem to foreshadow two very different lives. In being great Dos Passos may or may not have included his being a great artist. But if he did, he very likely envisaged much besides. For Dos Passos had been listening to the Choate headmaster praise the sort of person who "changes the condition of affairs."[9]

Dos Passos' writings as a young adult certainly show that he had complex personal standards. These included multitudinous sensitivity to life, responsible action, and artistic skill. In ordinary life all this meant behaving well and sensitively towards people (witness his relationship with McComb) and getting the joys the world has to offer, joys as different as knowledge, travel, architecture, and good food and drink. In his literary life it involved recognizing an intellectual's duty to his civilization and performing it.

Differences in temperament provide a large part of the drama of human life, to the delight of playwrights, novelists, and historians, and Dos Passos' temperament was far different from McComb's. Like McComb, Dos Passos grasped the horrors of the twentieth century, especially total war, and he found the mass media of communication ridiculous and sinister. But he did not flee these phenomena, but instead got to know and describe them. Living in the twentieth century, he found his work there. Perhaps Arthur's puzzlement at the sign "Dr.

---

*See p. 2 above.

McComb says there is hope"* is significant symbolically. When later in life Arthur McComb wrote of modern society that he had no use "for it," Dos Passos answered him: "Still I'm all for saving the it you despair of. It's all we've got: there isn't any more."[10]

*See p. 2 above.

Notes to the Narrative

Some of the biographical material in the narrative was presented and documented in detail in the editor's *Dos Passos' Path to "U.S.A.": A Political Biography, 1912–36* (Boulder: Colorado Associated University Press, 1972 [1973]), which was written during Dos Passos' lifetime. The editor refers interested readers to that biography as a whole for fuller treatments than the present edition of letters permits. Needless to say, the narrative in *"Learn to sing the Carmagnole"* has benefited from many primary biographical sources that were unavailable when the editor wrote the earlier work.

The present work was substantially completed before the appearances of two full-length biographies of Dos Passos, by Townsend Ludington and Virginia Spencer Carr; however, for a number of reasons, it remained in its double-checking and galley-reading stages a long time.

INTRODUCTION (PAGES 1–15)

1. Dos Passos, *The Best Times* (New York: New American Library, 1966), pp. 8, 10–11, 12, 15; Dos Passos, *U.S.A.: The 42nd Parallel* (New York: Harcourt, Brace and Co., 1937 [1938]), pp. 81, 206–7, 223–24; Melvin Landsberg, *Dos Passos' Path to "U.S.A.*,*"* pp. 3, 6, 8, 10.

2. [Dos Passos], "Diary etc J. R. Madison: 1911. . . ."

3. J. Madison [John Dos Passos], "Diary 1911–1912."

4. Obituaries of McComb's father: *New York Times,* September 12, 1938, p. 17, and *Times* (London), September 28, 1938, p. 13; letter from McComb to Dos Passos, February 9, 1965; two undated curricula vitae of McComb; "Arthur Kilgore McComb," *Harvard Class of 1918: Fiftieth Anniversary Report* (Cambridge: printed at the Harvard University Printing Office, 1968), pp. 405–6.

5. The information about the placard, McComb's relationship with his parents, his unhappiness prior to college, and his response to Harvard is from interviews with Constance R. Worcester (Dr. Elwood Worcester's daughter), in Boston, July 11 and 13, 1975.

6. [Dos Passos], "Literary Diary," September 1, 1914–September 1, 1915. Two notebooks.

7. Dos Passos, "Conrad's 'Lord Jim,' " *Harvard Monthly* 60 (July 1915): 151–54; [Dos Passos, unsigned], "Summer Military Camps: Two Views. I," *Harvard Monthly* 60 (July 1915): 156; Dos Passos, "The Evangelist and the Volcano," *Harvard Monthly* 61 (November 1915): 59–61 (the quotation is on p. 60).

8. McComb, "The Meaning of Pacifism," *Harvard Monthly* 62 (March 1916): 10–11 (the quotations are on p. 11); McComb, "Of Individuality," *Harvard Monthly* 62 (April 1916): 40–42 (the quotation is on p. 42).

9. McComb, Review of *The World Decision* by Robert Herrick, *Harvard Monthly* 62 (March 1916): 24–26. The quotation is on p. 25.

10. D.P. [Dos Passos], "The World Decision," *Harvard Monthly* 62 (March 1916): 23–24. The quotation is on p. 24.

11. Dos Passos, "A Humble Protest," *Harvard Monthly* 62 (June 1916): 115–20. The quotations are on pp. 116 and 119 respectively. The spelling "tentactular" is in the original.

12. McComb, "Art and Industry," *Harvard Monthly* 62 (June 1916): 121–23.

13. Interview with Dudley Poore at his home, near Amber, New York, summer 1971; telephone interview with him, October 28, 1979.

14. John Maynard Keynes, *The Economic Consequences of the Peace* (New York: Harcourt, Brace and Howe, 1920), pp. 9–26 (long quotation, pp. 19–20). The book appeared in England in 1919.

15. Ernest L. Bogart, *Direct and Indirect Costs of the Great World War* (New York: Oxford University Press, 1920), pp. 272, 277, 282.

16. Leonard Woolf, *Barbarians Within and Without* (New York: Harcourt, Brace and Co., 1939), pp. 5–18 (long quotation, p. 6). For the British edition, which Woolf says he finished writing prior to the Russo-German nonaggression pact in August, see Woolf, *Barbarians at the Gate* (Left Book Club edition; London: Victor Gollancz, 1939). The American edition has changes which color the Soviet scene darker.

17. William Henry Chamberlin, *Russia's Iron Age* (Boston: Little, Brown, and Co., 1934), pp. 80–82, 88. On the purges initiated in 1934, see Robert Conquest, *The Great Terror* (New York: Macmillan Co., 1968), pp. 43–44. Woolf condemned Stalin's methods but credited him with civilized motives, and he underestimated tremendously the numbers Stalin had killed or imprisoned.

18. George W. Baer, *Test Case: Italy, Ethiopia, and the League of Nations* (Stanford, California: Hoover Institution Press, 1976); Lucy S. Dawidowicz, *The War against the Jews, 1933–1945* (New York: Holt, Rinehart and Winston, 1975), 54–103.

19. Hugh Thomas, *The Spanish Civil War* (New York: Harper and Brothers, 1961), pp. 631–32. See also the third edition (London: Hamish Hamilton, 1977), 926–27.

20. The range for total dead in World War II is from Henri Michel, *The Second World War,* trans. Douglas Parmée (London: André Deutsch, 1975), p. 781. On the murders of Jews, see Dawidowicz, *The War against the Jews,* p. 403. On the murders of Gypsies, see Donald Kenrick and Grattan Puxon, *The Destiny of Europe's Gypsies* (London: Sussex University Press, in association with Heinemann Educational Books, 1972), pp. 183–84, and see *New York Times,* April 10, 1978, p. B2.

21. Conquest, *The Great Terror,* pp. 532–33. Woolf's "tens of thousands" is in *Barbarians Within and Without* (p. 157). In *Barbarians at the Gate* (p. 196) he has "thousands."

22. For Dos Passos' comment in October 1919, see the narrative below, p. 130. His statement about broader creeds was in "The Caucasus under the Soviets," *Liberator* 5 (August 1922): 7. The article bore a 1921 dateline. On Stalin, see the narrative below, p. 229, note marked †.

23. For McComb's references to himself as a liberal, see Letters 64 and 65 below; for his use of the term conservative-pacifist, see Letter 115 below; for his references or allusions to a strong role for the church, see his comments on T. S. Eliot and Pope Pius IX in Letters 145 and 150 respectively.

24. H. R. Trevor-Roper, "The Phenomenon of Fascism," in *European Fascism,* ed. S. J. Woolf (New York: Random House, 1968), pp. 23–24 (for long quotation), and 28.

25. See Letter 129 below.

26. Lawson's feelings may be gauged by his letter to Dos Passos, dated "August 24th [1937?]," which ends with a warning that Dos Passos' course will destroy the friendship. Dos Passos not long afterwards wrote Lawson a letter (n.d.) beginning "You must have patience with the unbelievers. . . ." In a letter Dos Passos wrote Wilson on October 3, 1964, he said: "The time has probably come to admit that two moderately reasonable people can reach diametrically opposite conclusions from the same set of facts."

27. For Chaucer, see Dos Passos, *Occasions and Protests* (n.p.: Henry Regnery Co., 1964), pp. 53–57. For Cummings, see Dos Passos, Review of *The Enormous Room* by E. E. Cummings, *Dial* 73 (July 1922): 98.

28. See *College in a Yard,* ed. Brooks Atkinson (Cambridge: Harvard University Press, 1957), pp. 33–39, 139–42.

29. Dos Passos, *The Best Times,* p. 25.

30. Harvard records credit Dos Passos with preparatory school or college work, or both, in Greek, Latin, French, Spanish, and German, and McComb with such work in Latin, French, German, and Italian. Their stays in continental Europe were, of course, invaluable for learning modern languages. Dos Passos had an excellent command of French; McComb, according to Dudley Poore, spoke "perfect" French, German, and Italian. Interview with Poore, summer 1971.

LETTERS: JULY 1916–FEBRUARY 1917 (PAGES 17–18)

Dos Passos' activities may be followed in his letters to Walter Rumsey Marvin written during the period. See also Dos Passos, *The Best Times,* pp. 3–4, 20, 24–27, 30–34, 40, and Landsberg, *Dos Passos' Path to "U.S.A.,"* p. 44 and p. 233, n. 1.

1. Letter from Dos Passos to Walter Rumsey Marvin, July 30, 1916.

2. [McComb], "A Foreign Dye: Some Spanish and Italian Reminiscences." This manuscript is not paginated well enough to allow page references.

3. Dos Passos, "Against American Literature," *New Republic* 8 (October 14, 1916): 269–71.

LETTERS: SPRING 1917–OCTOBER 1917 (PAGES 40–41)

Dos Passos' activities may be followed in his letters to Marvin written during the period. See also Dos Passos, *The Best Times,* pp. 42–59.

1. Letter from Dos Passos to Marvin begun February 20, 1917, and continued on later dates.

2. Letters from Dudley Poore to Stewart Mitchell, January 29, February 23, and April 11, 1917.

3. Dos Passos, *The Best Times,* pp. 23–24, 51; Dos Passos, draft (n.d.), Alderman Library, confirmed in letter from Dos Passos to ML, October 4, 1965. The name appeared as Nagel in the *Harvard Alumni Directory* for 1919. However, Dos Passos' friend spelled his name "Nagle" in the *Dial,* which published art work by him between 1920 and 1929.

LETTERS: NOVEMBER 1917–MAY 1919 (PAGES 73–77)

Dos Passos' activities may be followed in his letters to Marvin written during this period. His diary of November-December 1917 helps date his stay in Milan in 1917. For Dos Passos' retrospective account of events described in his letters, see his *The Best Times*, pp. 58–78. McComb's activities may be followed in his "Notes" (a diary) for 1918 and in his "A Foreign Dye."

1. Dos Passos, diary of November-December 1917. December 10 entry.

2. Letter from Dos Passos to Marvin, December 30, 1917.

3. Dos Passos, *The Best Times*, p. 63.

4. Letter from Dos Passos to Mrs. Edward Cummings (Rebecca Haswell Clarke Cummings), December 16, 1917.

5. Dos Passos, *The Best Times*, p. 70.

6. Letter from Dos Passos to Poore, May 21, 1919; Dos Passos, *The Best Times*, pp. 70–71.

7. Letters from Dos Passos to Marvin, July 13, 1919 (for discharge), July 25 and August 2, 1919 (for visit to England); letter from Dos Passos to Stewart Mitchell begun July 19, 1919, and continued July 25.

8. McComb, "The Russian Revolution," *Harvard Monthly* 63 (Spring 1917): 56.

9. Dos Passos, *One Man's Initiation—1917* (London: George Allen and Unwin, 1920); Dos Passos, *The Best Times*, p. 71.

LETTERS: JULY 1919–SUMMER 1920 (PAGES 127–33)

1. Interview with Poore, summer 1971, and telephone interviews with him, July 4, 1976, and September 17, 1977; McComb, "Notes," August 12 and 13, 1919; Dos Passos, *The Best Times*, pp. 77–81. I have followed Poore's memory of events, as McComb's "Notes" makes it seem more reliable than Dos Passos' account.

2. Elizabeth Sweeney Schneider, "A Family Chronicle," 1924. Interviews with Arthur, Nora, and Alice Sweeney, in Andover, Massachusetts, July 26, 1975. "Everywhere" statement from summer 1971 interview with Poore.

3. Quotation from postcard to Mitchell (n.d.).

4. McComb, "Notes," August 14–24, 1919; Dos Passos, diary in Spain, from August 19, 1919, entry to "Oviedo" entry; letter from Dos Passos to Marvin, August 24 and (same letter) September 20, 1919; telephone interview with Poore, July 4, 1976.

5. McComb, "Notes," August 24–September 23, 1919; Dos Passos, diary in Spain, from Oviedo entry to September 17, 1919, entry; telephone interview with Poore, July 4, 1976.

6. McComb, "A Foreign Dye"; interview with Poore, summer 1971.

7. Dos Passos, diary in Spain, September 17–October 10, 1919; postcard from Dos Passos to Mitchell, September 25, 1919; letter from Dos Passos to Marvin, October 15 and November 17, 1919; letter from McComb to Poore, October 28, 1919; McComb, "Notes," October 14–November 20, 1919; McComb, "A Foreign Dye"; Dos Passos, *The Best Times*, pp. 81–82; telephone interview with Poore, July 4, 1976.

8. McComb, "A Foreign Dye."

9. Letter from Dos Passos to Marvin, November 17, 1919, tells duration of illness. The identifications for Dos Passos' letter to McComb (Letter 72 below) are based on McComb's "A Foreign Dye" and his notes to Dos Passos' letters to him.

10. Letter from Dos Passos to Marvin, December 6, 1919; letter from Dos Passos to Mitchell, December 8, 1919; McComb, "Notes," December 20, 1919–February 14, 1920; interview with Poore, summer 1971.

11. Poore described his own view in the interview of summer 1971 and the telephone interview of October 28, 1979.

12. Letters from Dos Passos to J. H. Lawson, February 27, 1920 (which includes quotations), and n.d.; letter from Dos Passos to Marvin, March 14, 1920; letter from Dos Passos to managing editor, George Allen and Unwin, March 13, 1920; McComb, "Notes," March 11–17, 1920; interview with Poore, summer 1971.

13. Letter from McComb to Dos Passos, April 10, 1920 (on "fling"); McComb, "Notes," March 19–August 6, 1920.

14. Letter from Dos Passos to Marvin, March 14, 1920, and postcard from Dos Passos to him (n.d.); letters from Dos Passos to J. H. Lawson, March 26 and 29, 1920; interview with Adelaide (Lawson) Gaylor at Glenwood Landing, New York, September 4, 1971, and telephone interview with her, July 7, 1974; telephone interview with Kate Drain Lawson, September 21, 1974.

15. Letter from Dos Passos to J. H. Lawson, April 8, 1920 (for arrangements to meet, money problem, departure of Lawson family); letter from Dos Passos to Marvin, n.d. at start but continued May 1, 1920 (on Marseilles and Paris).

16. Interview with Poore, summer 1971. A letter from Poore to Stewart Mitchell, June 21, 1920, has Poore in Liverpool waiting to help his parents debark the next day.

17. Letter from Dos Passos, in Paris, to Thomas Pym Cope, May 15, 1920. Poore's letter of June 21, 1920, to Mitchell speaks of Poore's coming to England with Dos Passos and spending two days boating with him at Cambridge before going on to Liverpool.

18. Interview with Poore, summer 1971; letter from Dos Passos (off Galician coast) to Marvin, August 7, 1920; letter from Dos Passos (at sea) to Cope, n.d.; letter from Dos Passos (on Ward Line boat the *Monterey*) to Poore, postmarked August 31, 1920; letter from Dos Passos to Mitchell, postmarked New York, August 31, 1920.

LETTERS: AUGUST? 1920–JANUARY 1922 (PAGES 161–63)

1. Letter from Dos Passos to Cope, probably November 1, 1920; letter from Dos Passos to Robert Hillyer, n.d.

2. See Jack Potter, *A Bibliography of John Dos Passos* (Chicago: Normandie House, 1950), p. 69. Dos Passos, *The Best Times,* p. 90, speaks of commitments.

3. Dos Passos, *The Best Times,* pp. 86–87 (which include quotation), 88; Dos Passos, travel notes for March 1921; letter from Dos Passos to Marvin, n.d.

4. Two letters from Dos Passos to Marvin, n.d.; Dos Passos, travel diary, July 1921; Dos Passos, *The Best Times,* pp. 88–89; Richard S. Kennedy, *Dreams in the Mirror: A Biography of E. E. Cummings* (New York: Liveright Publishing Corp., 1980), pp. 226–30; interview with Poore, summer 1971.

5. Dos Passos, travel diaries for Venice-Persia journeys and trip with camel caravan; letters from Dos Passos to J. H. Lawson, October 23, 1921, to Cope, November 13, 1921, to Eugene Saxton, January 7, 1922, to Mitchell, January 15, 1922; Dos Passos, *The Best Times,* pp. 90–124.

6. Information on McComb's visits to Spain and Portugal is from his postcard to Dos Passos, August 29, 1921, and from his letter to Dos Passos, September 13, 1921.

LETTERS: FEBRUARY? 1922–MARCH 1923 (PAGES 185–86)

1. Cablegram from Dos Passos to Poore, February 8, 1922 (for Dos Passos' route).

2. For Dos Passos' problems with Doran and for his stay in Cambridge, postcard from Dos Passos to Marvin, postmarked March 13, 1922, and letter from Dos Passos to Marvin, n.d. Other information from interview with Poore, summer 1971, telephone interviews with Poore, September 17, 1977, June 4 and July 20, 1978, and October 28, 1979.

3. Interview with Poore, summer 1971 (on Poore's joining parents in Italy); letter from Dos Passos to Mrs. Sweeney, March 8, 1923 (from *Roussillon*); letter from Dos

Passos to Mrs. Sweeney, postmarked April 27, 1923 (for Dos Passos' doings in France and Italy); letter from Dos Passos to Poore, August 15, 1923 (on Spain and Dos Passos' return to New York).

LETTERS: AUGUST 1924–DECEMBER 1925 (PAGES 204–5)

1. McComb, "The Life and Works of Francesco di Giorgio," *Art Studies* 2 (1924): 2–32.

2. Two undated curricula vitae of McComb (for employment data); letter from Pamela Askew to ML, September 10, 1975 (on marriage).

3. Postcard from McComb to Dos Passos, June 21, 1924 (for McComb quotation); letter from Dos Passos to J. H. Lawson, n.d. (for Dos Passos quotation).

4. Dos Passos, *The Best Times,* p. 162 (on rheumatic fever).

LETTERS: JULY 1926–DECEMBER 1929 (PAGES 211–15)

1. For Dos Passos' political biography, 1926–29, see Landsberg, *Dos Passos' Path to "U.S.A.,"* pp. 124–60.

2. McComb, "Francesco Ubertini (Bacchiacca)," *Art Bulletin* 8 (March 1926): 140–67.

3. Letter from Dos Passos to J. H. Lawson, n.d. (for quotation). The storm and rescue are described in Dos Passos, *The Best Times,* pp. 150–51.

4. Postcard from Dos Passos to Mitchell, with Christmas greeting and 1926 postmark; postcard from Dos Passos to Hillyer, postmarked March 27, 1927; Dos Passos, *The Best Times,* pp. 170–71. On Dos Passos' articles on Mexico, see Landsberg, *Dos Passos' Path to "U.S.A.,"* pp. 153–54, 263.

5. On his efforts in behalf of Sacco and Vanzetti, see particularly Dos Passos' 127-page pamphlet *Facing the Chair* (Boston: Sacco-Vanzetti Defense Committee, 1927). Dos Passos appears originally to have gone to Boston in 1926 to do an article on the Sacco-Vanzetti case for *New Masses.* The Boston anarchist printer Aldino Felicani got him to write the pamphlet for the committee. See Dos Passos, *The Best Times,* p. 166; Gardner Jackson, "The Reminiscences of Gardner Jackson" (New York: Oral History Research Office, Columbia University, 1959), pp. 157–58.

6. The dates of Dos Passos' stay in the U.S.S.R. are from his U.S. passport issued November 17, 1926.

7. Dos Passos, *The Best Times,* pp. 177–92; interview with W. Horsley Gantt, in Baltimore, Maryland, January 7, 1974.

8. Letter from Dos Passos to Hillyer (n.d.) and letter from Dos Passos to Mitchell, postmarked February 10, 1928 (on Dos Passos' presence at rehearsals); Dos Passos, *The Best Times,* pp. 199–200, and Carlos Baker, *Ernest Hemingway: A Life Story* (New York: Charles Scribner's Sons, 1969), pp. 200, 598 (on Key West); Dos Passos, *The Best Times,* pp. 171–72 (on Dos Passos' early work on novel); two postcards from Dos Passos to Marvin, postmarked April 29, 1929, and July 16, 1929 (on Dos Passos' racing to complete book).

9. On McComb's unfaithfulness: interview with Constance R. Worcester, July 11, 1975, and interview with Gurdon S. Worcester, near Gloucester, Massachusetts, July 12, 1975. On separation and divorce: letter from Pamela Askew to ML, September 10, 1975.

10. Letter from Dos Passos to Mitchell, postmarked April 8, 1929 (for breakfasts); postcard from Dos Passos to Poore, in envelope postmarked June 26, 1929, and postcard from Dos Passos to Marvin, postmarked July 16, 1929 (for duration of stay with Poore); telephone interview with Poore, July 20, 1978 (for Dos Passos' being guest of Poore's mother); letter from Dos Passos to Poore, postmarked August 20 or 26, 1929, and postcard

from Dos Passos to Poore, September 13, 1929, asking about songs; interview with Poore, summer 1971 (for Dos Passos' not talking much about *The 42nd Parallel* and for Poore's research in library); letter from Dos Passos to Poore, postmarked July 26, 1929 (for Dos Passos' library work in Chicago).

11. Letter from Dos Passos to Poore, postmarked October 28, 1929 (on Dos Passos' living in Provincetown and visiting Boston); letter from Dos Passos to Poore, postmarked December 18, 1929 (shows the proofs completed); interview with Eben and Phyllis Given in Truro, Massachusetts, summer 1971 (on house); letter from Dos Passos to Ernest Hemingway, postmarked October 1, 1929 (helps establish date Dos Passos finished *The 42nd Parallel*); postcard from Dos Passos to Mitchell, postmarked December 5, 1929 (on boarding *Roussillon*); Dos Passos, *The Best Times,* p. 202 (quotation).

LETTERS: 1933?–MARCH 1935 (PAGES 228–31)

1. See Landsberg, *Dos Passos' Path to "U.S.A.,"* pp. 163–70 (on miners), 173 (on presidency).
2. Letters from Dos Passos to Hemingway in 1933: April 24 (dictated to wife), May 3, May 7, May 10, May 18; letter from Hemingway to Dos Passos, n.d.; Dos Passos, *The Best Times,* p. 209; interview with Gantt, in Charlottesville, Virginia, July 1978; W. A. Baker and Tre Tryckare, *The Engine Powered Vessel* (New York: Crescent Books, 1965), p. 166.
3. Landsberg, *Dos Passos' Path to "U.S.A.,"* pp. 178–82.
4. Letter from Dos Passos to Wilson, n.d.

LETTERS: JULY 1937–JANUARY 1967 (PAGES 234–47)

1. Friends' memories of Dos Passos' routine include those of Charles and Isobel (Ing) Mayo (interview in Provincetown, August 11, 1971) and of Mr. and Mrs. Robert Ball (interview in Provincetown, summer 1971). Mrs. Marjorie Roza, who before Katy's death worked for the Dos Passoses about a year, says that if any extraneous problems came up while John Dos Passos was working, his wife would take care of them (interview with Mrs. Roza, in Provincetown, July 26, 1973). Descriptions of Dos Passos' working habits while he was a house guest are based on interviews with Poore, summer 1971 (in which he spoke of Dos Passos' visit in 1929) and with Helen Sawyer Farnsworth, in North Truro, Massachusetts, July 25, 1973.
2. Dos Passos, "Grosz Comes to America," *Esquire* 6 (September 1936): 105, 128, 131. The quotation is on p. 128.
3. Dos Passos, *The Theme Is Freedom* (New York: Dodd, Mead and Co., 1956), p. 161.
4. Dos Passos, *The Theme Is Freedom,* pp. 115–18, 127–30, 136–37, 140–42, 145–46, 148; Baker, *Ernest Hemingway,* pp. 300, 305–6, 308, 312, 620, 621; interview with Archibald MacLeish, in Conway, Massachusetts, August 26, 1974; Dos Passos, "Farewell to Europe!" *Common Sense* 6 (July 1937): 9–11; Dos Passos, "The Communist Party and the War Spirit," *Common Sense* 6 (December 1937): 11–14.
5. Interview with Sydney J. Freedberg, in Cambridge, Massachusetts, August 3, 1973, and telephone interview with him, August 7, 1975 (for Mussolini, black shirt, Nazis, gentleness); interview with Gurdon S. Worcester, July 12, 1975 (for Franco, Italian Fascists, strong hand, McComb's being an observer).
6. Nicky Mariano, *Forty Years with Berenson* (New York: Alfred A. Knopf, 1967), p. 112 (for McComb as guest).
7. McComb, "The Anglo-Americans in Florence," in *English Miscellany* 17, ed. Mario Praz (Rome, Italy: British Council, 1966), pp. 288–89.
8. Mariano, *Forty Years with Berenson,* p. 112 (on McComb as habitué); McComb,

Agnolo Bronzino: His Life and Works (Cambridge: Harvard University Press, 1928); McComb, *The Baroque Painters of Italy: An Introductory Historical Survey* (Cambridge: Harvard University Press, 1934).

9. Letter from Berenson to McComb, January 25, 1953, in Arthur K. McComb, ed., *The Selected Letters of Bernard Berenson* (Boston: Houghton Mifflin Co., 1964), p. 274. Freedberg says that McComb did not get tenure because of "extremely rigorous" new requirements, but he also says that some faculty members had "rather bourgeois" objections to his love affairs (interview with Freedberg, August 3, 1973). Poore speaks of McComb's unwillingness to ingratiate himself with Professor Paul J. Sachs (see Letter 95, n. 7 above); in addition, he thinks that McComb's unconventional private life hurt him with Professor Chandler R. Post. Telephone interviews with Poore, August 15 and September 12, 1976.

10. After McComb lost his position at Harvard, he told Poore: "I'm not going to try to get anything. I'll be poor and be my own boss." The quotation is from Poore (telephone interview with Poore, June 18, 1980). Freedberg said that many major institutions would have welcomed McComb. He also spoke of McComb's inheriting money and of his inclination to enjoy an independent gentleman's life (interview with Freedberg, August 3, 1973). The comment on McComb's liking for Boston is based on the general tenor of his correspondence with Dos Passos.

11. The description of McComb's apartment is based on ML's interview with Freedberg, August 3, 1973. "V for Vichy" was McComb's postscript in a letter of September 4, 1941, sent to Mitchell at his home in Gloucester, Massachusetts. The information on McComb's reaction to aircraft noise is based on ML's interview with Gurdon Worcester, July 12, 1975. Richard R. Beatty, a mutual friend of McComb's and Mitchell's, says that in December 1941 McComb was terrified that the Germans would bomb Boston. Mitchell took pity on McComb and invited him to stay with him in Gloucester (telephone interview with Beatty, June 28, 1980). McComb stayed with Mitchell in Gloucester in the winter of 1941–42, according to a letter McComb wrote Mitchell on March 19, 1942. A letter from McComb to Mitchell dated April 4, 1942, helps establish the time of McComb's coming to Asheville. McComb wrote Mitchell about opting for and obtaining citizenship in Eire in letters of July 24, 1942, and November 26, 1943. McComb's comment about having convictions on record is in the *Harvard Class of 1918: 25th Anniversary Report* (Cambridge: printed for the Class, 1943), pp. 526–27.

12. *New York Times,* September 14, 1941, sec. 1, p. 28 (for P.E.N.); Dos Passos, *State of the Nation* (Boston: Houghton Mifflin Co., 1944).

13. Dos Passos, *Tour of Duty* (Boston: Houghton Mifflin Co., 1946). He arrived in the Pacific area in December 1944.

14. Dos Passos, *The Theme Is Freedom,* p. 164.

15. Dos Passos, "England in the Great Lull," *Harper's Magazine* 184 (February 1942): 242 (for ritual); letter from Dos Passos to Wilson, July 19, 1945; Dos Passos, "The Failure of Marxism," *Life* 24 (January 19, 1948): 96–98, 100, 102, 105, 106, 108. In presenting "The Failure of Marxism" I have to a slight extent interpreted Dos Passos in the light of his *The Prospect before Us* (Boston: Houghton Mifflin Co., 1950), pp. 117, 131, and his *The Theme Is Freedom,* pp. 3–4.

16. For Dos Passos' having favored British socialism, see Dos Passos, "Some Glasgow People," *Harper's Magazine* 184 (April 1942): 478–80, and Harvey Breit, "Talk with Mr. Dos Passos," *New York Times,* November 12, 1950, sec. 7, p. 53. For Dos Passos' attitude towards the Labour government in 1947, see Dos Passos, "Britain's Dim Dictatorship," *Life* 23 (September 29, 1947): 120–22, 124, 127–28, 130, 133–34, 136, 139, and Dos Passos, "The Failure of Marxism," pp. 102, 105, 106, 108.

17. Dos Passos, *The Theme Is Freedom,* p. 161 (for third term), pp. 169–71 (for Hopkins); Dos Passos, "Washington Sketches," *Fortune* 28 (December 1943): 200, 202, 212, 214 (for failings of the Administration and for Hopkins); Dos Passos, *Tour of Duty,*

pp. 309–10, 324 (for yielding areas of Europe); Dos Passos, *The Grand Design* (Boston: Houghton Mifflin Co., 1949).

18. Dos Passos, "The Failure of Marxism," p. 98 ("vested interests" quotation); Dos Passos, *The Prospect before Us*, pp. 118 (a similar "vested interests" statement), 82 ("struggle for power" quotation), 294, 359 (for trend), 120, 363–74 (for critical stage and for way to save republic); Dos Passos, "There Is Only One Freedom," *'47: The Magazine of the Year* 1 (April 1947), p. 76 ("one basic truth").

19. Letter from Dos Passos to Wilson, January 27, 1948. The account of the accident is from the *New York Times*, September 14, 1947, sec. 1, p. 9.

20. Information on farm based on interview with Elizabeth Dos Passos, at her home, in Westmoreland, Virginia, July 23, 1976.

21. Elizabeth Dos Passos furnished much of the information for this paragraph, which she examined for accuracy during the interview of July 23, 1976.

22. Letter from Dos Passos to Wilson, May 22, 1951.

23. Dos Passos, *Brazil on the Move* (Garden City, New York: Doubleday and Co., 1963), pp. 13, 62, 101 (for years of first three visits); letter from Dos Passos to Carol Brandt, July 14, 1962 (for P.E.N. conference); interviews with Elizabeth Dos Passos and Lucy Dos Passos Coggin, in Westmoreland, July 23–24, 1976. In addition to *Brazil on the Move,* Dos Passos published numerous articles on Brazil.

24. Dos Passos, "Unexpected Brazil," *Holiday* 42 (September 1967): 52, 54, 56, 58, 104. The quotation "When people. . . ." is on p. 52, and the quotation "There is nothing. . . ." is on p. 58.

25. For losses: interviews with Freedberg, August 3, 1973, and Gurdon Worcester, July 12, 1975.

26. Letter from Gordon T. Banks, of Goodspeed's Book Shop, to Chauncey B. Tinker, January 11, 1951. Tinker's note, handwritten beneath the close of Banks' typed letter, records the purchase.

27. For apartment: interview with Freedberg, August 3, 1973, interview with David McKibbin, at Boston Athenaeum, July 15, 1975, interview with Robert and Kelly Lynch, in Boston, November 6, 1977. Robert Lynch says that McComb had his own bed and lamps in the room. For pictures of Mussolini: interview with Robert and Kelly Lynch, November 6, 1977. For McComb's honoring Mussolini: telephone interview with Poore, October 30, 1977. Poore said: "To Arthur, Mussolini was the savior of order and civilization." On bathroom fixture and McComb's looking unshaven: interview with McKibbin, July 15, 1975, and interview with Robert Lynch, November 6, 1977.

28. Interview with Freedberg, August 3, 1973 (for McComb on privilege); interview with Robert and Kelly Lynch, in Boston, November 18, 1971 (for McComb on elite); interviews with McKibbin, July 15, 1975, and with Robert and Kelly Lynch, November 18, 1971 (for restaurants); interviews with Robert and Kelly Lynch, November 18, 1971, and November 6, 1977, and interview with McKibbin, July 15, 1975 (for clothing). Robert Lynch says that the seersuckers, McComb's summer clothes, were of cotton and had a rumpled look, which Arthur liked, and that despite a fourth day, the shirts were always clean.

29. Interview with Freedberg, August 3, 1973 (for McComb's having been a teacher of his, McComb's teaching jobs, McComb and scholarship); interview with McKibbin, July 15, 1975 (for McComb's authenticating). A curriculum vitae of McComb's, extending to 1953, listed him as Lecturer at Wellesley College, 1947, 1949–50, and in the Harvard Summer School, 1951.

30. Interview with Laurette Murdock, in Boston, August 5, 1975.

31. Interview with McKibbin, July 15, 1975.

32. Letter from Dorothy de Santillana to ML, December 12, 1975 (chief source); interview with Laurette Murdock, August 5, 1975; interview with McKibbin, July 15, 1975 (for McComb's passage first class).

33. Letter from Robert Lynch, October 14, 1976 (for McComb and young people); interview with Constance Worcester, July 11, 1975.

34. "Over twenty-seven": interview with Constance Worcester, July 11, 1975, and interview with Kelly Lynch, November 6, 1977. Kelly Lynch observed that McComb meant romantically interested. Athenaeum incident: interview with McKibbin, July 15, 1975, and interview with Robert Lynch, November 6, 1977. Robert Lynch says that it was McKibbin who objected.

35. Attribution of charm, dignity, sensitivity based on interviews with Constance Worcester, Sydney Freedberg, and Robert and Kelly Lynch. Gurdon Worcester thought McComb highly affected (interview, July 12, 1975), and McKibbin said he grew irritated at his posturing (interview, July 15, 1975). Laurette Murdock's description is from the interview of August 5, 1975.

36. Interview with Poore, summer 1971, and telephone interview with him, June 4, 1978.

37. For instances of Mitchell's helping Dos Passos with money, see their correspondence between 1937 and 1940. For Mitchell's helping him with American historical scholarship, see their correspondence beginning with 1939. Mitchell sold his house in Gloucester in 1945. On his extending hospitality in Cambridge, see letter from Dos Passos to Mrs. Lloyd Lowndes, postmarked September 22, 1947. For Mitchell and McComb on Spain, see letter from Mitchell to Dos Passos, October 1, 1936. For Mitchell on Roosevelt and on the election of 1952, see his letter to Dos Passos, December 19, 1952. Gurdon Worcester spoke of Mitchell's twitting and mimicking in ML's interview with him on July 12, 1975. The McComb–Mitchell and the Dos Passos–Mitchell correspondences contain numerous references to McComb's and Mitchell's seeing one another. McComb's letters to Mitchell between December 21, 1941, and July 28, 1944, speak of Mitchell's hospitality and favors to him.

38. Mitchell's papers at the Boston Athenaeum provide much information about his relationships with his family, his friendship with Mrs. Thomas, and his finances. A carbon copy of a letter he wrote Sydney G. Soons on July 10, 1940, to help in settling the Thomas estate, is a helpful chronicle of his relationship with Mrs. Thomas. In 1916 Dos Passos wrote Poore that he had visited Mitchell and Mrs. Thomas, and he praised Mitchell's "aunt" most highly (telephone interview with Poore, August 15, 1976). Dos Passos' outburst against her was in a letter to Poore written in the spring of 1921 (earliest legible postmark, May 19, 1921).

39. A letter from Katharine Dos Passos to Mitchell (September 21, 1939) and an enclosed note from Dos Passos urge Mitchell, along with Cowan, to come to Provincetown as their guests. Mitchell wrote Dos Passos about Cowan's death in letters of October 24, 1939, and January 5, 1940. Mrs. Thomas' bequest was reported in the *New York Times,* March 9, 1940, p. 8. Mitchell once told McKibbin that he got $57,000 a year from Mrs. Thomas' estate (interview, ML with McKibbin, July 15, 1975). Mitchell was drinking heavily in the 1930s, when Poore was teaching at Harvard (telephone interview with Poore, August 15, 1976). Gurdon Worcester spoke of Mitchell's aggressive and notorious homosexuality (interview, July 12, 1975), and McKibbin spoke of Mitchell's expenditures on young men. Evidence of such expenditures may be found among Mitchell's papers. Dos Passos, who got an account of Mitchell's death through E. E. Cummings, wrote Hillyer of the circumstances in a letter of April 18, 1958.

40. McKibbin said that McComb was bitterly disappointed at not inheriting any money (interview, July 15, 1975). A letter from Slater Brown to ML, November 21, 1973, states that McComb told him that Mitchell promised to leave McComb $5,000. Dos Passos' appreciation was "In Memoriam: Stewart Mitchell," *New England Quarterly* 30 (December 1957): 513–14.

41. Carbon copy of letter from Mrs. Matthew Josephson (Academy librarian) to Dos Passos, June 7, 1961; letter from Dos Passos to Mrs. Josephson, June 16, 1961.

42. Carbon copy of letter from Mrs. Matthew Josephson to Daniel Aaron, December 18, 1961. Aaron apologized for a slipup. Letter from Aaron to Mrs. Josephson, December 20, 1961.

43. Letter from Bernardin to director of Academy, October 28, 1962; letter from Felicia Geffen to Dos Passos, October 30, 1962, with Dos Passos' note to McComb beneath the signature; carbon copy of the same letter, with Dos Passos' note of permission written on it; letter from Dos Passos to Wilson, April 26, 1965.

44. A letter from Edward Kuhn, Jr., of New American Library, to Carol Brandt, of the Brandt and Brandt literary agency, November 19, 1965, offered an initial $25,000 advance; a letter from Dos Passos to Lovell Thompson, of Houghton Mifflin, November 24, 1965, indicates that Dos Passos accepted. Dos Passos in a letter to Carol Brandt, January 11, 1966, said that he would work to keep the memoirs paperback size, under a hundred thousand words. The information from Poore is from ML's interview with him, summer 1971.

45. McComb, "The Anglo-Americans in Florence," pp. 279–310. The "back-slapper" quotation is on p. 292.

46. McComb, ed. "Some Letters of Edith Wharton," *Boston Review* 1 (Fall 1966): 81–92; McComb, "Notes on the Dodo," *Boston Review* 1 (Fall 1966): 10–14.

CODA (PAGES 296–300)

1. Letter from Poore to Dos Passos, April 26, 1968; *Harvard Class of 1918: Fiftieth Anniversary Report,* p. 405 (for date of death); letter from Robert Lynch to ML, October 14, 1976 (for Boston City Hospital).

2. *Harvard Class of 1918: Fiftieth Anniversary Report,* p. 406.

3. Interview with Dr. Edwin Cowles Andrus, in Baltimore, August 10, 1975.

4. Dos Passos, *Easter Island* (Garden City, New York: Doubleday and Co., 1971), p. 122 (for month of visit to island); interview with Elizabeth Dos Passos, July 23, 1976 (for visit to Cape Kennedy).

5. Dos Passos, *On the Way to a Moon Landing* (n.p.: United States Information Service, n.d.). Unpaginated.

6. Interview with Dr. Andrus, August 10, 1975.

7. Dos Passos, *Easter Island,* p. 141.

8. Interview with Dr. Andrus, August 10, 1975 (on Dos Passos' medical history and movements); letter from Elizabeth Dos Passos, August 25, 1976, on Dos Passos' travels, physical condition, and death.

9. Dos Passos, "Diary etc J. R. Madison." Entry of April 9, 1911.

10. See Letters 148 and 149 above.

Manuscripts of the Dos Passos–McComb Letters

Most of John Dos Passos' letters, cards, notes, etc., to McComb through 1928 are at the American Academy and Institute of Arts and Letters, in New York City, and most of those from 1951 through 1966 are on deposit in the Manuscript Division of Alderman Library, University of Virginia. The exceptions are Letters (etc.) 4, 69, 110, 190, 192, 194, 195, 197, and 200, which have been lent to the editor by Robert Lynch, of Boston.

Almost all of McComb's letters and cards to John Dos Passos are on deposit in the Manuscript Division of Alderman Library. The only exception is Letter 42, which is part of the permanent collection there.

The manuscripts on deposit at Alderman Library were placed there by Elizabeth Dos Passos.

June 1990

Index

322 / INDEX

Great Terror, The (Conquest), 12
Greco, El, 28, 85, 87, 89, 92, 93,
102 (n. 5)
Greece, 2, 91, 96, 103, 212, 219
Greeks, 218
Greenwich Village (New York City),
185, 190, 237
Gregory, Lady Augusta (Persse), 21
Grosz, George, 234
"Grosz Comes to America" (Dos
Passos), 234, 307 (n. 2)
Guardi, Francesco, 198
Guercino (Italian painter), 225
Guild socialism, 130
Gunn, Peter, 275
Guns of August, The (Tuchman), 272
Gypsies, 12

Habana/Havana (Cuba), 160, 163,
232
Hairy Ape, The (O'Neill), 193
Hals, Frans, 156
Hamish Hamilton Ltd. (publisher),
275
Hardinge. See Scholle, Hardinge
Harper and Brothers (publisher), 215,
218
Harvard Advocate, 41, 291
Harvard Business School, 47
Harvard Class of 1918: Fiftieth Anniversary Report (McComb's commentary for), 296
Harvard Class of 1918: 25th Anniversary Report (McComb, con-
tributor), 237
Harvard Cooperative Society (Coöp),
175
Harvard Monthly, 2, 25, 30, 33, 36,
37, 42, 104, 121, 172; Dos Passos'
friends from, 5; Dos Passos' writings in, 5, 6, 7, 175, 255; McComb
editor of, 40, 43; McComb's writings in, 5, 6, 7, 77, 114; past
editors of, 96 (n. 4), 125 (n. 5);
World War I destroys, 40–41, 43,
45, 51, 52, 55
Harvard Union, 43 (n. 2)
Harvard University, 43, 45, 47, 51,
55, 56, 156, 165, 175, 185, 200,
205–6 (n. 3), 228, 263 (n. 7). See
also under Dos Passos, John;
McComb, Arthur Kilgore. See also
Cambridge (Mass.)

Harvard University Press, 236, 291
Hassan Khan (Dr. Hassan Tabataba),
176, 177, 178
Hayek, Friedrich August von, 233
Hemingway, Ernest, 205 (n. 2), 213,
229, 234
Henderson, Lawrence Joseph, 170
Herrick, Robert, 6
Heures d'Italie (G. Faure), 151
Hibben, Paxton, 162
Hillyer, Robert Silliman, 5, 40 (n.
marked †), 45, 53, 63, 183, 202 (n.
1), 233, 254, 260 (n. 2), 310 (n.
39); identified, 45 (n. 6); col-
laborates with Dos Passos on novel,
60, 76, 97, 103, 189; with Dos
Passos in France (1917), 56, 57,
59, 60; teaches at Harvard, 175,
228
Hiroshima (Japan), 12
"History and Significance of the
Human Nose" (Dos Passos' jest),
143
Hitler, Adolf, 9, 10, 11, 12, 13, 14,
196 (n. 2), 290
Hofmann, Konrad von, 256
Hofmannsthal, Hugo von, 151
Holbein, Hans, the younger, 132,
142, 143, 152
Holdridge, Christopher (Kiffy) (Eliza-
beth Dos Passos' son), 239, 251
(port.), 287 (n. 2)
Holiday (magazine), 240
Homer, 26
Hoover, Herbert Clark, 139, 224 (n.
6)
Hopkins, Harry, 238
Houghton Mifflin (publisher), 242,
244, 249, 258, 260, 261, 262, 263,
265, 274, 276, 277, 294
House of Mirth, The (Wharton), 66
Howe, George Locke ("Gazelle"), 30,
33, 37, 42, 45, 48, 55, 70, 108,
113, 120; identified, 30 (n. 4)
Huebsch, B. W., 166
Huguet, Jaime, 140 (n. 1)
"Humble Protest, A" (Dos Passos),
6–7, 13
Humphrey, Hubert H., 282
Hungarians, 158–59
Hungary, 156, 196, 295

Imperialism, 10

Lawson, Kate Drain, 132–33, 141, 142
League of Nations, 11
Lebe das Leben, Es (Sudermann), 83
Lechería de la Castellana (Madrid restaurant). *See* Vaquería
Lee, Vernon (pseudonym of Violet Paget), 222, 247, 275
Lenin, V. I., 121, 136
Leningrad (Soviet Union), 213
León (Spain), 129, 295
"Leonardo" (Berenson), 169
Leonardo da Vinci, 150, 156, 169
Liberal Bourgeoisie, 114, 119, 120
Liberal Fiction, 157
Liberal Party, 104
Liberals, 54, 64, 233. *See also* American liberals; German liberals
Liberator (journal), 156, 161
Liebknecht, Karl, 25, 119 (n. 5)
Liechtenstein, 123
Life (magazine), 237–38, 240, 259 (n. 4)
"Life and Works of Francesco di Giorgio, The" (McComb), 204
Liliom (Molnár), 192, 194
Liluli (Rolland), 147, 154
"Lines Written among the Euganean Hills" (Shelley), 73
Lippmann, Walter, 282, 282 (n. 1)
Lisbon (Portugal), 162, 215
Littell, Robert, 96, 99, 103, 104
Little, Brown (publisher), 258
Little Theatre. *See* Toy Theatre
Lloyd George, David, 136
Lluch, Nuestra Señora de (Mallorcan church), 141, 218
Lodge, Henry Cabot, 247, 254 (n. 1)
Loeser, Charles Alexander, 205, 247
London (England), 152, 263
Lorenzo da Viterbo, 189
Louisburg Square (Boston), 122
Louis IX (St. Louis, king of France), 144
Louis Salvator (Austrian archduke), 141
Louvre (Paris museum), 148 (n. 16), 150
Lowell, A. Lawrence, 47
Lowell, Amy, 31, 54, 130
Lucas-Champonnière, Germaine, 218
Ludovisi reliefs, 174
Lugubrio dei Funghi (Dos Passos' spoof), 185, 193, 199

Luxembourg, Musée du (Paris), 145
Luxemburg, Rosa, 119 (n. 5)
Lynch, Kelly (friend of A. K. McComb), 310 (n. 34)
Lynch, Robert (friend of A. K. McComb), 309 (nn. 27, 28), 310 (n. 34)

McComb, Arthur Kilgore (1895–1968) (*see also* McComb, Arthur Kilgore, writings of): and airplanes, 183, 236, 242, 254; Alhambra, delighted by, 116–17; at American consulate (Madrid), 76, 99, 103, 108, 113–15; on Americans, 84, 172, 232, 252; appearance of, 241–42, 244, 291 (*see also* subentry photographs of); art history, plans career in, 132; in Asheville (N.C.) (1942–44), 236, 237, 246, 248 (n. 2), 275; in Austria (1920), 132, 155–56, 158–59; (1922), 192, 194, 195–96; on automobiles, 254; Berenson, does "stunt" of, 196; birthplace of, 2, 288; on Bolsheviks/Bolshevism, 8, 12–13, 77, 114, 116, 119, 120, 121, 122, 125, 156–57, 232; in Boston, 2, 213, 226, 228, 236, 241–44, 247, 248, 248 (n. 2), 249–95 (passim), 296; boyhood of, 2, 9, 242, 299; on capitalism, 8, 232; on Church, 13, 151, 232; in Cuba (1915), 232; (1916), 18, 27; on Cuba, 232; daughter of (*see* McComb, Pamela); death of (1968), 296; divorce of (1929), 213; on Dos Passos and Élie Faure, 151; with Dos Passos in Boston, 104, 226, 228, 262, 283; on Dutch art, 156 (*see also* individual artists); Edgell, studies with, 27; editorial work of, 242, 258 (*see also* subentry as indexer); education, early, of, 2; on fascism, 13, 14, 221, 232, 235; father of, 2, 41, 166 (n. 8); financial straits of, 236, 241–42, 245, 249, 253, 258; on Flemish art, 27, 87, 117, 156, 165, 176 (*see also* individual artists); in France (1961), 263; in Gibraltar (1937), 247; on Goya, 87; Granja, La, enchanted by, 215; in Great Britain (1961), 263; on Great Britain, 232, 288; Greco, El, finds too subjective, 87; in Greece (1926), 212, 219; in Hanover, Germany, 2; at Harvard as student (1914–17), 2, 5, 6–7, 27, 40–41, 42, 43, 45, 56, 66, 71–72, 77–78, 79; (1920–22), 161, 162, 163, 164, 165, 169, 172 (n. 16), 172–73, 174–75, 180, 183; as Harvard instructor and assistant professor (1927–39), 213, 224–25, 226, 228, 236; at Harvard Summer School, as teacher, 242, 258; as Harvard traveling fellow (1922–23), 188 (n. 3); on heroism, 27–28, 58; and Houghton Mifflin, 242, 249, 258, 260, 261, 263, 265, 274, 277; in Hungary (1922), 196; illnesses of, 219, 262–63, 265, 290; as indexer, 242, 249, 250, 252; Irish citizenship of (1943), 237; on Italian art, 27, 77–78, 95, 154, 169, 176, 189, 192, 198, 199, 205, 206, 211, 225, 236 (*see also individual artists, museums, works, and styles in art and architecture*); in Italy (1920), 132, 149, 151, 152, 154–55, 156–59; (1921), 162, 174; (1922), 183, 185, 188–89, 191–92, 194, 195, 198–99; (1923), 186; (1924), 205; (1926), 212, 220; (1927), 221–22; (1933?), 231; (1937), 247; (1961), 242, 263; on Jamaica, 231–32; languages of, 80, 81, 81 (n. 5), 95, 303 (n. 30); on Leonardo da Vinci, 156, 169; Ludovisi reliefs, thrilled by, 174; marries (1923), 204; at Metropolitan Museum of Art, 204; on Moorish architecture in Granada, 116–17; mother of, 2; on "negro revolution" (1960s), 280; in New Hampshire, 41, 48, 52, 158; in New York City, 18, 26, 27, 45, 77–78, 165, 166, 183, 204, 220, 222, 225, 225 (n. 6), 248 (n. 2), 276; on New York City, 207, 276; on Northern Europe, 108; on old age, 261, 263, 267, 282, 291, 293; personality of, 7, 8, 14–15, 72, 242; photographs of, 4, 227, 230, 243; plaque over bed of, 2, 299; political identification of by Dos Passos, 131, 138, 210; political self-identification of, 13, 54, 85, 116, 119,

120, 191, 230, 235, 237, 241, 252, 256, 280, 309 (n. 27); in political talks with Dos Passos, 7, 131, 155, 155 (n. 5), 228–29, 249–50; in Portugal (1921), 163, 174; (1926), 215; on Portugal, 274; Prado overpowers, 86; on religion, 13, 139–40, 232; Rembrandt, dissatisfied with, 156; reproves Dos Passos, 125, 151, 207, 232; on revolution (code word *Nagel*), 62, 122; romances of, 150, 213, 215, 236, 242, 291, 293, 294, 296, 310 (n. 34); on Roosevelt, Franklin D., 280; on royalty, 215, 255, 256, 290–91; on Russia (August 1917), 58; on Russian Revolution, 8, 41, 43, 55, 77, 114, 116, 119, 120, 121, 123, 125, 156–57, 158; and sketch for Dos Passos, 28 (illus.); in Spain (1918–20), 8, 76, 83–88, 89–90, 94–96, 98–99, 103–4, 107–8, 113–25, 127–29, 130, 131, 132, 136–37, 248; (1921), 163; (1926), 211, 215–17, 220; on Spain, 45, 85, 94, 104, 108, 114, 116, 118, 150, 235–36, 274; on Spanish art and architecture, 85, 87, 95–96, 99, 116–17, 140, 172, 175, 215 (*see also individual artists, museums, works, and styles in art and architecture*); in Switzerland (1920), 132, 138–40; (1961), 242, 263; on teaching, 172, 224, 236; as Tenoya, Arturo de, 86; on theater, 226; on time as pixie, 270; in Turkey (1926), 212, 219; Vassar, teaches at (1924–26), 204, 206; Velázquez, lauds, 87; on Vichy government (1941), 236; wife of (*see* McComb, Constance); during World War I, 8, 40–41, 52, 55, 76, 77, 83; on World War I, 6, 15, 27–28, 52, 55, 77, 83, 113–14; during World War II, 236–37, 248; on World War II, 236–37, 280

McComb, Arthur Kilgore, writings of: **articles and essays** (*see* "Consular Appointment of 1900, A"; "Francesco Ubertini [Bacchiacca]"; "Life and Works of Francesco di Giorgio, The"; "Notes on the Dodo"; "Some Letters of Bernard Berenson" [McComb, ed.]; "Some Letters of